The *Shakespeare* Encyclopedia

The *Shakespeare* Encyclopedia

The Complete Guide to the Man and His Works

FIREFLY BOOKS

A Firefly Book

Published by Firefly Books Ltd. 2009

First printing

Publisher Cataloging-in-Publication Data (U.S.)
Cousins, A.D., 1950-
The Shakespeare encyclopedia : the complete guide to the man and his works / Professor A.D. Cousins.
[304] p. : photos.(chiefly col.) ; cm.
Summary: Companion to Shakespeare's complete works, including an introduction to his life.
ISBN-13: 978-1-55407-479-2
ISBN-10: 1-55407-479-7
1. Shakespeare, William, 1564-1616 -- Encyclopedias. I. Title.
822.33 dc22 PR2892.C68 2009

Library and Archives Canada Cataloguing in Publication
Cousins, A. D., 1950-
The Shakespeare encyclopedia : the complete guide to the man and his works / A.D. Cousins.
Includes bibliographical references and index.
ISBN-13: 978-1-55407-479-2
ISBN-10: 1-55407-479-7
1. Shakespeare, William, 1564-1616--Encyclopedias.
2. Shakespeare, William, 1564-1616--Criticism and interpretation. I. Title.
PR2892.C68 2009 822.3'3 C2009-902928-6

Published in the United States by
Firefly Books (U.S.) Inc.
P.O. Box 1338, Ellicott Station
Buffalo, New York 14205

Published in Canada by
Firefly Books Ltd.
66 Leek Crescent
Richmond Hill, Ontario L4B 1H1

The moral rights of the contributors have been asserted.

Printed in China by 1010 Printing International Ltd
Color separation Pica Digital Pte Ltd, Singapore

Developed by Global Book Publishing
Level 8, 15 Orion Road
Lane Cove, NSW 2066
Australia
Ph: (612) 9425 5800 Fax: (612) 9425 5804
Email: rightsmanager@globalpub.com.au

Managing Director	Chryl Campbell
Publishing Director	Sarah Anderson
Art Director	Kylie Mulquin
Project Manager	John Mapps
New Title Development Manager	David Kidd
Chief Consultant	A.D. Cousins
Contributors	Helen Barr, Line Cottegnies, Pascale Drouet, Sarah Dustagheer, Alan W. Friedman, Rosemary Gaby, Barry Gaines, Bradley Greenburg, Ronald Huebert, Gwilym Jones, Gillian Murray Kendall, Ros King, Jane Kingsley-Smith, James Loehlin, Margaret McPhee, Richard Madelaine, Marea Mitchell, Dani Napton, Kevin Quarmby, Alison V. Scott, R.S. White, George Walton Williams
Editors	Emma Driver, Scott Forbes, John Mapps, Mary Trewby
Proofreader	Dannielle Viera
Index	Jo Rudd
Cover Design	Kylie Mulquin
Design Concept	Kerry Klinner, Kylie Mulquin
Designers	Cathy Campbell, Susanne Geppert, Kerry Klinner, Kylie Mulquin
Photo Researcher	Tracey Gibson
Production Manager	Ian Coles
Rights Manager	Belinda Vance
Publishing Assistant	Jessica Luca

FRONT COVER The Cobbe portrait (unknown artist), thought to be of Shakespeare, *c.* 1610 (Getty Images)
BACK COVER (top to bottom) Al Pacino as Richard III, in the film *Looking for Richard* (1996) (The Picture Desk/Kobal Collection); *Hamlet and Horatio in the Cemetery* (1839) by Eugène Delacroix (The Picture Desk/Art Archive); scene from the film *A Midsummer Night's Dream* (1935), with Mickey Rooney as Puck and Olivia de Havilland as Hermia (The Picture Desk/Kobal Collection)

EXIT

Contributors

Chief Consultant

A.D. Cousins is Professor of English and Head of the English Department at Macquarie University, Sydney, Australia. He is a member of the Australian Academy of the Humanities and of the General Division of the Order of Australia. His books include *Shakespeare's Sonnets and Narrative Poems* (1999) and, with Alison V. Scott, *Ben Jonson and the Politics of Genre* (2009). He has published widely in the United States and Europe on English Renaissance literature and has been a Visiting Scholar at the University of Massachusetts, Princeton, and Pennsylvania State University.

The Two Gentlemen of Verona; The Tempest; Shakespeare's Enduring Appeal

Helen Barr, Fellow and Tutor at Lady Margaret Hall, University of Oxford, United Kingdom, teaches Shakespeare, medieval literature, and English language. She is the author of *The Piers Plowman Tradition* (1993); *Signes and Sothe: Language in the Piers Plowman Tradition* (1994); *Socioliterary Practice in Late Medieval England* (2001); and *The Digby Poems: A New Edition of the Lyrics* (2009).

Henry VI, Parts 1, 2, and 3

Line Cottegnies, Professor of English Literature at the University of Paris 3–Sorbonne Nouvelle, France, has published widely on seventeenth-century literature, from Shakespeare to Mary Astell. She is the author of a study of the Cavalier poets, *L'Eclipse du regard: La poésie anglaise du baroque au classicisme (1625–1660)* (1997), and has coedited *Authorial Conquests: Essays on Genre in the Writings of Margaret Cavendish* (2003). She has edited the three parts of *Henry VI* (2008).

Richard II

Pascale Drouet, Senior Lecturer, University of Poitiers, France, is the author of *Le vagabond dans l'Angleterre de Shakespeare, ou l'art de contrefaire à la ville et à la scène* (2003), and editor and joint editor of *Shakespeare au XXème siècle: Mises en scène, mises en perspective de Richard II* (2007) and *"The True Blank of Thine Eye": Approches critiques de King Lear* (2008). In 2007, she launched the online journal *Les Cahiers Shakespeare en devenir / The Journal of Shakespearean Afterlives* (http://edel.univ-poitiers.fr/licorne/sommaire.php?id=3680).

Richard III; All's Well That Ends Well

Sarah Dustagheer, Collaborative Doctoral Award student at King's College London, United Kingdom, and Shakespeare's Globe, London, is completing a thesis on the production of theater space at the early modern Globe and Blackfriars, and modern reconstructed playhouses. She has published on drama education in *Arts Professional Magazine* and on Shakespearean staging conditions and history in *Around the Globe*.

The Merchant of Venice

Alan W. Friedman, Thaman Professor of English and Comparative Literature at the University of Texas at Austin, United States, specializes in twentieth-century British and American literature, although he has published articles on *Hamlet* and *The Jew of Malta* and regularly teaches Shakespeare. He has written and edited 11 books, including *Fictional Death and the Modernist Enterprise* (1995) and *Beckett in Black and Red* (2000).

The Winter's Tale

Rosemary Gaby lectures at the School of English, Journalism, and European Languages, University of Tasmania, Hobart, Australia. Her research interests include Shakespeare in performance and Australian theater history. She is currently editing *Henry IV, Part 1* for the Internet Shakespeare Editions and completing a book on the history of open-air Shakespeare production in Australia.

A Midsummer Night's Dream; Cymbeline

Barry Gaines is Professor of English in the University of New Mexico, Albuquerque, United States. He is the joint editor of *A Yorkshire Tragedy* for the Revels Plays (1986), *Q1 Romeo and Juliet* for the Malone Society (2000), and *Antony and Cleopatra* for the Applause Shakespeare (2001). He is presently editing a volume of *The Complete Works of Thomas Heywood.*

King John; Henry IV, Parts 1 and 2; Henry V; Henry VIII; The Merry Wives of Windsor

Bradley Greenburg is Associate Professor of English at Northeastern Illinois University in Chicago, United States. His recent articles on Shakespeare's history plays and early modern historiography have appeared in *Shakespeare Studies, Criticism, Studies in Medieval and Renaissance History,* and *Quidditas.* He is working on a book project on the Henriad, chronicle history, Lollardy, and Wales.

The World Before Shakespeare

Ronald Huebert is Professor of English, Dalhousie University, and Carnegie Professor, University of King's College, both in Halifax, Nova Scotia, Canada. He is also a Life Member of Clare Hall, Cambridge University, United Kingdom. He is the editor of *James Shirley's The Lady of Pleasure* (1986) and the author of *The Performance of Pleasure in English Renaissance Drama* (2003).

Julius Caesar

Gwilym Jones is completing his D.Phil. thesis, "Shakespeare's Storms," at the University of Sussex, Brighton, United Kingdom. He is a visiting lecturer at Shakespeare's Globe, London, leading undergraduate and MA courses on Shakespeare and Renaissance reading and contributing to the Globe's publications. He also teaches early modern drama at the University of Kent.

Twelfth Night; Titus Andronicus

Gillian Murray Kendall is an Associate Professor at Smith College, Massachusetts, United States. She has written articles on Shakespeare and has edited (and contributed to) a volume of essays, *Shakespearean Power and Punishment* (1998).

Othello; Language of the Soul

Ros King is Professor of English Studies at the University of Southampton, United Kingdom, and Director of the interdisciplinary Centre for Medieval and Renaissance Culture. Her books include *The Works of Richard Edwards: Politics, Poetry and Performance in Sixteenth Century England* (2001); *Cymbeline: Constructions of Britain* (2005); and a handbook on *The Winter's Tale* (2008). She is coeditor of *Shakespeare and War* (2009).

Hamlet; Romeo and Juliet; The Poems
JANE KINGSLEY-SMITH, Senior Lecturer at Roehampton University, London, United Kingdom, has published widely on Shakespeare and early modern literature and is a regular guest speaker at Shakespeare's Globe, London. Her first monograph was *Shakespeare's Drama of Exile* (2003) and she is currently working on her next book, *Cupid in Early Modern Literature and Culture,* to be published in 2010.

Canonical Works; Shakespeare or Not?
JAMES LOEHLIN, Shakespeare at Winedale Regents Professor at the University of Texas at Austin, United States, writes on the performance history of Shakespeare on stage and film. He has published books on *Henry V* (1996), *Romeo and Juliet* (2002), and *Henry IV: Parts 1 and 2* (2008), as well as Chekhov's *The Cherry Orchard* (2006).

Shakespeare the Man
MARGARET MCPHEE has worked as a researcher, writer, and editor in the general reference field for more than 20 years. She was a member of the team that produced the first edition of the *Macquarie Dictionary,* has written for the *Australian Encyclopaedia,* and is author of or has contributed to more than 30 reference, travel, and lifestyle books in Australia and the United Kingdom.

Much Ado about Nothing; Antony and Cleopatra
RICHARD MADELAINE, Associate Professor in the School of English, Media, and Performing Arts at the University of New South Wales, Sydney, Australia, has published widely on Shakespearean staging issues and stage history. He is author of *Antony and Cleopatra* in the Shakespeare in Production series (1998) and joint editor of *"O Brave New World": Two Centuries of Shakespeare on the Australian Stage* (2001).

The Taming of the Shrew; Love's Labor's Lost; Troilus and Cressida; A Universal Phenomenon
MAREA MITCHELL, Associate Professor in the Department of English at Macquarie University, Sydney, Australia, has most recently contributed to the Norton critical edition of *The Taming of the Shrew* (2009). Her research and teaching focus on gender in the early modern period of Shakespeare and his contemporaries.

Coriolanus
DANI NAPTON is completing her doctoral dissertation at Macquarie University, Sydney, Australia, and has published articles on Renaissance literature and nineteenth-century fiction. She is currently coediting a collection of essays on nineteenth-century novelists' engagement with the concepts and consequences of revolution, and writing a monograph, *Revolution, Restoration, Riot and Rebellion: A Counter-Revolutionary Continuum of Politics and Place in Scott.*

As You Like It; Measure for Measure; Macbeth; King Lear
KEVIN QUARMBY, after a 30-year professional career in British theater, recently completed a PhD on Shakespeare and Jacobean drama at King's College London, United Kingdom, where he also lectured and taught courses on Literature and Drama of the English Renaissance. He regularly reviews plays in London and Stratford.

The Sonnets
ALISON V. SCOTT lectures in English at the University of Queensland, Brisbane, Australia, where she specializes in early modern literature. Her books include *Selfish Gifts: The Politics of Exchange and English Courtly Literature, 1580–1628* (2006) and, with A.D. Cousins, *Ben Jonson and the Politics of Genre* (2009).

Timon of Athens; The Two Noble Kinsmen; Pericles
R.S. WHITE is Winthrop Professor of English and Cultural Studies at the University of Western Australia, Perth, Australia. His books on Shakespeare include Palgrave New Critical Casebooks on *Twelfth Night, The Tempest,* and *Romeo and Juliet.* His latest book is *Pacifism and English Literature: Minstrels of Peace* (2008).

The Comedy of Errors
GEORGE WALTON WILLIAMS, Professor of English (Emeritus), Duke University, North Carolina, United States, is Associate General Editor (History Plays) of the Arden Shakespeare series and was contributing editor of the *Beaumont and Fletcher Canon* (1966–96). He has published critical and bibliographical studies on Shakespeare, with particular interests in textual problems and stagecraft.

Contents

Foreword

Nearly four hundred years after his death in 1616, Shakespeare still speaks to us. His plays are a global phenomenon, on both stage and screen, and his poems are some of the best known in the English language. Not only does he speak to us, he puts words in our mouths. Almost everyone has heard or quoted, "To be or not to be," or "Shall I compare thee to a summer's day?" Beyond the words, of course, lies the world of characters he created, with all their desires, flaws, and contradictions. Delighting to observe them, we are led to ask questions about ourselves and our world.

Now, perhaps more than ever, people are seeking to find out about the man who fashioned those words and those characters, and how he related to the society for which he created them. Now, as much as ever, people are intensely interested in what Shakespeare has to tell us about the scope, pleasures, and challenges of human experience.

The aim of this book is, then, to offer an illuminating, companionable guide to the life and writings of the most famous of English dramatists. Drawing on some of the best current research, and written by a team of scholars from

around the world, it focuses first on Shakespeare's life, and shows how he related to the Elizabethan and Jacobean literary world, especially to the world of the theater.

The book thereafter discusses each of Shakespeare's plays and all his nondramatic verse. With the assistance of lavish illustrations and useful charts, each of Shakespeare's works is considered in terms of its main themes or preoccupations and its uses of imagery. Stage technique is of course taken into account, as is the survival of the plays in landmark—particularly, recent—productions for stage and screen.

The account of every work examines both how it connects with events or concerns of Shakespeare's times and how it has something to say to our own. If it is true that Shakespeare still speaks to us, then this book seeks to help us hear more clearly what he is saying.

A.D. Cousins
Macquarie University
Sydney, Australia

Shakespeare for All Time

The World Before Shakespeare

The culture Shakespeare inherited was still medieval in many respects: in its insistence on hierarchy, in its emphasis on religion, and in its reliance on authority, for example. But there were unmistakable signs of change, especially in the urban centers such as London; when taken together, the signs of change amounted to a vast cultural upheaval now known as the Renaissance.

The European Renaissance

In the half century preceding Shakespeare's birth in 1564, Ferdinand Magellan, the Portuguese navigator, set out on the first successful circumnavigation of Earth (1519–22); the Polish astronomer Nicolaus Copernicus, in *Six Books Concerning the Revolutions of the Heavenly Orbs* (*De revolutionibus orbium coelestium libri vi*, 1543), was the first scientific thinker to propose a heliocentric (sun-centered) model of the universe; and the Venetian painter Titian—in *The Venus of Urbino* (*c.* 1538), for example—was the first to treat a reclining female nude as a completely natural subject. Each of these initiatives owes something to the philosophical humanism that had become part of the European Renaissance with the publication of the Italian scholar Pico della Mirandola's *Oration on the Dignity of Man* (*Oratio de hominis dignitate*, 1486). The human figure was now at the center of the created universe; henceforth man would be making a special effort to exert mastery over the world.

During Shakespeare's lifetime (1564–1616), the achievements in geography, science, and art would escalate. Exploration of the New World led to the first permanent English (Jamestown in Virginia, 1607) and French (Quebec, 1608) settlements in North America. Improvements to the telescope allowed Galileo to be the first to observe sunspots (in 1611), and thence to declare that the solar system was demonstrably the right hypothesis. These important "firsts" would have been of less immediate interest to Shakespeare than construction of the first professional playhouse, The Theatre, by James Burbage in 1576.

Literary London

By the time Shakespeare arrived in London—and the first evidence of this event is dated 1592—literature was a thriving enterprise. Many English writers began as translators: Sir Thomas Wyatt (1503–42) made English versions of Petrarch's *Rime;* Henry Howard, Earl of Surrey (1517–47), translated two of the books of Virgil's *Aeneid* into English blank verse; Arthur Golding (1536–1605) rendered all of Ovid's *Metamorphoses* into rhyming couplets; and a distinguished list of translators, beginning with William Tyndale (*c.* 1490–1536), produced a series of biblical translations leading up to the publication of the King James Bible in 1611.

BELOW: *This plan of the City of London in about 1580 was published in* Civitates Orbis Terrarum (Atlas of Cities of the World). *The city expanded greatly during the reign of Elizabeth I: by 1600 its population was around 90,000.*

RIGHT: *This miniature, said to be of Sir Philip Sidney, is by Isaac Oliver. Sidney was a poet, courtier, and soldier, and died in battle in 1586. He wrote the first of the great English sonnet sequences,* Astrophil and Stella.

FAR RIGHT: *Edmund Spenser's* The Faerie Queene, *an epic poem written in praise of Queen Elizabeth, was published in 1590.*

THE FAERIE QVEENE.

Diſpoſed into twelue books,

Faſhioning

XII. Morall vertues.

LONDON

Printed for William Ponſonbie.

1590.

Reading Classical and biblical texts written in the vernacular seems to have provoked a great wave of creativity among English authors. Sir Philip Sidney (1554–86), a much admired and perhaps unfairly neglected figure at the court of Queen Elizabeth I, was also the author of a sequence of 108 sonnets *(Astrophil and Stella)* and of the first work of literary criticism in English *(The Defense of Poesy)*. Both of these works were published shortly after Sidney's early death, and were therefore available to the young Shakespeare as he negotiated the early years of his career.

The same is true for the first three books of *The Faerie Queene* by Edmund Spenser (1552–99), published in 1590 with the explicit intention of conferring epic stature upon "the most excellent and glorious person of our soveraine the Queene." This quotation, from "A Letter of the Authors" appended to the first edition, shows the degree to which literary publication was, in Shakespeare's early years, highly dependent upon patronage. Writers needed the blessing—and the financial support—of literary noblemen and women. Shakespeare, too, would rely on such support when he dedicated his narrative poems, *Venus and Adonis* (1593) and *The Rape of Lucrece* (1594), to Henry Wriothesley, Earl of Southampton.

The Virgin Queen

At the very top of the literary system, standing above the top rung of the precarious patronage network, was the figure of the queen. Her long and celebrated rule—from 1558 to 1603—was at the height of its prestige when Shakespeare began his theatrical career. Among her most remarkable achievements was the creation and maintenance of the kind of English national spirit that would lead, for example, to the defeat of the Spanish Armada in 1588. Elizabeth was revered by those close to her, and she was admired for her unerring political judgment; but she was also feared for something close to ruthlessness, a quality she needed simply to survive as England's queen. Had she chosen to marry one of the many suitors who presented themselves early in her reign, she would certainly have lost her position of preeminence.

Elizabeth I was much more than a political figure; she was a cultural icon of the first order, and in that role she inspired great ambitions and splendid achievements in a wide circle of friends, followers, and admirers. The list of writers who dedicated works to the queen includes Sir Walter Raleigh, Sir Philip Sidney, Fulke Greville, Samuel Daniel, and Richard Hakluyt. Shakespeare did not use this direct approach, but in *A Midsummer Night's*

ABOVE: *Elizabeth I is depicted at prayer in the frontispiece of* Christian Prayers and Meditations, *published in 1569, in the early and uncertain years of her long reign.*

Dream, he did have Oberon, the king of the fairies, refer to "a fair vestal throned by [the] west" who seems invulnerable to Cupid's arrows, and therefore lives "[i]n maiden meditation, fancy-free" (Act 2, Scene 1, lines 158, 164). Although not an overt request for sponsorship, these lines do amount to a thinly disguised compliment to the queen.

The Entertainment Industry

Shakespeare's regular income was earned in the newly established professional theater world that he encountered in London. The playhouses, and the companies who performed in them, were highly commercial enterprises. Between two and three thousand spectators could enter one of the open-air playhouses to watch an afternoon's performance, and everyone would pay: just a penny for standing room in the yard; an extra penny for a seat in the top gallery; two additional pennies for a seat in the (middle) twopenny gallery; and considerably more than this for the best seats, which were at ground level and near the stage.

People of all social classes and income levels attended the theaters, although the experience was clearly not the same for an apprentice on his afternoon off (who could afford standing room only) as for a gentleman and his female companion (who might be comfortably seated where they could not only see but be seen as well). The gate receipts were sufficient to pay running expenses and to earn profits for managers or shareholders. The demand for new plays was virtually limitless, and this meant plenty of opportunities for writers who could work quickly and adapt their pens to the needs of performance.

Trouble at the Margins

The optimistic ambitions of the Renaissance, the leadership of an exceptional monarch, unprecedented literary energies, and an innovative environment for theatrical performance—if all this sounds too good to be true, perhaps it is time to acknowledge that there was plenty of trouble just offstage, and that the precarious success of the Elizabethan moment was in part an exercise in damage control.

Although England was officially a Protestant country, this bland description of religious practice does not do justice to the tensions that were bubbling just below the surface. Even within the bracket of Protestantism, there was profound disagreement—most of it created, or at least augmented, by Puritan thinkers and preachers, who believed that the Reformation, initiated by Martin Luther in the early sixteenth century and pursued in Europe by John Calvin, had not gone far enough. The English Puritans believed the official (Protestant) church, in its adherence to traditional ceremonies and its love of elaborate vestments, for example, was merely following in the footsteps of Roman Catholicism.

The radical Puritans called for a more decisive break with the past, and their voices were gaining momentum in London. Puritan writers, such as Stephen Gosson in *The Schoole of Abuse* (1579), made the case that theatrical entertainment had no place in a godly society. Since the lords mayor of London and their influential supporters tended to be Puritans, the theatrical culture of the metropolitan area had to be constructed outside the city limits, either far to the north in Shoreditch (the location of The Theatre), or on the south bank, across the Thames River from the City of London proper, where the Globe theater would eventually be built in 1599.

If the Puritans believed the Reformation had not gone far enough, a beleaguered minority of

Catholics thought it had gone too far. Catholics were on the whole left unmolested if they did nothing to draw attention to themselves. But attempts to proselytize for the Roman Catholic Church were defined as high treason, therefore meeting with stiff opposition and heavy penalties. Jesuit missionaries who came to England to seek recruits for their seminaries on the Continent could do so only at the risk of their lives. One such missionary, the Jesuit Robert Southwell, a poet of considerable power and the author of *An Humble Supplication to her Majestie* (1595), was captured on his way to celebrate mass in 1592 and eventually executed at Tyburn in 1595.

Religious toleration had not been achieved in the culture Shakespeare inhabited, and it would require further bloodshed on both sides before it could be seen (a century later) as desirable.

ABOVE: *In 1555, bishops Nicholas Ridley and Hugh Latimer were burned at the stake for supporting the claim to the throne of the Protestant Lady Jane Grey over that of the Catholic Queen Mary I. Religion was to divide England until the 1700s.*

Pestilence, Policing, and Potions

Even if the Puritans could not close the theaters, the plague could at any moment do the job. When the weekly tally of deaths by bubonic plague went above 30, the civic authorities stopped all public assemblies, including theatrical productions, and therefore deprived the actors and playwrights of their usual opportunities to earn a living.

Under these circumstances, the actors might go on tour, and the playwrights might turn their hands to other kinds of writing. But whatever they chose to do, their lives were full of risk and uncertainty. There was no regular police force in the City of London; there was very little attention to public sanitation; there was no street lighting; there was no reliable contraception. Fresh food was rare, and water unclean. The medical advice available to those few who could afford it was, by our modern standards, lamentably inadequate.

It would have been very difficult for any of us to enjoy living in Shakespeare's London, but that thought should not prevent us from enjoying and celebrating what has been bequeathed to us from another time, another place.

Christopher Marlowe

The first playwright to achieve dazzling success on the London stage was not Shakespeare, but Christopher Marlowe, born in the same year as Shakespeare, and stabbed to death at the age of 29 in 1593. Marlowe's first great success was *Tamburlaine the Great, Part 1*, a play in which the hero sets himself the task of conquering the world. When he speaks out to justify his vast ambition, Tamburlaine sounds like the spirit of the European Renaissance itself:

> Nature, that framed us of four elements
> Warring within our breasts for regiment,
> Doth teach us all to have aspiring minds[.]
> (ACT 2, SCENE 7, LINES 18–20)

One of the signs of the newness of Renaissance culture is the conviction, on the part of many artists, writers, and thinkers, that they are encountering challenges never faced before. Marlowe has a compelling way of capturing the exhilaration that arises from this conviction.

RIGHT: *This portrait, dating from 1585, is believed to be of Christopher Marlowe. He wrote for Lord Strange's Men, as did Thomas Kyd, who enjoyed great success with* The Spanish Tragedy *the year before* Tamburlaine *was first performed.*

Shakespeare the Man

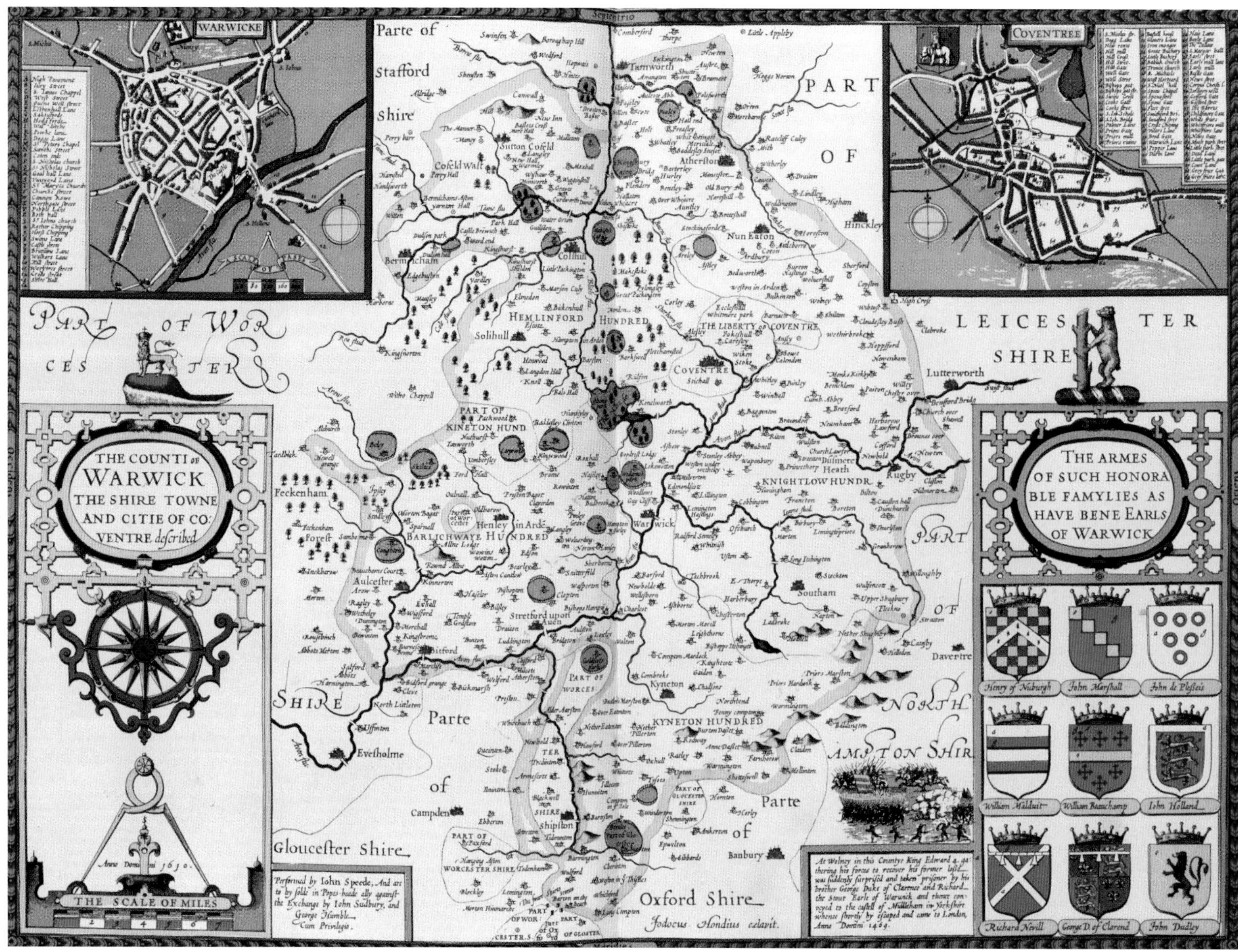

ABOVE: *Stratford was one of the important market towns of the sixteenth-century "County of Warwick." This map, engraved by Jodocus Hondius, from John Speed's* Theatre of the Empire of Great Britain, *was published in 1611–12.*

William Shakespeare's precise birth date is a matter of conjecture. It is known that he was christened on April 26, 1564, probably within days of his birth. He died almost exactly 52 years later, on April 23, 1616—St. George's Day—a date that is now traditionally celebrated as his birthday.

He was born and lies buried in Stratford-upon-Avon, Warwickshire, a rural town in the heart of England, sited where several routes met to cross the Avon River. To the north of the river stretched the forests of Arden, to the south was the fertile plain of Feldon. At the time of Shakespeare's birth, Stratford was a long-established, thriving market center. Although he made his name and fortune amid the crowded streets of London, the playwright retained a close, continuing involvement in his home town and the Warwickshire countryside, both of which provided a wealth of detailed images and settings for his writings.

Forebears

William's father, John Shakespeare, hailed from farming stock. In the early years of his working life, he appears to have been ambitious and hard-working, rising to become a respected merchant (a maker and seller of leather goods, specifically gloves), landholder, and a member of Stratford's ruling elite, first as a municipal officer, and later, in 1568, as mayor. However, from 1577, William's thirteenth year, John's fortunes and his reputation began to decline; borne low by debt and business woes, he neglected his duties as an alderman, and in 1586 was removed from the council.

William's mother, Mary Arden, came from a prosperous local farming family with pretensions to gentility. Some biographers have described her as capable, strong-minded, and quick-witted; it is not known whether she could read or write. As the favored youngest of eight daughters, Mary had brought some property to the marriage.

Childhood and Family Life

Shakespeare's first months were overshadowed by the terror of bubonic plague. More than 230 of Stratford's townsfolk—mostly women, and almost one-tenth of its population—were claimed by the epidemic in the first year of his life. Mary, having suffered the earlier loss of two infant daughters, would have been anxious to protect her baby son from the disease. But by the boy's fourth year, the danger was over, and young William enjoyed the security and stability of being the cherished eldest son of a prominent family.

His boyhood home on Henley Street, a main road out of town, was large (it was two buildings joined into one), with gardens and an orchard to the rear, plus the outbuildings and pits associated with the glover's trade. At the front, opening onto the busy thoroughfare, was the shop where his father conducted his business; neighbors included a tailor, blacksmith, haberdasher, and shepherds. At his mother's knee, William would have learned local folk tales of fairies, goblins, ghosts, witches, and enchanted forests. From Henley Street, he set off on rural rambles, acquiring a keenly observed knowledge of the countryside in all its seasons, and the details of its flowers, meadows, woodlands, and wildlife, particularly birds. From his father he learned about the glover's craft and the rewards of prosperity and social status that flow from hard work. William was also well acquainted with the practices and terms of both the hunt and falconry, and it has been suggested that, like many Tudor lads, he may have taken part in a spot of poaching. He had an ear, too, for the local dialect: its words and country talk flow through his later writings.

School Days

As the son of an alderman, William was entitled to free education at the King's New School, the grammar school in Stratford. His attendance there would have begun at the age of six or seven, after he had acquired, at a junior, or petty, school, basic proficiency in reading, writing, and simple arithmetic. His school day was long and arduous. Boys arrived at about 6 or 7 AM and, with breaks for breakfast and lunch, were at their desks until 5 PM, six days a week with few holidays. Attendance at church was compulsory, and the rote learning of Latin grammar and the translating of texts by Classical writers, ranging from Aesop's *Fables* to works by Cicero and Virgil, were the order of the day—young William no doubt developed skills for memorizing, which would serve him well as an actor. He proved a receptive student. The Roman poet Ovid made a particular impression, revealing to the incipient poet and dramatist an elegantly crafted imaginary world, which inspired his later sonnets and provided rich material for many of the plots of his plays: some 90 percent of the allusions to Classical mythology in Shakespeare can be traced to stories contained in the *Metamorphoses*, the epic compendium of heroic tales by Ovid.

Marriage and Children

After leaving school, probably at around the age of 15, Shakespeare may have worked briefly for his father, taken a post as a lawyer's clerk, or he may even have become a schoolmaster. In any event, in November 1582, there was marriage to a pregnant

BELOW: *Shakespeare's childhood home in Henley Street, Stratford-upon-Avon, was also the busy working premises of a craftsman.*

BOTTOM: *It is known that Shakespeare attended the King's New School, and he would have studied in this classroom.*

Theatrical Career

By 1592, Shakespeare was well drilled in the skills of the theater and had written the first of his plays, possibly as a member of Lord Strange's Men, an acting troupe that favored politically bold dramas. Three years later, he was a leading actor and the principal dramatist for London's most prestigious company, the Lord Chamberlain's Men (after the accession of James I in 1603, known as the King's Men), an association that continued throughout his working life. Enjoying royal patronage, the company performed at court regularly, with many of the works by Shakespeare. From 1609, he seems to have withdrawn from London, spending more time in Stratford, although he continued to write plays until 1613, in collaboration with the company's new dramatist, John Fletcher.

Anne Hathaway. At 18, William was still a minor and needed his father's permission to marry; Anne was eight years his senior and from an old country family. Their first child, Susanna, was born the following May, and twins, Hamnet and Judith, in 1585. William, not yet 21, was the father of three, with the responsibility of supporting his family.

His solution was to pursue a theatrical career, and to do so in London, where fortunes could be made. He may have joined a touring company of players, such as the Queen's Men who had visited Stratford in 1587. Apart from a reference in a court case, no documentary evidence of his activities exists from the time of his twins' baptism to his reappearance in the records at the end of 1592, in London. This latter reference was from a minor playwright, Robert Greene, who dismissed his younger rival (and social inferior), as "an upstart Crow … [who] supposes he is able to bombast out a blank verse as the best of you: and being an absolute Johannes factotum [jack of all trades]." It was clear that by this time William Shakespeare was not only an actor, but also a poet and a writer of scripts, and sufficiently well established to irritate the university-educated Greene.

Shakespeare's family remained in Stratford, living with his parents and his younger siblings in the Henley Street house. He may have returned home frequently: a two-day journey on horseback or carrier's wagon; four days on foot. This separation must have compounded his distress when his son Hamnet died in 1596. The following year, he bought New Place, the second-largest house in Stratford and an indication of his prosperity and accompanying status. This provided William with a comfortable base in his home town to retreat to; he appears to have done so increasingly from 1609.

Later investments proved him to be an astute businessman. He amassed substantial estates in Stratford, as well as financial interests in London,

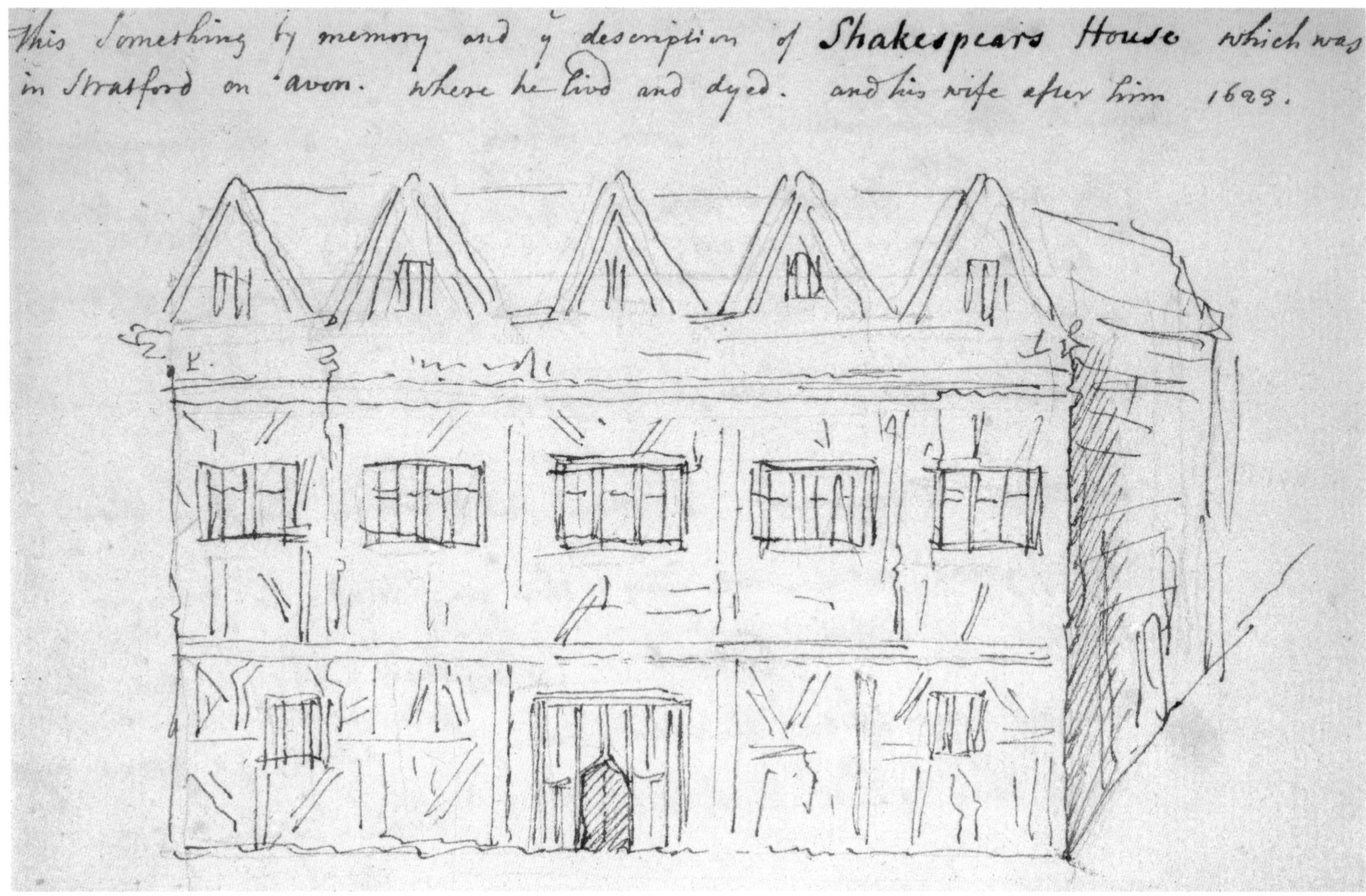

BELOW: *The drawing of Shakespeare's New Place, in Stratford, was made by George Vertue in 1737, 35 years after the house had been demolished. The artist relied on a description by a distant relative of Shakespeare.*

RIGHT: *The Shakespeare Birthplace Trust announced in 2009 that the painting of the man with a ruff (near right) was an authentic portrait of Shakespeare—a number of experts have since expressed doubt. Known as the Cobbe portrait, it was painted in about 1610 when Shakespeare was 46. The Chandos portrait (far right) is regarded by many as the painting most likely to be of the playwright. We cannot be sure, however, exactly what Shakespeare looked like.*

including, in 1599, becoming the part-owner of the Globe theater. From 1602, he was financially secure; he would never suffer the fate of his father.

William died in New Place in April 1616, at the age of 52. Anne outlived her husband by seven years, dying in 1623 aged 67. Shakespeare's last direct descendant, Susanna's daughter Elizabeth Hall, died in 1670.

Religious Beliefs and Sexuality

Shakespeare was born into the political and social turmoil following the Reformation and the break with the old Catholic faith. Shakespeare's parents were raised as Catholics and, in 1583, his mother's cousin, Edward Arden, was among those executed for his involvement in a "papist" plot to murder the queen. Some have suggested that William's father, John, retained his Catholic faith even though he did attend the local Protestant church, and that William was brought up in a covertly Catholic household. William's own religious beliefs, if any, are a matter of speculation: in London it seems he was not a regular churchgoer and, on the evidence found in his plays, he was remarkably evenhanded toward both the old and the new orders.

Similarly, his sexuality is also a matter of a great deal of gossip and guesswork. Much has been made of the dedication of narrative poems to the young Henry Wriothesley, who is sometimes supposed to be the "fair youth" of his sonnets; at the very least, this suggests Shakespeare had an understanding of male friendships. In an age known for its promiscuity, it is unlikely that Shakespeare remained faithful to his absent wife; indeed, contemporary tittle-tattle hints at philandering.

Shakespeare the Enigma

Shakespeare's death received little public attention, and his fellow dramatists paid few tributes to his memory. During his lifetime, he attracted very few negative comments, apart from those of the jealous Robert Greene. In 1623, Ben Jonson, in his dedicatory poem in the First Folio—the first published collection of Shakespeare's works—described him as "not of an age, but for all time." Still, no scholars recorded the impressions he had made on his contemporaries; while his work was valued, it seems his personality was not deemed to be of any significant interest.

Apart from his will, none of the personal papers of Shakespeare has survived; there are no letters from him or to him. Throughout the course of his career he is revealed as determined, hardworking, and ambitious; he appears to have been shrewd and successful in his business dealings; and his extraordinary body of work displays keen intelligence, wit, and passion. Nevertheless, Shakespeare the man remains elusive.

BELOW: *There are only six known examples of Shakespeare's signature in existence—the sole authenticated examples of his handwriting. Three of them are on his will, which was made in January 1616, three months before he died. This signature was on the third and final page of the will.*

Canonical Works

The collection of plays and poems that we know as the "complete works" of William Shakespeare has remained relatively stable since the seventeenth century, but it might never attain a definitive form. Many questions about collaborative plays, variant readings, and lost works continue to forestall a fixed Shakespearean canon. Nonetheless, the provisional assembly of texts that we ascribe to Shakespeare's creative imagination constitutes one of the most remarkable achievements in world literature, and it provides a firm enough foothold for myriad enterprises of scholarship, performance, and enjoyment.

What we consider to be the canon consists of 38 plays, a collection of 154 sonnets, two long narrative poems, and a handful of shorter poetic works (some of disputed authorship). All these works come to us in mediated forms, shaped by the practices of playhouses and of publishers in Renaissance England. The only example we have of creative work believed to be in Shakespeare's own hand consists of a few pages of manuscript contributed to the collaboratively written play *Sir Thomas More*. Everything else comes to us at one remove at least from the author's pen, in printed editions of variable provenance.

Textual scholars study, research, and compare the various editions in which Shakespeare's works were printed, as well as historical documents such as the Stationers' Register (a record of publications, which was maintained by the Stationers' Company, a trade guild associated with printers, booksellers, and publishers, in order to document publishers' rights to print a particular work), the records of performances at court, and other writings. By examining these traces, we have developed a fairly coherent picture of the shape of the literary and theatrical career of Shakespeare.

BELOW: *In 1596, Shakespeare played a part in fruitless negotiations for the Lord Chamberlain's Men to move to the Swan theater on the south bank of the Thames. This sketch of the Swan, made by Johannes de Witt the same year, gives an idea of the type of stage—and theater—for which Shakespeare wrote his plays.*

Quartos and Folios

Like most of his contemporaries apart from Ben Jonson (who published his own plays in 1616), Shakespeare appears to have given little attention to the publication of his plays. Only about half of them appeared during his lifetime, in single-volume editions called "quartos" because they were made up of sheets of printers' paper folded into fourths. Several of these were unauthorized—what Shakespeare's colleagues called "stolen and surreptitious copies, maimed and deformed by the

frauds and stealths of injurious imposters." Seven years after Shakespeare's death, two of his fellow players from the King's Men, John Heminges and Henry Condell, compiled *Mr. William Shakespeares Comedies, Histories, & Tragedies*, that were "published according to the true original copies." This volume, known as the First Folio of 1623, is a landmark in literary history, and it remains the primary source for the Shakespeare canon. It contains all the plays now considered to be canonical except for *Pericles* and *The Two Noble Kinsmen*, both of which are partly by other hands. It includes 18 plays that were never published in any other form, and would have been lost forever without it. Among them are some of the greatest works by Shakespeare: *As You Like It* and *Twelfth Night; Macbeth* and *Antony and Cleopatra; The Winter's Tale* and *The Tempest*.

Despite the claims of its two editors, the First Folio is not definitive. Many of the quartos contain readings that appear to be superior, or material absent from the Folio versions. The Folio text of *Hamlet*, for instance, lacks the important scene in Act 4 in which Hamlet reflects on his Norwegian counterpart, Fortinbras, including the soliloquy beginning "How all occasions do inform against me, / And spur my dull revenge!" (Act 4, Scene 4, lines 32–66). The Folio and quarto texts of *King Lear* differ so greatly that in 1986 *The Oxford Shakespeare* took the radical step of printing both versions. The most recent Arden edition of *Hamlet* includes three distinct versions, including the First Quarto, a text previously dismissed as corrupt. Several early printed texts were long considered to be "bad quartos," perhaps pirated versions that were reconstructed from memory by actors who had left the company. But scholars are now giving these increased attention, suggesting they may contain valid variant readings, and that they have much to tell us about Elizabethan performances.

Shakespeare and Genre

The editors of the First Folio divided Shakespeare's works into the three genres of comedy, history, and tragedy. This remains a convenient designation, although in the past century or so other categories have often been adopted. Each genre has certain distinctive characteristics, and studying them can help us understand the breadth of Shakespeare's outlook and the structure of his career.

A quick glance at the table of contents of the First Folio suggests that generic distinctions are evident even in the titles of Shakespeare's plays. Comedies never use the names of the principal characters; if characters are designated at all, it is by their social identity. Such titles as *The Merchant of Venice, The Two Gentlemen of Verona,* and *The Merry Wives of Windsor* suggest an orientation toward

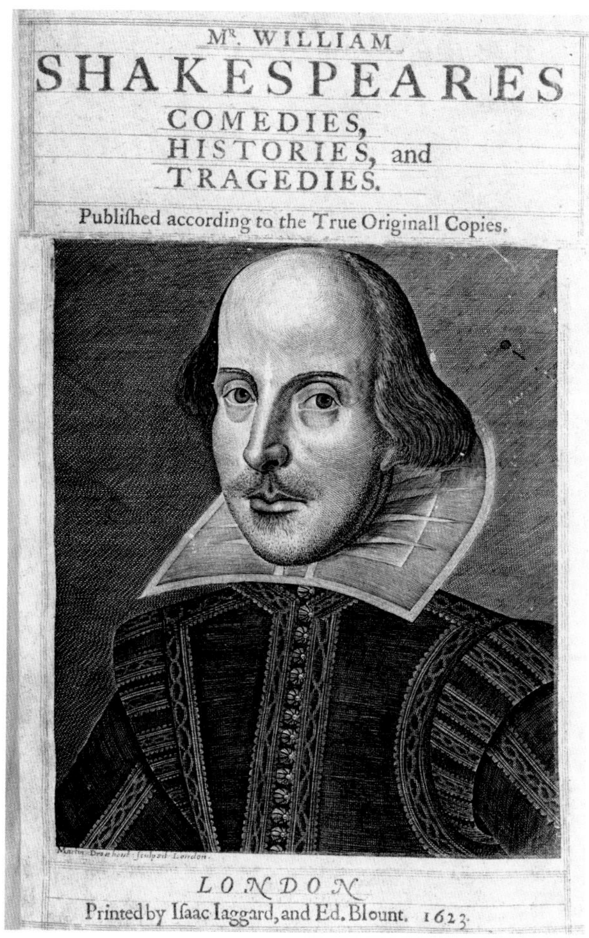

LEFT: *The engraving of Shakespeare by Martin Droeshout on the title page of the First Folio published in 1623 is believed to be a good likeness, since it would have been approved by his fellow players. The First Folio included 18 plays that had not appeared in print and would otherwise have been lost.*

personal and domestic affairs rather than political life; there are no kings or emperors named in the titles of these plays. Just as often, however, brief thematic phrases are used as the titles of comedies, suggesting that their content is not to be taken too seriously: *Much Ado about Nothing, As You Like It, All's Well That Ends Well.*

Histories, by contrast, are always designated by names and numbers that indicate the reigns of English monarchs, or portions thereof. Sometimes the individual life of the ruler is given less importance than political events that occurred during his rule. *Henry VI, Part 1,* for example, is concerned much less with King Henry himself than with the French wars and the civil conflicts that troubled the early years of his reign; Henry does not appear until Act 3, Scene 1.

The titles of the tragedies contain names but no numbers: they are concerned with the fates of particular people, and limited by the ends of lives. The names in tragic titles are generally foreign—even exotic—and they suggest figures of power and grandeur: *Hamlet, Prince of Denmark; Othello, the Moor of Venice.* Sometimes the titles of tragedies contain not one name but two, hinting at the entwined destinies of star-crossed lovers: *Romeo and Juliet; Antony and Cleopatra.*

The consistency of these titling strategies, at least in the Folio versions (in some of the quartos

OPPOSITE: *The builder of the Globe theater, Richard Burbage, was also the actor-manager of the Lord Chamberlain's Men. Burbage, who was regarded as one of the great tragedian actors of his time, originated many of the principal roles Shakespeare wrote.*

LEFT: *Shakespeare's quartos and the First Folio were set in movable type—a process developed by Johannes Gutenberg in about 1450—in print shops like the one in this sixteenth-century engraving.*

plays had different titles), indicates the degree to which Shakespeare's writing can be understood in terms of strong generic categories.

Comedy

During the first decade of Shakespeare's career, the 1590s, he wrote primarily in the genres of comedy and history. Shakespeare's early comedies are somewhat imitative of Classical and continental models: *The Comedy of Errors* derives from Plautus's Roman comedy *Menaechmi;* and *The Taming of the Shrew* has elements of the Italian *commedia dell'arte,* a form of improvisational farce based on stock characters. These early plays are full of slapstick vitality but are lacking in psychological nuance. In *A Midsummer Night's Dream,* Shakespeare demonstrates his ability to incorporate materials from diverse sources into an original and intricately layered plot. The basic story line of *Midsummer* is typical of Shakespeare's comic structures: young lovers, thwarted by a harshly unsympathetic authority, undergo transformative experiences in a topsy-turvy pastoral world, and thus achieve a final happy ending marked by multiple marriages.

Several elements remain consistent throughout Shakespeare's comic writing. Multiple story lines offer differing perspectives on the basic theme of romantic love. The natural world often provides a temporary haven from the corrupt city or court. Disguise, mistaken identity, and various forms of deception generate conflict and misunderstanding, until everything gets sorted out in the final act.

The protagonist is often a resourceful young woman, who may adopt male disguise. In the end, social harmony is restored: youth triumphs over age, and love over irrational law. Sometimes hostile or marginalized characters are excluded from the final celebrations—as Shylock is in *The Merchant of Venice* or Malvolio in *Twelfth Night*—

THE TABLE OF CONTENTS OF SHAKESPEARE'S FIRST FOLIO, 1623

The first collected edition of Shakespeare's works grouped the plays into three genres—comedy, history, and tragedy—a division that survives, with some modifications, to the present. Here are the plays as they appear in the First Folio table of contents.

Troilus and Cressida appears in the First Folio between the histories and the tragedies, but is not listed in the table of contents. *Pericles* and *The Two Noble Kinsmen* are not included in the First Folio.

COMEDIES	HISTORIES	TRAGEDIES
The Tempest	King John	Coriolanus
The Two Gentlemen of Verona	Richard II	Titus Andronicus
The Merry Wives of Windsor	Henry IV, Part 1	Romeo and Juliet
Measure for Measure	Henry IV, Part 2	Timon of Athens
The Comedy of Errors	Henry V	Julius Caesar
Much Ado about Nothing	Henry VI, Part 1	Macbeth
Love's Labor's Lost	Henry VI, Part 2	Hamlet
A Midsummer Night's Dream	Henry VI, Part 3	King Lear
The Merchant of Venice	Richard III	Othello
As You Like It	Henry VIII	Antony and Cleopatra
The Taming of the Shrew		Cymbeline
All's Well That Ends Well		
Twelfth Night		
The Winter's Tale		

RIGHT: *Josie Lawrence and Michael Sidberry are Katherina and Petruchio in* The Taming of the Shrew, *one of Shakespeare's earliest comedies and often criticized for its misogyny.*

and their fate might darken the comic resolution. In some of the later comedies, such as *Measure for Measure,* the unresolved conflicts and the proximity of death are so pronounced that some editors have assigned them to the supplemental category of "problem plays." *Troilus and Cressida,* Shakespeare's most generically puzzling play, is often placed in this category, along with *All's Well That Ends Well.*

History

Shakespeare wrote ten history plays, which examined questions of power and authority in the context of the English monarchy from medieval to Tudor times. Eight of these are grouped into two "tetralogies," linked cycles of four plays comprising a single, epic sweep of action; whether Shakespeare conceived them as four-play cycles is unknown.

The first tetralogy contains the three parts of *Henry VI* plus *Richard III*, and depicts the bloody struggle between the families of Lancaster and York that took place between 1455 and 1485 and is known as the Wars of the Roses: the prize they were fighting for was the English crown.

The second tetralogy explores the origins of that conflict in the deposition of Richard II by his cousin, Henry IV, whose reign was fraught with rebellion, but whose son, Hal, went on to triumph over the French as Henry V. The *Henry IV* plays challenge the conventions of the history genre, in that they include Shakespeare's greatest comic character, Falstaff, whose tavern world of anarchic revelry provides a strong counterpull to the plays' main action, the political education of Prince Hal.

BELOW: *In the 1995 London production of the history play* Richard II, *directed by Deborah Warner, Fiona Shaw plays the title role, reversing the tradition of men playing women's roles in Shakespeare's time.*

RIGHT: *Helena Kaut-Howson directed a production of one of Shakespeare's greatest tragedies,* King Lear, *at the Young Vic in London—with Kathryn Hunter playing Lear and Robert Pickavance as Gloucester.*

Tragedy

Shakespeare experimented with tragedy early in his career, with the gory *Titus Andronicus* and the lyrical *Romeo and Juliet*, which are believed to have been written in about 1593–94 and 1594–95, respectively. But the majority of Shakespeare's tragedies were written just after the end of the sixteenth century, when his work enters a new phase of darkness and pessimism that is reflected in other literature of the Jacobean period (the reign of King James I, beginning in 1603).

Shakespeare's greatest tragedies depict a world filled with human evil, in a universe that is either implacably indifferent (as in *King Lear*) or inhabited by ominous supernatural agents (as in *Hamlet* and *Macbeth*). Roman tragedies, such as *Julius Caesar* and *Antony and Cleopatra,* present the world in political rather than in moral terms, but even they are infused with imagery of loss and waste. The tragic protagonists that Shakespeare created are figures of dignity and grandeur, but they are also animated by destructive passions, such as pride, ambition, and jealousy (as in *Othello,* for example). Above all, they are defined by the suffering they inflict and endure.

BELOW: *The bodies of the doomed young lovers are carried through the streets of Verona in Franco Zeffirelli's 1968 film of* Romeo and Juliet. *The play, which dates from* c. *1594-95, was one of Shakespeare's earliest tragedies.*

Romance

Late in Shakespeare's career, he wrote plays that seem to extend beyond the Folio's threefold generic scheme. The Victorian critic Edward Dowden coined the term "romances" to refer to them; they are also sometimes called tragi-comedies, or simply the "late plays." They reflect the vogue for tragicomedy on the English stage that was being led by John Fletcher, who was Shakespeare's collaborator on two of his last works, *Henry VIII* and *The Two Noble Kinsmen*.

These late works, which also include *Pericles, Cymbeline, The Winter's Tale,* and *The Tempest,* generally combine the story of a near-tragic father with a redemptive story of a comic daughter. Shakespeare, by encompassing two generations, is able to explore both passion and loss while allowing the possibility of forgiveness and reconciliation. These late works are clear evidence of Shakespeare's ability to work creatively within and across the generic boundaries. A play such as *Cymbeline* might fit Polonius's hybrid category of "tragical-comical-historical-pastoral" (*Hamlet*, Act 2, Scene 2, lines 398–99).

ABOVE: Cymbeline, *written around 1609–10, is one of the late works often referred to as romances. Here, Ben Kingsley plays Jachimo, the play's villain, in a 1979 London staging.*

Shakespeare's Poetry

The only works that we know Shakespeare took pains to publish in his lifetime were the narrative poems, *Venus and Adonis* and *The Rape of Lucrece*. They appeared in 1593 and 1594, respectively, and both were dedicated to Henry Wriothesley, Earl of Southampton, from whom Shakespeare sought, and evidently found, patronage. The poems seem to have been popular and, in addition, to have helped Shakespeare make his name in literary circles. In 1598, Francis Meres, in his *Palladis Tamia: Wit's Treasury,* mentions them favorably, noting that "the sweete wittie soule of Ovid lives in mellifluous and honeytongued Shakespeare."

The Classical influence of the Roman poet Ovid is especially clear in *Venus and Adonis*. The story comes from Ovid's *Metamorphoses,* a collection of tales of erotic pursuit and magical transformation. In Shakespeare's poem, Venus is an aggressively sexy goddess of love who pursues a bashful young man. But Adonis would prefer to spend his time hunting; after his death at the tusks of a wild boar, he is transformed into a flower. Despite Adonis's death, the tone of the poem is witty, playful, and titillating. *The Rape of Lucrece,* by contrast, is much graver in tone. Based in part on Ovid's story *Fasti,* the poem deals with the rape of a noble Roman matron by the tyrant Tarquin, as well as Lucrece's subsequent heroic suicide, which helped to bring about the founding of the Roman republic.

Undoubtedly the best known of Shakespeare's poems are his *Sonnets*. Some of them were probably written in the 1590s, during a vogue for sonnet sequences that also produced works by Sir Philip Sidney and Edmund Spenser, but they are believed to have been composed over several decades. They were not published as a collection until 1609, although two of the sonnets appeared in a poetry anthology in 1599. Shakespeare may have circulated them among a literary coterie: Meres speaks of "his sugred Sonnets among his private friends." It is not known if Shakespeare determined the order in which the sonnets were eventually published, nor whether they relate to particular people in his life. The identities of the "fair young man" and "dark lady" who seem to populate *The Sonnets* have occasioned a great deal of fruitless speculation.

The other poems most widely believed to be by Shakespeare are two shorter works: *The Phoenix and Turtle* and *A Lover's Complaint*. The latter was included in the 1609 edition of *The Sonnets*. A 1599 collection entitled *The Passionate Pilgrim* was published under Shakespeare's name, but only five of the poems included are known to be his. Recent scholars have given him the credit for other poems, including "A Funeral Elegy for William Peter" and a song beginning "Shall I die, shall I fly," but these attributions have not been broadly accepted.

Shakespeare or Not?

ABOVE: *The title role in* Edward III *was played by David Rintoul (center) at the Swan Theatre, Stratford, in 2002.* Edward III *is regarded as a semi-canonical work, a play that Shakespeare is believed to have written or at least contributed to.*

Scholars continue to seek "new" Shakespeare works—any texts that have been previously unknown, or attributed to other writers, or listed as anonymous. It is entirely possible—even likely—that the Shakespeare canon will continue evolving as new discoveries are authenticated and new methods of textual analysis are employed.

Semicanonical Works

Some plays that were not published in the First Folio are now generally accepted into the canon, notably *Pericles* and, more recently, *The Two Noble Kinsmen*. Most scholars agree that Shakespeare was at least coauthor of both.

Two other plays are now on the margins of the canon, and are sometimes included in modern editions of Shakespeare's works. *Edward III,* published anonymously in 1596, has elements in common with Shakespeare's other history plays, and some scholars now believe that Shakespeare made a substantial contribution to the play. *Sir Thomas More,* originally written in the early 1590s by Anthony Munday and others, seems to have been revised by a team of playwrights that included Shakespeare. It is thought that Shakespeare's likely contribution was only a few pages, but these make a compelling addition to the canon, especially as the manuscript pages are probably in the playwright's own hand. In Britain, the Royal Shakespeare Company has performed both of these plays as works at least partly by Shakespeare.

Lost Works

There are convincing references, from his own lifetime, to two plays that Shakespeare seems to have written but for which we have no surviving texts. Francis Meres, in a 1598 list of Shakespeare titles, mentions a play called *Love's Labour's Won,* and a 1603 fragment of a bookseller's inventory seems to confirm the existence of such a work. It is also possible that one of Shakespeare's other comedies was known by this title.

There are three seventeenth-century references to a play called *Cardenio*, apparently performed by the King's Men in 1613, which was attributed to Shakespeare and John Fletcher, his collaborator on *The Two Noble Kinsmen* and *Henry VIII*. Cardenio is a character in Miguel de Cervantes's novel, *Don Quixote,* which was published in English in 1612, so presumably the story comes from that novel. In 1728, the Shakespearean editor Lewis Theobald published *Double Falsehood, or the Distressed Lovers,* which he claimed was adapted from an unpublished Shakespearean manuscript that was later lost in a fire. Theobald's play does draw on Cervantes, and may reflect an earlier Shakespeare version. There are other candidates for the lost *Cardenio,* including a play called *The Second Maiden's Tragedy,* which is usually ascribed to Thomas Middleton.

Apocryphal Works

A number of surviving plays have appeared under Shakespeare's name or have since been ascribed to him, although most scholars reject them from the canon. *Sir John Oldcastle, The London Prodigal, The Birth of Merlin,* and *A Yorkshire Tragedy* have all been published as Shakespeare's; *Thomas Lord Cromwell, Locrine*, and *The Puritan* were all attributed to "W. S." Some of these plays were performed by the King's Men, so it is possible that Shakespeare was involved in the writing of them, but none has won general acceptance as belonging to the canon. The Oldcastle play is noteworthy, since it presents a more positive view of the Protestant martyr who inspired Shakespeare's character, Falstaff. It is possible it was written in response to the *Henry IV* plays, though almost certainly not by Shakespeare.

Three anonymous plays in Charles II's library were bound together and ascribed to Shakespeare: *Mucedorus, The Merry Devil of Edmonton,* and *Fair Em. Mucedorus* may at least have influenced Shakespeare, since it contains a prominent role for a bear, as does Shakespeare's *The Winter's Tale*. There are other Elizabethan plays of unknown authorship for which Shakespeare has sometimes been credited; the most important of these is *Arden of Faversham,* a domestic tragedy of adultery and murder based on a real sixteenth-century case.

The Afterlife of Cardenio

Cardenio is a lost play that will not stay lost; it keeps coming back in various speculative versions. Lewis Theobald's *Double Falsehood* (1728) is only the first in a series of reconstructions. Gary Taylor, the Shakespeare scholar, has prepared a version that attempts to get beyond Theobald's eighteenth-century language to the supposed Shakespeare/Fletcher original underneath, and incorporates material from the 1612 translation of *Don Quixote* on which the play may have been based. Taylor's version has had a number of public readings and workshop performances. Stephen Greenblatt, another Shakespeare scholar, recently collaborated with postmodern playwright Charles Mee on a new version of *Cardenio,* which is set in the present day but is inspired by the lost original; it incorporates the Shakespearean device of a play-within-the play. Greenblatt has also encouraged writers around the world to adapt their own versions of this tantalizing lost work.

BELOW: *The Spanish first edition of* The Life and Times of Don Quixote *by Miguel de Cervantes (title page below) was published in 1608, and the English translation four years later. The novel is thought to be the source for the lost play* Cardenio, *believed to be by Shakespeare and John Fletcher.*

BELOW RIGHT: Sir Thomas More, *a play about Henry VIII's defiant chancellor, is now recognized as including a few pages written by Shakespeare. The Royal Shakespeare Company produced the play in 2005 with Nigel Cooke (center) as Thomas More.*

EL INGENIOSO
HIDALGO DON QVI-
XOTE DE LA MANCHA.
Compueſto por Miguel de Ceruantes Saauedra.
DIRIGIDO AL DVQVE DE BEIAR, Marques de Gibraleon, Conde de Benalcaçar, y Bañares, Vizconde de la Puebla de Alcozer, Señor de las villas de Capilla, Curiel, y Burgillos.
Año 1608.
Con priuilegio de Caſtilla, Aragon, y Portugal.
EN MADRID, Por Iuan de la Cueſta.

Language of the Soul

During Shakespeare's lifetime, the English language was at the end of a period of great change, but still contained many elements of middle English—the language used, for instance, by the poet Geoffrey Chaucer in the fourteenth century. There were two different ways of framing questions and negatives; multiple ways of forming the possessive; verbs were inflected to a greater extent than they are now; and "thou" and "thy" were used, inconsistently, rather than "you" and "your" to address an individual person and to denote familiarity. Because the concept of the dictionary was still in its infancy, there was no practical need for fixed spellings, and individual writers displayed their own preferences, and they were often inconsistent.

English was also embracing large numbers of new words. Writers were consciously attempting to make the English language less "barbarous" and more fit for poetry: they borrowed words from Latin, as well as from other modern European languages, and invented new words to match the intellectual and global explorations that marked the age. Thus, the state of the English language at that time offered Shakespeare unprecedented choice and freedom.

Meaning and Ambiguity

It is often assumed that Shakespeare is difficult to understand because his language is more than four centuries old. Though it is true that words change their meanings over time, the greater part of the vocabulary of Shakespeare is perfectly familiar to us. Most of the difficulty for readers comes from his *combinations* of words, and the fact he is writing poetry. The great joy—and the opportunity—of poetry is that, through the subtle use of rhetorical and aural patterns, it can both create and compress complex ideas. Its power often lies in its ambiguity.

The multiple latent meanings contained in a piece of Shakespeare's dialogue contribute to our sense that the highly structured, artificial language he uses is a convincing simulation of the tensions and undercurrents in real human interactions. The dramatist's poetic sleight of hand is to provide an illusion of a character's complexity and inner life.

Words in Performance

In fact, Shakespeare's language must always have been difficult to understand, if understanding is taken to mean supplying an instantaneous running paraphrase while reading. However, the plays do not seem to be so difficult when we watch them,

BELOW: *Shakespeare's language is better understood in performance rather than in reading. Here, an audience watches* Henry V *in Central Park, New York, in 1960.*

provided the actors comprehend what it is they are saying—which, sadly, is not always the case. A good actor's intonation will enable an audience to hear the rhetorical structure of whole speeches, while experiencing the pulling of emotional focus between one phrase and the next. In an effective performance of *The Winter's Tale,* for instance, we do not agonize about not making sense of Leontes' speeches—or indeed of the editor's attempts to paraphrase them in the footnotes. Instead, the non sequiturs and disjointed grammar convince us of the character's deteriorating mental health.

In a performance, visual clues are supplied by gestures and by the arrangement of characters on the stage. Although it is often said that the plays of Shakespeare contain very little in the way of stage directions, in fact the dialogue is studded with prompts for obligatory actions as characters comment on their own actions or describe those of others. Sometimes, however (as often in *The Winter's Tale*), these descriptions are deliberately at odds with what the play demands we see. Leontes describes as gross animal lust his wife's gesture as she takes his friend's arm, "How she holds up the neb! the bill to him!" (Act 1, Scene 2, line 183). Though she says nothing audible at this point, the characterization of Hermione elsewhere in the play will demand that the actor playing her is making gestures of open, honest friendship. Thus, the visual/aural discrepancy created by the writing lets us see, hear, and feel a marital relationship that is breaking down.

ABOVE: *Artist Joshua Reynolds painted this portrait of Samuel Johnson in 1756–57. In the English dictionary that he compiled, Johnson illustrated the meanings of words with quotations, the greatest number of which were from Shakespeare's works.*

LEFT: *When Visscher's map of London was published in 1616, its illustration of the Globe theater was out of date: the playhouse where many of Shakespeare's words had first been spoken had burned down three years earlier while* Henry VIII *was being performed.*

Vocabulary and Soundscape

Shakespeare possessed an enormous vocabulary—although the much-quoted 29,000 words is both rounded up and includes single words in all their variant forms. But just as a visual artist limits the palette of colors for each painting, so in each play Shakespeare limits his vocabulary, employing his facility for word play and pun to repeat words and sounds, thus creating a distinctive soundscape. It is this that contributes to the sense that his created worlds have coherence and probability.

In *Othello,* for example, the storm of passion that causes Desdemona to marry Othello (Act 1, Scene 3, line 249) echoes in the storm that wrecks the Turkish fleet. There, waves like "mountains" meld the sea and land, concealing sands, "traitors ensteep'd"—that is, both "submerged" and in great "banks"—that "enclog the guiltless keel" (Act 2, Scene 1, lines 8 and 70). Later, Shakespeare again repeats the prefix "en" in a word that he invents for Iago to describe his plans to "enmesh" them all (Act 2, Scene 3, line 362). The word casts Iago as a huntsman catching rabbits or birds, but it also prefigures the finer mesh of the woven handkerchief, which becomes central to his scheme. Later still, in another new coinage, Iago invites Othello to "encave" himself (Act 4, Scene 1, line 81). Each character in turn throughout the play repeats this

ABOVE: *The director moves an actor during a rehearsal of* Macbeth *at Stratford in 1968. The ways in which actors use the stage are part of the language of a play.*

sense of enclosure and entrapment. Bianca feels herself to be "circumstanc'd" (Act 3, Scene 4, line 201), for instance, the only time that word occurs in Shakespeare, and here carrying a range of its possible meanings, from "governed by circumstances" and "limited with conditions," to "subordinate." Similarly, although the play never says so explicitly, the evidence against Desdemona is entirely circumstantial.

Many of Shakespeare's more striking inventions and coinages have passed into the English language and therefore are more familiar to us than they would have been to his first audiences and readers. To use one of Shakespeare's own invented phrases, which was later taken up by Charles Dickens, they are as familiar to us as "household words" (*Henry V*, Act 4, Scene 3, line 52). Some, equally striking, have never caught on, and they would have been as strange and disturbing then as they are now.

Meter and Rhythm

Shakespeare's usual metrical unit is the iambic pentameter, a ten-syllable line divided into five sections, or feet, each comprising an unstressed syllable followed by a stressed one: ti tum / ti tum / ti tum / ti tum / ti tum. If slavishly followed for more than a few lines at a time, however, the effect is soporific. Instead, Shakespeare introduces great variation. He frequently reverses the pattern of unstressed and stressed syllables (tum ti), or adds an extra unstressed syllable to the end of a line. Rather than saying that the majority of his lines are "irregular," it is better to draw a distinction between meter and rhythm, and to think of the iambic pentameter as the underlying metrical pulse around which the rhetorical patterns and verbal rhythms of his poetry dance and riff, creating pace and mood.

Punctuation Marks

One reason Shakespeare is sometimes difficult to read, both in the earliest printed texts and in modern editions, is because we have not always fully understood the punctuation of his time. The same marks were used to denote three distinct functions: grammar, oratorical length of pause, and metrical structure.

The most problematic of these marks is the colon ":", which originally designated a section ("colon") of a sentence ("period")—in the biblical psalms, for instance, two colons balance each other in each verse-sentence. In Shakespeare's time, the colon was often used to indicate a pause in speaking, longer than a comma and shorter than a period, or full stop; but it is also found marking the ends of rhyming couplets, whether or not the sense runs on. In all cases, it marks off a distinct but intrinsically related idea. This usage was most helpfully defined by Francis Clement in his 1587

The Petty Schole, as a pause "in expectation of as much more to be spoken, as is already rehearsed."

Shakespeare often writes in extended sentences of a dozen or more lines. In the early printed texts these are divided into sections by colons. The most common editorial practice has been to substitute periods for one or more of these colons, using the modern semicolon for the remainder. The effect is often to lose the momentum and connectedness of Shakespeare's sentence, so that by the end of the speech, it is difficult to remember where it began. Taking the cue provided by Clement, it is more helpful to think of the Shakespearean colon as marking a sideways comment or digression on the main theme or flow of the sentence. The dash is often the nearest modern equivalent, although that mark is usually explicitly discouraged by the editors of modern Shakespeare series.

LEFT: *Stagings of the plays have to take into account silences that frame the dialogue. Shakespeare may have used incomplete lines to indicate silence in* Coriolanus. *In this scene from the play, Jonathan Cake is Coriolanus in a 2006 production at the Globe in London.*

Silence

Silence is the backdrop against which sounds make meaningful patterns, but the First Folio text of Shakespeare contains just two stage directions calling for silence: he "*holds her by the hand, silent*" (*Coriolanus,* Act 5, Scene 3, line 183), and "*Silence*" as Hermione walks in to face her trial (*The Winter's Tale,* Act 3, Scene 2, line 10). Modern editions often reduce the impact of the latter by making it an officer's spoken command.

There are some instances in Shakespeare, however, where incomplete lines of verse in the Folio may also indicate intended silences. In the following passage, Coriolanus's family come to him to plead for the safety of Rome:

CORIOLANUS *These eyes are not the same*
I wore in Rome.
VIRGILIA *The sorrow that delivers us thus*
chang'd
Makes you think so.
CORIOLANUS *Like a dull actor now,*
I have forgot my part,
And I am out, even to a full disgrace.
Best of my flesh,
Forgive my tyranny: but do not say
For that, "forgive our Romans."
(FOLIO LINEATION AND PUNCTUATION:
ACT 5, SCENE 3, LINES 37–44)

In Coriolanus's agitatedly rhythmic observation that he is like an actor who has "dried," the important, and therefore stressed, syllables are: dull; act; now; got; part; I; out; ev; full; grace. The two half lines—"Makes you think so" and "Best of my flesh"—create gaps and offer space for an excruciatingly painful silence between husband and wife. The Folio text's colon after "tyranny" (usually changed to a comma or semicolon in modern editions), combined with the repetition of "forgive," marks both a separation and a connection: an antithesis, rather than a conjunction. These eight lines in *Coriolanus* are often rearranged and regularized into seven complete pentameter lines by modern editors, ignoring that Shakespeare's most emotional, psychologically compelling moments are sometimes constructed in the gaps of his verse.

BELOW: The Winter's Tale *contains the stage direction "Silence," one of two instances it occurs in the First Folio, as well as the famous stage direction: "Exit, pursued by a bear." This scene is from a 1968 film directed by Frank Dunlop.*

A Universal Phenomenon

To say William Shakespeare is a universal phenomenon is an understatement. With the publication of the complete works in over 30 languages, and individual plays in closer to 100, Shakespeare's work is universally available, in print, electronically, on film, and via the Internet. However indisputable this is, there is considerable discussion, and very different political, aesthetic, and philosophical views, about why Shakespeare has such appeal. Broadly, the arguments fall into two distinct camps.

First, there is the argument that Shakespeare's words and body of work are inherently timeless and universal, that they speak to all people across time periods and continents in ways that are still understood. Within this camp, there are those who argue that this involves a sense of his work as constant, eternal, and unchanging, and others who believe that the timelessness is a product of adaptability—that Shakespeare's work survives because of its capacity to be altered and remade.

The second argument is that the longevity of Shakespeare's work is at least partly attributable to colonialism, that it has become part of a kind of cultural capital in which initially English—and later more generally Western—values could be imposed on diverse colonial territories in the name of the superior intellectual and aesthetic codes of the colonizing powers. Learn the language of Shakespeare, the argument goes, and you learn the language and values of civilization.

Perhaps the reasons behind Shakespeare the global phenomenon lie somewhere in between: a combination of appreciation of the poetry and its power, and the success of the British Empire in exporting the work of one of its favored sons. But in the twenty-first century, the postcolonial states have exercised their own dominion over Shakespeare, and today part of the history of any Shakespeare studies must include the myriad ways in which his work has become a part of so many different histories—how it has been used in very many different forms to support indigenous struggles and triumphs.

Referencing Shakespeare

The Tempest, Shakespeare's last sole-authored play, focuses closely on the enterprises of making and writing, in relation to the discovery of new worlds and the control over existing worlds. In its own time, the play was seen to engage with the explorations of new lands, new goods, and new peoples; in the late twentieth century, it was held up as a model for identifying the exploitation of indigenous peoples, with Caliban in particular the focus of extensive criticism. Indeed, over the centuries, writers and producers have turned to Shakespeare as a source of ideas and as a significant cultural

BELOW: *The great Spanish tenor Plácido Domingo sings the title role in Giuseppe Verdi's opera* Otello *in the 1986 film version directed by Franco Zeffirelli.*

Building the New Globe

In 1970, US actor and film director Sam Wanamaker established the Globe Playhouse Trust to build a new Globe in London near the site of the original theater, of which Shakespeare was a shareholder. The Globe theater had been erected in late 1598, constructed from the timbers taken from the playhouse known as The Theatre. The Globe was destroyed by fire in 1613 during a performance of *Henry VIII*, and again, finally, in 1644. Wanamaker's Globe opened in 1997. It had been constructed based on detailed research about the original. The new Globe gives audiences the opportunity to experience Shakespeare's plays near the site where his works were first performed for his contemporaries, who regarded them as popular entertainments.

LEFT: *Reconstructing the Globe was the "great obsession" of Sam Wanamaker. He persevered, despite widespread skepticism, dying four years before it was completed.*

authority for their own work. Shakespeare becomes one way of fighting back against colonial authorities, with audiences finding support for their own projects and political agendas in his work.

The popular British television series *Doctor Who* has included many Shakespearean references. In 2007, it played up the sense of familiarity with Shakespeare, naming one of its alien peoples the Sycorax, after the unseen mother of Caliban in *The Tempest*, demonstrating that Shakespeare is an international and intertextual icon.

Shakespeare, Language, and Languages

Part of Shakespeare's power and longevity lies in his use of language. Much of the impact of *Macbeth* as a play is that it is not simply a story of a bloody "butcher and his fiend-like queen" (Act 5, Scene 9, line 35). When informed of the death of his wife, Macbeth makes one of the most moving speeches in the play, a speech that is full of desperation and futility. How one squares such poetry with a man who has been so contemptuous of the lives of others in the pursuit of his own career is unclear, but the words ring loud of the loss that all human beings might experience in life:

To-morrow, and to-morrow, and to-morrow,
Creeps in this petty pace from day to day,
To the last syllable of recorded time;
And all our yesterdays have lighted fools
The way to dusty death. Out, out, brief candle!
Life's but a walking shadow, a poor player,
That struts and frets his hour upon the stage,
And then is heard no more. It is a tale
Told by an idiot, full of sound and fury,
Signifying nothing.

(ACT 5, SCENE 5, LINES 19–28)

Shakespeare has been described as contributing more to the English language than any other writer. But he has also been the source of creativity in language for others. In 1945, for example, the Maori scholar, Dr. Pei Te Hurinui Jones, translated *The*

BELOW: *Veeshayne Armstrong (left) plays Nerissa (Nerita) and Ngarimu Daniels Portia (Pohia) in the Maori-language film* The Maori Merchant of Venice *(2002).*

ABOVE: *The jazz trumpeter Louis Armstrong played Bottom in* Swingin' the Dream, *a "swing" adaptation of* A Midsummer Night's Dream, *in 1939.*

Merchant of Venice into the Maori language; when, in 2002, Don C. Selwyn used this translation for a film version, at least one aim of the project was to help young indigenous New Zealanders engage with their own native language. As in this example, Shakespeare's works can be the vehicle employed to reengage people with their own native cultures.

Words and Beyond Words

The globalization of Shakespeare's works has gone beyond words. His works have been adapted, rewritten, and reinterpreted in many different contexts, cultures, languages, and forms. In India, for example, there have been numerous translations of the plays into many local languages, including Hindi and Urdu, and the plays have also been given particular Indian flavor by incorporating specifically Indian cultural forms. *Barnam Vana,* a Hindi version of *Macbeth* produced in 1979, used the Yakshagana dance–drama style that is popular in the southern Indian state of Karnataka, and versions of *Othello* and *King Lear,* using another style, Kathakali, have been staged in India and at the Globe theater, London.

In musical forms, versions of Shakespeare's works exist in all shapes and sizes, from comic operas, such as Adolphe-Charles Adam's *Falstaff* of 1856 and the Cole Porter Broadway musical *Kiss Me, Kate* (1948, film 1953), which is based on *The Taming of the Shrew*, to Leonard Bernstein and Stephen Sondheim's *West Side Story* (1957, film 1961) using the *Romeo and Juliet* plot. Cleo Laine and Duke Ellington recorded Shakespeare-inspired jazz albums, *Shakespeare and All That Jazz* (1964) and *Such Sweet Thunder* (1957), respectively. Shawn Northrip and Peter Sanfilippo wrote the punk rock *Titus X: The Musical* (2006), and Serge Prokofiev composed the ballet *Romeo and Juliet* (1935–36). Painters have been just as enthusiastic, illustrating Shakespeare's drama and reworking his subjects: among them, William Hogarth, William Blake, Dante Gabriel Rossetti, and, most famously, John Everett Millais, whose *Ophelia* of 1851–52 is one of the key works of the Pre-Raphaelite movement.

Ideas for All Seasons

The deep themes in the works of Shakespeare have resonated across time and place. In the early seventeenth century, one of the great philosophical debates concerned free will versus determinism: whether the level of free will that people might have is counterbalanced by a sense that events and conclusions had been predetermined. Hamlet's belief that "There's a divinity that shapes our ends, / Rough-hew them how we will" (Act 5, Scene 2, lines 10–11) might be less commonly held in the secular cultures of the twenty-first century, but anxiety over personal agency remains common. The 1988 adaptation *Macbeth: The Witches Scenes* by the video artist Miroslaw Rogala foretells a post-apocalyptic world that is paranoid about technology

RIGHT: *In the first public performance in Afghanistan of a Shakespeare play for 25 years, the Afghan television star Sabar Sahar (right) played the Princess in* Love's Labor's Lost. *The outdoor performance in Kabul in 2005 was in the local dialect of the Farsi language.*

ABOVE: *This* King Lear *at the Globe theater in London in 1999 used Kathakali, a traditional Indian dance-drama form.*

(standing in for Shakespeare's witches), which has been designed to control human beings.

Although cultural understandings of love may differ widely, what love is and how it is manifested are of recurring and abiding universal interest. In Shakespeare's work, there is ample treatment of the topic, from Orsino's affected "If music be the food of love, play on, / Give me excess of it; that surfeiting, / The appetite may sicken, and so die" (*Twelfth Night,* Act 1, Scene 1, lines 1–3), to the calm affirmation in Sonnet 116 that "love is not love / Which alters when it alteration finds" (lines 2–3), to Adonis's clever and plangent attempt to deter the amorous Venus:

Love comforteth like sunshine after rain,
But Lust's effect is tempest after sun;
Love's gentle spring doth always fresh remain,
Lust's winter comes ere summer half be done;
Love surfeits not, Lust like a glutton dies;
Love is all truth, Lust full of forged lies.
(*VENUS AND ADONIS*, LINES 799–804)

The relationships between words and truth, appearance and reality, are also abiding concerns. When Iago says that "he that filches from me my good name / Robs me of that which not enriches him, / And makes me poor indeed" (*Othello,* Act 3, Scene 3, lines 159–61), the validity of his words is undercut by the audience's knowledge of their irony. Even as he is speaking, we are aware of his plan to bring Othello down. And, again, we are to learn how costly will be Duncan's naive belief in his own abilities to judge people, when he says to Macbeth, "I have begun to plant thee, and will labor / To make thee full of growing" (*Macbeth,* Act 1, Scene 4, lines 28–29).

"All the World's a Stage"

Perhaps more than anything else, Shakespeare's works, and especially his plays, have survived in so many very different forms because of the ways they engage the imagination of others. Perhaps, too, this is partly because of their provisionality. As stage texts, the plays are less determined, less fixed, than, say, a novel, a tract, or an essay. To perform them requires acts of interpretation, adaptation, and rewriting that breathe new life into these familiar words and stories, revealing aspects that have not been seen before.

Shakespeare is remade with every new performance, and every new production. His name is synonymous with his works, as those works are re-created with an eye to new audiences in ways that, as the consummate populous playwright, he would probably have understood very well.

Shakespeare's Enduring Appeal

ABOVE: *When William Dieterle and Max Reinhardt directed a Hollywood version of* A Midsummer Night's Dream *in 1935, their interpretation was in the extravagant tradition of the nineteenth century.*

The enduring appeal of Shakespeare's plays can be seen from their rich and diverse stage history. No other English dramatist has had his or her works performed on stage more consistently than Shakespeare, and indeed with more variety in performance. This is not necessarily because the plays have transcendent "universal" appeal. Rather, their richness of theme, language, and character allows each age to interpret them to suit the cultural tastes of their own time.

Free Interpretation

In the earliest printed texts of Shakespeare's plays there are no stage directions. So crucial decisions about what actually happens fall to directors and performers. Shakespeare left no cues to tell his (then) boy actor how to deliver Katherina's final speech in *The Taming of the Shrew.* It can be performed as an act of submission to Petruchio (as delivered by Peggy Ashcroft in the 1960 Royal Shakespeare Company production); spoken with complete sincerity, but as a tour de force that upstages everyone (Paola Dionisotti in the 1978 RSC staging); or, frighteningly, in the 1986 production by Turkish director Yücel Erten, as a prelude to Katherina laying her hands on the floor to reveal that she has slashed her wrists and is about to die. The absence of precise dramatic guidance from the playwright creates interpretative versatility, and, in this instance, the play continues to be part of a cultural dialogue about relationships between men and women.

Shakespeare provided no detailed accounts of the settings for his plays. Where the action takes place, both literally and symbolically, depends on verbal description used by characters within the plays, not the playwright's direction. Once again, this leaves room for variety of interpretation. Late nineteenth-century theater realized the wood in *A Midsummer Night's Dream* with extravagant painted stage scenery replete with foliage and balletic fairies (in productions directed by Augustine Daly in 1873, 1888, and 1895–96, and by Herbert Beerbohm Tree in 1900 and 1911). In the later twentieth century, the wood has been rendered more figuratively: a white box (in Peter Brook's production for the RSC, 1970); a mud pool (in Canadian director Robert Lepage's 1992 National Theatre production in Britain); and an open space with closets and hanging lightbulbs (in the 1994 RSC production directed by Adrian Noble).

Visual Metaphor

Directors may take their cue for the design of a play from the metaphors in the text. So, Hamlet's "the time is out of joint" (Act 1, Scene 5, line 188), in the production Henry Woronicz directed for the Oregon Shakespeare Festival in Ashland in 1994, prompted a set full of construction lamps and scaffolding. Great statues were covered in plastic, although one left recognizable was clearly that of Julius Caesar. A fascist flag center stage bore the name "Fortinbras." The set "portrayed the limbo of an interregnum between drastically different styles of leadership," Woronicz said.

This practice of updating is compatible with Shakespeare's own method of treating history and location. In *Julius Caesar*, Romans wear hats (Act 2, Scene 1, line 73), and ask the time by the clock (Act 2, Scene 2, line 114), and the Egyptians play billiards in *Antony and Cleopatra* (Act 2, Scene 5). Shakespeare's history plays continue to be staged with very contemporary relevance, and sometimes timely issues "overtake" the play. The modern-dress production of *Henry V* directed by Nicholas Hytner at the National Theatre, London, in 2003 placed cameramen among Henry's troops; they produced video coverage of the war against the French for the English at home. The political resonance of this scene would have changed between planning, rehearsal, and opening the production to the public. To the audiences, whatever Hytner's original reasons for modernization, his directorial decisions suggested news broadcasts of British and US forces at war in Iraq.

"[D]ressing Old Words New"

Every year, more books, academic articles, and literary journalism are published on Shakespeare than any other author. Shakespeare has been reinvented across space and time to keep pace with changing scholarly pursuits; the widening access to academia of people from diverse social, cultural, and national backgrounds; and popular interests.

A.C. Bradley's seminal *Shakespearean Tragedy*, published in 1904, with its exploration of character within an Aristotelian framework of good versus evil, may sit, in a present-day university curriculum, alongside a feminist inquiry that analyzes, for instance, the absence of mothers in Shakespeare's plays. G. Wilson Knight's Christian metaphysical readings of the plays—*The Wheel of Fire* (1930) and *The Crown of Life* (1946)—might keep company with Marxist-based discussion of the treatment of the "underdogs" in Shakespeare: the prostitutes in *Measure for Measure*, for example, or the apothecary in *Romeo and Juliet*. Studies of Shakespeare's sources and analogues, known as Early Modern performance practices, coexist with New Historicist interventions, such as Stephen Greenblatt's book *Shakespearean Negotiations* (1989), which read Shakespeare through political

ABOVE: *A strikingly original treatment of* A Midsummer Night's Dream *was the production at the 2007 Salzburg Festival, Austria, by the Salzburg Marionettes company, which used puppets and Felix Mendelssohn's music.*

LEFT: *Alfred Lunt and Lynn Fontanne were Petruchio and Katherina in a 1935 stage version of* The Taming of the Shrew. *They successfully toured the play throughout the United States, playing it as a farce.*

pamphlets or anecdotes buried in chronicles, giving equal weight to both kinds of materials.

Linguistic studies—such as William Empson's detailed analysis of the word "dog" in *Timon of Athens* (*The Structure of Complex Words,* 1951), or Caroline Spurgeon's examination of the imagery Shakespeare uses (published in 1935)—may keep company with books such as *Shakespeare's Queer Children* (1995) by Kate Chedgzoy. In recent years, increasing attention has been devoted to matters of religious intolerance, ethnicity, and colonization in Shakespeare—for example, by Ania Looma in *Shakespeare, Race and Colonialism* (2002).

ABOVE: *Ethan Hawke plays Hamlet and Diane Venora is Gertrude in Michael Almereyda's film of* Hamlet, *which uses a contemporary setting and technology such as video and Polaroid cameras but retains the dialogue of Shakespeare's play.*

Shifting Ground

The translation of Shakespeare into the media of film, television, and animation has given rise to new types of performance criticism alongside the more traditional theater reviews. Advances in information technology have spawned electronic texts, and made available digitized images of early text and performance diaries. Popular and specialized biographies continue to be written, and Shakespeare's position as an icon in academic, pedagogic, and cultural arenas is questioned by critics who are concerned to interrogate "high" versus "popular" culture. Shakespeare the Bard is recognized also as Shakespeare the brand name.

In his own time, Shakespeare's plays were performed both at court and alongside the inns and brothels of London's Southwark, a sign of their adaptability in terms of audience and place. There has been a very long history of adapting Shakespeare for other media: novels, musicals, films, operas, and versions of the stories for children, notably Charles and Mary Lamb's *Tales from Shakespeare* (1810).

The continuing influence of Shakespeare can be seen in the proliferation of loose adaptations in a variety of media worldwide. The animated film *The Lion King* (1994) echoes *Hamlet*. *Fools in Love,* a jukebox musical version of *A Midsummer Night's Dream* produced mainly for young children

The World's Stage

Theater companies continue to find new ways to make Shakespeare's plays contemporary. Tim Supple of the Royal Shakespeare Company directed an Indian cast for *A Midsummer Night's Dream* in 2006–7. Staged in both India and Britain, replete with Indian dance, song, and costume, this staging featured seven different Indian languages alongside roughly half of Shakespeare's text. In a 2009 collaboration, the RSC and the Baxter Theatre Centre staged *The Tempest* with an entirely South African cast in Cape Town before taking the production to Britain. Rich use of African dance, song, and ritual re-created the magic of the play. Starring Antony Sher (a white South African who has made a stage career in Britain) as Prospero, and the legendary black South African actor John Kani as Caliban, it explored parallels between political control, vengeance, and forgiveness on Shakespeare's island and the aftermath of the truth and reconciliation process in postapartheid South Africa.

LEFT: *Antony Sher is Prospero (center) in the colorful Baxter Theatre Centre and Royal Shakespeare Company joint production of* The Tempest *in 2009.*

(first staged in New York in 2005), used pop hits of the 1950s and early 1960s to explain the action. Contemporary singers have continued to draw on Shakespeare: for example, rap artist Sylk E. Fyne's "Romeo and Juliet" on his 1998 album, *Raw Sylk,* or Bob Dylan's "Po' Boy" from his *Love and Theft* album (2001), where Desdemona gets her revenge, *Hamlet*-style, on Othello:

Othello told Desdemona, "I'm cold, cover me with a blanket.
By the way, what happened to that poisoned wine?"
She says, "I gave it to you, you drank it."

The series *Shakespeare: The Animated Tales* (1992–94) was developed by a Welsh-language television channel. Twelve plays were adapted by Leon Garfield, voiced by British actors, and animated, using a variety of techniques, by Russian filmmakers working for Soyuzmultfilm.

The Cinematic Shakespeare

Shakespeare on film has now come into its own. Directors are unapologetic in creating cinematic Shakespeare rather than simply holding up a camera reverently to his plays.

In Kristian Levring's *The King Is Alive,* a 2000 Danish production—which translates *King Lear* to an abandoned mining town in a Namibian desert and follows the fortunes of a group of marooned Western tourists—the stripped-down cinematic style and extensive use of voiceover is an explicit rejection of lush mainstream film. *Titus,* directed by Julie Taymor (2000), is one of many films that reference visual media: for instance, when Anthony Hopkins playing Titus reproduces the grotesque jaw-juddering salivation that was such a defining feature of his portrayal of Hannibal Lecter in *Silence of the Lambs* (1991). The director Billy Morrissette set *Scotland PA* (2001) in an economically depressed Pennsylvania: Joe MacBeth and his wife Pat work in dead-end jobs in a burger joint where they murder the Duncan figure in a Fryolator, and the Macduff equivalent is modeled on the American TV detective Columbo. Morrissette explores the potential of his medium by an extensive soundtrack and images jostled by print. Dependence on junk food and the recycling of popular culture are referenced through the characters performing riffs on key lines of the play such as "fair is foul." A version of *Hamlet,* directed by Michael Almereyda (2000), has Ethan Hawke deliver Hamlet's "to be or not to be" speech in a Blockbuster video store.

With the global availability of recordings of films and performances on VHS, DVD, and with resources on the Internet, Shakespeare is now more likely to be seen or heard in one's home rather than read in a book, or watched on stage.

LEFT: *Jennifer Jason Leigh is one of the tourists stranded in the Namibian desert in Kristian Levring's 2000 film* The King Is Alive. *To keep their spirits up, the tourists stage* King Lear.

The Plays

The Histories

In his ten history plays, Shakespeare gave his Elizabethan audiences a vivid representation of their past, and his modern audiences a penetrating insight into power politics and human nature. Each bears the name of a king and dramatizes the often turbulent events of medieval and early Renaissance English history, charting the ambition of nobles, the downfall of kings, and the bloody chaos of war.

Henry VI, Part I

THE PLOT: *The play begins with the funeral of Henry V of Lancaster, who is succeeded by the young Henry VI, with his uncle Gloucester as Protector. The French, under Charles, rebel and attack English possessions in France. Led by Joan de Pucelle (Joan of Arc), they win Orleance (Orléans), lose the city to Lord Talbot in the same day, then lose Rouen.*

In England, the rivalry between Richard Plantagenet, Duke of York, and John Beauford, Duke of Somerset, creates two factions. The supporters are asked to wear a white rose for York or a red rose for Somerset; the king later declares himself for the latter. This strife causes Lord Talbot's death, when the other lords fail to come to his aid.

York exposes his secret claim to the throne to his supporters. In France, he takes Joan prisoner and sends her to be executed. The Earl of Suffolk, hoping to control Henry, arranges for him to marry Margaret of Anjou.

ABOVE: *This fifteenth-century manuscript depicts Henry VI investing Lord Talbot with the sword of office as Constable of France. Shakespeare has Talbot die at the hands of Joan de Pucelle, but in reality he died more than 20 years after Joan was burned at the stake by the English.*

Dramatis Personae

King Henry the Sixth
Duke of Gloucester, *uncle to the king, and Protector*
Duke of Bedford, *uncle to the king, and Regent of France*
Thomas Beauford, Duke of Exeter, *great-uncle to the king*
Henry Beauford, Bishop of Winchester, *and afterward Cardinal, great-uncle to the king*
John Beauford, Earl, *afterward* **Duke, of Somerset**
Richard Plantagenet, *son of Richard, late Earl of Cambridge, afterward* **Duke of York**
Earl of Warwick
Earl of Salisbury
Earl of Suffolk
Lord Talbot, *afterward Earl of Shrewsbury*
John Talbot, *his son*
Edmund Mortimer, *Earl of March*
Sir John Falstaff
Sir William Lucy
Sir William Glansdale
Sir Thomas Gargrave
Mayor of London
Woodvile, *Lieutenant of the Tower*
Vernon, *of the White Rose or York faction*
Basset, *of the Red Rose or Lancaster faction*
Lawyer
Jailers, *to Mortimer*
Charles, *Dolphin, and afterward king, of France*
Reignier, *Duke of Anjou, and titular King of Naples*
Duke of Burgundy
Duke of Alanson
Bastard of Orleance
Governor of Paris
Master Gunner of Orleance, and his Son
General of the French forces in Bordeaux
French Sergeant
Porter
Shepherd, *father to Joan de Pucelle*
Margaret, *daughter to Reignier, afterward married to King Henry*
Countess of Auvergne
Joan de Pucelle, *also called Joan of Aire*
Fiends appearing to Joan de Pucelle
Lords, Warders of the Tower, Papal Legate, Ambassadors, Heralds, Officers, Soldiers, Messengers, and Attendants, English and French

WRITTEN
c. 1592

SETTING AND PERIOD
England and France during part of the reign of Henry VI (1422–44)

CHARACTERS 34

ACTS 5

SCENES 27

LINES 2,695

This play is the first of a tetralogy of plays—a series of four, which includes *Richard III*—retracing a crucial episode in the history of England: the Wars of the Roses, a vicious civil war that broke out in the fifteenth century during the reign of Henry VI of Lancaster, between Henry's followers and those of Richard Plantagenet. The subject matter was dear to Queen Elizabeth I: it was her Tudor grandfather, Henry VII, who eventually killed the bloodthirsty Richard III and put an end to the feud. The whole tetralogy shows the evils of division; *Part 1* stages the decline of feudal England.

From History to Drama

For inspiration, Shakespeare turned to historians such as Raphael Holinshed (*Chronicles of England, Scotland and Ireland,* 1587), but also to the Tudor propagandist Edmund Hall's *The Union of the ... Families of Lancaster and York* (1548). Shakespeare did not write as a historian and did not feel bound to historical accuracy. He freely reorganized the historical material to suit his dramatic purposes, superimposing characters (for instance, in representing two dukes of Somerset as one), collapsing events (the loss of the French provinces is shown as simultaneous with Henry V's death), and even inventing episodes (like the meeting between Talbot and Joan, and her execution by York).

A Clash of Values

The play focuses on the evils of division and shows the decadence of heroism: the chivalric Talbot is depicted as a fossil from Henry V's reign, mocked by the more opportunistic Joan, who refuses to engage in single combat with him (Act 3, Scene 2). This clash of values is best exemplified by the level of disrespect shown by the French toward Talbot's corpse, and their disregard for his aristocratic titles, as Joan makes clear:

The Turk, that two and fifty kingdoms hath,
Writes not so tedious a style as this.
Him that thou magnifi'st with all these titles
Stinking and fly-blown lies here at our feet.
(ACT 4, SCENE 7, LINES 73–76)

This late dissension grown betwixt the peers/
Burns under feigned ashes of forg'd love,/
And will at last break out into a flame:/
As fest'red members rot but by degree.

—*Exeter* (ACT 3, SCENE 1, LINES 188–91)

England's Troubles

Glory is like a circle in the water,
Which never ceaseth to enlarge itself,
Till by broad spreading it disperse to nought.
With Henry's death the English circle ends,
Dispersed are the glories it included.
—*Joan de Pucelle* (ACT 1, SCENE 2, LINES 133–37)

O Warwick, Warwick, I foresee with grief
The utter loss of all the realm of France.
—*York* (ACT 5, SCENE 4, LINES 111–12)

Shakespeare's satirical treatment of the French was already present in his sources; the French are invariably shown as cowardly and changeable. But the English, irascible and selfish, fare little better. The ambitious Duke of York, in particular, emerges as Machiavellian, biding his time; but he also has a legitimate title to the crown. Meanwhile, Henry VI, the young devout king, appears incapable of domesticating his fiery vassals, and the play ends with intimations of disaster.

The play has an episodic structure. It is full of the swift movements of troops, sieges and countersieges, sudden victories and losses; there is no respite in the action, the English court being the scene of more strife. The war is shown as indecisive, as the French and the English alternatively win and lose indiscriminate battles. The English seem to have secured their position in France at the end of the play, but the loss of Talbot and the intended marriage between Henry and Margaret of Anjou bring this into question. The overriding image is that of simmering division, which will lead to worse evils, as Henry says:

Believe me, lords, my tender years can tell,
Civil dissension is a viperous worm
That gnaws the bowels of the commonwealth.
(ACT 3, SCENE 1, LINES 71–73)

Critical Fortune

Of the three *Henry VI* plays, which are usually staged as a whole, *Part 1* is most often cut, perhaps because it has no dominant parts and presents a gallery of two-dimensional characters. Moreover, its outstanding warriors, Talbot and Joan, are both short-lived. In fact, the play is mainly famous for the cameo appearance of Joan of Arc. Although made a saint by the Catholic Church in 1920, in *Henry VI, Part 1* she is represented as a hilarious antiheroine, not a virgin (a "Pucelle") inspired by God, but a lewd witch (a "Puzzel," or prostitute) with a good sense of humor.

Henry VI, Part 2

THE PLOT: *Henry VI welcomes his new queen, Margaret of Anjou, who is Suffolk's secret lover. Gloucester objects to a marriage that implies the surrender of Anjou and Maine. The peers worry about his influence on the devout king and plot his downfall. Gloucester's wife Eleanor, hoping to be queen, dabbles in witchcraft, and is then banished. Gloucester is accused of treason, imprisoned, and murdered. Suffolk is banished by the king for his part in the conjuration and is murdered by pirates. In Ireland, York represses an uprising, and enlists Jack Cade to lead a rebellion in England. Cade enters London with an army of commoners and declares himself Protector; the rebels are routed and Cade killed. York claims the throne, and triumphs at the battle of Saint Albons where Somerset is killed.*

Dramatis Personae

King Henry the Sixth
Humphrey, Duke of Gloucester, *his uncle*
Cardinal Beauford, Bishop of Winchester, *great-uncle to the king*
Richard Plantagenet, Duke of York
Edward and Richard, *his sons*
Duke of Somerset
Duke of Suffolk
Duke of Buckingham
Lord Clifford
Young Clifford, *his son*
Earl of Salisbury
Earl of Warwick
Lord Scales
Lord Say
Sir Humphrey Stafford
William Stafford, *his brother*
Sir John Stanley
Vaux
Matthew Goffe
Alexander Iden, *a Kentish gentleman*
Lieutenant, Shipmaster, and Master's Mate, and Walter Whitmore
Two Gentlemen, *prisoners with Suffolk*
John Hume, John Southwell, *priests*
Roger Bolingbrook, *a conjurer*
Thomas Horner, *an armorer*
Peter Thump, *his man*
Clerk of Chartam
Mayor of Saint Albons
Simpcox, *an impostor*
Jack Cade, *a rebel*
George Bevis, John Holland, Dick the butcher, Smith the weaver, Michael, etc., *followers of Cade*
Two Murderers
Margaret, *queen to King Henry*
Eleanor, *Duchess of Gloucester*
Margery Jordan, *a witch*
Wife *to Simpcox*
Spirit
Lords, Ladies, Attendants, Petitioners, Aldermen, Herald, Beadle, Sheriff and Officers, Citizens, Prentices, Falconers, Guards, Soldiers, Messengers, etc.

LEFT: *An anguished Queen Margaret (Penny Downie) carries the head of her murdered lover Suffolk in* The Plantagenets, *a Royal Shakespeare Company adaptation of the tetralogy in 1988-89: "Here may his head lie on my throbbing breast;/But where's the body that I should embrace?" (Act 4, Scene 4, lines 5-6).*

Henry VI, Part 2 is the second episode of Shakespeare's first tetralogy, and shows the actual beginning of the Wars of the Roses between the followers of Henry VI (a Lancastrian) and those of Richard Plantagenet. It is primarily concerned with questions of legitimacy and the specter of civil disorder. Like *Henry VI, Part 1,* this play is based on the work of Hall and Holinshed, but Shakespeare did not feel bound by accuracy. By collapsing historical events, the play concentrates its action on domestic issues. Jack Cade's 1450 uprising is historical, but Shakespeare turned Cade into an agent provocateur in York's pay, with a ferocious sense of humor.

Turmoil and Rebellion

The main themes of the play are disorder and rebellion, which are repeated on several levels. While Eleanor's mindless plot is easily repressed, the courtiers' machinations against Gloucester remove Henry's last bulwark against York. Cade's uprising, which echoes riots in Shakespeare's time among textile workers and peasants, reflects popular concerns about land use, escalating food prices, and the arrogance of the aristocracy. The rebellion also includes carnivalesque elements: Cade, as a Lord of Misrule, promises free wine, food, land, and sexual freedom to his followers. The barbarity and inconstancy of the rabble, however, reflect Shakespeare's ambivalent attitude toward the people, which can be seen later in *Coriolanus.*

Cade also offers a distorted echo of York. Not only is York's title to the crown legitimate, but York sees Henry VI as an incompetent king:

That head of thine doth not become a crown:
Thy hand is made to grasp a palmer's staff
And not to grace an aweful princely sceptre.
That gold must round engirt these brows of mine[.]

(ACT 5, SCENE 1, LINES 96–99)

Yet York's rebellion leads to a vendetta that will cease only with the deaths of all the protagonists. Witness Young Clifford's vow to take indiscriminate revenge on his father's murderers:

Meet I an infant of the house of York,
Into as many gobbets will I cut it
As wild Medea young Absyrtus did;
In cruelty will I seek out my fame.

(ACT 5, SCENE 2, LINES 57–60)

Images of Division

The play is dominated by a bestiary of cruel predators and serpents, and by the vocabulary of illness and the suffering body. The gangrene of division threatens the whole kingdom: "Send succors, lords, and stop the rage betime, / Before the wound do grow uncurable" (Act 3, Scene 1, lines 285–86). But the dominant image is that of decapitation, also an emblem of the divided body politic, from strangled Gloucester to the decapitated bodies of Suffolk, Somerset, and Cade's victims.

Modern Performances

The play has often been performed since World War II, thanks to playwright Bertolt Brecht's interest in epic drama. A famous production of the tetralogy (including *Richard III*), titled *The Wars of the Roses,* was directed by Peter Hall and John Barton for the Royal Shakespeare Company (RSC) in 1963–64; it was filmed as a series for BBC TV, again directed by Hall and Barton, in 1965. King Henry VI was represented as a martyr, and Cade as a legitimate working-class ruler who gradually evolved toward a Hitler-like figure. In a touring RSC production in 1977, with Terry Hands as director, Cade became a bloodthirsty anarchist, while in a 1965 production by Italian director Giorgio Strehler, Cade became a circus clown. Director Michael Bogdanov's English Shakespeare Company production, which toured internationally in 1986, transformed the rebel leader into a punk.

WRITTEN
c. 1591

SETTING AND PERIOD
England and France during part of the reign of Henry VI (1445–55)

CHARACTERS **69**

ACTS **5**

SCENES **24**

LINES **3,130**

And you that love the commons, follow me./
Now show yourselves men, 'tis for liberty./
We will not leave one lord, one gentleman;/
Spare none but such as go in clouted shoon.

—*Cade* (ACT 4, SCENE 2, LINES 182–85)

Uprising and Upheaval

CADE [T]here shall be no money; all shall eat and drink on my score, and I will apparel them all in one livery, that they may agree like brothers, and worship me their lord.
DICK The first thing we do, let's kill all the lawyers.
(ACT 4, SCENE 2, LINES 72–77)

Is not this a lamentable thing, that of the skin of an innocent lamb should be made parchment? that parchment, being scribbled o'er, should undo a man?
—*Cade* (ACT 4, SCENE 2, LINES 78–81)

But then are we in order when we are most out of order. Come, march forward.
—*Cade* (ACT 4, SCENE 2, LINES 189–90)

Henry VI, Part 3

THE PLOT: *Henry VI agrees to let York have the crown after his death, thereby disinheriting his son Edward. The queen, outraged, declares war on the Yorkists, followed by Clifford and others. She is victorious at Wakefield. Clifford murders York's youngest son, Edmund, and York is killed. The Yorkists, led by Warwick and York's son Edward, kill Clifford. Edward is proclaimed king, while his brothers George and Richard become the Dukes of Clarence and Gloucester. Warwick defects to the queen's party when Edward marries Lady Grey. Edward IV is taken prisoner, then rescued by Richard. Henry VI, restored to the throne, is overthrown again by Edward, who kills Warwick at Barnet. The queen is sent into exile; Prince Edward is killed. After Gloucester has murdered Henry in the Tower, Edward IV celebrates his victory and his newborn son.*

ABOVE: *Henry VI's decision to relinquish his throne to York sparks another bloody episode in the Wars of the Roses. King Henry (played by Chuk Iwuji) is joined here by Queen Margaret (Katy Stephens) and Exeter (Roger Watkins) in the Royal Shakespeare Company's production at Stratford in 2006.*

Dramatis Personae

King Henry the Sixth
Edward, *Prince of Wales, his son*
Lewis the Eleventh, *King of France*
Duke of Somerset
Duke of Exeter
Earl of Oxford
Earl of Northumberland
Earl of Westmerland
Lord Clifford
Richard Plantagenet, Duke of York
Edward, *Earl of March, afterward* **King Edward IV** *(son of the Duke of York)*
Edmund, Earl of Rutland *(son of the Duke of York)*
George, *afterward Duke of Clarence (son of the Duke of York)*
Richard, *afterward* **Duke of Gloucester** *(son of the Duke of York)*
Duke of Norfolk
Marquess of Montague
Earl of Warwick
Earl of Pembroke
Lord Hastings
Lord Stafford
Sir John Mortimer, Sir Hugh Mortimer, *uncles to the Duke of York*
Henry, *Earl of Richmond, a youth*
Lord Rivers, *brother to Lady Grey*
Sir William Stanley
Sir John Montgomery
Sir John Somervile
Tutor, *to Rutland*
Mayor of York, Mayor of Coventry
Lieutenant of the Tower
Nobleman
Two Keepers
Huntsman
Son that has killed his father
Father that has killed his son
Queen Margaret
Lady Grey, *afterward queen to Edward IV*
Bona, *sister to the French queen*
Soldiers, Attendants, Messengers, Watchmen, etc.

WRITTEN
c. 1591

SETTING AND PERIOD
England during part of the reign of Henry VI (1455–71)

CHARACTERS 39

ACTS 5

SCENES 28

LINES 2,915

Henry VI, Part 3 covers the central period of the Wars of the Roses. It depicts the rise of the cruel, misshapen Richard—Duke of Gloucester, son of York, and the future Richard III—who embarks on a quest for power against a background of increasing anarchy.

Like the first two *Henry VI* plays, *Part 3* is once again based on the work of Hall and Holinshed, but also on Sir Thomas More for its monstrous portrait of Richard of Gloucester. Although more faithful to his sources in this play, Shakespeare still effaces the reign of Edward IV, who ruled for ten years before Henry VI returned briefly to the throne, and brings Gloucester to the fore, who historically was still a child when his father died.

Legitimacy and Obedience

The play foregrounds the question of legitimacy. Henry VI, as the grandson of Henry IV, who murdered Richard II, is aware that his title is tainted; moreoever, he only descends from the fourth son of Edward III, while York derives from the third. This is why he offers York a compromise, which angers both his own son's and York's supporters. The military and political situation becomes more and more confused as notions of loyalty and obedience become relative. Henry VI is depicted as a devout but weak monarch, while Margaret appears as the real ruler, even though it is Henry who "do[es] wear the crown" (Act 2, Scene 2, line 90).

The play stages a radical questioning of the code of honor and chivalry in its representation of a world in which warriors in arms kill children and desecrate their enemies' corpses. This allows the rise of the Machiavellian Richard, whose will to power and envy derive from his misshapen body and radical loneliness. This fascinating character, presented as a kind of Antichrist figure, allows Shakespeare to reflect on the origin of evil in a world of murderous ambition.

A Theater of Cruelty

The dominant imagery in the play is that of sick, maimed, or monstrous bodies, which goes together with the denaturing of blood relationships. One of the most frequent words in the play is "unnatural." Richard's misshapen body appears as a dramatization of unnaturalness. The evils of civil war are perfectly illustrated by the scene in which Henry witnesses two soldiers attempting to rob their victims, only to discover that they have killed, respectively, their own father and son:

Woe above woe! grief more than common grief!
O that my death would stay these ruthful deeds!
O, pity, pity, gentle heaven, pity!
The red rose and the white are on his face,
The fatal colors of our striving houses;
The one his purple blood right well resembles,
The other his pale cheeks, methinks, presenteth.
Wither one rose, and let the other flourish;
If you contend, a thousand lives must wither.
(ACT 2, SCENE 5, LINES 94–102)

Blood on the Boards

This play, best known as a blueprint for *Richard III,* has been performed many times in the post–World War II period. Most productions focus on Richard of Gloucester as a symptom of the decline of England's glorious past. Several productions have been influential: the 1963–64 Royal Shakespeare Company production under the direction of Peter Hall and John Barton, and filmed for BBC television in 1965; the 1977 Royal Shakespeare Company production directed by Terry Hands; and director Michael Bogdanov's 1986 English Shakespeare Company version. An independent 2002 English production entitled *Rose Rage,* directed by Edward Hall and Roger Warren and featuring the all-male Propeller Company, won critical acclaim by setting the play in a slaughterhouse and using raw meat to represent the bodies of the civil war's victims.

I have no brother, I am like no brother;/ And this word "love," which greybeards call divine,/ Be resident in men like one another,/ And not in me: I am myself alone.

—*Richard of Gloucester* (ACT 5, SCENE 6, LINES 80–83)

Richard of Gloucester's Monstrous Ambition

I'll make my heaven to dream upon the crown,
And whiles I live, t' account this world but hell,
Until my misshap'd trunk that bears this head
Be round impaled with a glorious crown.
(ACT 3, SCENE 2, LINES 168–71)

Why, I can smile, and murther whiles I smile[.]
(ACT 3, SCENE 2, LINE 182)

I can add colors to the chameleon,
Change shapes with Proteus for advantages,
And set the murtherous Machevil to school.
Can I do this, and cannot get a crown?
(ACT 3, SCENE 2, LINES 191–94)

Richard III

WRITTEN
c. 1592–93
SETTING AND PERIOD
England, 1471–85
CHARACTERS 40
ACTS 5
SCENES 28
LINES 3,667

THE PLOT: *The Lancastrian King Henry VI has been overthrown by Edward IV of York. Edward's brother Richard, the physically deformed Duke of Gloucester, harbors ambitions for the throne. Richard's scheming creates animosity between Edward and another brother, Clarence. While Clarence is imprisoned, Richard's assassins kill him. Richard woos Lady Anne, the widow of Henry VI's son, Prince Edward, whom Richard had murdered. Margaret, Henry VI's widow, prophesies that Richard will destroy the Yorkists. After his brother Edward dies, Richard imprisons Edward's two young sons. Aided by the Duke of Buckingham, Richard manipulates the nobles into crowning him Richard III. He pays James Tyrrel to kill the two imprisoned young princes (the "Princes in the Tower") because Buckingham is unwilling to do so. After having Anne killed, Richard attempts to negotiate with Elizabeth, the widow of Edward IV, in order to marry her daughter (who is also called Elizabeth), and so secure his claim to the throne. A Lancastrian, the Earl of Richmond, leads a rebellion against Richard, joined by Buckingham. Buckingham is captured and executed. Before battle, ghosts of his victims visit Richard. Richmond kills Richard, is crowned Henry VII, and ends the civil warring by marrying Elizabeth, Edward IV's daughter.*

ABOVE: *In the 1996 film* Looking for Richard, *directed and starring Al Pacino, the actor explores approaches to Shakespeare, and in particular preparations for a production of* Richard III.

Richard III compresses the events that took place between 1471 and 1485 and concludes Shakespeare's first set of history plays, which concern the bitter war (Wars of the Roses) between the houses of York and Lancaster. The three *Henry VI* plays depict the treacherous and bloody events preceding Edward IV's reign, the situation that opens *Richard III*. The fourth play in the chronological sequence, *Richard III* refers to previously staged events, and thus evokes a strong sense of history. Characters pay for past misdeeds in a cycle of retributive violence. The conclusion of the play breaks this cycle with the resolution of England's civil wars, a significant historical event for Shakespeare's audience. The marriage between Henry VII and Elizabeth unites the houses of York and Lancaster and launches the Tudor royal line that produced Elizabeth I. Without doubt, the Tudors were keen to promote the notion that their recent ancestors—Henry VII was the grandfather of Elizabeth I—had resolved the civil warring and secured England's prosperity. But *Richard III* is more than mere Tudor propaganda.

The propelling force of *Richard III* is the evil but engaging Richard, arguably Shakespeare's first compelling depiction of a villain. Richard's skillful machinations drive forward a play that, with no subplot, is a focused and relentless series of violent

Dramatis Personae

King Edward the Fourth
Edward, *Prince of Wales, afterward King Edward V (son to the king)*
Richard, *Duke of York (son to the king)*
George, *Duke of Clarence (brother to the king)*
Richard, *Duke of Gloucester, afterward King Richard III (brother to the king)*
Edward Plantagenet, *Earl of Warwick, a young son of Clarence*
Henry, *Earl of Richmond, afterward King Henry VII*
Cardinal Bourchier, *Archbishop of Canterbury*
Thomas Rotherham, *Archbishop of York*
John Morton, *Bishop of Ely*
Duke of Buckingham
Duke of Norfolk
Earl of Surrey, *his son*
Earl Rivers (Anthony Woodvile), *brother to Queen Elizabeth*
Marquess of Dorset, Lord Grey, *sons to Queen Elizabeth*
Earl of Oxford
Lord Hastings
Lord Stanley, *called also Earl of Derby*
Lord Lovel
Sir Thomas Vaughan
Sir Richard Ratcliffe
Sir William Catesby
Sir James Tyrrel
Sir James Blunt
Sir Walter Herbert
Sir Robert Brakenbury, *Lieutenant of the Tower*
Sir William Brandon
Christopher Urswick, *a priest*
Another Priest
Hastings, *a pursuivant*
Tressel, Berkeley, *gentlemen attending on the Lady Anne*
Keeper in the Tower
Lord Mayor of London
Sheriff of Wiltshire
Elizabeth, *queen to King Edward IV*
Margaret, *widow of King Henry VI*
Duchess of York, *mother to King Edward IV, Clarence, and Gloucester*
Lady Anne, *widow of Edward, Prince of Wales, son to King Henry VI; afterward married to Richard, Duke of Gloucester*
Margaret Plantagenet, *Countess of Salisbury, a young daughter of Clarence*
Ghosts of those murdered by Richard III; Lords, Gentlemen, and other Attendants; Page, Scrivener, Citizens, Bishops, Aldermen, Councillors, Murderers, Messengers, Soldiers, etc.

events. Richard inhabits multiple roles—dutiful brother, caring uncle, loyal subject, bitter outsider, courting lover, and tyrannical king—so it is little wonder that leading actors seek out the role.

Contemporary references to *Richard III* suggest that it was also one of Shakespeare's most popular plays with audiences. A poetry anthology published in 1600, *England's Parnassus,* contains five quotations from the play alone. Combining historical realism, scheming villainy, and political tyranny through poetry that is evocative and memorable, *Richard III* deserves its popular acclaim.

England and Rebellion

Shakespeare's sources for *Richard III* were histories written during the Tudor period. They created the image of a monstrous Richard by manipulating, by ignoring, or by fabricating the historical evidence. Richard was, in fact, a popular Yorkist nobleman for most of Edward IV's reign; there are no contemporary references to any physical deformity, and he was not involved in Clarence's death. In reality, Clarence angered Edward IV by organizing a rebellion and was put on trial, with the king—his brother—as prosecutor, and was executed. Richard was so maligned by Tudor historians because the more evil he was made to appear, and the more dubious his claim to the throne, the more justified the rebellion and subsequent crowning of the Earl of Richmond as Henry VII. In this narrative, Henry is the savior of England, who purges it of Richard's tyrannies.

Shakespeare is dealing with politically sensitive material in the play: the very events that provided the Tudor monarchy with the reasons and authority to govern. It would have been a dangerous strategy to explicitly undermine or to question this narrative in a society where royal censorship was the norm and where treasonable writing led to imprisonment or worse. Nevertheless, in *Richard III,* Shakespeare manages to subtly challenge the simplicity of this Tudor propaganda through the play's powerful themes.

BELOW: *This 1877 advertisement shows John McCullough as Richard III, who he played on the New York stage. The* New York Tribune *noted that McCullough based his Richard "on intellect, conscience, sardonic humor, latent sensibility and fiery physical vitality," and his performance "reveals ... a prodigy of structural power."*

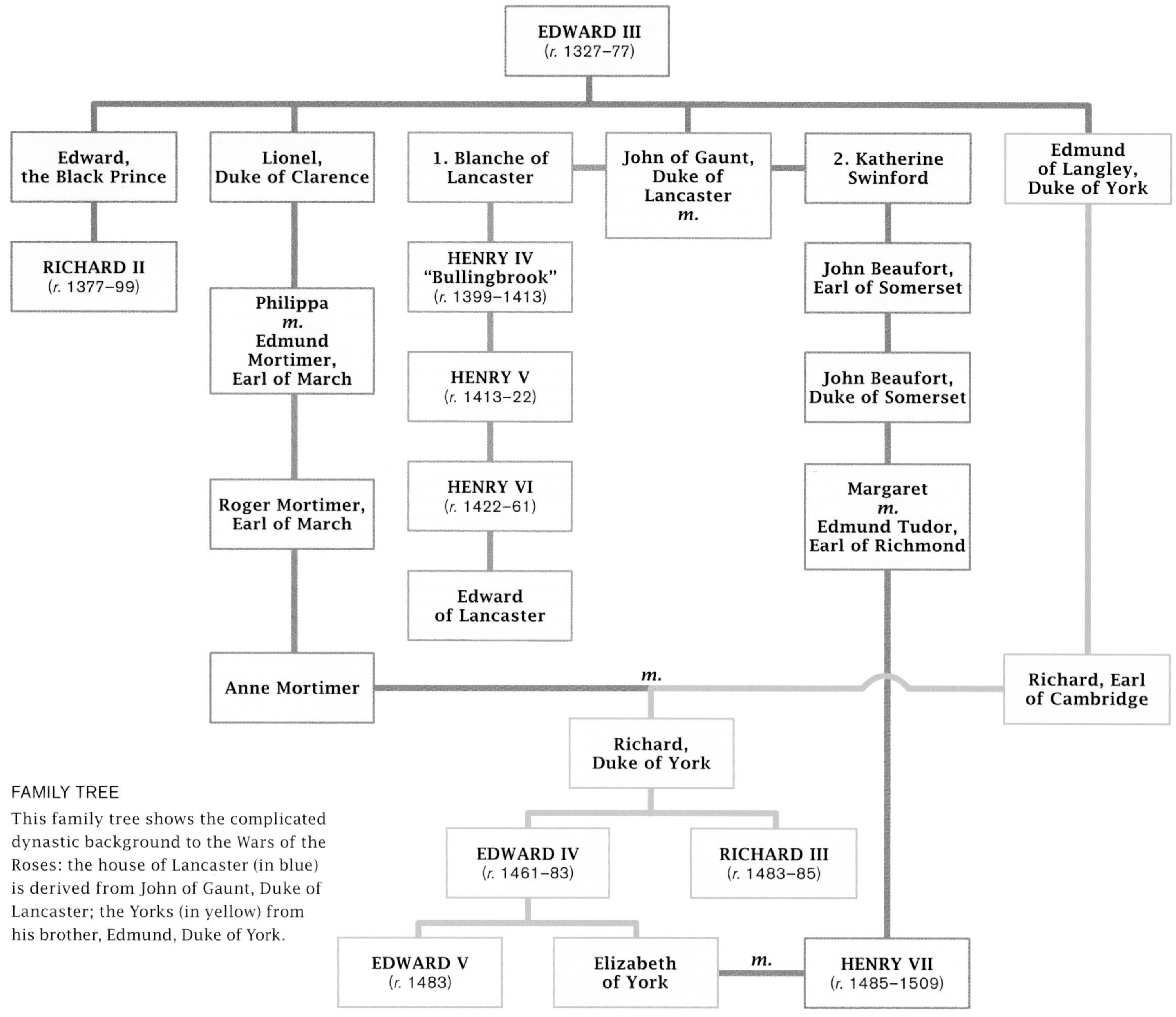

FAMILY TREE
This family tree shows the complicated dynastic background to the Wars of the Roses: the house of Lancaster (in blue) is derived from John of Gaunt, Duke of Lancaster; the Yorks (in yellow) from his brother, Edmund, Duke of York.

A Cycle of Murder

In *Richard III*, the history of England is portrayed as a cycle of violent murders committed by both the Yorkist and the Lancastrian factions. When Margaret bitterly laments the death of her husband and son, Henry VI and Prince Edward, Richard reminds her that these deaths were responses to her murder of his father and brother, the Duke of York and Earl of Rutland. The Yorkists curse the murder of the young Earl of Rutland—"O, 'twas the foulest deed to slay that babe" (Act 1, Scene 3, line 182)—but this only foreshadows Richard's infanticide of the young princes.

The fact that dead and living characters have the same name, or inherit the same title, serves to enhance this complex and confused succession of blame, revenge, and bloodshed. Late in the play, Margaret tells the queen:

I had an Edward, till a Richard kill'd him;
I had a [Harry], till a Richard kill'd him:
Thou hadst an Edward, till a Richard kill'd him;
Thou hadst a Richard, till a Richard kill'd him.

(ACT 4, SCENE 4, LINES 40–43)

The Duchess of York, who is also present, is very quick to remind Margaret of the past: "I had a Richard too, and thou didst kill him" (line 44).

Richard's manipulations suggest that history is often a biased fabrication. Act 3, Scene 6 consists of a short speech from the Scrivener, the scribe who produced the legal documents that provide a record of events. The scene does not contribute to the plot in any way and exists only to highlight how Richard is creating his own history. When

A horse, a horse!
my kingdom for a horse!

—*Richard* (ACT 5, SCENE 4, LINE 7)

the Scrivener produces a legal record on the basis of an indictment that had been given to him by Richard's henchman, Catesby, outlining how and why Richard had Lord Hastings executed, he notes that within the last five hours, Hastings was living "Untainted, unexamin'd, free, at liberty" (line 9). Yet Catesby brought the Scrivener the indictment "yesternight" (line 6); the scribe has spent 11 hours producing the record and concludes it must have taken a similar amount of time to write the indictment. Clearly the indictment, an account of Hastings' execution, is a "palpable device" (line 11) written well before he was accused or convicted.

An Evil and Fatalistic Force

Richard is often compared to the Vice, a stock character popular in medieval drama. The Vice was an embodiment of the ills that afflicted humankind, yet was traditionally a charismatic character who engaged directly with the audience. It is easy to understand the reason why Richard compares himself to "the formal Vice" (Act 3, Scene 1, line 82). Richard is presented as an otherworldly embodiment of evil: a "dreadful minister of hell" (Act 1, Scene 2, line 46), "the son of hell" (Act 1, Scene 3, line 229), and "devil" (Act 4, Scene 4, line 418). So, although historical events are presented in a tangibly realistic world, the play seems driven by fatalistic force (in the earliest printed edition it is termed a "tragedy").

BELOW: *In the film he directed in 1955, Laurence Olivier played Richard as a physically and psychologically deformed character, a ruthless, devious, and unstoppable force who devoured his enemies.*

Enduring Mystery

The fate of the real-life young princes in the Tower of London has become an enduring historical mystery, capturing the imaginations of academics, artists, and the public alike. Shakespeare's contribution to the cult of the princes is Tyrrel's evocative account of their murder in Act 4, Scene 3. In contrast to earlier rhetoric, the murderous thug, Tyrrel, renders the princes' murder a poetical subject:

> "O thus," quoth Dighton, "lay the
> gentle babes."
> "Thus, thus," quoth Forrest, "girdling
> one another
> Within their alabaster innocent arms.
> Their lips were four red roses on a stalk,
> [Which] in their summer beauty kiss'd
> each other.["]
> (LINES 9–13)

The imagery of this speech seems to have inspired Richard Northcote's 1805 painting, *The Murder of the Princes in the Tower.*

Margaret articulates this in Act 1, Scene 3 when she outlines specific curses for the York family and invokes heaven to aid her revenge:

> *Can curses pierce the clouds and enter heaven?*
> *Why then give way, dull clouds, to my quick*
> *curses!*
> *Though not by war, by surfeit die your king,*
> *As ours by murther, to make him a king!*
> *Edward thy son, that now is Prince of Wales,*
> *For Edward our son, that was Prince of Wales,*
> *Die in his youth by like untimely violence!*
> (LINES 194–200)

As each one of her specific curses is realized, it seems that a tragic inevitability is at work in the narrative of the play. Characters who face death often recognize Margaret's invocation of heaven; Grey, Hastings, and Buckingham all lament that her curses have fallen upon their heads. In revenge tragedy from Shakespeare's time, murdered ghosts appear to direct the retributive action onstage. According to the Elizabethan historical record, Margaret was dead by the time of Edward IV's

Pithy Richard

And therefore, since I cannot prove a lover
To entertain these fair well-spoken days,
I am determined to prove a villain[.]
(ACT 1, SCENE 1, LINES 28–30)

Was ever woman in this humor woo'd?
Was ever woman in this humor won?
(ACT 1, SCENE 2, LINES 227–28)

So wise so young, they say do never live long.
(ACT 3, SCENE 1, LINE 79)

Off with his head!
(ACT 3, SCENE 4, LINE 76)

I am not made of stones,
But penetrable to your kind entreaties,
Albeit against my conscience and my soul.
(ACT 3, SCENE 7, LINES 224–26)

Besides, the King's name is a tower of strength[.]
(ACT 5, SCENE 3, LINE 12)

O coward conscience, how dost thou afflict me!
(ACT 5, SCENE 3, LINE 179)

ABOVE: *The women in* Richard III *act as a Classical Greek chorus, lamenting the evil that has been done. Nancy Price and Nadje Compton were Queen Margaret and Lady Anne in the 1930 production directed by Baliol Holloway at the New Theatre, London.*

reign, so her presence in the play is Shakespeare's invention. Her appearance as an eerily powerful prophetess who is working on behalf of the dead and initiating divine retribution turns *Richard III* from historical drama to revenge tragedy.

Margaret is one of many women who enrich the play with a language of loss and grief. In Act 4, Scene 4, Margaret, Queen Elizabeth, and the Duchess of York expound their sufferings at length. The Duchess tells Elizabeth to mourn:

> *Woe's scene, world's shame, grave's due by life usurp'd,*
> *Brief abstract and record of tedious days,*
> *Rest thy unrest on England's lawful earth[.]*
> (LINES 27–29)

The women contribute to *Richard III*'s tone, functioning like a chorus in Classical Greek tragedy that laments violent, evil acts.

The Play as Theater

Richard plays a variety of roles to hide his true evil intentions and manipulate events and people to his advantage. He summarizes his ability: to "seem a saint, when most I play the devil" (Act 1, Scene 3, line 337). Richard melodramatically woos Anne, kneeling before her, asking to be killed: "Take up the sword again, or take up me" (Act 1, Scene 2, line 183). Richard, working with Buckingham, in effect stages his own coronation. Buckingham, who assures Richard that he can convincingly lie to the citizens, promises: "I can counterfeit the deep tragedian" (Act 3, Scene 5, line 5). Richard appears with two bishops deep in prayer when the Lord Mayor arrives, then proceeds to reject the throne, before unwillingly and humbly accepting.

Richard's skill as an actor is confirmed by those who believe he is good and honest. To the assassins Richard has sent to kill him, Clarence says that his brother loves him. Hastings believes that Richard is always direct because "by his face straight shall you know his heart" (Act 3, Scene 4, line 53). Richard proves to be a master of simulating emotions—he feigns love for Lady Anne, genuine concern for his brother Clarence, as well as playful affection with his two doomed nephews.

Richard III is metatheatrical, constantly drawing attention to itself as a piece of theater, frequently controlled by Richard.

Evocative Imagery

Richard's deformity, which is physically embodied onstage, is also embedded in the play's imagery. In his opening soliloquy, Richard is quick to comment about his "rudely stamp'd" and "[d]eform'd" body

(Act 1, Scene 1, lines 16, 20). In Shakespeare's time, there was a perceived correlation between physical deformity and a warped mentality, and Richard seems to confirm this. He is depicted as inhuman—associated with animal imagery: he is a "toad" (Act 1, Scene 2, line 147), a "bottled spider" (Act 1, Scene 3, line 241). One of the most evocative descriptions of Richard's unnatural evil is provided by Margaret:

Thou elvish-mark'd, abortive, rooting hog!
Thou that wast seal'd in thy nativity
The slave of nature and the son of hell!
(ACT 1, SCENE 3, LINES 227–29)

Richard associates himself with the image of shadows (Act 1, Scene, 1, line 26; Act 1, Scene 2, line 263), which is suitable for a dark, lurking character who conceals his murderous intentions. Actors were sometimes referred to as "shadows," for their ability to create an ethereal reflection of reality. Richard is the ultimate shadow-actor, who morphs into a variety of characters. Shadow imagery also reinforces the otherworldly tone of the play. After having seen the ghosts of his victims, Richard complains that "shadows to-night / Have struck ... terror" into him (Act 5, Scene 3, lines 216–17). The Duke of Clarence has dreams of an afterworld of shadows:

Then came wand'ring by
A shadow like an angel, with bright hair
Dabbled in blood, and he shriek'd out aloud,
"Clarence is come—false, fleeting, perjur'd Clarence,
That stabb'd me in the field by Tewksbury[."]
(ACT 1, SCENE 4, LINES 52–56)

Clarence's dream is considered one of the most impressive poetic episodes in the Shakespeare canon. But he is just one of many of the play's characters—including Richard, Richmond, and Stanley—who recount the vivid imagery of their dreams. Often the dreams represent characters' subconscious articulations of their fate; Clarence tragically dreams of his death before being murdered. Indeed, Shakespeare mentions the word *"dream"* and its derivatives more times in *Richard III* than in any other of his plays; the dreams represent how events may be influenced by a range of forces—such as ghosts, divine will, fate, or devilry—that are outside reality.

Now is the winter of our discontent/
Made glorious summer by this son of York;/
And all the clouds that low'r'd upon our house/
In the deep bosom of the ocean buried.

—*Richard* (ACT 1, SCENE 1, LINES 1–4)

The Message Play

Richard III has become a powerful way of commentating on violent political tyranny. A bold 1937 German production in Nazi Berlin made oblique comparisons between Joseph Goebbels, Hitler's propagandist, and Richard. After World War II, productions identifying Richard with right-wing totalitarianism increased. As late as 1995, a film version starring Ian McKellen and directed by Richard Loncraine was set in a fascist England.

Performances rest heavily on the success of the central role, and there have been many fine interpretations of the character by leading actors. In 1984, Antony Sher literalized the description of Richard as a "bottled spider," appearing in black almost doubled over on long, insectlike crutches. This acclaimed physical performance highlighted the psychologically grotesque villainy of Richard. The 1996 film *Looking for Richard,* directed by Al Pacino, charts Pacino's quest to play Richard and comprehend the character's history.

Richard III is sometimes performed alongside the three parts of *Henry VI,* an approach foregrounding the retributive violence of the play and its function as conclusion—and solution—to a historical crisis. The Royal Shakespeare Company performed all of Shakespeare's history plays in 2008. In *Henry VI,* Jonathan Slinger's Richard disguised the large red birthmark on his scalp with a wig. For *Richard III,* he exposed his "deformity"—the evil outsider had developed over the play cycle.

BELOW: *In Richard Loncraine's freely adapted 1995 film of* Richard III, *with Ian McKellen (left) playing Richard and Annette Bening as Elizabeth, the setting was a fascist 1930s-style England.*

Richard II

THE PLOT: *The play opens with Bullingbrook, in the presence of Richard, accusing Mowbray, the king's agent, of having used royal funds improperly and having been involved in the murder of the Duke of Gloucester (which Bullingbrook believes to have been the work of Richard). The two agree to a duel, but Richard prevents it and banishes both, Mowbray permanently and Bullingbrook for six years. Bullingbrook's father, John of Gaunt, then dies and the king seizes his lands. With Richard in Ireland, Bullingbrook returns at the head of an army to claim his inheritance, and defeats Richard's allies. On his return, Richard submits to Bullingbrook's power, repeals his banishment, and restores his lands. Bullingbrook claims the throne, and Richard abdicates before being imprisoned and then murdered by Exton. The newly crowned Henry IV banishes the killer and plans a redeeming pilgrimage to the Holy Land.*

WRITTEN
c. 1595

SETTING AND PERIOD
England and Wales, late 1390s

CHARACTERS 39

ACTS 5

SCENES 19

LINES 2,796

Dramatis Personae

King Richard the Second
John of Gaunt, *Duke of Lancaster, uncle to the king*
Edmund of Langley, *Duke of York, uncle to the king*
Henry, surnamed Bullingbrook, *Duke of Herford, son to John of Gaunt; afterward* **King Henry IV**
Duke of Aumerle, *son to the Duke of York*
Thomas Mowbray, *Duke of Norfolk*
Duke of Surrey
Earl of Salisbury
Lord Berkeley
Sir John Bushy, Sir John Bagot, Sir Henry Green, *favorites to King Richard*
Earl of Northumberland
Henry Percy, surnamed Hotspur, *his son*
Lord Ross
Lord Willoughby
Lord Fitzwater
Bishop of Carlisle
Abbot of Westminster
Lord Marshal
Sir Stephen Scroop
Sir Pierce of Exton
Captain of a band of Welshmen
Two Gardeners
Queen to King Richard
Duchess of York
Duchess of Gloucester, *widow of Thomas of Woodstock, Duke of Gloucester*
Lady attending on the Queen
Lords, Heralds, Officers, Soldiers, Keeper, Messenger, Groom, Servingman, and other Attendants

In terms of the historical chronology, *Richard II* is the first in Shakespeare's series of eight history plays, divided into two tetralogies, covering the period from the reign of King Richard II (1377–99) to that of King Richard III (1483–85). When writing the play, Shakespeare was influenced by several chronicles, the main one being Raphael Holinshed's *Chronicles of England, Scotland and Ireland* (1587), the playwright's favorite historical chronicle and one of the most detailed. He was also inspired by *The Mirror for Magistrates* (1559), a collection of poems by various authors about the lives of historical figures; the anonymous morality play entitled *Woodstock* (1591–95), which challenged the kingly notion of divine right; and Samuel Daniel's *The Civile Wars Between the Two Houses of Lancaster and York* (1595), a history in verse of the Wars of the Roses. Shakespeare added three female characters who were not mentioned in the other sources—the Queen and the Duchesses of York and Gloucester—and focused in his story on Richard's tragic failure and deposition rather than Bullingbrook's triumph, attributing to the king a defeatist psychology.

Although acknowledged in the play as the rightful heir of Edward III, Richard is shown to be a wasteful king who misgoverns his kingdom, while Bullingbrook is depicted as a pragmatic politician who is willing to breach traditional laws of royal inheritance if it ensures more effective and honorable government for the nation. Two conceptions of kingship are thus opposed: a king elected by God *(rex imago Dei)* versus a king supported both by the lords and the commons *(rex in parliamento)*. The traditional vision of monarchy is questioned and shaken, and the Bishop of Carlisle is ultimately proven to be wrong when he tells Richard "that Power that made you king / Hath power to keep you king in spite of all" (Act 3, Scene 2, lines 27–28).

One of Shakespeare's sources, *The Mirror for Magistrates*, can be regarded as an anthology of notable unfortunates and part of a tradition of works about the downfalls of the powerful dating back to Giovanni Boccaccio's *On the Falls of Famous Men (De casibus virorum illustrium)*, written in the mid-fourteenth century. Richard alludes to this *de casibus* tradition when he gloomily suggests:

For God's sake let us sit upon the ground
And tell sad stories of the death of kings:
How some have been depos'd, some slain in war,
Some haunted by the ghosts they have deposed,
Some poisoned by their wives, some sleeping kill'd,
All murthered ...
(ACT 3, SCENE 2, LINES 155–60)

BELOW: *In the Wilton Diptych* (c. *1395–99*), *which was painted for Richard II, the king kneels in front of (from left to right) St. Edmund, last King of the Angles; Edward the Confessor, King of England (reigned 1042–66); and St. John The Baptist.*

The play, as a whole, follows the traditional pattern: King Richard, "God's substitute, / His deputy anointed in His sight" (Act 1, Scene 2, lines 37–38), is deposed, dethroned, sent to jail, and murdered.

A Weapon of Propaganda

Richard II was first performed in late 1595 by the Lord Chamberlain's Men, the company Shakespeare had joined on its formation at James Burbage's The Theatre, in Shoreditch, in 1594. The play was revived at the Globe in London on February 7, 1601, in response to a request from Robert Devereux, Earl of Essex, a former favorite of Queen Elizabeth I, who had been stripped of his standing and offices of state after losing a campaign in Ireland and signing a peace treaty with the Irish that had enraged Elizabeth. At the time of his request, Essex was plotting to overthrow the queen and viewed Shakespeare's play as a perfect weapon of propaganda for his rebellion: spectators would see a historical precedent for the deposition of an ageing monarch, be favorably influenced, and rally to his cause. (Elizabeth, who saw through Essex's plan, allegedly said: "I am Richard II. Know you not that?") The rebellion, launched the day after the performance, was checked, and Essex executed.

The issue of the deposition of monarchs was so politically sensitive that the scene in which Richard II hands over his crown (Act 4, Scene 1) was not allowed to be printed in Elizabeth I's lifetime. It was printed five years after her death, in 1608, in the Fourth Quarto, the title of which explicitly read *The Tragedy of King Richard the Second: With new additions of the Parliament Scene, and the deposing of King Richard.*

Quotable Richard

Not all the water in the rough rude sea
Can wash the balm off from an anointed king[.]
(ACT 3, SCENE 2, LINES 54–55)

All souls that will be safe, fly from my side,
For time hath set a blot upon my pride.
(ACT 3, SCENE 2, LINES 80–81)

I wasted time, and now doth time waste me[.]
(ACT 5, SCENE 5, LINE 49)

Mount, mount, my soul! thy seat is up on high,
Whilst my gross flesh sinks downward, here to die.
(ACT 5, SCENE 5, LINES 111–12)

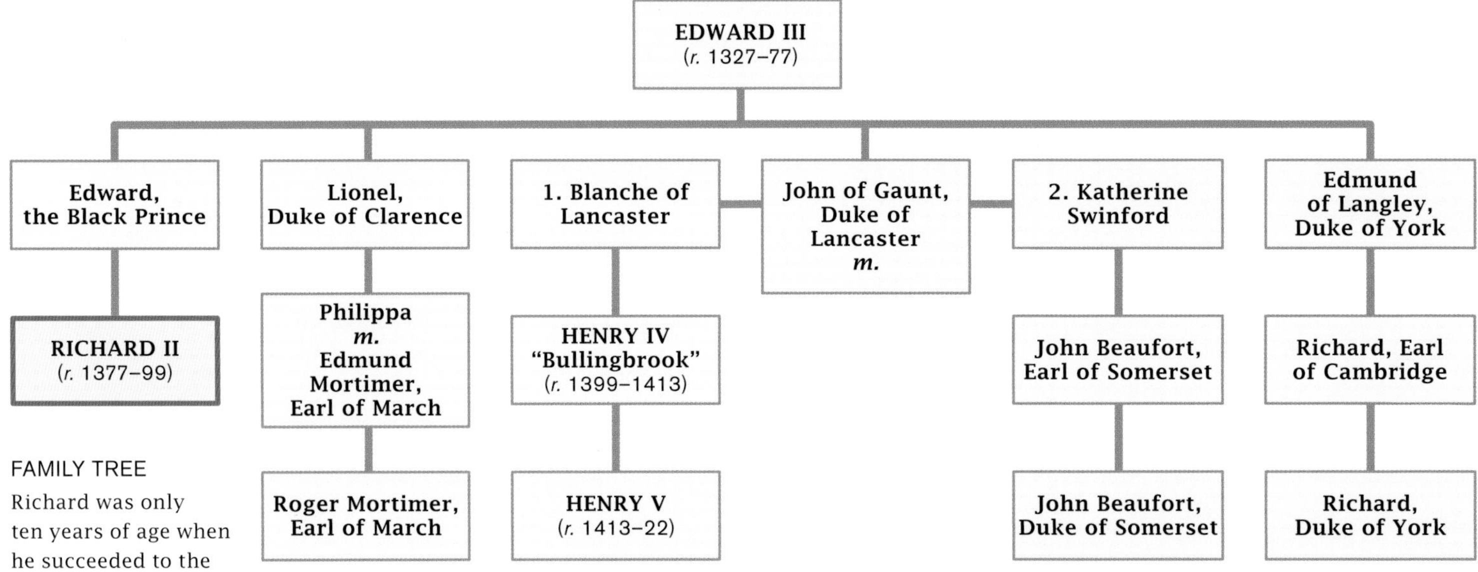

FAMILY TREE
Richard was only ten years of age when he succeeded to the throne. His uncle, John of Gaunt, backed him, but it was John's son, Bullingbrook, who would later depose him.

The Use and Abuse of Power

Richard II is a play about the legitimacy and illegitimacy of power, rivalry and challenges (many characters "throw down their gages"), pride, abuses of power and the consequences of treason, deposition, and regicide. It touches both the political and the private spheres, and shows how kingship and kinship are intertwined: Richard and Bullingbrook are cousins, and their quarrels trigger civil wars. More precisely, the play tackles the issues of unjust banishment, unlawful seizing of property—Bullingbrook is "Bereft and gelded of his patrimony" (Act 2, Scene 1, line 237)—and the perils of ignoring wise counsel. It also examines the forced transfer of power and the use of military intimidation, imprisonments, and summary executions.

Abuses of power are answered with curses and chilling prophecies by powerless people. John of Gaunt prophesies Richard's fall and the ruin of England as a result of his misgovernment; the Bishop of Carlisle predicts the Wars of the Roses as a consequence of Bullingbrook's ambition and usurpation. More generally, the rise and fall of kings, and the turn of the Wheel of Fortune, are announced by omens. Salisbury foretells:

Ah, Richard! with the eyes of heavy mind
I see thy glory like a shooting star
Fall to the base earth from the firmament.
(ACT 2, SCENE 4, LINES 18–20)

BELOW: *Jeremy Irons played Richard in a Royal Shakespeare Company production at Stratford-upon-Avon in 1986.*

Binary Opposites

Richard II is known for its profusion of metaphors, personifications, and oppositions. Grief is recurrently personified by various characters, such as the Duchess of Gloucester, John of Gaunt, and the Queen. Throughout the play, Bullingbrook and Richard are presented as binary opposites: Bullingbrook epitomizes day while Richard stands for night; Richard wishes he were melting snow just as Bullingbrook has turned into the shining sun (the king's emblem). They are also compared and contrasted in the images of a pair of scales and two buckets in a well.

Animal and bird metaphors are also used. At the beginning of the play, Richard is the lion while Mowbray and Bullingbrook are leopards, and the common people curs. Richard's enemies are

Distorted Vision

Shakespeare had in mind anamorphic pictures—images that need to be viewed from a particular perspective to be seen correctly—when he gave the following lines to Bushy:

> For sorrow's eyes, glazed with blinding tears,
> Divides one thing entire to many objects,
> Like perspectives, which rightly gaz'd upon
> Show nothing but confusion; ey'd awry
> Distinguish form[.]
> (ACT 2, SCENE 2, LINES 16–20)

RIGHT: *A famous example of an anamorphic image is the skull in the lower half of Hans Holbein the Younger's* The Ambassadors *(1533). It can only be seen in normal perspective by looking at the painting from an acute angle.*

vipers, dogs, and snakes. But Richard is also associated with birds: he is, for example, an "insatiate cormorant" (Act 2, Scene 1, line 38) and a cannibalistic pelican feeding on the family blood, before he appears "plume-pluck'd" (Act 4, Scene 1, line 108) at the end.

One of the most famous similes of the play is that of the garden. The Gardener compares Richard's realm to an ill-kept garden full of weeds and caterpillars, whereas his garden is like a mini kingdom that is well governed. He wishes the king had been a better gardener:

> *O, what pity is it*
> *That he had not so trimm'd and dress'd his land*
> *As we this garden ...*
> (ACT 3, SCENE 4, LINES 55–57)

Last but not least, the play is full of biblical imagery, especially when treason is at stake. There are references to Cain and Abel, and Pilate and Christ, and Richard identifies with the suffering Christ betrayed by Judas.

Twentieth-century Productions

Because it deals with both political rivalry and internecine quarrels, *Richard II* has had wide, international appeal in the modern era, and has been staged by a number of influential directors. In Britain, noteworthy are the productions of directors Peter Hall (1964), Richard Cottrell (1968; with Ian McKellen in the title role), John Barton (1971, 1973), David William (1972), Terry Hands (1980), Barry Kyle (1986), Derek Jacobi (1988), Michael Bogdanov (1989), Ron Daniels (1990), Deborah Warner (1995), Steven Pimlott (2000), Jonathan Ken (2000), Mark Rylance (2003), and Trevor Nunn (2005). Across the Channel, the productions of French directors such as Jean Vilar (1947), Patrice Chéreau (1970), and Ariane Mnouchkine (1981) have also been memorable. In the United States, actor Maurice Evans secured the play's reputation as early as 1937, and it has since been a favorite, being regularly produced for festivals such as the Oregon Shakespeare Festival (Ashland, 1995) and the Colorado Shakespeare Festival (1959, 1977, 1984, and 1998).

Three twentieth-century productions merit particular mention: director John Barton's 1973 production with the Royal Shakespeare Company, in which the actors Richard Pasco and Ian Richardson played the parts of Richard and Bullingbrook on alternate nights, thus offering an interesting experience to spectators who saw the two versions; director Ariane Mnouchkine's 1981 kabuki-style version with the Théâtre du Soleil; and director Deborah Warner's 1995 production with the National Theatre Company, in which Richard was brilliantly impersonated by a woman, actress Fiona Shaw, thus radically departing from the traditional male rivalries.

> *Now is this golden crown like a deep well/ That owes two buckets, filling one another,/ The emptier ever dancing in the air,/The other down, unseen, and full of water:/That bucket down and full of tears am I,/Drinking my griefs, whilst you mount up on high.*
>
> 
>
> —*Richard* (ACT 4, SCENE 1, LINES 184–89)

WRITTEN
c. 1595–96
SETTING AND PERIOD England and France, 1203 and 1212–16
CHARACTERS 27
ACTS 5
SCENES 16
LINES 2,638

King John

THE PLOT: *The play begins with a French ambassador delivering King Philip II's demand that John hand over his crown to Arthur (John's nephew). John refuses; war breaks out and rages inconclusively until a marriage between Philip's son and John's niece brings a temporary peace. When John refuses to approve Pope Innocent III's choice for Archbishop of Canterbury, however, decrying papal interference, the papal legate, Pandulph, forces Philip to break the peace.*

Arthur is captured by the English and taken to England. It is falsely reported that he has been executed, causing outraged English nobles to join the French. Attempting to escape, Arthur leaps from a castle wall and falls to his death. John reconciles with Pandulph, but too late to stop the French invading England. French reinforcements are, however, wrecked at sea, and John is poisoned by a monk. Pandulph concludes a peace, and the dying John declares his son Henry heir.

ABOVE: *Franklin McLeay donned chain mail for his role as Hubert de Burgh in director Herbert Beerbohm Tree's 1899 film of* King John.

Dramatis Personae

King John
Prince Henry, *son to the king*
Arthur, *Duke of Britain, nephew to the king*
Earl of Pembroke
Earl of Essex
Earl of Salisbury
Lord Bigot
Hubert de Burgh
Robert Faulconbridge, *son of Sir Robert Faulconbridge*
Philip the Bastard, *his half-brother (also called* **Richard***)*
James Gurney, *servant to Lady Faulconbridge*
Peter of Pomfret, *a prophet*
Philip, *King of France*
Lewis, *the Dolphin*
Lymoges, *Duke of Austria*
Cardinal Pandulph, *the Pope's legate*
Melune, *a French lord*
Chatillion, *ambassador from France to King John*
Queen Elinor, *widow of Henry II, mother to King John*
Constance, *widow of Geoffrey, John's elder brother, mother to Arthur*
Blanch of Spain, *daughter to the King of Castile, niece to King John*
Lady Faulconbridge, *widow of Sir Robert Faulconbridge*
Lords, Citizens of Angiers, Sheriff, Heralds, Officers, Soldiers, Executioners, Messengers, and Attendants

Shakespeare's *King John* is unusual in that it is the only history play from the 1590s that is not part of a sequence. It is also unusual in its cynicism with regard to politics, honor, and the rule of law. One of the most famous historical events in John's rule, the signing of Magna Carta in 1215, an early affirmation of baronial rights and the limits of monarchy, goes unmentioned.

A King Rehabilitated

Written in the mid-1590s, Shakespeare's *King John* stitches together two periods of early thirteenth-century history: the early part of John's reign, to 1203, and the later, to his death in 1216. In Shakespeare's time, people were ambivalent about John. By signing Magna Carta, he had gained a reputation as a weak ruler; yet his reputation had been rehabilitated in the sixteenth century by the Protestant writers John Bale and John Foxe, who saw him as an exemplar of proto-Protestantism.

The Vagaries of Fate

King John's main conflict is between family ties and political maneuvering, while the theme of legitimacy is also a recurrent source of debate. But the overriding theme of the play is the variable nature of power politics. The question of who is right is never certain. As fortunes change, it becomes clear that John's insistence on his "strong possession and our right" is correctly qualified by his mother's response: "Your strong possession much more than your right" (Act 1, Scene 1, lines 39–40).

Foiled by Fate

Images of viewing and spectating represent political conflict as a stage play:

> BASTARD *By heaven, these scroyles of Angiers*
> *flout you, kings,*
> *And stand securely on their battlements*
> *As in a theatre, whence they gape and point*
> *At your industrious scenes and acts of death.*
> (ACT 2, SCENE 1, LINES 373–6)

Characters often claim that a failed strategy demonstrates that nature itself is against them. The French are twice foiled by storms that sink their navy. Portents plague John's attempts to stave off French invasion and appease his nobles:

> HUBERT *My lord, they say five moons were seen*
> *to-night;*
> *Four fixed, and the fift did whirl about*
> *The other four in wondrous motion.*
> (ACT 4, SCENE 2, LINES 182–84)

When Arthur jumps from the wall trying to escape captivity, he imagines that it is the ground that kills him: "O me, my uncle's spirit is in these stones. / Heaven take my soul, and England keep my bones!" (Act 4, Scene 3, lines 9–10).

Legitimacy in Question

> Thus, after greeting, speaks the King of France
> In my behavior to the majesty,
> The borrowed majesty, of England here.
> —*Chatillion* (ACT 1, SCENE 1, LINES 2–4)

> Now powers from home and discontents at home
> Meet in one line; and vast confusion waits,
> As doth a raven on a sick-fall'n beast,
> The imminent decay of wrested pomp.
> —*Bastard* (ACT 4, SCENE 3, LINES 151–54)

Political Allegory

King John's popularity was highest in the eighteenth and early nineteenth centuries, when the play functioned as political allegory in a period of colonial retreat and Anglo-French conflict. Subsequently, its contradictions proved too considerable for it to be used to promote British nationalism or imperialism. In the last 25 years, however, the play's political ambivalence has seemed more relevant, and many productions have capitalized on its contradictions. Recent stagings—such as director Karin Coonrod's 2000 version of the drama with the Theatre for a New Audience, and Gregory Doran's Royal Shakespeare Company production of 2001—have garnered enthusiastic reviews, suggesting that *King John* may be on its way to renewed popularity.

King John was the first of Shakespeare's plays to be filmed, by Herbert Beerbohm Tree, in 1899. Tree made the film not to capture Shakespeare on film, ironically, but to promote his upcoming stage production of the play.

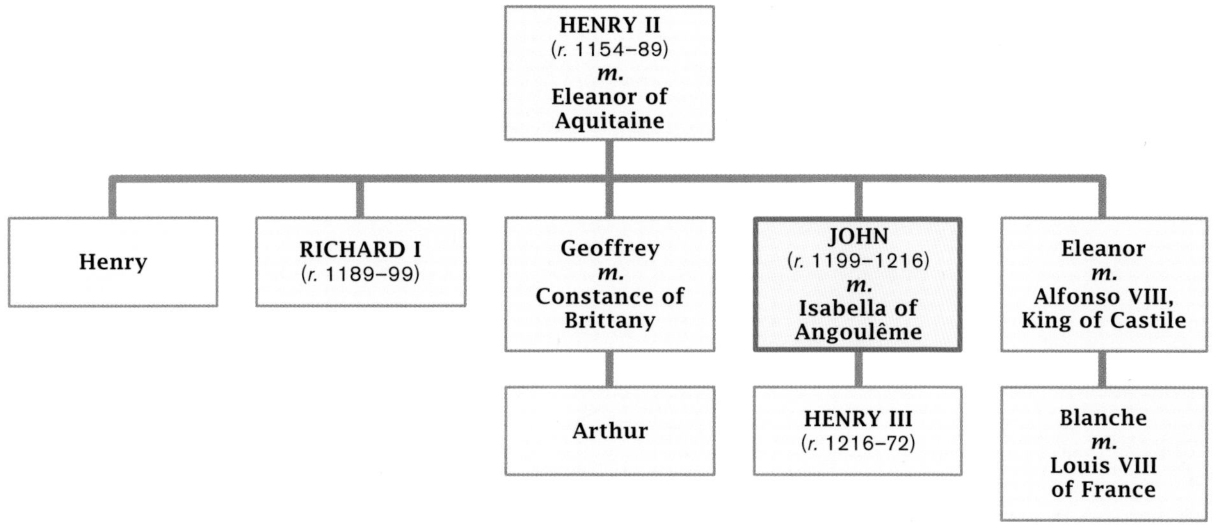

FAMILY TREE

The second son of Henry II to become king, John claimed the throne on the death of his brother, Richard. Richard had, however, nominated as heir his nephew, Arthur, son of another brother, Geoffrey, who had died in 1186.

Henry IV, Part 1

THE PLOT: *Henry IV, having taken the crown from his cousin Richard II, reigns in unquiet fashion, beset on his Welsh and Scottish borders with rebellion and incursion. He despairs when reminded of his oldest son and heir, Prince Henry (also known as Harry or Hal), who spends all his time in taverns consorting with disreputable characters. These include Sir John Falstaff and his friends, who involve the prince as they carouse and commit highway robbery. Nevertheless, Hal reveals in a soliloquy that he only pretends to be bad and that he will redeem himself when the right time comes.*

Rebellion grows more serious when Henry falls out with the powerful Percy family of Northumberland, the youngest being Henry Percy, known as Hotspur. Hotspur joins the Welsh rebel Owen Glendower and Edmund Mortimer, whose claim to the throne threatens Henry's legitimacy. They agree to divide the realm in thirds if they defeat the king. At the Battle of Shrewsbury, Hal saves his father's life, kills Hotspur, and redeems, for the time being, his reputation.

Dramatis Personae

King Henry the Fourth
Henry, Prince of Wales, *son to the king*
Prince John of Lancaster, *son to the king*
Earl Of Westmerland
Sir Walter Blunt
Thomas Percy, *Earl of Worcester*
Henry Percy, *Earl of Northumberland*
Henry Percy, *surnamed* **Hotspur,** *his son*
Edmund Mortimer, *Earl of March*
Richard Scroop, *Archbishop of York*
Archibald, *Earl of Douglas*
Owen Glendower
Sir Richard Vernon
Sir John Falstaff
Sir Michael, *of the household of the Archbishop of York*
Edward Poins, *gentleman-in-waiting to Prince Henry*
Gadshill
Peto
Bardolph
Lady Percy, *wife to Hotspur, and sister to Mortimer*
Lady Mortimer, *daughter to Glendower, and wife to Mortimer*
Mistress Quickly, *hostess of the Boar's Head Tavern in Eastcheap*
Lords, Officers, Sheriff, Vintner, Chamberlain, Ostler, Drawers, two Carriers, Travellers, and Attendants

WRITTEN
c. 1596
SETTING AND PERIOD
England and Wales, 1402–3
CHARACTERS 33
ACTS 5
SCENES 19
LINES 3,081

This second play in Shakespeare's sequence dramatizing the reigns of Richard II, Henry IV, and Henry V demonstrates the playwright's consummate skill in bringing English history to life for his Elizabethan audience. First performed in the winter of 1596–97, *Henry IV, Part 1* presents Henry's tumultuous reign as a surprising sequel to the play that preceded it. In *Richard II*, Henry was a young courtier who, in avenging his father John of Gaunt's treatment at the hands of the king, galvanized the unhappy nobility and deposed Richard. Seizing the crown, as Richard had warned him, turns out to be much easier than wearing it. The first line of the play attests to this sense of the burden of kingship: "So shaken as we are, so wan with care ..." Instead of leading a united English army on crusade to the Holy Land, as he devoutly wishes, Henry will spend the entire play staving off rebellion across his realm as well as in his own family.

Henry IV, Part 1 introduces us to Hal, the Prince of Wales (the title of the heir to the English throne), as a prodigal son whose father wishes he had been switched at birth with the heroic Hotspur (Henry Percy), son of the Earl of Northumberland. The future Henry V is, at this point, known for his antics, showing little promise to the court. He does this, he tells us, to diminish opinion of him to such a low point that when he does reveal his true nature everyone will find him that much more extraordinary:

> *So when this loose behaviour I throw off*
> *And pay the debt I never promised,*
> *By how much better than my word I am,*
> *By so much shall I falsify men's hopes[.]*
> (ACT 1, SCENE 2, LINES 208–11)

The play alternates between court scenes, or scenes featuring nobles, and scenes in taverns or inns with characters drawn from the lower levels of society. It is Shakespeare's first history play to offer his audience a thorough experience of English history, moving beyond the king and court to present the everyday life of English citizens.

Altering History

Written in 1596, Shakespeare's *Henry IV, Part 1* encompasses the years 1402 to 1403, early in Henry's reign (1399–1413). His sources were Raphael Holinshed's *Chronicles of England, Scotland and Ireland* (1587), Samuel Daniel's poem *The Civile*

Wars Between the Two Houses of Lancaster and York (1595), and the anonymous play *The Famous Victories of Henry the Fifth* (1580s). Shakespeare follows fact with just a few alterations. Most notably, following Daniel, he makes Hotspur a younger character in order to serve as a contemporary of Hal (Hotspur was actually a few years older than Henry IV).

In Shakespeare's time, Henry IV was well known as the first king of the House of Lancaster, a dynasty that would have a troubled future after its beginning with usurpation. Henry was also remembered, none too fondly in Protestant England, as the first king to issue a statute for the burning of heretics (*De heretico comburendo*, 1401; repealed by Elizabeth I in 1559).

A Troubled Legacy

The dramatic tension in *Henry IV, Part 1* derives from two main themes: political instability and father-son relations. Both revolve around the question of disputed legitimacy that haunts the kingship of Henry IV in the wake of seizing the crown from Richard.

Henry becomes increasingly anxious about his legacy, and evermore intent on leaving his heir a quieter, more stable rule than he has experienced. But the English nobility are also anxious about having replaced what they perceived to be one overreaching, corrupt king with another. Hotspur pointedly upbraids Northumberland and Worcester, his father and uncle respectively,

FALSTAFF *[B]ut for sweet Jack Falstaff, kind Jack Falstaff, true Jack Falstaff, valiant Jack Falstaff, and therefore more valiant, being as he is old Jack Falstaff, banish not him thy Harry's company, banish not him thy Harry's company—banish plump Jack, and banish all the world.*
PRINCE *I do, I will.*

(ACT 2, SCENE 4, LINES 475–81)

Falstaff or Oldcastle?

The character Sir John Falstaff was originally named Sir John Oldcastle after a real historical figure (*c.* 1378–1417), who, following a distinguished military career, became Lord Cobham by marriage; Oldcastle was also a well-known Lollard (religious radical), and was finally burned to death for his beliefs. Shakespeare was forced to change Oldcastle's name because he was a famous proto-Protestant martyr and/or because the contemporary Lord Cobham objected.

LEFT: *The relationship between Falstaff and the young Prince Henry is central to the play. In a 2005 National Theatre production, Michael Gambon starred as Falstaff and Matthew MacFadyen played the young Hal.*

ABOVE: *Numerous versions of this seventeenth-century portrait of Henry IV exist. But historians have cast doubt on its authenticity as a portrait of the king, given that it was painted many years after his death.*

for their part in the deposition of Richard and his replacement with Bullingbrook:

> *Shall it for shame be spoken in these days,*
> *Or fill up chronicles in time to come,*
> *That men of your nobility and power*
> *Did gage them both in an unjust behalf*
> *(As both of you—God pardon it!—have done)*
> *To put down Richard, that sweet lovely rose,*
> *And plant this thorn, this canker, Bullingbrook?*
> (ACT 1, SCENE 3, LINES 170–76)

Henry may care more about good governance than his predecessor, but the play is relentless in its presentation of incessant rebellion. Henry's judgment regarding those two subjects is questionable. He misjudges Hotspur, with disastrous results for his rule, a disagreement over captured prisoners leading to the Northumberland rebellion. Only one scene before this, Henry had described Hotspur glowingly as "the theme of honor's tongue" (Act 1, Scene 1, line 81). He misjudges Hal, whom he sees as dishonorable and irresponsible. When we learn that Hal is only pretending prodigality, we wonder how a father could so poorly understand his own son. The double theme of family strife and political instability is the dominant theme of all four plays in this cycle.

Strength of Character

Characters in this play are often distinguished by language that invokes physical attributes or states of being. Thus, Falstaff is perhaps the most famous fat character in all of English literature; Hal is well known by his contrasted skinniness; the king is tired, worn out with worry; Hotspur's very name indicates his fiery temper; and so on. This is Shakespeare's first history play to offer such a variety and dynamism of character. That is strikingly reflected in the play's formal composition: coming just after *Richard II*, a court play composed entirely in verse, *Henry IV, Part 1* is half in verse (for the court scenes) and half in prose (for the tavern and other everyday-life scenes), the language thus becoming more supple and varied and reflecting English society more fully.

A persistent image is that of seizing something, indicated by the repeated use of the word "pluck," as when Hotspur indicates his desire to displace Henry, who has, he asserts, plucked the crown from where it ought not have been touched:

> *By heaven, methinks it were an easy leap,*
> *To pluck bright honor from the pale-fac'd moon,*
> *Or dive into the bottom of the deep,*

Falstaff's Philosophy

There lives not three good men unhang'd in England, and one of them is fat and grows old ...
(ACT 2, SCENE 4, LINES 130–32)

I was as virtuously given as a gentleman need to be, virtuous enough: swore little, dic'd not above seven times—a week, went to a bawdy-house not above once in a quarter—of an hour, paid money that I borrow'd—three or four times, liv'd well and in good compass, and now I live out of all order, out of all compass.
(ACT 3, SCENE 3, LINES 14–20)

To the latter end of a fray and the beginning of a feast
Fits a dull fighter and a keen guest.
(ACT 4, SCENE 2, LINES 79–80)

To die is to be a counterfeit, for he is but the counterfeit of a man who hath not the life of a man ... The better part of valor is discretion ...
(ACT 5, SCENE 4, LINES 115–17, 119–20)

Where fadom-line could never touch the ground,
And pluck up drowned honor by the locks[.]
(ACT 1, SCENE 3, LINES 201–5)

The characteristic known in English as "pluck," a dogged resoluteness and energetic attitude, is something that Henry wishes for but eventually rues. The play makes it clear that characters such as Henry and Hotspur, who act impulsively, come to a bad end, while a character such as Hal, who plans ahead and plots carefully, is the type who will succeed in the dangerous and intricate world of monarchical politics.

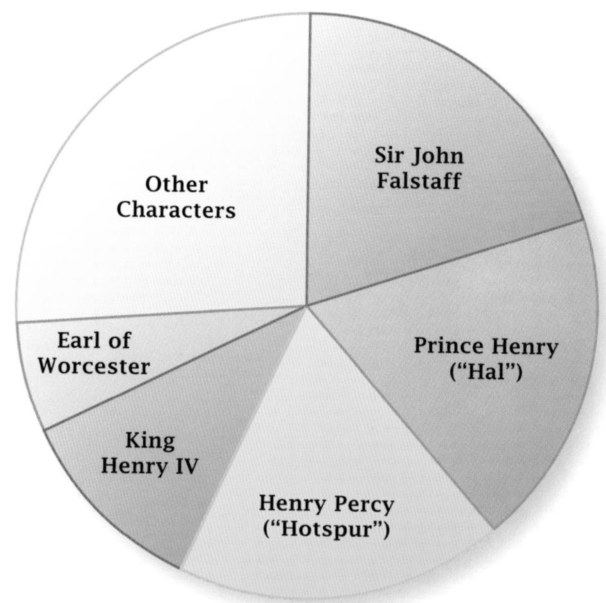

MAJOR ROLES
Despite the title of the play, the character of King Henry IV speaks a far smaller proportion of the play's lines than Prince Henry, Hotspur, or Falstaff.

Continuing Impact

Henry IV, Part 1 has thrilled audiences since the late 1590s with its combination of court intrigue; violent rebellion; Welsh magic, music, and language; the bluster of comic characters (Falstaff) and chivalrous characters (Hotspur); and the coming of age of a famous prince (Hal). The role of Falstaff is a staple of the comic tradition on stage, a signature role for generations of older actors. The most celebrated Falstaffs include Thomas Betterton (1700), James Quin (1721–51), Stephen Kemble (1802–20), James Hackett (1832–70), Ralph Richardson (1945), Anthony Quayle (1951), and John Woodvine (1986).

Two significant film adaptations feature Falstaff and the tavern and robbery scenes. Orson Welles's *Chimes at Midnight* (1965) features Welles as Falstaff, John Gielgud as Henry IV, and Jeanne Moreau as Doll Tearsheet, in a production that uses scenes from five plays to construct a narrative of London low life. It is acknowledged to be one of Welles's best films. The other is Gus Van Sant's *My Own Private Idaho* (1991), which in part tells the story of street hustlers in Portland, Oregon, by casting them in the roles of the characters in the tavern scenes in *Henry IV, Part 1*. Though set in a US city and modernized, these scenes are generally faithful to Shakespeare's play.

LEFT: *River Phoenix (left) and Keanu Reeves (right) starred in Gus Van Sant's movie* My Own Private Idaho *(1991), which incorporated the tavern scenes from* Henry IV, Part 1.

Henry IV, Part 2

THE PLOT: *Following the Battle of Shrewsbury, the Earl of Northumberland receives the news that Henry IV has defeated the army led by his son Hotspur, and that his son has been killed by Prince Henry. The Archbishop of York and other powerful nobles take up arms in rebellion, though without Northumberland.*

Meanwhile, Falstaff is busy securing a livelihood for himself by exploiting his relationship with Hal. But Hal, having distinguished himself at Shrewsbury, is now preparing himself to act the proper prince. The king is reported ill. Rebellion comes to a head at Gaultree Forest in Yorkshire. The rebels and their army confront the king's forces and present their grievances. Prince John, Hal's younger brother, standing in for his ill father, agrees to peaceful terms and the rebels dismiss their army. But immediately John revokes the peace and arrests these men for treason. This trick crushes the rebellion without a battle. On his deathbed, Henry and Hal are reconciled. Henry dies and Hal is crowned Henry V. He rejects Falstaff publicly and looks toward France.

ABOVE: *In a highly symbolic gesture, in Act 4, Scene 5, Prince Henry tries on his father's crown as the king sleeps, then takes it out of the room—to the alarm of the king, when he wakes soon after.*

Written around 1597 and first performed in 1598, *Henry IV, Part 2* brings to a conclusion Henry's troubled reign, as he encounters further rebellion and renewed anxiety about his son Hal's fitness to rule. Although the Battle of Shrewsbury had concluded *Henry IV, Part 1* on a note of triumph, rebellion now breaks out in new quarters. As Shakespeare portrays it, Henry is unable to find peace in the role of king. His usurpation of Richard and questions regarding the legitimacy of his rule will not go away. The Archbishop of York mentions this explicitly, blaming Henry's greed in seizing the crown, and the people for hastily supporting him. Conveniently, he glosses over the role of the nobility and the church in Richard's downfall, ignoring the way they have switched sides for political convenience. Henry, already weary from the strain of civil strife at the opening of *Part 1*, here fades from view as a major character until the middle of the play. He is ill and begins to confront his succession and legacy. His first speech in the play occurs in Act 3, ending with the ominous couplet, "Then (happy) low, lie down! / Uneasy lies the head that wears a crown" (Scene 1, lines 30–31).

In the Wake of Usurpation

The play encompasses the years 1403–13. Instead of focusing on a few years of Henry's reign (1399–1413) as *Henry IV, Part 1* does, *Part 2* compresses ten years of history into a seamless narrative of Henry's physical collapse and his son's ascension to kingship. Shakespeare's sources are again Holinshed's *Chronicles of England, Scotland and Ireland* (1587), Samuel Daniel's poem *The Civile Wars Between the Two Houses of Lancaster and York* (1595), and the anonymous play *The Famous Victories of Henry the Fifth* (1580s). Alterations of historical fact in this play largely involve portraying the most unsettled events and leaving out the periods of calm. This continues to emphasize the point, introduced in *Henry IV, Part 1*, of the difficulty of ruling in the wake of usurpation.

WRITTEN
c. 1597

SETTING AND PERIOD
England, 1403–13

CHARACTERS 50

ACTS 5

SCENES 19 plus Induction and Epilogue

LINES 3,326

Dramatis Personae

Rumor, *the Presenter*
King Henry the Fourth
Prince Henry, *afterward crowned* **King Henry the Fifth**
Prince John of Lancaster, Humphrey Duke of Gloucester, Thomas Duke of Clarence, *sons to Henry the Fourth and brethren to Henry the Fifth*

OPPOSITES AGAINST KING HENRY THE FOURTH
Earl of Northumberland
Scroop, *the Archbishop of York*
Lord Mowbray
Lord Hastings
Lord Bardolph
Travers, Morton, *retainers of Northumberland*
Sir John Colevile

OF THE KING'S PARTY
Earl of Warwick
Earl of Westmerland
Earl of Surrey
Sir John Blunt
Gower
Harcourt
Lord Chief Justice

Poins, Sir John Falstaff, Bardolph, Pistol, Peto, Falstaff's Page, *irregular humorists*
Shallow, Silence, *both country justices*
Davy, *servant to Shallow*
Fang, Snare, *two sergeants*
Mouldy, Shadow, Wart, Feeble, Bullcalf, *country soldiers*
Francis, *a drawer*
Northumberland's Wife
Lady Percy, *Percy's widow*
Hostess Quickly *of the Boar's Head Tavern, Eastcheap*
Doll Tearsheet
Epilogue
Lords and Attendants; Porter, Drawers, Beadle, Officers, Strewers, Servants, etc.

Scenes of rebellion and court politics only serve to punctuate the drama of *Part 2*. The play spends much of its time following Falstaff's efforts to borrow money and to support his lifestyle at others' expense while he travels the Gloucestershire countryside waiting, at first, to join the king's army or, later, for his old friend Hal to become king. Either way, Falstaff turns necessity into virtue, using his relationship with Hal to garner credit from anyone who will believe his copious falsehoods.

While Falstaff retains his wit and charm, his scenes gradually reveal an old man who is vulnerable to the depredations of a dissolute life.

MAJOR ROLES
As this pie chart of the proportion of lines spoken by each character shows, Falstaff dominates *Henry IV, Part 2*. The play has a wide range of significant minor characters.

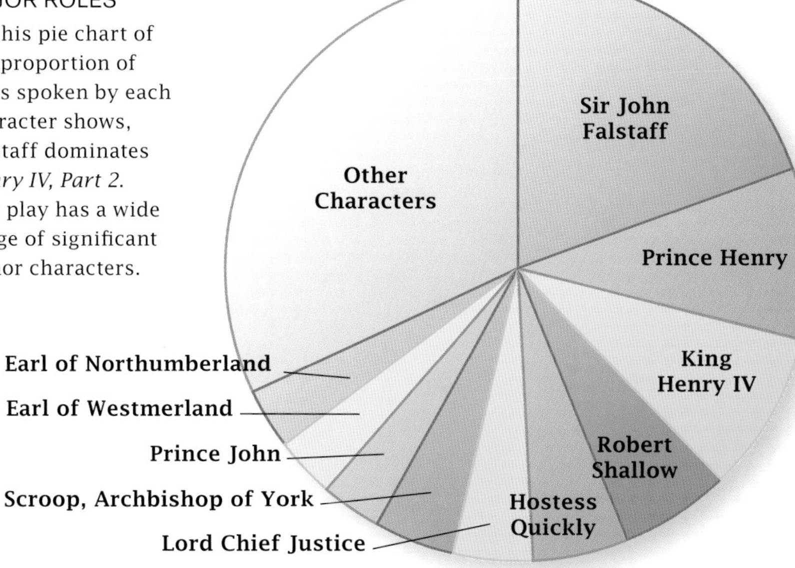

Gone are the easy insults and bantering moments with Hal from the earlier play, so full of potential, when the fat knight was securely in his element. Falstaff is now forced to curry favor with old friends such as Justice Robert Shallow, whom he despises, in the hope that he can borrow money.

Falstaff's belief that Hal will make a place for him once he becomes king results in a desperate rush to him, all other means of support exhausted. Hal's rejection of Falstaff just after his being crowned Henry V is a crushing blow, felt keenly by the audience and readers.

Finding a Place in the World

Henry IV, Part 2 continues the dramatic tension between political instability and father-son relations that was already present in *Part 1*. The disputed legitimacy that plagues Henry's kingship is extended by a new group of rebels and made more acute by Henry's failing health. Henry remains anxious about Hal's ability to rule after his own death, which now seems imminent.

In this play, instead of using martial glory to propel himself into the good graces of his father and others, Hal must overcome his own misgivings about the responsibility of governing. The prince's absence from the scenes in which the king's forces confront the rebels raises questions once again about his suitability. Emblematic is the scene in which Hal picks up the dying king's crown and takes it into the next room. When the king awakens, he jumps to conclusions:

I stay too long by thee, I weary thee.
Dost thou so hunger for mine empty chair
That thou wilt needs invest thee with my honors
Before thy hour be ripe? O foolish youth,
Thou seek'st the greatness that will overwhelm
thee.
(ACT 4, SCENE 5, LINES 93–97)

This scene of accusation, which ends in reconciliation, demonstrates the paradox at the heart of Henry's kingship: having gained the crown via questionable means, and now suffering from the responsibilities of rule, he wants both to pass on the title and warn his son of its debilitating effects.

Another prominent theme is time. The characters are highly self-conscious not only about the passage of time and their place in it, but about the way the past and future intrude upon the present. One way this manifests itself is through nostalgia:

SILENCE *That's fifty-five year ago.*
SHALLOW *Ha, cousin Silence, that thou hadst seen that that this knight and I have seen! Ha, Sir John, said I well?*
FALSTAFF *We have heard the chimes at midnight, Master Shallow.*
(ACT 3, SCENE 2, LINES 210–15)

Falstaff's Drink of Choice

In Act 4, Scene 2, Falstaff speaks in effusive praise of "sack," an alcoholic beverage he has mentioned numerous times. Sack is a strong, sweet or dry white wine. In 1615, English poet Gervase Markham wrote: "Our best sack are of Seres in Spain, your smaller of Galicia and Portugal; your strong sacks are of the islands of the Canaries, and of Malaga."

This backward-looking tendency is matched by the disruption of future actions by vestiges of past errors and regrets:

WARWICK *There is a history in all men's lives,*
Figuring the natures of the times deceas'd,
. . . .
Such things become the hatch and brood of time[.]
(ACT 3, SCENE 1, LINES 80–81, 86)

Both examples demonstrate the ways guilt and anxiety affect characters who muse about their place in this world. Henry will only find a way to

BELOW: *References to lost youth and the inevitability of death color the exchanges between Falstaff (center), Shallow (left), and Silence (right), seen here in a 2001 Royal Shakespeare Company production in London.*

I know thee not, old man, fall to thy prayers./How ill white hairs becomes a fool and jester!/I have long dreamt of such a kind of man,/So surfeit-swell'd, so old, and so profane;/ But being awak'd, I do despise my dream.

—*King Henry V to Falstaff*
(ACT 5, SCENE 5, LINES 47–51)

articulate this in terms of political functioning when he counsels Hal to "busy giddy minds / With foreign quarrels, that action, hence borne out, / May waste the memory of the former days" (Act 4, Scene 5, lines 213–15).

"Smooth Comforts False"

The play is dominated by images of paradox: what ought to heal kills; what ought to bring relief brings pain; what is supposed or expected to be one thing turns out to be another. This theme is signaled in the very opening of the play by imagery in Rumor's Induction: "From Rumor's tongues / They bring smooth comforts false, worse than true wrongs" (lines 39–40). Examples abound, and taken together this imagery suggests that political wrangling results in gross distortions of language. This language has consequences for the political action of history as the play represents it. It is deceptive language that drives much of the plotting, from Falstaffian comedy to tragic double-dealing (Prince John), underscoring what a perilous, Machiavellian world is Henry's England.

The Fortunes of Falstaff

The fortunes of *Henry IV, Part 2* have largely followed the fortunes of Falstaff. While other characters have a number of famous lines, productions of the play have centered on Sir John and his prominent role. Indeed, in the eighteenth and nineteenth centuries, many adaptations pared the play down to the Falstaff portions, cutting out the political plot.

While *Part 2* has often been performed as a standalone play, since the 1930s it has commonly been part of a cycle, accompanied by *Part 1* and often *Henry V*. A memorable example is the London production of 1945 that featured Laurence Olivier as Hotspur and then as Justice Shallow, and Ralph Richardson as Falstaff.

ABOVE: *In 1945, the Old Vic company performed both parts of* Henry IV *along with* Henry V *at the New Theatre, London. Ralph Richardson's performance as Falstaff was widely hailed as one of the best ever in the role.*

Falstaff's Insults

Well, he may sleep in security, for he hath the horn of abundance, and the lightness of his wife shines through it[.]
(ACT 1, SCENE 2, LINES 45–47)

The young prince hath misled me. I am the fellow with the great belly, and he my dog.
(ACT 1, SCENE 2, LINES 145–46)

He a good wit? Hang him, baboon! his wit's as thick as Tewksbury mustard, there's no more conceit in him than is in a mallet.
(ACT 2, SCENE 4, LINES 240–42)

When 'a [Justice Shallow] was naked, he was for all the world like a fork'd redish, with a head fantastically carv'd upon it with a knife. 'A was so forlorn, that his dimensions to any thick sight were [invisible]. 'A was the very genius of famine[.]
(ACT 3, SCENE 2, LINES 310–14)

Henry V

WRITTEN
c. 1599

SETTING AND PERIOD
England and France, 1413–22

CHARACTERS 43

ACTS 5

SCENES 23 plus Prologue, 4 Choruses, and an Epilogue

LINES 3,297

THE PLOT: *The play opens with Henry's negotiations with the church and with the French ambassador regarding his claim to the French throne. From the church he needs money and moral support, and from the French he seeks either acquiescence or provocation. Henry makes it clear to the defiant French that he means business and announces his intention to make his claim through force. Action moves swiftly to Southampton, where the English army prepares to invade France. Here a plot is discovered among three of the king's closest courtiers. Henry is one step ahead of the conspirators, and they are seized and executed.*

The English army, composed of a unified force that includes Irish, Scottish, and Welsh soldiers, then invades France and lays siege to Harfleur. Successful, the English occupy the town and move on until they encounter the French at Agincourt. The night before what will come to be considered one of the greatest battles in English history, Henry visits his troops in disguise in order to gauge their mood. The next morning he rallies them in preparation for battle against a larger and better-rested force. Against long odds, the English win the Battle of Agincourt. As a consequence, Henry is betrothed to the French king's daughter; their son, Henry VI, will, for a time, unite the English and French crowns.

Broken Promises

The Epilogue to *Henry IV, Part 2* promises that, "our humble author will continue the story, with Sir John in it ... where (for any thing I know) Falstaff shall die of a sweat ..." (lines 27–30). Shakespeare breaks this promise in *Henry V*, since Falstaff does not appear. He is, however, described in two scenes as dying and then dead (Act 2, Scenes 1 and 3). Hostess Quickly suggests he is indeed dying of a fever; but Falstaff's tavern companions link his demise to Hal's public rejection of the old man at the end of *Henry IV, Part 2*.

First performed in 1599, *The Life of Henry the Fifth*, to give it its full title from the 1623 First Folio, is Shakespeare's final play of the two historical tetralogies he wrote in the 1590s. The full title is somewhat misleading, since the play is chiefly concerned with Henry's conquests in France during the years 1414–15.

Henry V is the culmination of the four-play sequence that began with *Richard II* and the dynastic, familial, and political struggle that resulted in his usurpation and the crowning of Henry IV, then moved through that king's unquiet reign, marred by dissent, bloody insurrection,

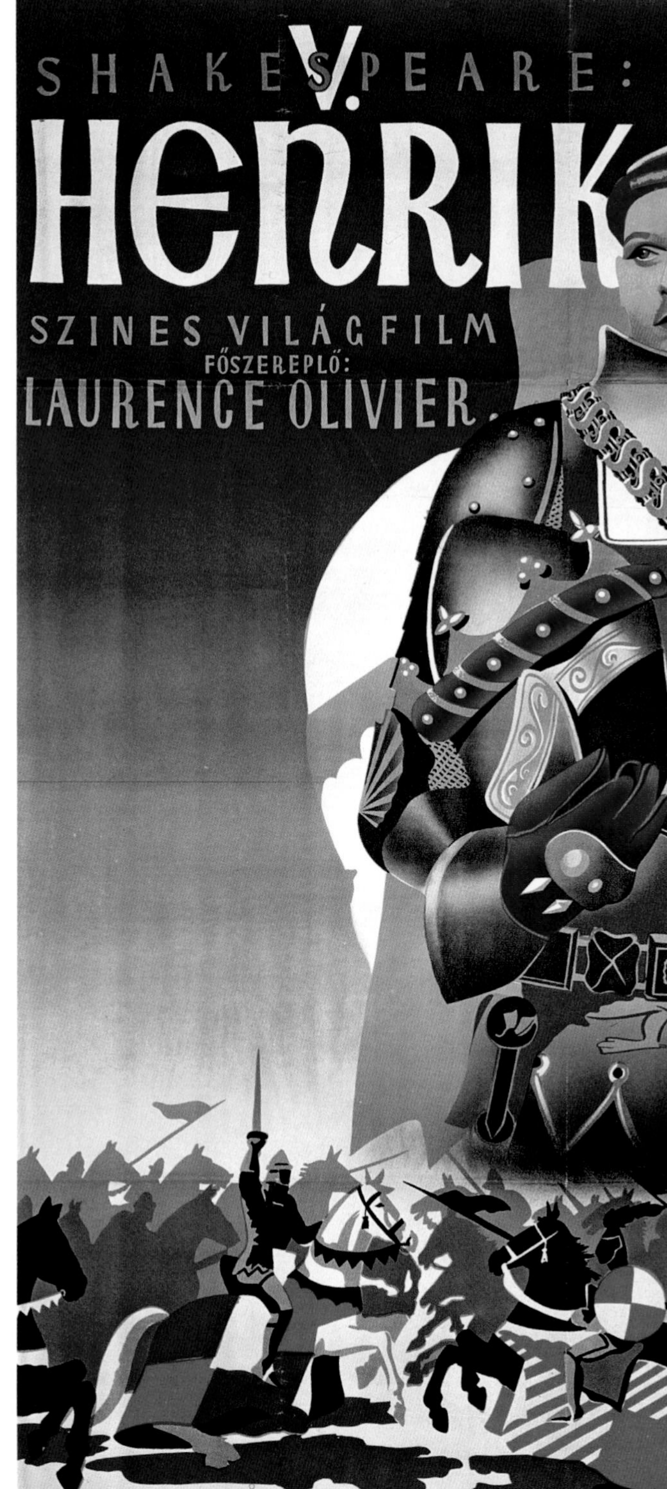

RIGHT: *This boldly designed poster was created in 1944 to advertise the Hungarian release of the film version of* Henry V, *starring Laurence Olivier as the king.*

and border wars with Wales and Scotland. In *Henry IV, Part 1*, Shakespeare introduced his audience to Henry (also called Hal or Harry), Prince of Wales and heir to the English throne, as a ne'er-do-well scoundrel who inhabits the London underworld with his pal Falstaff and other ruffians. But, as the prince tells us in a soliloquy at the end of Act 1 of *Henry IV, Part 1*, he is only feigning prodigality in order to appear more miraculous when he becomes king. He upholds the promise of this soliloquy in the opening of *Henry V* with his audacious claim to the French throne. This, along with masterful management of his army, courageous campaigning, and rousing speeches to his men, accomplishes what his father could never do: unite a fractious nobility and establish a peaceful dynasty.

The play, and the four-play sequence, ends on a note of caution, however. Though Henry succeeds in subduing France and securing his claims through his son, the Epilogue tells us that Henry VI

> *in infant bands crown'd King*
> *Of France and England, did this king succeed;*
> *Whose state so many had the managing,*
> *That they lost France, and made his England*
> *bleed[.]*
>
> (LINES 9–12)

A Fascinating Figure

Thanks to his stunning victory at Agincourt, Henry took his place in history as a warrior king. His death at a relatively young age, his son Henry VI's mismanagement and loss of French territory, and an ensuing period of political and civil unrest that came to be known as the Wars of the Roses all contributed to the chroniclers' fascination with this "mirror of all Christian kings" (Act 2, Chorus, line 6). Shakespeare's history plays drew large audiences in the 1590s, a period in which the writing of history had become a popular subject and an important concern for the developing English nation. This interest is reflected in the abundance of historical source material that was available to Shakespeare when he sat down to write this and his other history plays. The major source for his portrayal of Henry and of late medieval history was Raphael Holinshed's *Chronicles of England, Scotland and Ireland* (1587); he also drew on an anonymous play, *The Famous Victories of Henry the Fifth* (1580s).

The play's action is relatively faithful to the description in these sources of Henry's preparation for, and execution of, his efforts to gain the French crown. However, any drama that takes as its subject a king of heroic status is likely to provoke readers and viewers to wonder whether the playwright intended that king to be viewed as genuinely heroic or as dangerously manipulative. In *Henry V*, the opening act, in which the king agrees to suppress a bill in Parliament that would cut deeply into church revenues in exchange for church support for and funding of his war in France, introduces a ruler who feigns neutrality

Dramatis Personae

Chorus
King Henry the Fifth
Humphrey Duke of Gloucester, John Duke of Bedford, Duke of Clarence, *brothers to the king*
Duke of Exeter, *uncle to the king*
Duke of York, *cousin to the king*
Earl of Salisbury
Earl of Westmerland
Earl of Warwick
Archbishop of Canterbury
Bishop of Ely
Earl of Cambridge
Lord Scroop
Sir Thomas Grey, Sir Thomas Erpingham, Gower, Fluellen, Macmorris, Jamy, *officers in King Henry's army*
Bates, Court, Williams, *soldiers in the same*
Pistol
Nym
Bardolph
Boy
Herald
Charles the Sixth, *King of France*
Lewis, *the Dolphin*
Duke of Burgundy
Duke of Orleance
Duke of Bourbon
Duke of Britain
Duke of Berri
Duke of Beaumont
Constable of France
Rambures, Grandpré, *French lords*
Governor of Harfleur
Montjoy, *a French herald*
Ambassadors to the King of England
Isabel, *Queen of France*
Katherine, *daughter to Charles and Isabel*
Alice, *a lady attending on her*
Hostess *of the Boar's Head Tavern in Eastcheap, formerly Mistress Quickly, and now married to Pistol*
Lords, Ladies, Officers, Soldiers, Citizens, Messengers, and Attendants

THE HISTORY BEHIND THE PLAY

1387	Henry is born at Monmouth Castle, Wales, eldest son of Henry Bullingbrook (Bolingbroke) and Mary de Bohun
1398	Bullingbrook is banished by Richard II
1399	Bullingbrook deposes Richard II; Henry becomes Prince of Wales
1400	Henry accompanies his father on campaigns against the Scots; outbreak of rebellion in Wales
1403	Henry takes command of the war against the Welsh rebels; takes part in the Battle of Shrewsbury against Hotspur and the Percy family
1409	End of the Welsh rebellion
1413	Henry succeeds to the throne on his father's death
1414	Henry suppresses the Lollard rising; lays claim to French territories including Aquitaine, Normandy, Touraine, and Maine
1415	Henry foils the conspiracy led by Richard of York, Earl of Cambridge, and Henry, Lord Scroop; he then sails for France, captures the port of Harfleur, and defeats the French at the Battle of Agincourt
1416	Henry makes an alliance with the Holy Roman Emperor, Sigismund
1417	War with France is renewed
1420	Treaty of Troyes recognizes Henry as heir and regent of France; Henry marries Katherine of Valois, daughter of the King of France
1421	Birth of Henry's son, the future Henry VI
1422	Henry dies at Bois de Vincennes, France

RIGHT: *Taken in 1922, this photograph shows Corsican actress Irène Bordoni—who later gained fame as a Broadway singer—elaborately garbed to play the role of Princess Katherine.*

and self-righteousness while working behind the scenes to engineer his objectives. We may thus greet with some suspicion Henry's claim at the end of the act, once he has secured the approval of the church and nobility, that "we have now no thought in us but France, / Save those to God, that run before our business" (Act 1, Scene 2, lines 302–3). He has, to be sure, done something Henry IV was never able to do, but he has also followed closely his father's advice to "busy giddy minds / With foreign quarrels" (*Henry IV, Part 2*, Act 4, Scene 5, lines 213–14).

Honor Restored

When Henry V is crowned at the end of *Henry IV, Part 2*, he knows that he will have to behave differently in an effort to rule successfully. If *Henry V* breaks with its predecessors in presenting a king who is able to avoid the troubling themes of preceding plays, it still cannot steer clear of the durable issues of the history play genre: honor, identity, national unity, and responsibility.

In *Henry IV, Part 1*, the king admiringly referred to Hotspur as "the theme of honor's tongue" (Act 1, Scene 1, line 81) in order to contrast him with his unruly son, the Prince of Wales. Honor is constantly at issue throughout these plays, and to restore this to the crown is one of Henry's concerns as he plans and manages his French campaign. The dishonorable prince turns for political ends into an honorable king. This potential contradiction, that honor is a relative concept, is one that Shakespeare explores doggedly in the tetralogy. In *Henry V*, the idea of honor is placed squarely in the context of national loyalty and service by the king himself. The more individualized examinations of honor that occur in the plays leading up to this one—such as Falstaff's famous "What is honor? A word. What is in that word honor? … Air" (*Henry IV, Part 1*, Act 5, Scene 1, lines 133–35), in which discretion is the better part of valor, and Hotspur's obsessive adherence

No, it is not possible you should love the enemy of France, Kate; but in loving me, you should love the friend of France; for I love France so well that I will not part with a village of it; I will have it all mine.

—*King Henry* (ACT 5, SCENE 2, LINES 171–75)

to the code of chivalry, in which valor is all—give way to expressions of the importance of honor to the success of a nation led by a strong king.

Inspiring National Unity

Closely tied to this idea of honor, as it manifests itself in the context of a military campaign, are the related themes of identity and national unity. Act 3 of *Henry V* presents a conspicuously mixed group of soldiers comprising the "English" army. Captains Fluellen (Welsh), Macmorris (Irish), and Jamy (Scottish), all speaking in accented English, fight alongside their English compatriots without visible nationalist distinction. This suggests that Henry has somehow been able to muster an army that represents the whole of greater Britain, endowing him with an almost magical ability to unify as no other king has had. These captains are, however, interested in declaring pride in their national identities. The touchy Macmorris, while fighting loyally in an English army, nonetheless will not stand to have his "nation" called into question:

> FLUELLEN *Captain Macmorris, I think, look you, under your correction, there is not many of your nation—*
> MACMORRIS *Of my nation? What ish my nation? Ish a villain, and a basterd, and a knave, and a rascal? What ish my nation? Who talks of my nation?*
> (ACT 3, SCENE 2, LINES 120–24)

ABOVE: *A vital victory against a numerically superior French army at the Battle of Agincourt, on October 25, 1415, swung the tide of war in Henry's favor. The battle is shown here in a fifteenth-century illustration.*

Henry Galvanizes His Men

Once more unto the breach, dear friends, once
more;
Or close the wall up with our English dead.
In peace there's nothing so becomes a man
As modest stillness and humility;
But when the blast of war blows in our ears,
Then imitate the action of the tiger[.]
(ACT 3, SCENE 1, LINES 1–6)

The game's afoot!
Follow your spirit; and upon this charge
Cry, "God for Harry, England, and Saint George!"
(ACT 3, SCENE 1, LINES 32–34)

He that shall see this day, and live old age,
Will yearly on the vigil feast his neighbors
And say, "To-morrow is Saint Crispian."
Then will he strip his sleeve and show his scars,
[And say, "These wounds I had on Crispin's day."]
Old men forget; yet all shall be forgot,
But he'll remember with advantages
What feats he did that day ...
(ACT 4, SCENE 3, LINES 44–51)

tell the Constable
We are but warriors for the working-day;
Our gayness and our gilt are all besmirch'd
With rainy marching in the painful field[.]
(ACT 4, SCENE 3, LINES 108–11)

This exchange touches on the recurring theme of responsibility, or loyalty, which is signally important to a king whose father had enjoyed so little of it. Henry plots obsessively so that he does not run the risk of becoming dependent upon his nobles or the church.

It is a feature of Shakespeare's Henry V, and one not found elsewhere in the historical record, that he anticipates the actions of others at almost every turn. Exemplary in this is his walking alone and disguised among his troops the night before the Battle of Agincourt. The lengthy discussion that ensues concerns the loyalty of a subject to a king and of the responsibility of a king toward his subjects. The soldier Bates responds to the disguised king's assertion that his cause is just and his quarrel honorable:

> *[F]or we know enough, if we know we are the King's subjects. If his cause be wrong, our obedience to the King wipes the crime of it out of us.*
> (ACT 4, SCENE 1, LINES 130–33)

The other soldier, Williams, adds, "But if the cause be not good, the King himself hath a heavy reckoning to make" (lines 134–35). Henry's lengthy reply is notable for the way it takes these common soldiers seriously, but also for how much moral anxiety it reveals beneath his confident exterior. "The King," says the muffled monarch, "is not bound to answer the particular endings of his soldiers" (lines 155–56). While it is unclear whether these articulate, skeptical men agree with

ABOVE: *Played by Kenneth Branagh, Henry addresses his troops prior to the Battle of Agincourt, in Branagh's 1989 film adaptation.*

this, they certainly raise a question for the play's audience: if Henry is not, in the end, responsible for them, why should they be responsible to him and his regal desires?

Image Clusters

One of the most striking images in the play occurs early on in Henry's first major speech. The Dolphin, or Dauphin, heir to the French throne, has sent a mocking gift of a barrel of tennis balls to Henry in order to show his contempt for the new English king's audacity and as a reminder of Henry's youthful reputation. In this rhetorically masterful, chilling speech, Henry establishes himself as a man to be reckoned with, and one who can turn language to his advantage:

We are glad the Dolphin is so pleasant with us,
His present and your pains we thank you for.
When we have match'd our rackets to these balls,
We will in France, by God's grace, play a set
Shall strike his father's crown into the hazard
. . . .
And tell the pleasant prince this mock of his
Hath turn'd his balls to gun-stones, and his soul
Shall stand sore charged for the wasteful vengeance
That shall fly with them . . .
(ACT 1, SCENE 2, LINES 259–63, 281–84)

Thus do tennis balls become "gun-stones" in our mind's eye, and Shakespeare begins the transformation of prodigal prince into warrior king.

Image clusters also animate the speeches of the character called the Chorus, who introduces each act. The Prologue, spoken by the Chorus, appeals directly to the audience to "Piece out our imperfections with your thoughts" (line 23). Shakespeare addresses the idea of the theater itself in the first lines of the play, as the Chorus prepares the audience for the sometimes frustrating fact that presenting sweeping action, including major battles, on a tiny, relatively prop-free stage on an English afternoon is not very lifelike:

O for a Muse of fire, that would ascend
The brightest heaven of invention!
A kingdom for a stage, princes to act,
And monarchs to behold the swelling scene!
(PROLOGUE, LINES 1–4)

Elizabeth's General

The analogy used by the Chorus in Act 5 to describe the enthusiasm for Henry's return to London after his Agincourt victory was highly topical for the play's first audiences:

> Were now the general of our gracious Empress,
> As in good time he may, from Ireland coming,
> Bringing rebellion broached on his sword[.]
> (LINES 30–32)

Shakespeare was referring to Robert Devereux, Earl of Essex (1566–1601), the popular and dashing young courtier who was a favorite of the ageing Queen Elizabeth and the hero of a successful 1596 raid on Càdiz in Spain. At the time of writing, Essex was leading a campaign to subdue a rebellion in Ireland headed by Hugh O'Neill, the Second Earl of Tyrone.

The playwright's enthusiasm in early 1599 would not have lasted out the year, however. Essex's campaign turned out to be a failure, ending with a truce and terms of peace that enraged Elizabeth. Instead of continuing his command, Essex hurried, against orders, to London, argued with the queen, was placed under house arrest, and eventually stripped of all offices of state. Early in 1601, he led a disastrous coup attempt. Captured by the queen's forces, he was beheaded on February 25, 1601.

LEFT: *This portrait of Robert Devereux was painted* c. *1596 by the studio of the Dutch-born, English-based artist Marcus Gheeraerts the Younger. Essex was then at the height of his renown following the capture of Càdiz.*

The Role of the Chorus

In each of the subsequent introductions by the Chorus, too, a cluster of images sets the scene. For Act 2, "all the youth of England are on fire" (line 1), and we get a clear feeling for the enthusiasm that attends the preparations for war. But "a nest of hollow bosoms" (line 21) threatens English unity with individual treachery, and we learn of the conspiracy that Henry will foil.

At the start of Act 3, the Chorus provides vivid images of Henry's fleet crossing the English Channel to do battle in France—"behold the threaden sails, / Borne with th' invisible and creeping wind" (lines 10–11)—and the ensuing siege of Harfleur—"Behold the ordinance on their carriages, / With fatal mouths gaping on girded Harflew" (lines 26–27).

At the beginning of Act 4, the Chorus employs a series of striking images to bring to life the scene on the night before the Battle of Agincourt. The English soldiers can hear the "confident and overlusty French" (line 18) because they are camped so close. The soldiers, "like sacrifices" (line 23), await anxiously the morning's battle like "So many horrid ghosts" (line 28).

Introducing Act 5, the Chorus describes Henry returning home to London to be greeted by streets full of cheering people. This topical image brings to a conclusion the motif of military triumph shadowed by dismal defeat:

> *Like to the senators of th' antique Rome,*
> *With the plebeians swarming at their heels,*
> *Go forth and fetch their conqu'ring Caesar in;*
> *As by a lower but by loving likelihood,*
> *Were now the general of our gracious Empress,*
> *As in good time he may, from Ireland coming,*
> *Bringing rebellion broached on his sword[.]*
> (LINES 26–32)

Bringing the Past to Life

In England, nineteenth-century productions were drab affairs until director William Charles Macready's 1839 staging introduced elaborate dioramas for each Chorus, including the Chorus as Time, with scythe and hourglass; a great fleet setting sail and a siege; and a crowd welcoming Henry back to London. This practice culminated in director Charles Kean's 1859 production, which employed six hundred extras to play the throng that greeted Henry's return.

A Mirror to Modern Conflict

Of all Shakespeare's plays, only *Hamlet* has been as often produced to reflect current events. The two most famous film adaptations of *Henry V* are Laurence Olivier's (1944) and Kenneth Branagh's (1989). Olivier's film, financed by the British government, gave its war-weary audience a surge of national pride, portraying an English fighting force struggling against all odds to victory. Branagh's film is not nearly as clear-cut. It celebrates Henry's nationalist speeches and offers a charming and triumphant English conqueror at the film's end. However, it also presents the brutality of war and the killing of innocents in a graphic and affecting way. In this respect, the film was reflecting then-recent experiences of trauma, atrocities, and collateral damage in conflicts in Vietnam, the Falkland Islands, and elsewhere, as well as the fact that images of warfare were by then much more conspicuous—mainly due to the advent of television—than they had been in the 1940s. As a king, Branagh's Henry is simultaneously an attractive and dangerous figure.

Cheerly to sea! The signs of war advance!/ No king of England, if not king of France!

—*King Henry* (ACT 2, SCENE 2, LINES 192–93)

Four hundred years after it was written, Shakespeare's depiction of an English victory over the French was first played in France, at the Cour d'Honneur du Palais des Papes in Avignon, on July 9, 1999, directed by Jean-Louis Benoit. In 1997, a Belgian/Dutch production, entitled *Ten Oorlog (To War)*, by Luk Percival and Tom Lanoye, incorporated material from both of Shakespeare's historical tetralogies (encompassing the reigns of Richard II, Henry IV, Henry V, Henry VI, Edward IV, and Richard III) into a three-part drama. This production was lauded for its adaptation of Shakespeare's historical material to the social and political context of 1990s Belgium.

BELOW: *The Royal Shakespeare Company's 1997 production of the play transferred the action to a modern war zone. Here, Henry, played by Michael Sheen, leads his troops into battle.*

Henry VIII

THE PLOT: *The Duke of Buckingham becomes suspicious of Cardinal Wolsey and complains about his influence over the king. Buckingham is arrested and charged in the king's name with high treason. He learns that his Surveyor has informed on him, but suspects that it is Wolsey's doing. The cardinal appears to be in political control, but his unpopularity with the people and his overreaching in the king's name put this in jeopardy. Henry meets Anne Bullen at a dinner at Wolsey's.*

Buckingham goes to his execution. Meanwhile, Henry plans his divorce from his wife, Katherine. She defends herself in front of the court and the pope's representative and refuses the divorce. Cardinal Wolsey, who is disgraced, is stripped of his offices. Despite the pope's opposition, Henry divorces Katherine. Anne becomes the queen, and shortly afterward gives birth to a daughter. Wolsey dies. Gardiner, Bishop of Winchester, does not approve of Anne's Protestant leanings, and he accuses Cranmer, Archbishop of Canterbury, of heresy; Cranmer is saved by his friendship with Henry. In the final scene, Anne's daughter, Elizabeth, is christened with much fanfare.

ABOVE: *The* c. *1540 portrait of Henry VIII by Hans Holbein the Younger captures the king's overbearing bullheadedness and lust for power.*

Dramatis Personae

King Henry the Eighth
Cardinal Wolsey
Cardinal Campeius
Capuchius, *ambassador from the Emperor Charles V*
Cranmer, *Archbishop of Canterbury*
Duke of Norfolk
Duke of Buckingham
Duke of Suffolk
Earl of Surrey
Lord Chamberlain
Lord Chancellor
Gardiner, *secretary to the king, afterward Bishop of Winchester*
Bishop of Lincoln
Lord Aburgavenny
Lord Sands *(called also* **Sir Walter Sands***)*
Sir Henry Guilford
Sir Thomas Lovell
Sir Anthony Denny
Sir Nicholas Vaux
Cromwell, *servant to Wolsey*
Secretaries *to Wolsey*
Griffith, *gentleman usher to Queen Katherine*
Three Gentlemen
Doctor Butts, *physician to the king*
Garter King-at-Arms
Surveyor *to the Duke of Buckingham*
Brandon, and a Sergeant-at-Arms
Doorkeeper of the Council-chamber
Porter, and his Man
Page to Gardiner
Crier
Queen Katherine, *wife to King Henry, afterward divorced*
Anne Bullen, *her Maid of Honor, afterward queen*
Old Lady, *friend to Anne Bullen*
Patience, *woman to Queen Katherine*
Spirits
Several Bishops; Lords and Ladies in the dumb shows; Women attending upon the Queen; Scribes, Officers, Guards, and other Attendants

WRITTEN
c. 1612
SETTING AND PERIOD
England, 1508–33
CHARACTERS 71
ACTS 5
SCENES 16, plus Prologue and Epilogue
LINES 3,221

Written in about 1612, in collaboration with the playwright John Fletcher, *Henry VIII,* or *All Is True,* is the final history play of Shakespeare's career. Instead of the clashes between dynastic factions (as in the Wars of the Roses plays, culminating in *Richard III*), or between the king and his nobles (as in the *Henry IV* plays), or England and France (as in *Henry V* or in parts of the *Henry VI* plays), *Henry VIII* focuses on political intrigue at court.

LORD CHAMBERLAIN *It seems the marriage with his brother's wife/Has crept too near his conscience.*

SUFFOLK [ASIDE] *No, his conscience/ Has crept too near another lady.*

(ACT 2, SCENE 2, LINES 16–18)

Close to the Bone

This first and only play to take the Tudor dynasty as its subject treads carefully: for example, it presents the Crown's dispute with the Catholic Church in Rome over Henry's request for divorce and the fall of Cardinal Wolsey, but it does not include the nastier, more sordid details of Henry's relationship with Anne Bullen (Boleyn) while he is still married to Katherine of Aragon. The play's most striking omission is that it does not dramatize Henry's break with Rome and the beginning of England's conversion to Protestantism.

These omissions are understandable because in 1613, when the play was first staged, the Tudors were recent history. Elizabeth I had died ten years previously, bringing to an end just over a century of Tudor rule. Now, under James I, Elizabeth's chosen successor, for reasons of political sensitivity, Shakespeare and Fletcher had to finely balance the backstabbing and double-dealing endemic in the English court with the providential anticipation of Elizabeth's birth. Henry VIII's court may have been a place of danger and bloody contention, but it did produce Elizabeth, the great virgin queen.

The importance of Elizabeth's reputation is evident in the language that greets Henry and Anne's new daughter in the play's final scenes:

This royal infant—heaven still move about her!—
Though in her cradle, yet now promises
Upon this land a thousand thousand blessings,
Which time shall bring to ripeness. She shall be
(But few now living can behold that goodness)
A pattern to all princes living with her,
And all that shall succeed ...

(ACT 5, SCENE 4, LINES 17–23)

Another reason Shakespeare and Fletcher had for accentuating Elizabeth I's future greatness is to offer the promise that the daughter of the current king might follow in her footsteps (in February 1613, James's daughter, who was also named Elizabeth, married Frederick, Elector Palatine of the Rhine and director of the Protestant Union).

A Dual Structure

Henry VIII freely incorporates episodes from the historical sources, covering 25 years of Henry's reign. These sources—Raphael Holinshed's *Chronicles of England, Scotland and Ireland* (1587), and English Puritan John Foxe's monumental *Actes and Monuments* (four editions beginning in 1563)—provided the raw materials for a play whose plot is a combination of two different generic structures: history play and romance.

Shakespeare and Fletcher's audiences would have been familiar with the main characters, such as Wolsey, who are represented in the *de casibus,* or "fall of great men," manner—named after Boccaccio's *De casibus virorum illustrium* (*On the Fates*

Cranmer Anticipates Queen Elizabeth

All princely graces
That mould up such a mighty piece as this is,
With all the virtues that attend the good,
Shall still be doubled on her ...

(ACT 5, SCENE 4, LINES 25–28)

Good grows with her;
In her days every man shall eat in safety
Under his own vine what he plants, and sing
The merry songs of peace to all his neighbors.
God shall be truly known, and those about her
From her shall read the perfect [ways] of honor,
And by those claim their greatness, not by blood.

(ACT 5, SCENE 4, LINES 32–38)

She shall be, to the happiness of England,
An aged princess; many days shall see her,
And yet no day without a deed to crown it.
Would I had known no more! but she must die,
She must, the saints must have her; yet a virgin,
A most unspotted lily shall she pass
To th' ground, and all the world shall mourn her.

(ACT 5, SCENE 4, LINES 56–62)

ABOVE: *Cardinal Wolsey—portrayed here by nineteenth-century English actor Henry Irving—is one of the masters of intrigue in this play about political power.*

of Famous Men) and well known to Shakespeare's audience through *The Mirror for Magistrates* (1559), a book that also collected the stories of a number of exemplary figures. This *de casibus* style drives the plot of *Henry VIII* when it focuses on issues of political intrigue within the court.

The play's other structure is that of providential romance: all roads lead to the birth of the future Queen Elizabeth I—a teleological structure that ensures that any crisis that looms for Henry and, later, Anne, is overcome in order to enable the birth of their daughter.

Behind the Spectacle

As the alternative title suggests, *All Is True* is concerned with "truth" and "truthfulness." It is not, however, easy to discern exactly what "the truth" is or how certain we can be that the play of *Henry VIII* is offering the truth of Henry's reign or Tudor rule. At the very end of the play, the optimism of Cranmer's prophecy of Elizabeth's future success is belied by the cynicism that characterizes many earlier scenes. The play opens, for example, with a scene in which the Duke of Norfolk reports what he has witnessed at the Field of the Cloth of Gold meeting between Henry and Francis I of France outside Calais, in the summer of 1520. Norfolk's description of the famous tournament spectacle is, on the surface, complimentary of the lavishness and grandeur on display:

To-day the French,
All clinquant, all in gold, like heathen gods,
Shone down the English; and, to-morrow, they
Made Britain India . . .
(ACT 1, SCENE 1, LINES 18–21)

But considered more closely, Norfolk implies that all this pomp and spectacle does not result in anything practical for England's political interests:

Grievingly I think
The peace between the French and us not values
The cost that did conclude it.
(ACT 1, SCENE 1, LINES 87–89)

When Norfolk and Buckingham learn that the meeting was Cardinal Wolsey's doing, Buckingham dismisses the spectacle as "fierce vanities" (Act 1, Scene 1, line 54). Impressive appearances, the play suggests, often cover over disappointment.

Another important theme is the fortunes, or otherwise, of highly placed men and women. The play consistently explores how a cardinal, a queen, and an archbishop, for example, grasp power and status and then lose everything.

Political Imagery

Two significant events occurred just before the play's first performance in the late spring or early summer of 1613: James I's eldest son and heir to the throne, Henry, died in November 1612, and the king's daughter, Elizabeth, married the Elector Palatine in February 1613.

The national mood is registered in the somber tone of the Prologue, a warning to the audience that the drama they are about to see will not be humorous, it will be "noble":

[T]hings now
That bear a weighty and a serious brow,
Sad, high, and working, full of state and woe:
Such noble scenes as draw the eye to flow,
We now present . . .
(LINES 1–5)

Ready. Aim. Fire?

Henry VIII was the play that brought the house down. Literally. At a performance on June 29, 1613, a cannon shot ignited the thatch roof atop the Globe theater in London. It caused the building to burn to the ground. Only one of the audience members was injured when his pants caught fire. He was lucky, though, as it was put out with a handy bottle of ale.

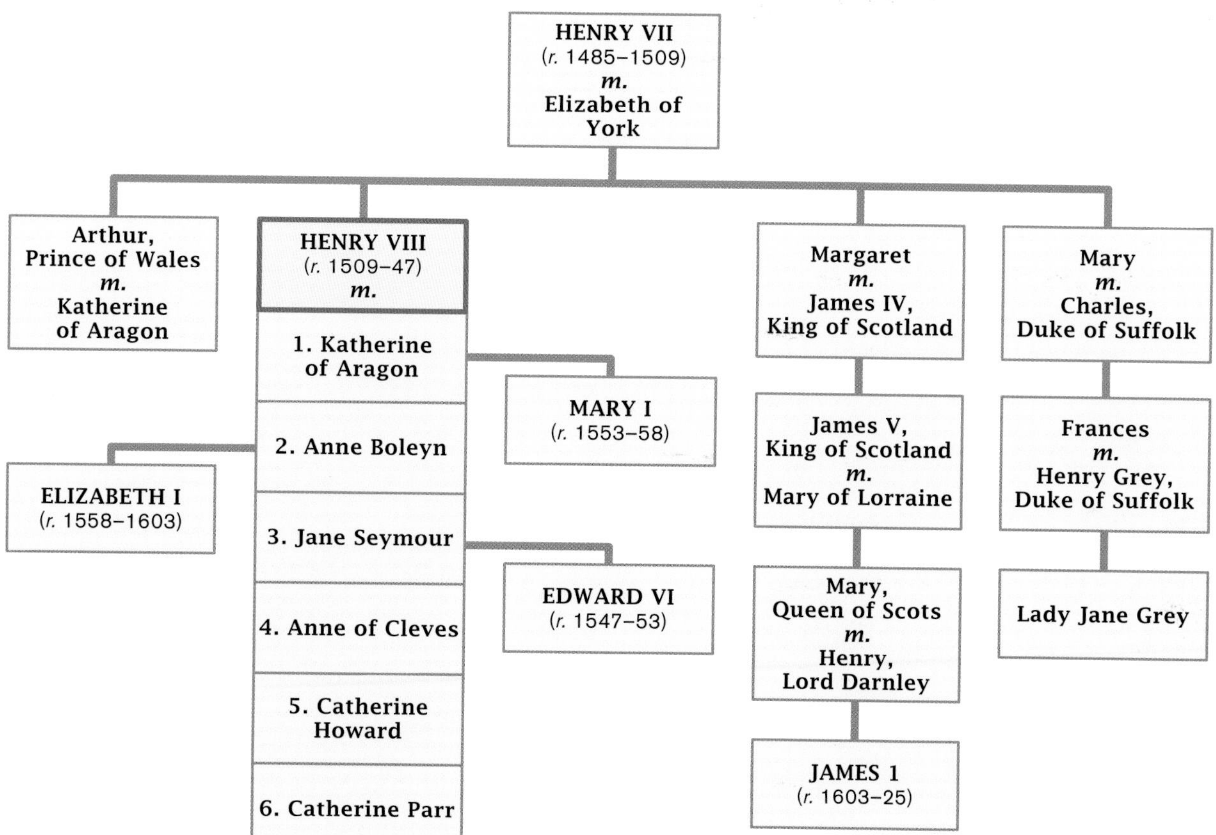

FAMILY TREE
Although the Wars of the Roses ended in 1485, the familial intrigues involving the English crown continued for more than a century, until James Stuart took the throne in 1603. So ended the Tudor line.

The images of high and low used here anticipate a dominant theme in *Henry VIII*: the rise and fall of political fortunes and status.

Henry is largely left out of the political intrigue. Religious figures such as Cardinal Wolsey and Gardiner are the instigators of the strategies designed to crush opposition, further their own causes, or influence those in power. Such behavior is often attended by images of natural predation: Cardinal Wolsey, says Buckingham, is a "holy fox, / Or wolf," as "rav'nous / As he is subtile" (Act 1, Scene 1, lines 158–60). And when Katherine defends herself during the divorce proceedings, she compares herself to "… the lily, / That once was mistress of the field, and flourish'd" (Act 3, Scene 1, lines 151–52).

Significant Adaptations

Henry VIII was one of the few Shakespeare plays staged without significant adaptation during the Restoration period in late seventeenth-century England. It was staged by the poet and dramatist William Davenant nearly uncut and with the emphasis on its spectacle and court pageantry.

In England during the eighteenth century, productions of *Henry VIII* followed Davenant, continuing to emphasize royalist imagery through lavish costumes and scenery. Nineteenth-century productions in London, beginning with actor–manager John Philip Kemble in 1788, shifted the action toward a more realistic setting. Productions such as actor–director Charles Kean's in 1855 combined lavish sets and costumes (extensive research providing accurate period costumes and props) with an emphasis on a more realistic presentation of historical events.

Recently, in productions in Britain, the United States, and Japan, the play has been interpreted as conservative pageantry and biting political satire. For contemporary theater, *All Is True* lends itself to myriad interpretations of that most playful title.

BELOW: *In the 2006 Royal Shakespeare Company production of* Henry VIII *at the Holy Trinity Church, Stratford, Patience (Amy Finegan, left) supports Katherine, played by Corinne Jaber, agonizing over her divorce.*

The Comedies

Shakespeare's comedies are rich with witty wordplay and humorous situation, often involving mistaken identity. Their plots move from confusion and trouble to social reconciliation and harmony. Changes of scene often produce benign transformations. But while most of the comedies end in marriage, the "happy ending" rarely expels all discord.

The Two Gentlemen of Verona

THE PLOT: *Valentine leaves Verona to serve the Duke of Milan and falls in love with his daughter Silvia. Valentine's friend Proteus pledges his love to Julia but, sent by his father to Milan, also falls in love with Silvia. Proteus betrays Valentine's elopement plans to the Duke. Banished, Valentine joins a band of outlaws. Julia goes to Milan disguised as a page, Sebastian, only to find herself employed by Proteus to woo Silvia on his behalf. Silvia escapes in search of Valentine but is kidnapped by the outlaws. Proteus, having gone in search of Silvia with the Duke and Julia/Sebastian, rescues her from the outlaws, but then threatens to rape her. Valentine arrives at that moment and Proteus repents, yet Valentine offers him Silvia anyway. Julia/Sebastian faints and reveals her true identity. Julia and Proteus are reunited and a double wedding is planned.*

Dramatis Personae

Duke of Milan, *father to Silvia*
Valentine, Proteus, *the two Gentlemen*
Antonio, *father to Proteus*
Thurio, *a foolish rival to Valentine*
Eglamour, *agent for Silvia in her escape*
Host, *where Julia lodges*
Outlaws, *with Valentine*
Speed, *page to Valentine*
Launce, *a clownish servant to Proteus*
Panthino, *servant to Antonio*
Julia, *beloved of Proteus*
Silvia, *beloved of Valentine*
Lucetta, *waiting-woman to Julia*
Servants; Musicians

WRITTEN
c. 1590–91

SETTING AND PERIOD
Verona, Milan, and a forest near Mantua, c. sixteenth century

CHARACTERS 13

ACTS 5

SCENES 20

LINES 2,288

Possibly Shakespeare's earliest play, *Two Gentlemen* explores the potentially devastating conflict between love and friendship. Only Valentine's abrupt intervention saves Silvia from rape, and the hurried reconciliation that follows seems lightweight. The language of the play is highly stylized, with characterization often coming second to quick-fire wit:

> JULIA *His little speaking shows his love but small.*
> LUCETTA *Fire that's closest kept burns most of all.*
> JULIA *They do not love that do not show their love.*
> LUCETTA *O, they love least that let men know their love.*
> (ACT 1, SCENE 2, LINES 29–32)

Comic stage business abounds: contrived letters are torn to pieces; a clown laments his family's dispersal by conversing with his shoes; and a rope ladder discovered on Valentine's person prevents an elopement. But there are also dramatically poignant scenes: Julia, disguised as a boy, watches her lover woo another woman; and through the guise of recounting a performance of a play feelingly expresses her anguish at Proteus's betrayal to Silvia herself.

Friendship and Romance

Shakespeare interweaves two parallel plots in *Two Gentlemen*. He adapted the triangular love story from Jorge de Montemayor's Spanish prose romance *Diana*, published around 1559 and subsequently translated into French and English. For the friendship plot, he drew on the tale of Titus and Gisippus in Sir Thomas Elyot's *The Boke Named the Governour* (1531)—"a right goodly example of friendship," as Elyot described it.

Ever-changing Proteus

Thou, Julia, thou hast metamorphis'd me[.]
(ACT 1, SCENE 1, LINE 66)

O, how this spring of love resembleth
The uncertain glory of an April day[.]
(ACT 1, SCENE 3, LINES 84–85)

O heaven, were man
But constant, he were perfect …
(ACT 5, SCENE 4, LINES 110–11)

Friendship, indeed, is the major theme of the play, as encapsulated by Proteus's question, "In love / Who respects friend?" (Act 5, Scene 4, lines 53–54). But *Two Gentlemen* also explores gentlemanliness. Panthino lists its qualities: travel to wars or undiscovered islands, university study, prowess in tournaments, civil discourse with noblemen, and service of a great lord (Act 1, Scene 3). Proteus falls far short of such civility, and the play's clowns comment ironically. Launce recounts how his dog Crab thrust himself

> *into the company of three or four gentleman-like dogs, under the Duke's table. He had not been there (bless the mark!) a pissing-while, but all the chamber smelt him.*
> (ACT 4, SCENE 4, LINES 17–20)

Speed parodies the traditional language of courtly love by listing his mistress's qualities in domestic terms: "*Item*, she brews good ale" (Act 3,

LEFT: *Angelica Kauffmann's 1788 painting depicts the moment in Act 5, Scene 4 when Valentine prevents Proteus from forcing himself on Silvia, as an aghast Julia/Sebastian looks on.*

Scene 1, line 303). A further important theme is fatherly authority: Antonio sends Proteus to Milan against his will, and the Duke determines that Silvia will marry his courtier Thurio rather than love whom she chooses.

The Moods of Love

The lovers lace their language with religious terms: "penance," "holy," "altar," "love's firm votary," "true devoted pilgrim," "beadsman," and "heavenly saint." Animal references, supplied chiefly by Launce and Speed, undercut the idealism: "fish," "crow," "fox," "water-spaniel," "sheep," and "mutton" (this last being Elizabethan slang for prostitute). Selfhood and identity are questioned through the motifs of "picture," "painting," or "shadow." Imagery drawn from the natural world shows the mutability of love: the bud loses its verdure; the summer-swelling flower is blasted by rough winter; love melts like ice or changes as the tide.

Rewritten and Redirected

Director Benjamin Victor's Drury Lane production in London in 1762 staged a rewritten text. New scenes were created for the clowns, and Valentine's "All that was mine in Silvia I give thee" (Act 5, Scene 4, line 83) was cut. This version of the play proved influential. With the exception of director Charles Macready's 1841 Drury Lane production, eighteenth- and nineteenth-century audiences would have seen an "easier" play.

The Bristol Old Vic successfully revived the play's fortunes in 1957 through lavish spectacle. Some subsequent stagings suggested sexual ambivalence among the lovers, especially director Leon Rubin's 1984 Stratford, Ontario, production, where Valentine announced "All my love to Silvia I also give to thee" before embracing Proteus. In 2006, a Brazilian company, Nos do Morro, cast a human actor as Crab; the "dog" growled mistrustfully at Proteus whenever he appeared on stage.

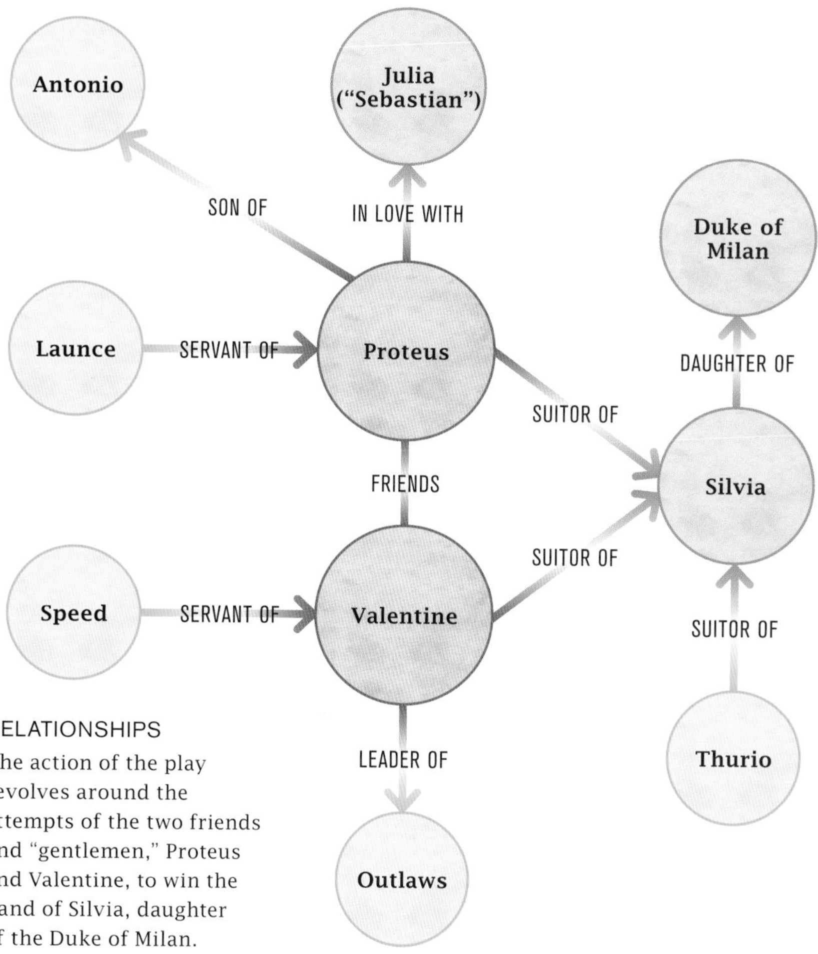

RELATIONSHIPS
The action of the play revolves around the attempts of the two friends and "gentlemen," Proteus and Valentine, to win the hand of Silvia, daughter of the Duke of Milan.

The Comedy of Errors

THE PLOT: *Egeon, a merchant from Syracuse, his wife, Aemilia, their twin sons, and twin servants are separated by a storm at sea. Egeon, one son, and one servant are rescued and taken to Syracuse; Aemilia, one son, and one servant are rescued but separated. Some years later, this threesome comes to the city of Ephesus separately. The Syracusan son and then Egeon travel to find the lost brother and son. They, too, come to Ephesus separately.*

Egeon is sentenced to death for violating a law banning travel between Syracuse and Ephesus. The Syracusan son and servant, however, are greeted warmly, having been mistaken for their Ephesian brothers. Adriana, wife of the Ephesian, dines with the Syracusan and locks her husband out of the house. A goldsmith and a Courtezan make similar mistakes. Meanwhile, the Ephesians are mistaken for the Syracusans. They all come by chance to the door of a Priory. The twin brothers and servants recognize one another; Aemilia, the Abbess, recognizes Egeon as her husband, and he is pardoned.

RIGHT: *A nineteenth-century engraving depicts Aemilia and the babies Antipholus and Dromio being saved from the shipwreck. The separation of the family is recounted by Egeon in Act 1, Scene 1 as he faces the death penalty. Death and disaster hover at the edges of the play.*

Dramatis Personae

Solinus, *Duke of Ephesus*
Egeon, *a merchant of Syracuse*
Antipholus of Ephesus, Antipholus of Syracuse, *twin brothers, and sons to Egeon and Aemilia*
Dromio of Ephesus, Dromio of Syracuse, *twin brothers, and bondmen to the two Antipholuses*
Balthazar, *a merchant*
Angelo, *a goldsmith*
First Merchant of Ephesus, *friend to Antipholus of Syracuse*
Second Merchant of Ephesus, *to whom Angelo is a debtor*
Doctor Pinch, *a conjuring schoolmaster*
Aemilia, *wife to Egeon, an Abbess at Ephesus*
Adriana, *wife to Antipholus of Ephesus*
Luciana, *her sister*
Luce, *servant to Adriana (also known as Nell)*
Courtezan
Jailer, Headsman, Messenger, Officers, and other Attendants

With about 1,800 lines, *The Comedy of Errors* is the shortest of Shakespeare's plays, but it is by no means a slight work. Its particular merits lie in the intricacy of its plotting and in the reworking and blending of its disparate source materials into an organic whole. It is the only play in the canon that exhibits an exact display of the Classical unities of time, place, and action. And it is also, surprisingly, a farce that takes the human condition seriously.

WRITTEN
c. 1592
SETTING AND PERIOD
Ephesus, Classical times
CHARACTERS 16
ACTS 5
SCENES 11
LINES 1,787

Contexts: Setting and Tone

Roman dramatist Plautus's *Menaechmi*, on which the play is partly based, is set in Epidamnum; Shakespeare transferred the setting to Ephesus. He did so probably because he knew that his audiences were familiar with Ephesus from the Bible, as a city both of dealers in magic and exorcists (Acts 19:13), and of the site of the Temple of Diana (Acts 19:27). To the Ephesians, St. Paul wrote his instructions for marital relationships and the duties of servants to masters (Ephesians 5, 6). As a play based on a Classical original, the comedy fitted neatly into the Pauline context of this city.

So Shakespeare used these associations. The background of magic justifies the fears of the Syracusan travelers: "Thou art, as all you are, a sorceress" (Act 4, Scene 3, line 66). And the emotional and religious power of the Great Temple of Diana transposes into a Priory, a Christian Abbess, and a final call for baptism.

The Christian tone that concludes the play and the play's frequent references to the Christian tradition are responsible also for the morality that characterizes the relations between the married couples in the play. In Plautus's play, it is clear that the Ephesian twin has been carrying on an intimate affair with a prostitute; in Shakespeare's version, it is not at all clear that that relationship is sexual. Shakespeare has diminished the emphasis that the Classical text gives to that association and has made it less explicit.

Fidelity and Harmony in Marriage

Why should their [men's] liberty than ours be more?
—*Adriana* (ACT 2, SCENE 1, LINE 10)

Man, more divine, the master of all these,
Lord of the wide world and wild wat'ry seas,
Indu'd with intellectual sense and souls,
Of more pre-eminence than fish and fowls,
Are masters to their females, and their lords:
Then let your will attend on their accords.
—*Luciana* (ACT 2, SCENE 1, LINES 20–25)

In food, in sport, and life-preserving rest
To be disturb'd, would mad or man or beast:
The consequence is then, thy jealous fits
Hath scar'd thy husband from the use of wits.
—*Abbess* (ACT 5, SCENE 1, LINES 83–86)

Marriage and Fidelity

The Comedy of Errors includes Shakespeare's most extensive treatment of loyalty in marriage. In Act 2, Scene 2, Adriana's comment is a powerful argument for the sanctity of the marriage bond and the rights of women:

Ah, do not tear away thyself from me;
For know, my love, as easy mayst thou fall
A drop of water in the breaking gulf,
And take unmingled thence that drop again,
Without addition or diminishing,
As take from me thyself and not me too.
(ACT 2, SCENE 2, LINES 124–29)

Though the play presents us with a double standard of conduct for husband and for wife, Adriana's heartfelt comments argue strongly for Shakespeare's belief in mutuality and the rightness of marital fidelity. Luciana's submissiveness is obsolete, and the play does not admit it as effective. The Abbess—in Classical terms the *dea ex machina* (the goddess from the machine), a figure who emerges at just the right moment to solve an apparently insoluble crisis—chides Adriana for her failure to provide a proper atmosphere at home ("thy jealous fits / Hath scar'd thy husband from the use of wits," Act 5, Scene 1, lines 85–86), which Adriana accepts as, in part, at least, her own fault: "She did betray me to my own reproof" (Act 5, Scene 1, line 90).

Thus, we must take seriously Adriana's insistence that her husband come home to dinner. That dinner scene (Act 3, Scene 1)—the critical scene of the play—is the culmination of Adriana's actions in the first two acts to bring together the wife and the husband (supposed). Its source is the scene in another play by Plautus, *Amphitruo*, in which Jupiter descends in the likeness of the husband and seduces the wife. Shakepeare's treatment greatly modifies this source. In his play, the Syracusan—in the likeness of the husband (his twin)—does not seduce the wife: he has dinner with her and her sister (as later reported to the Duke in Act 5, Scene 1, lines 207–8). He is terrified at the aspect of Adriana—whom he regards as a witch ("none but witches ... inhabit here,"

BELOW: *In a 2006 staging at the Globe, London, Antipholus of Syracuse (his servant Dromio behind him) listens, mystified, as Adriana, who believes she is talking to her husband, gives a heartfelt speech on marital fidelity (Act 2, Scene 2).*

ANTIPHOLUS OF SYRACUSE *Then she bears some breadth?*

DROMIO OF SYRACUSE *No longer from head to foot than from hip to hip: she is spherical, like a globe; I could find out countries in her.*

(ACT 3, SCENE 2, LINES 112–15)

Act 3, Scene 2, line 156), but at first sight he falls in love with her sister, Luciana, and courts her in Act 3, Scene 2. The juxtaposing of these two scenes, Scenes 1 and 2 of this act, exhibits Shakespeare's masterful blending of his sources seamlessly. For Scene 2, a scene of romantic lovers, derives, not from Plautus, but from Italian romantic comedy of the Renaissance. Luciana has no original in the Classical tradition.

Poetical and Theatrical Treatment

Some readers complain that the play lacks the poetic intensity of Shakespeare's later work. That complaint, accurate enough, is not as significant as it might seem. The concentrated interests of this play do not lie in poetic treatment or in the development of character, but those lacks do not of necessity constitute defects. We might as well complain that the later tragedies do not have the intricate plotting and movement of characters that are found in this comedy. Every play in the canon has its virtues, uniquely appropriate to it.

In place of a rich stream of poetic imagery, we have the visual images on stage of the ring and the chain. In the last scene of the play, the ring is returned to its rightful owner (Act 5, Scene 1, line 393); that gesture represents the termination of the association between the Ephesian and the Courtezan. The chain, conspicuously worn by the Syracusan twin throughout the second half of the play, is given publicly by the Syracusan to the Ephesian (line 380) and then by the Ephesian to his wife, for whom it was ordered (Act 3, Scene 2, line 173). It is the visible symbol of the links that bind together husband and wife. Its transfer here must be taken to symbolize the reunion of the young husband and wife, a movement parallel to the reunion of the parents and the reunion of the two pairs of twins.

Another notable detail of stagecraft is the juxtaposition of the twins at the beginning and again at the end of Scene 1 of Act 3, where one twin goes off stage as the other twin comes on. These choric juxtapositions occur significantly before and after the central critical scene, the scene that addresses most keenly the questions of identity and the self, and the scene in which both of the servant twins are on stage at the same time—both visible to the audience but not visible to one another. (If they saw and recognized one another, the search for the lost brother—and the play—would be over.) In the first act, the Syracusian has said that in losing his brother, he has lost himself, and in seeking him,

I to the world am like a drop of water,
That in the ocean seeks another drop,
Who, falling there to find his fellow forth,
(Unseen, inquisitive), confounds himself.

(ACT 1, SCENE 2, LINES 35–38)

RELATIONSHIPS
The activities of two sets of identical twin brothers, Antipholus and Dromio, form the comic center of the play. A pair of sisters, Adriana and Luciana, adds more complexity to an intricate plot.

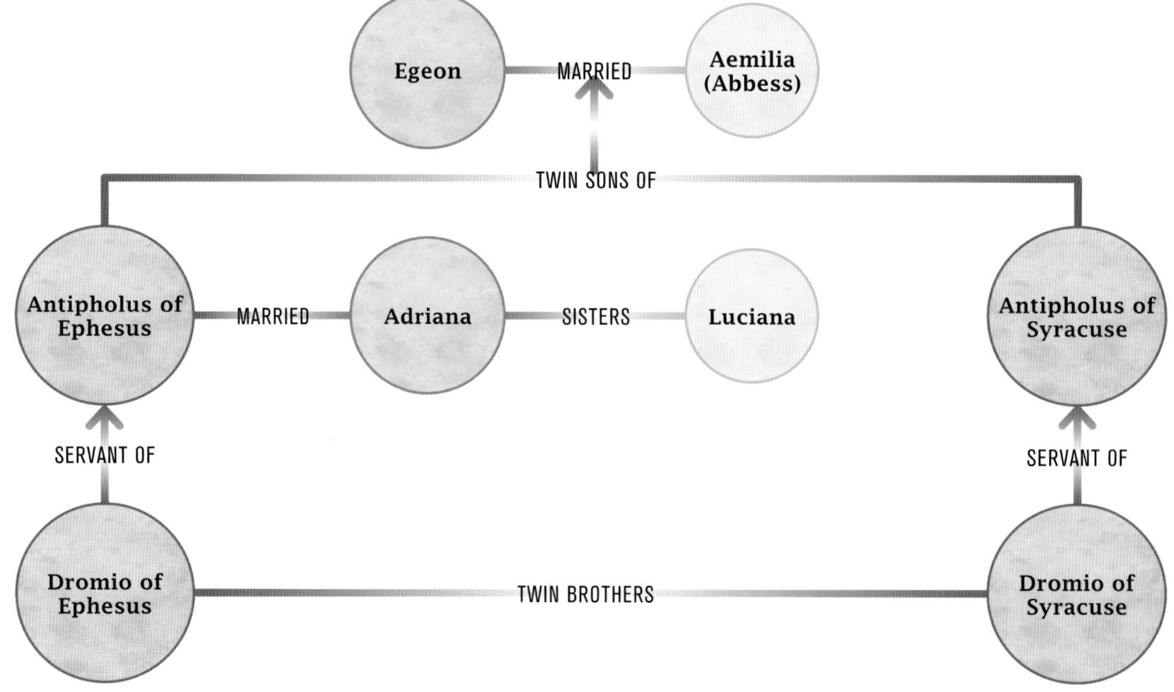

ABOVE: *Members of the Mansaku Nomura Company perform as Antipholus and Dromio in the 2001 London staging of* The Kyogen of Errors, *an adaptation of the play as a* kyogen, *a Japanese comic theatrical form.*

At these two moments, the Syracusan has almost found his brother, that other drop. Without a reunion at either of these near meetings, he still has lost himself.

Impact and Influences

This early play—Shakespeare's first comedy, according to some scholars—treats a surprising number of themes, interests, and situations that will receive extensive development in the later plays. The opening lines, for instance, discuss the sentence of death on Egeon; we do not expect comedy to open with a reference to death. But Shakespeare knew that life and death are inextricably woven in human experience. The threat of the executioner's ax darkens the hilarity of the play.

This play also presents initially the relationships between brothers, between fathers and sons, between loving couples, and between married couples—anguish, joy, reconciliation, and so on; the list is endless. The Abbess's prescription for the happy life—food, sport, rest—remains a standard throughout the later works.

If there is a shortcoming in this perfect little play, it is the absence of any indication of the power of music. Shakespeare soon learned to associate that feature with the excitement of young love and as a restorative in ill health. Songs and instrumental music grow in importance as the playwright's dramatic technique develops.

Noteworthy modern productions of the play include the Ethiopian Art Theater's jazz version, performed in New York in 1923 with an African-American cast; director Theodor Komisarjevsky's 1938 Stratford staging, featuring a colorful toy-town set; the 1996 Royal Shakespeare Company production at Stratford, directed by Tim Supple; and the Mansaku Nomura Company's Japanese-language adaptation, *The Kyogen of Errors*, at the Globe, London, in 2001.

Inspired By ...

There are several sources: for the errors of the Twins, the source is Plautus's *Menaechmi*; for the frame of Egeon and Aemilia, the tale of Apollonius of Tyre from English poet John Gower's *Confessio amantis*; for Adriana's dinner, Plautus's *Amphitruo*; and for the setting and the Priory, the Bible (Acts 19, Ephesians 5, 6).

The Taming of the Shrew

WRITTEN
c. 1592

SETTING AND PERIOD
Padua, Renaissance

CHARACTERS 32

ACTS 5

SCENES
12 plus 2 Induction scenes

LINES 2,676

THE PLOT: *In the Induction scenes, Christopher Sly, a drunken tinker, is tricked by a group of aristocrats into thinking himself a rich man. In his inebriated state, he watches a play, which forms the main action.*

Bianca Minola is unable to marry while her wild older sister, Katherina (Kate), has no suitor. Petruchio arrives from Verona determined to marry well, because wealthily, in Padua and begins to court Katherina by taming her. Bianca has a number of suitors, who have to disguise themselves to gain access to her, and she settles on Lucentio, who deceives his own father to pursue his love. Hortensio, another of Bianca's suitors, rejects her and marries a Widow. Both Bianca and the Widow fail the test of loyalty that the husbands carry out in the final scene. By the end of the play, Katherina appears to be the ideal, subordinated, and mild wife.

The Taming of the Shrew is one of the most popular comedies in the Shakespearean canon, despite the fact that attitudes toward women and gender roles have changed considerably since the play was written in the 1590s. It presents a challenge for modern producers and directors. How, for example, do you stage a play whose script ends with Katherina's advice to other wives that they should "place your hands below your husband's foot" (Act 5, Scene 2, line 177) if he should require it?

One possible reason for the play's continuing popularity is the focus on the relationship between Petruchio and Katherina, which is often staged as a lively battle of the sexes, a battle that can be reworked to end in mutual respect. Modern expectations about women's equality with men can be satisfied in this way.

The relationship between the two central figures is contrasted with the courtship and marriages between Bianca and Lucentio, and

Dramatis Personae

IN THE INDUCTION

Lord

Christopher Sly, *a tinker*

Hostess, Page, Players, Huntsmen, and Servants

IN THE PLAY-WITHIN-THE-PLAY

Baptista, *a rich gentleman of Padua*

Vincentio, *an old gentleman of Pisa*

Lucentio, *son to Vincentio, in love with Bianca*

Petruchio, *a gentleman of Verona, suitor to Katherina*

Gremio, Hortensio, *suitors to Bianca*

Tranio, Biondello, *servants to Lucentio*

Grumio, Curtis, *servants to Petruchio*

Pedant

Katherina *(the shrew),* **Bianca,** *daughters to Baptista*

Widow

Tailor, Haberdasher, and Servants attending on Baptista and Petruchio

LEFT: *This postcard advertised a 1904 staging of the play at London's Adelphi Theatre starring Oscar Asche and his wife, Lily Brayton. The production, like many before and since, staged the play as a farcical romp, ignoring the darker side of the play's sexual politics.*

Hortensio and the Widow. The first is characterized by deception and disguise, as Lucentio takes on the guise of Cambio, a lute teacher, to gain access to Bianca, who may not be courted until Katherina is married. Both these young people deceive their fathers, and Lucentio's father, Vincentio, has to make amends to Bianca's father, Baptista, for the fact that Lucentio has married Baptista's daughter without his permission. While Katherina is initially rebellious, she proves to have been a more obedient daughter than her younger sister. The play rehearses significant shifts in expectations, with the sisters swapping places as the play progresses.

Ideas about Marriage

In the sixteenth century, ideas about marriage were changing, and while it was still generally understood that wealthy parents would use marriage as a way of making useful political, economic, and social connections, there was also an increasing reaction against the idea of forced marriages in favor of marriages of companionship. Competing models of marriage, companionate and hierarchical, coexist within the play.

Katherina's behavior—her violence against her sister and her verbal anger against the suitors—would have been seen as comic by the play's original audiences. She is an example of the "shrew," a woman who disturbs the natural order by presuming to take control over men, and acting on her own initiative for her own benefit. She is, however, given lines in the play that suggest the tide is turning against the Elizabethan view of women as simply chattels to be disposed of as a father thought fit (although it should be kept in mind that it is not historically accurate to read Katherina as a sympathetic character or proto-feminist). Near the beginning of Act 1, Scene 1, Baptista offers Katherina to the richest suitor, which prompts the response from her: "I pray you, sir, is it your will / To make a stale [laughing

Control in Marriage

PETRUCHIO Good Lord, how bright and goodly
shines the moon!
KATHERINA The moon! the sun—it is not moonlight
now.
PETRUCHIO I say it is the moon that shines so
bright.
KATHERINA I know it is the sun that shines so
bright.
PETRUCHIO Now by my mother's son, and that's
myself,
It shall be moon, or star, or what I list,
Or ere I journey to your father's house.—
Go on, and fetch our horses back again.
(ACT 4, SCENE 5, LINES 2–9)

Thy husband is thy lord, thy life, thy keeper,
Thy head, thy sovereign; one that cares for thee,
And for thy maintenance; commits his body
To painful labor, both by sea and land;
To watch the night in storms, the day in cold,
Whilst thou li'st warm at home, secure and safe;
And craves no other tribute at thy hands
But love, fair looks, and true obedience—
Too little payment for so great a debt.
—*Katherina* (ACT 5, SCENE 2, LINES 146–54)

RELATIONSHIPS
The relationship between Petruchio and Katherina forms the main story line; Bianca and her suitors provide the subplot. Standing outside these events is the Induction, featuring Christopher Sly.

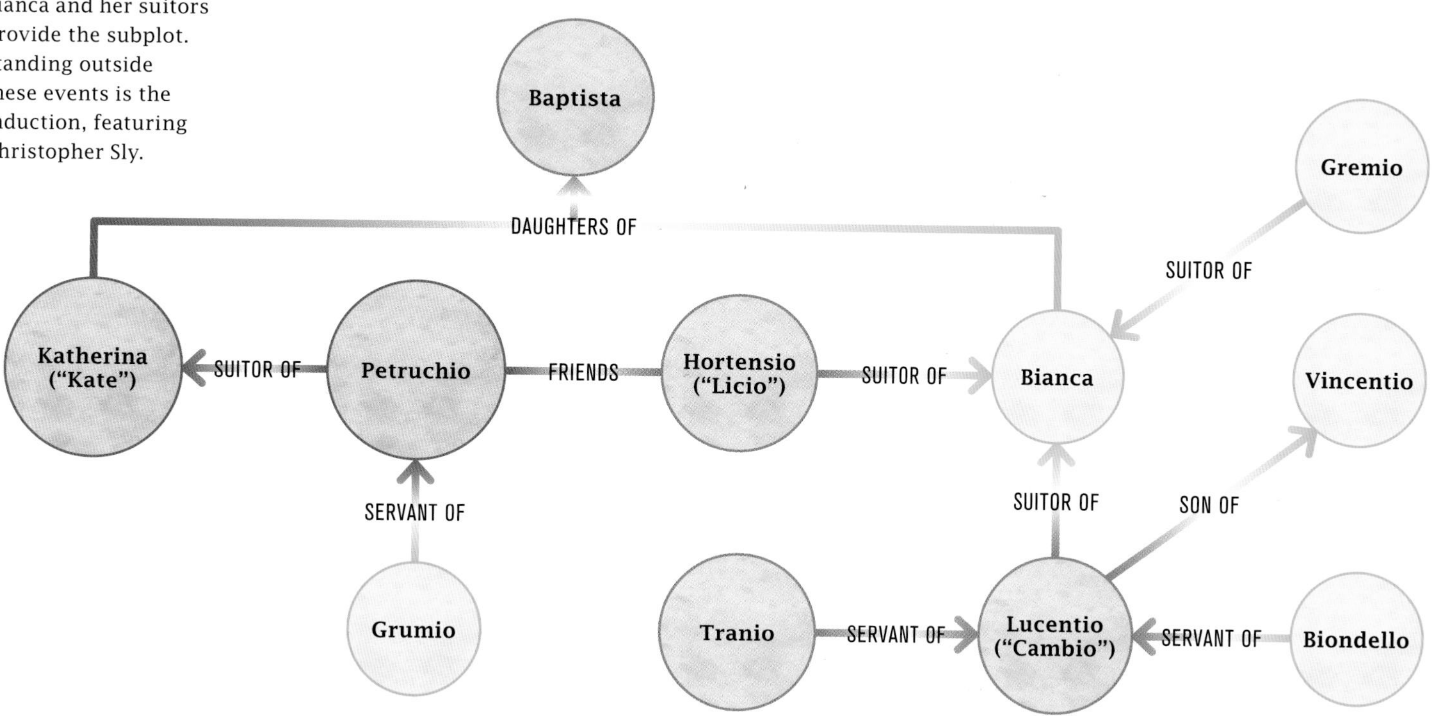

stock/prostitute] of me amongst these mates?" (lines 57–58). This question does not receive a convincing answer or rebuttal. Yet in the next act Baptista makes his policy concerning Bianca's marriage very clear:

'Tis deeds must win the prize, and he of both
That can assure my daughter greatest dower
Shall have my Bianca's love.
(ACT 2, SCENE 1, LINES 342–44)

"She Is My Goods, My Chattels"

Sixteenth-century English society was patriarchal in nature: there was a dominant belief in benign government carried out by men as head of state, and head of household. Women had complementary roles, but were nevertheless seen as properly subordinate to their husbands. In the play, this attitude is stated most famously by Petruchio, who asserts that women are simply men's possessions: "I will be master of what is mine own. / She is my goods, my chattels" (Act 3, Scene 2, lines 229–30). A good marriage would be one in which the roles of men, women, and children were properly understood and adhered to. Katherina's answering back, physical aggression, and verbal dexterity run against the ideal imagined woman.

Yet herein also lie some of the contradictions of the period. In this story of a woman's "taming," Shakespeare's Katherina also suggests that sixteenth-century imaginations found the notion of an assertive woman both comic and appealing. Katherina's energy and her rejection of Bianca's deceitful and foppish suitors linger in the mind of the audience.

Battle of the Sexes

Energetic verbal exchanges between Katherina and Petruchio form the heart of *The Taming of the Shrew*, and provide the core of the play's interest for modern-day actors, directors, and audiences. The pair's speeches are studded with puns, double entendres, insults, and witty imagery, which while designed to bring Katherina to submission, nevertheless demonstrate that Petruchio has met his intellectual equal in her.

In line after line of dialogue, the two seek to contradict and outdo one another, turning figures of speech back against each other, and contradicting the other's statements. While all the world may speak of "Kate the curst," the image that Petruchio creates of

bonny Kate ...
the prettiest Kate in Christendom,
Kate of Kate-Hall, my super-dainty Kate,
For dainties are all Kates, and therefore,
Kate[.]
(ACT 2, SCENE 1, LINES 186–89)

produces a new possibility for Katherina herself, and a new way for Katherina to be. Here the play stages parallel shifts. While Katherina becomes an eloquent helpmate for her husband by play's end, Bianca, the sought-after younger sister, becomes the strong-willed disdainer of her husband's authority. Shakespeare uses imagery

Why does the world report that Kate doth limp?/O sland'rous world! Kate like the hazel-twig/Is straight and slender, and as brown in hue/As hazel-nuts, and sweeter than the kernels.

—*Petruchio* (ACT 2, SCENE 1, LINES 252–55)

BELOW: *Katharine Hepburn and Robert Helpmann stage a literal battle of the sexes to promote a 1955 production of the play in which they starred. As the photo implies, physical comedy featured prominently in their performances.*

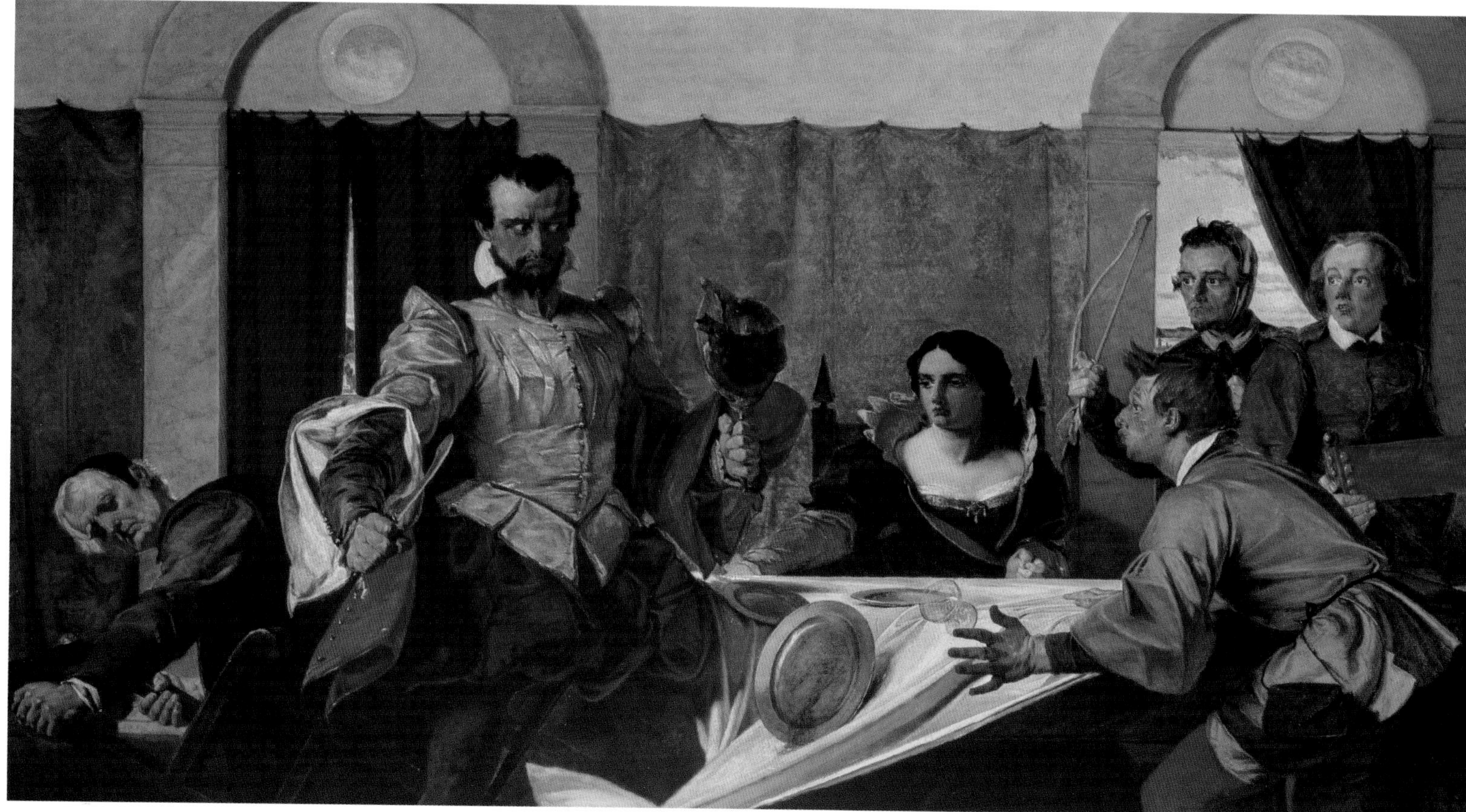

ABOVE: *Insisting the supper provided by his servants is unfit to eat, Petruchio sends the food flying in this 1860 painting by Augustus Egg of Act 4, Scene 1. This seemingly willful act is part of Petruchio's plan to keep his "falcon" hungry so as to curb her "mad and head-strong humor" (Act 4, Scene 1, line 209).*

drawn from the natural world, of order and disorder, to show how one sister reverts to a universal concord while the other sister ranges into destructive disorder.

Imagery of Battle

The play's imagery is full of contest and battle. The metaphor used by Petruchio concerning hawking, in Act 4, Scene 1, is a good case in point. Comparing Katherina to a falcon, he describes to the audience how he will train Katherina to be obedient by keeping her hungry and tired, and dependent on his will.

My falcon now is sharp and passing empty,
And till she stoop, she must not be full-gorg'd,
For then she never looks upon her lure.
(ACT 4, SCENE 1, LINES 190–92)

Elsewhere, Petruchio uses imagery of battles at sea, in which Katherina is a ship that he must "board" (Act 1, Scene 2, line 95)—the language suggests exerting control over her and sexual mastery of her. But throughout the play the imagery also highlights those things the two have in common. Says Petruchio:

I am as peremptory as she proud-minded;
And where two raging fires meet together,
They do consume the thing that feeds their fury.
(ACT 2, SCENE 1, LINES 131–33)

Rapid-fire Dialogue

One technique that gives *The Taming of the Shrew* its energy is Shakespeare's use of stichomythia. Short one-line exchanges between characters, rather than long one-sided monologues, create the sense that characters are actually engaging with one another in witty, verbal game-playing. In these rapid-fire exchanges, competition is also suggestive of intimacy.

Two strong people combine to overcome their weaknesses and the weaknesses of those around them, and the language and imagery are strongest and most memorable in the encounters and descriptions of the central couple.

Models of Womanhood

The play puts forward a number of different models of womanhood, both positive and negative. Early on, the audience hears of negative stereotypes of shrewish, nagging, and ugly women from medieval and Classical literature (Act 1, Scene 2, lines 68–70), as well as exemplars of female beauty such as Helen of Troy (Act 1, Scene 2, line 242). Elsewhere, there are emblems of patience such as Griselda, and emblems of chastity such as Lucrece (Act 2, Scene 1, lines 295–96). These contrasting images serve to emphasize the fact

ABOVE: *Richard Burton and Elizabeth Taylor brought Hollywood star power to the sumptuous and high-spirited 1967 film version of the play.*

Modern Shrews on Stage and Screen

Modern directors have dealt with the play's sexual politics in ways that reflect changing ideas about gender and romantic and sexual relationships. For example, in 1978 at Stratford, director Michael Bogdanov presented the play as a male wish-fulfillment fantasy, emphasizing Petruchio's abusive treatment of Katherina.

On the screen, the most famous Katherina and Petruchio were Elizabeth Taylor and Richard Burton in director Franco Zeffirelli's production, released in 1967. The play was also adapted as a musical, *Kiss Me, Kate* (1948, film 1953). More recently, in 1999 director Gil Junger transformed the play for a teen audience in *10 Things I Hate About You,* and the BBC produced a television version in 2005 with Katherina portrayed as a ruthless politician who ends up pregnant with triplets. The success of these very different versions might be linked to the original play's reliance on the use of dramatic stereotypes such as "the shrew" and the "tamer," taken from the Italian theatrical tradition of *commedia dell'arte,* in which easily recognizable types rather than complex characters are the focus of humor.

that ideas about femininity provide *The Taming of the Shrew* with some of its source material.

An interesting link here can be made between the role of the servants in the play and Katherina's change in behavior. When she sees just how badly Petruchio treats his men, which includes physical abuse, Katherina intercedes on their behalf, and begins to put herself in the position of those in need of consideration and compassion rather than merciless exploitation. She has been tyrannical in her treatment of others, but she begins to enact a more traditionally feminine gentleness when she sees the injustices meted out to others.

Taming and Reconciliation

Some of the sting of Katherina's taming is blunted because the audience knows that Petruchio is not being malicious in his treatment of Katherina, but strategic. "Say that she rail," he says, "why then I'll tell her plain / She sings as sweetly as a nightingale" (Act 2, Scene 1, lines 170–71). When Petruchio turns up at his and Katherina's wedding, "in a new hat and an old jerkin," as Biondello describes him in a long speech that vividly catalogs the eccentricity of Petruchio's outfit (Act 3, Scene 2, lines 43–63), we know that this is all part of his design. Petruchio performs the part of a demanding, inconsistent authoritarian to achieve the particular end of bringing Katherina into line. The fact that it is a performance, explained in private in the short soliloquies, gives the audience inside knowledge and empathy for Petruchio.

In a play where most characters are acting, pretending, or disguised, Petruchio's performance proves the most effective. It is studded with morals that would have sounded sensible to Elizabethan ears: "To me she's married, not unto my clothes" (Act 3, Scene 2, line 117).

While the relationship between the central protagonists is aggressive, it is nevertheless direct and open, contrasting strongly with the other relationships in the play. Lucentio, for example, swaps places with his servant Tranio, and then

> *A woman mov'd is like a fountain troubled,/Muddy, ill-seeming, thick, bereft of beauty,/And while it is so, none so dry or thirsty/Will deign to sip, or touch one drop of it.*
>
> 
>
> —*Katherina* (ACT 5, SCENE 2, LINES 142–45)

takes on a new identity of Cambio, tricking Gremio into thinking that he is working on Gremio's behalf to win Bianca when in fact he pursues his own ends.

At the end of the play, Petruchio rises to Baptista's accusation that he has married "the veriest shrew of all" (Act 5, Scene 2, line 64) by proposing a wager of one hundred crowns to see whose wife will come when her husband sends for her. Bianca refuses Lucentio, and the Widow refuses Hortensio, while Katherina comes when called, and then, at her husband's bidding, goes back to bring the other women with her, thus winning Petruchio's wager for him. The picture of Katherina's antagonism toward the world has been thoroughly rebutted, with husband and wife here projecting a united front in comparison with the play's other married couples.

Winners and Losers

Throughout *The Taming of the Shrew* money and marriage are inextricably linked, acknowledging the realities of sixteenth-century life for certain sections of the community. From Petruchio's frank statement that he has come to Padua to find a lucrative relationship, to Hortensio's declaration that should he find Bianca "ranging, / Hortensio will be quit with thee by changing" (Act 3, Scene 1, lines 91–92), it is very clear that love is not the only foundation for marriage. Hortensio's subsequent pursuit of the Widow indicates the pragmatism that governed many marriages.

While the Widow is a minor character in the play as a whole, she is important in that she represents the woman of experience, a woman who has been married before, and now has a combination of freedom and knowledge not known to the single or married woman. She puts that knowledge into practice in a second marriage, with the implication that she is able to outdo an unsuspecting husband. Hortensio soon finds himself bested by her, and it is significant that Katherina's long (44-line) final speech is specifically addressed to the Widow, at Petruchio's request. The best woman is the married compliant woman, as Katherina so succinctly puts it: "Such duty as the subject owes the prince, / Even such a woman oweth to her husband" (Act 5, Scene 2, lines 155–56).

And yet the play ends with a query rather than a firm statement, in spite of the declarations about right and wrong that have studded the story line. Hortensio declares that Petruchio has indeed tamed "a curst shrew," but Lucentio raises a doubt when he says: "'Tis a wonder, by your leave, she will be tam'd so" (Act 5, Scene 2, lines 188–89). The play ends, then, with doubts raised as to whether Katherina has been tamed at all, and with the suggestion that perhaps this married couple is performing yet again, this time in a partnership that has outwitted and out-thought the other married couples. The two have won not only the wager of one hundred crowns, but also Baptista's second dowry of twenty thousand crowns—a fine triumph over the forces of deception and disguise that have been the main focus of the play.

RIGHT: *An engraving shows US actor Edward H. Sothern as Petruchio in 1906. In a play full of pretence and disguise, Petruchio plays the role of tamer to the hilt, but soliloquies and asides let the audience know that he is not the domestic tyrant he seems.*

Love's Labor's Lost

WRITTEN
c. 1594–95

SETTING AND PERIOD
King of Navarre's grounds, *c.* sixteenth century

CHARACTERS 20

ACTS 5

SCENES 9

LINES 2,829

THE PLOT: *The play begins with an oath taken by Ferdinand, King of Navarre, and three of his lords to dedicate themselves to a period of three years' study, entailing their absence from high living, and in particular the company of women. Navarre, however, has forgotten that he is to receive a visit from the French king's daughter. When she arrives, accompanied by three of her ladies, the four men fall in love with them.*

Toward the end of the play, after scenes in which the men appear in disguise but are outwitted by the women, news arrives of the French king's death. The Princess now commits the men to 12 months' seclusion before they will be accepted by their ladies. The play ends with the men heading into an enforced retreat, and a song with contrasting verses on the merits of spring and winter.

Dramatis Personae

Ferdinand, *King of Navarre*
Berowne, Longaville, Dumaine, *lords attending on the King*
Boyet, Marcade, *lords attending on the Princess of France*
Don Adriano de Armado, *a fantastical Spaniard*
Sir Nathaniel, *a curate*
Holofernes, *a schoolmaster*
Dull, *a constable*
Costard, *a clown*
Moth, *page to Armado*
Forester
The Princess of France
Rosaline, Maria, Katherine, *ladies attending on the Princess*
Jaquenetta, *a country wench*
Lords, Attendants, etc.

RIGHT: *The irrepressible Berowne (David Tennant) displays his trademark verbal dexterity in the Royal Shakespeare Company production in 2008 at Stratford, while Dumaine (Sam Alexander) and Longaville (Tom Davey) lend an ear.*

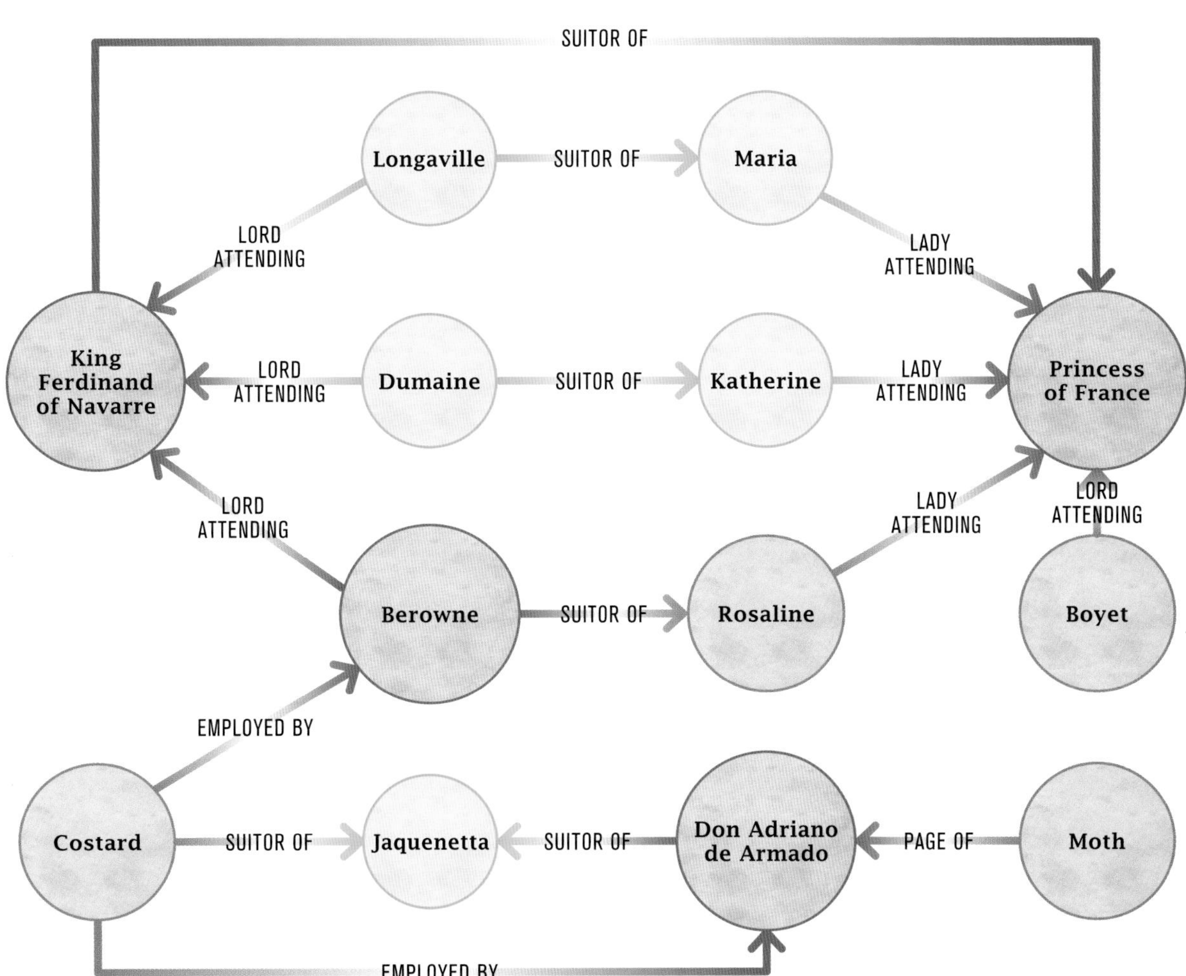

RELATIONSHIPS

The four female and four male aristocratic characters, led by the King of Navarre and the Princess of France, conveniently align themselves and fall in love; their amorous designs are parodied in Don Adriano's wooing of Jaquenetta, the "country wench."

While much of Shakespeare's reputation lies in his poetic use of language and verbal dexterity, no other play is quite as obsessed with language and its uses as *Love's Labor's Lost*. This focus made the play less popular with audiences than many other Shakespeare plays after the sixteenth century, as many of its jokes and puns were rendered obscure and difficult to follow. The absence of any real action in the play, and the very simple narrative, made it less attractive, and it has therefore been performed less often than many of the other comedies.

The play has a relatively simple structure, with only nine scenes. These scenes alternate between common and aristocratic characters, who all come together in the much longer final scene of more than 900 lines. In performance, the clustering of characters in the play can be brought out, with the four male and four female lovers; the groupings of additional characters such as Don Adriano de Armado, Holofernes, and Nathaniel; and the rustics Dull, Costard, and Jaquenetta. Moth the page, or clown, acts as a go-between and a link between the different groups.

Audience and Politics

We know that *Love's Labor's Lost* was performed at "Christmas time 1598," and the deliberately witty nature of the language may suggest that, unlike some of the other plays, its intended audience was a more educated one. In the play's concern with the making and breaking of oaths, critics have seen contemporary references to events in France under King Henry of Navarre, who gave up his Protestantism for Catholicism in 1593 to end the protracted religious wars. The sparring and cold intensity of the relations between Navarre and the French princess in the play are also thought to reflect in a lighthearted way on King Henry's relationship with his wife Marguerite de Valois, and their periods of separation and less-than-exemplary lifestyles. The gentle send-up of the regal and aristocratic Europeans is part of English comic traditions of the period, as is the depiction of the foppish, Spanish Don Adriano de Armado.

Language and Comedy

One of the central themes of the play concerns the disparity between fine words and less-than-fine deeds. The invitation to the audience to laugh at the pretentious and unrealistic King of Navarre is emphasized by Berowne's role in anticipating what will happen next. The first lines in the play, spoken by its highest ranking figure, sound well, and are concerned with life beyond death and reputation into eternity, a theme Shakespeare often explored:

But love, first learned in a lady's eyes,/ Lives not alone immured in the brain,/ But with the motion of all elements,/ Courses as swift as thought in every power,/ And gives to every power a double power,/ Above their functions and their offices.

—*Berowne* (ACT 4, SCENE 3, LINES 324–29)

Let fame, that all hunt after in their lives,
Live regist'red upon our brazen tombs,
And then grace us in the disgrace of death;
When spite of cormorant devouring Time,
Th' endeavor of this present breath may buy
That honor which shall bate his scythe's keen edge,
And make us heirs of all eternity.
(ACT 1, SCENE 1, LINES 1–7)

However, the King's high-minded plan to imitate a Classical "academe" is undercut immediately by Berowne's complaints that some of the rules are excessive, such as never seeing women, fasting one day a week, and only sleeping for three hours a night. Second, and more significant, as again Berowne points out, the visit of the French king's daughter will force the violation of the agreement. All of the grand and serious oaths are broken even before they have been properly made, and the end result and second conversion of the men to lovers undermines their short-lived dallying with eternity and scholarly reputations.

"The Mind Shall Banquet ..."

Another theme, which is related to the interest in the gap between words and deeds, is a concern about what knowledge is for, and how it should operate. In the first scene of the play, the debate between the four would-be scholars focuses on the purposes of the pursuit of knowledge, where the King advocates the pursuit of knowledge for its own sake—his "little academe" will be "Still and contemplative in living art" (Act 1, Scene 1, lines 13–14)—a position that did not sit easily with the idea that true virtue is demonstrated through actions. The complete reversal from the opening vows to abjure the company of women as obstacles to serious study is underlined later in Berowne's words; now, far from being the enemy of knowledge, women are in fact its source:

From women's eyes this doctrine I derive:
They sparkle still the right Promethean fire;
They are the books, the arts, the academes,
That show, contain, and nourish all the world,
Else none at all in aught proves excellent.
Then fools you were these women to forswear,
Or keeping what is sworn, you will prove fools.
(ACT 4, SCENE 3, LINES 347–53)

At a more directly comic level, characters such as Don Armado and Holofernes show that a little learning is a dangerous thing by their inappropriate use of language and ideas. In these examples there are circles or layers of knowledge, where one group of characters laughs at the ignorance of the others. Here knowledge is an indicator of social power and status. In attempting to ape their superiors, these comic figures clearly demonstrate that they might know the words, but they do not know how to apply them. By trying too hard to demonstrate their verbal sophistication, they demonstrate precisely the opposite, as we see in the following exchange:

ARMADO *Sir, it is the King's most sweet pleasure and affection to congratulate the Princess at her pavilion in the posteriors of this day, which the rude multitude call the afternoon.*
HOLOFERNES *The posterior of the day, most generous sir, is liable, congruent, and measurable for the afternoon. The word is well cull'd, chose, sweet, and apt, I do assure you, sir, I do assure.*
(ACT 5, SCENE 1, LINES 87–94)

The Ends of Knowledge

BEROWNE What is the end of study, let me know.
KING Why, that to know which else we should not know.
BEROWNE Things hid and barr'd (you mean) from common sense.
KING Ay, that is study's godlike recompense.
(ACT 1, SCENE 1, LINES 55–58)

Light, seeking light, doth light of light beguile[.]
—*Berowne* (ACT 1, SCENE 1, LINE 77)

Too much to know is to know nought but fame;
And every godfather can give a name.
—*Berowne* (ACT 1, SCENE 1, LINES 92–93)

The young Dumaine, a well-accomplish'd youth,
Of all that virtue love for virtue loved;
Most power to do most harm, least knowing ill;
For he hath wit to make an ill shape good,
And shape to win grace though he had no wit.
—*Katherine* (ACT 2, SCENE 1, LINES 56–60)

As Moth wittily observes, these characters "have been at a great feast of languages, and stol'n the scraps" (Act 5, Scene 1, lines 36–37).

Challenging Conventions

Consistent with the play's interest in language, how it is used, and by whom, much of the imagery in the play is concerned with turning expectations or conventions on their head. Berowne reverses the familiar patterns of female beauty and chastity in his description of Rosaline as "A whitely wanton with a velvet brow, / With two pitch-balls stuck in her face for eyes" (Act 3, Scene 1, lines 196–97). Part of this reversal involves imagery of darkness and blackness associated with Rosaline that challenges the conventions of female fairness but also casts questions on the wisdom of Berowne's choice, and the wisdom of love more generally.

In a similar challenge to convention, when faced with the prospect of hunting a deer—a pastime supposedly much enjoyed by royalty—the Princess asks of the forester, "Then, forester, my friend, where is the bush / That we must stand and play the murtherer in?" (Act 4, Scene 1, lines 7–8). In Act 5, Scene 2, the ladies swap the favors they have been given, so the men mistake their bearers and woo the wrong women, thus enacting another kind of pun on mistaking signs. What things mean is constantly the focus of attention in *Love's Labor's Lost*, with comic implications that nevertheless leave a sour taste. The play's ending enforces the retreat from society that the men promised at the beginning, with no tidy series of weddings to give romantic resolution.

Shakespeare's First Clowns

Shakespeare probably wrote the speeches of one character, Costard, specifically for a popular comic actor of the period, Will Kemp, who also performed the role of Bottom in *A Midsummer Night's Dream*. An appearance by Kemp, famous for his physical comedy, would no doubt have been an enticement for audiences to attend the play.

Afterlife

Love's Labor's Lost has traveled less successfully through time than many other Shakespeare plays. Comedy is more strongly based on its context than tragedy, and a comedy so reliant on language is particularly time-specific. However, its comic energy, particularly in relation to the undercutting of aristocratic pretensions, gives it a continuing relevance. The 2000 film version, directed by Kenneth Branagh, sought to play up the parodic elements; it was not a commercial success, unlike many other Shakespearean film adaptations, but its high-spirited musical focus brought the play to a new audience. In 2008, David Tennant gave an acclaimed performance as Berowne in a Royal Shakespeare Company production in Stratford, directed by Gregory Doran.

BELOW: *Taking its cue from musical comedies of the 1930s and 1940s, Kenneth Branagh's 2000 film adaptation features an all-singing, all-dancing cast, including Branagh as Berowne (second from right) and Natascha McElhone (right) as Rosaline.*

A Midsummer Night's Dream

THE PLOT: *The Athenian duke Theseus, anticipating his marriage to the conquered Amazonian queen Hippolyta, is confronted by Egeus, who is seeking support in his demand that his daughter Hermia marry Demetrius. But Hermia loves Lysander, and the couple decides to leave Athens. They tell their plan to Helena, who loves Demetrius, and she tells Demetrius of the plan.*

The four lovers enter the woods where fairy monarchs Oberon and Titania are quarreling. Oberon sends his henchman Puck for a floral love juice. Oberon anoints sleeping Titania and sends Puck to use the flower on Demetrius. Puck anoints Lysander by mistake, causing confusion among the lovers.

Puck finds Athenian artisans rehearsing a play and puts an ass's head on Bottom, the star performer. Titania awakens and falls in love with asinine Bottom. Oberon finally restores order and reconciles with Titania, the three human couples are married, and the six "mechanicals" perform their play for the entertainment of the newlyweds.

Dramatis Personae

Theseus, *Duke of Athens*
Egeus, *father to Hermia*
Lysander, Demetrius, *in love with Hermia*
Philostrate, *Master of the Revels to Theseus*
Quince, *a carpenter, presenting* **Prologue**
Bottom, *a weaver, presenting* **Pyramus**
Flute, *a bellows-mender, presenting* **Thisby**
Snout, *a tinker, presenting* **Wall**
Snug, *a joiner, presenting* **Lion**
Starveling, *a tailor, presenting* **Moonshine**
Hippolyta, *Queen of the Amazons, betrothed to Theseus*
Hermia, *daughter to Egeus, in love with Lysander*
Helena, *in love with Demetrius*
Oberon, *King of the Fairies*
Titania, *Queen of the Fairies*
Puck, *or* **Robin Goodfellow**
Peaseblossom, Cobweb, Moth, Mustardseed, *fairies*
Other Fairies attending their King and Queen; Attendants on Theseus and Hippolyta

RIGHT: The Marriage of Oberon and Titania by *John Anster Fitzgerald* (c. *1819–1906) depicts the kingdom of the fairies as a dreamlike yet faintly foreboding realm.*

WRITTEN
c. 1594–95

SETTING AND PERIOD
Athens and the surrounding woods; characters seem to be Shakespeare's English contemporaries

CHARACTERS 21

ACTS 5

SCENES 9

LINES 2,192

A *Midsummer Night's Dream* is a delightful early Shakespearean comedy filled with exquisitely lyrical verse, a diverse cast of characters, and fairy magic. Written and first performed around 1594–95, perhaps for a specific wedding (although there is no evidence connecting it to a particular event), the play demonstrates Shakespeare's skill in combining four groups of characters, suggested by different sources, in the elaborate plot. Unlike *King Lear*, in which the Duke of Gloucester's inability to recognize the goodness of one son and the evil of another parallels King Lear's blindness to the true nature of his daughters, in *A Midsummer Night's Dream* the plots are distinct though intertwined—and all of the plots are important.

Four Stories in One

In the Athenian court, Duke Theseus anxiously awaits his marriage to the Amazonian queen Hippolyta, whom he defeated in battle. Their wedding forms the foundation upon which the play is constructed.

The four young lovers—Hermia, Lysander, Helena, and Demetrius—form another focus. Hermia's father Egeus demands that she marry Demetrius (just as Capulet commands his daughter Juliet to marry Paris in *Romeo and Juliet,* a play written almost simultaneously with *Dream*). Demetrius had earlier courted Helena, who is desperately in love with him. Hermia, meanwhile, is in love with Lysander and he with her. This choice between two lovers is a frequent motif in comedy—although in this play Hermia is not forced to choose between her love and an older, wealthier man. Indeed, Lysander and Demetrius are virtually identical in every way.

While we have difficulty telling the two men apart, Hermia and Helena find special qualities in their loves that make them unique. Physically, Hermia and Helena are distinct: Hermia is short, with dark hair and features, while Helena is tall, with blonde hair and fair features. The contrasting ways they behave in the play, however, appear to be caused by the situations in which they find themselves, rather than by any great differences in their characters. Although Helena tells us, "Through Athens I am thought as fair as she [Hermia]" (Act 1, Scene 1, line 227), she later calls herself "as ugly as a bear" (Act 2, Scene 2, line 94) when rejected by Demetrius. The lovers will go through a variety of permutations before they are properly paired.

The third group of characters is made up of the "rude mechanicals," local artisans who seek their "15 minutes of fame" by performing a play as part of the Duke's nuptial celebrations. Shakespeare neatly delineates the amateur actors. Quince,

Bottom, Flute, Snout, Snug, and Starveling are "Hard-handed men" who "never labor'd in their minds till now" (Act 5, Scene 1, lines 72–73). Through them, Shakespeare is able to satirize theatrical activities while reminding audiences of their responsibility in observing a performance. The play they perform is unforgettable.

Finally, in the woods outside Athens, the play's fairies reside, led by their king and queen Oberon and Titania, and energized by Oberon's offsider Puck, also known as Robin Goodfellow. While to Shakespeare's contemporaries fairies were in some cases connected with evils, these fairies are, at worst, simply mischievous.

Shakespeare uses distinctive speech patterns and meters for the various groups. The Athenian court speaks in blank verse (unrhymed iambic pentameter), the lovers in rhymed couplets, the mechanicals in prose, and the fairies often in the incantational trochaic tetrameter style.

Love's Tribulations

A Midsummer Night's Dream makes many references to the tribulations of love as personified by Cupid. In one instance, Hermia swears to Lysander "by Cupid's strongest bow, / By his best arrow with the golden head" (Act 1, Scene 1, lines 169–70): Cupid's dull, lead arrows produce dislike. Helena provides another example:

Things base and vile, holding no quantity,
Love can transpose to form and dignity.
Love looks not with the eyes but with the mind;
And therefore is wing'd Cupid painted blind.
(ACT 1, SCENE 1, LINES 232–35)

The comical image of a blindfolded cherub flying around, wildly shooting arrows that make people fall in and out of love, does not, however, diminish the intensity of emotion that love produces. Shakespeare uses the love potion, the juice of the pansy (also called "love-in-idleness"), and its antidote to represent the vagaries of love. No one is immune from its effects, even the gods. The absurdity of love is most powerfully illustrated by the infatuation the enchanted queen Titania feels upon first seeing Bottom, complete with ass's head. Awakened by Bottom's singing, transformed now into a donkey's bray, Titania exclaims:

I pray thee, gentle mortal, sing again.
Mine ear is much enamored of thy note;
So is mine eye enthralled to thy shape;
And thy fair virtue's force (perforce) doth move me
On the first view to say, to swear, I love thee.
(ACT 3, SCENE 1, LINES 137–41)

Bottom, benighted in his ignorance, is able to see the absurdity of this declaration:

Methinks, mistress, you should have little reason for that. And yet, to say the truth, reason and love keep little company together now-a-days.

RELATIONSHIPS
Much of the play's action is a result of the comic collision between the worlds of the mortals and of the fairies, engineered by Oberon and dispensed, via love potion, by Puck. When the two worlds are contained again, the quarrels are resolved.

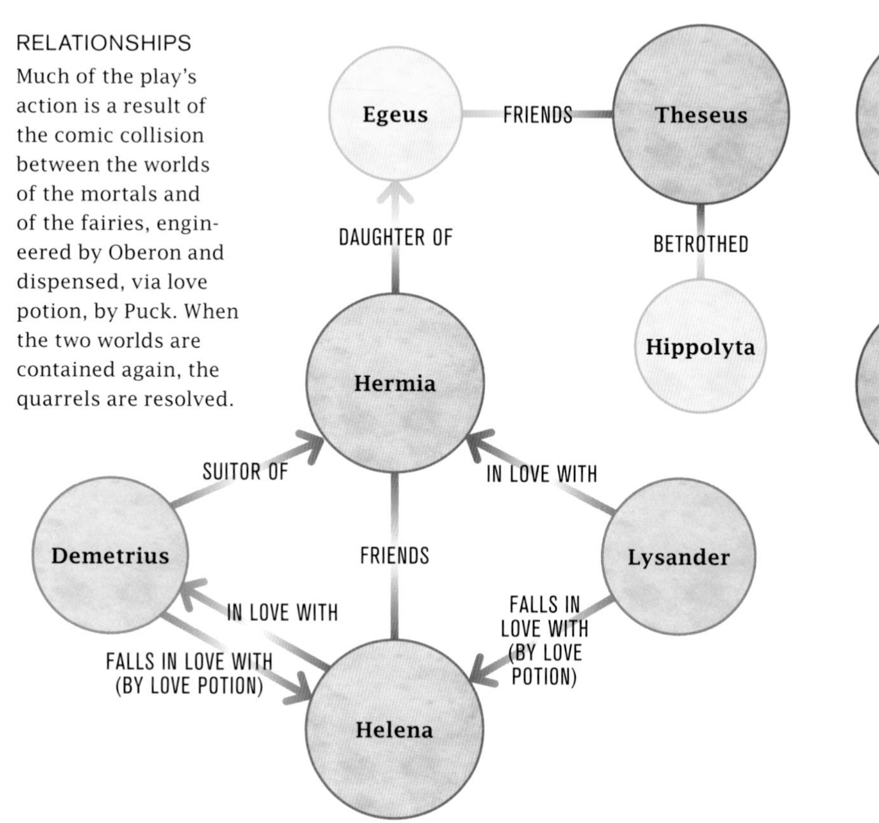

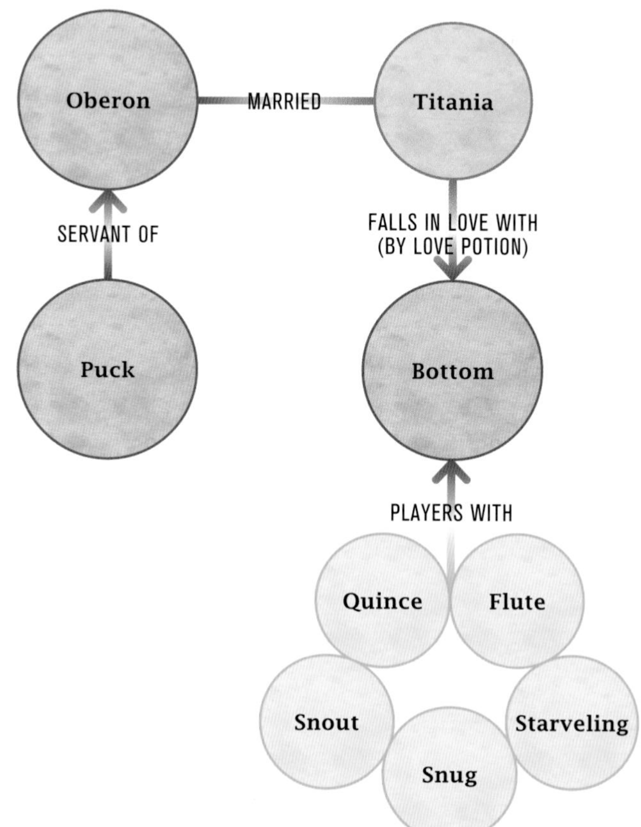

LEFT: *"Thou art as wise as thou art beautiful" (Act 3, Scene 1, line 148): Titania (Michelle Pfeiffer) is enchanted by Bottom (Kevin Kline) in Michael Hoffman's 1999 film. Other actors who have brought Bottom to life include James Cagney, Pete Postlethwaite, and Richard Griffiths.*

The more the pity that some honest neighbors will not make them friends.
(ACT 3, SCENE 1, LINES 142–46)

Yet Bottom accepts the offered love and follows Titania to her bower.

As is usual in his plays, in *A Midsummer Night's Dream* Shakespeare is an advocate for marriage. No matter how convoluted the path the lovers take, it eventually leads down the aisle. Once Oberon has correctly paired the four lovers, they join with Theseus and Hippolyta for a triple wedding. Oberon and Titania also resolve their differences, and together bless the marriage beds at play's end.

> *Ay me! for aught that I could ever read,/Could ever hear by tale or history,/The course of true love never did run smooth.*
>
> 
>
> —*Lysander* (ACT 1, SCENE 1, LINES 132–34)

Plays, Audiences, and Artifice

The play-within-the-play that is so memorably performed by the Athenian artisans, *The Most Lamentable Comedy and Most Cruel Death of Pyramus and Thisby,* is yet another story of thwarted love. Two lovers are separated by a wall that their fathers have constructed to keep them apart. They speak to one another through a chink in the wall and vow to meet each other. Through a fateful misunderstanding, the man believes his love is dead and takes his own life. The woman finds him dead and ends her own life. Resemblances to *Romeo and Juliet,* written around the same time, are anything but accidental.

The device of the play-within-the-play, used effectively in *Hamlet,* brings an audience composed of other characters onto the stage, so the larger audience in the theater watching Shakespeare's play can compare their responses to those of the onstage audience. Like unruly patrons of a local cineplex, Demetrius, Lysander, Theseus, and Hippolyta make quasi-clever comments about the performances, and take delight in pointing out the incompetence of the actors and the script. When Snout introduces himself as Wall, Theseus wisecracks, "Would you desire lime and hair to speak better?" (Act 5, Scene 1, line 165). When Pyramus and Thisby make their tryst through the wall, Hippolyta complains, "This is the silliest stuff that ever I heard" (Act 5, Scene 1, line 210). But Theseus responds, "If we imagine no worse of them than

A Contemporary Source

Although there is no clear source for this play, Shakespeare may refer to the elaborate entertainment that Robert Dudley, Earl of Leicester, prepared for Queen Elizabeth in 1575. Robert Langham, a minor official at the time, described a water show with "Triton on his mermaid skimming by" and Arion "riding aloft on his old friend the dolphin (that from head to tail was twenty-four foot long) ... began a delectable ditty ... resounding from the waters where [the] presence of her Majesty ... utterly damped all noise and din."

In *Twelfth Night* Shakespeare wrote of "[Arion] on the dolphin's back" (*Twelfth Night,* Act 1, Scene 2, line 15), and composed these lines in *Dream:*

Since once I sat upon a promontory,
And heard a mermaid on a dolphin's back
Uttering such dulcet and harmonious breath
That the rude sea grew civil at her song,
And certain stars shot madly from their spheres,
To hear the sea-maid's music[.]
—*Oberon* (ACT 2, SCENE 1, LINES 149–54)

they of themselves, they may pass for excellent men" (Act 5, Scene 1, lines 215–16). *A Midsummer Night's Dream* provides insight into what is expected from an audience and its imagination.

The mechanicals believe that the audience members at a theatrical performance take what they see as literally true. Bottom warns his fellow players, "Masters, you ought to consider with your[selves], to bring in (God shield us!) a lion among ladies, is a most dreadful thing" (Act 3, Scene 1, lines 29–31). To protect the audience from hysterical fear, Bottom suggests that Snug "must name his name, and half his face must be seen through the lion's neck, and he himself must speak" a speech of explanation (Act 3, Scene 1, lines 36–38). Audiences know, however, that players on the stage are not really the characters they portray. As Hamlet makes clear, "the purpose of playing" is "to hold as 'twere the mirror up to nature" (*Hamlet,* Act 3, Scene 2, lines 20–22). In the Prologue of *Henry V,* the Chorus urges the audience to let the players operate "On your imaginary forces"—the power of imagination—and to "Piece out our imperfections with your thoughts" (*Henry V,* Act 1, Prologue, lines 18, 23).

Imagination and Art

It is not surprising, then, that *A Midsummer Night's Dream* also explores the uses of the imagination. Theseus, for example, prides himself on being a rationalist and does not trust the powers of the imagination. He declares, "The lunatic, the lover, and the poet / Are of imagination all compact" (Act 5, Scene 1, lines 7–8), and he gives examples of the overexuberant misuse of fantasy. Hippolyta, however, notes that the four lovers tell the *same* imaginative tale of their night in the forest:

But all the story of the night told over,
And all their minds transfigur'd so together,
More witnesseth than fancy's images,
And grows to something of great constancy;
But howsoever, strange and admirable.
(ACT 5, SCENE 1, LINES 23–27)

If one person has a dream, that is an individual imaginative experience. If, however, the four lovers have the same dream, no matter how magical and unreal, then the experience is no longer merely a dream: it is art, namely *A Midsummer Night's Dream* by William Shakespeare. Art can give coherence and consistency to the imagination that distinguishes it from the imaginings of the lunatic and

RIGHT: *Oberon (Patrick de Jersey) invokes magic and mayhem in a Royal Shakespeare Company production in 2008, at Stratford. The King of the Fairies reflects Shakespeare's theme of transformation, as he wreaks havoc in the mortal and the fairy worlds alike.*

The poet's eye, in a fine frenzy rolling,/Doth glance from heaven to earth, from earth to heaven;/And as imagination bodies forth/The forms of things unknown, the poet's pen/Turns them to shapes, and gives to aery nothing/A local habitation and a name.

—*Theseus* (ACT 5, SCENE 1, LINES 12–17)

the romantic excesses of the lover. Art may capture and preserve the imagination, an idea that Theseus does not consider.

Ironically, we must turn to Nick Bottom for confirmation of this theory. Bottom's experiences during the night are extraordinary. When he wakes, he contemplates his encounters—"I have had a most rare vision. I have had a dream, past the wit of man to say what dream it was"—and decides to "get Peter Quince to write a ballet of this dream. It shall be call'd 'Bottom's Dream,' because it hath no bottom" (Act 4, Scene 1, lines 205–6, 214–16). To retain and reproduce an imaginative experience, one turns it into art.

Shadows

Shakespeare uses the word "shadow" in several interesting ways. He uses it in the conventional sense as the *umbra*—the area of darkness that occurs when an opaque object blocks the sun's rays. But he also applies the term "shadow" to any representation of an object that is not the object itself. The image in a mirror, for example, is referred to as a "shadow." Of more interest to *A Midsummer Night's Dream,* however, is when the word is also used for dreams, which can appear so real but are not. Finally, and most importantly, stage players are called "shadows" since they, too, often convincingly portray reality.

With this in mind, look at these lines spoken by Puck at the end of the play:

If we shadows have offended,
Think but this, and all is mended,
That you have but slumb'red here
While these visions did appear.
And this weak and idle theme,
No more yielding but a dream[.]
(ACT 5, SCENE 1, LINES 423–28)

ABOVE: *Since Peter Brook's seminal 1970 version, many productions of the play have employed spectacular staging. In this 2007 multilingual version at the Roundhouse in London, Archana Ramaswamy, as Titania, swings on red silk drapes. Colorful fight scenes and acrobatics also featured.*

Puck is speaking both as a character and as an actor. The "shadows" of line 1 refer to himself and his fellow players. Puck is saying that if one does not like the play, one can simply dismiss it as just a dream. But earlier, Shakespeare draws a distinction between dreams and art—the dream is the fleeting individual act of imagination while art is the enduring treatment of the imagination that can (and is) repeated over space and time. To have "slumb'red"

Shakespeare's Stagecraft

In Shakespeare's theater, all female roles were played by boys. Shakespeare's company clearly included both a tall and a short boy actor, since Helena is described as tall ("a painted maypole") and Hermia as short ("puppet"). The same is true in *As You Like It,* where Rosalind is tall and Celia short.

through *A Midsummer Night's Dream* is to have missed the play's power and magic. From those who have not slumbered, Puck asks for applause:

> *So, good night unto you all.*
> *Give me your hands, if we be friends,*
> *And Robin shall restore amends.*
> (ACT 5, SCENE 1, LINES 436–38)

On Stage: Pre-twentieth Century Productions

A Midsummer Night's Dream is today probably the most often performed of Shakespeare's plays, for it has long been a perennial favorite among performers and audiences around the world. The *Internet Shakespeare Editions* website lists 52 productions between 2000 and 2008.

Queen Elizabeth I may well have attended the first performance of *Dream,* and the play was periodically performed until the Puritans closed the theaters in 1642. Even during the interregnum, when public theater was banned, the play-within-the-play was presented as a "droll" or comic playlet called *Bottom the Weaver.*

After the Restoration, the play was adapted for "refined" theatrical sentiments. Much of the plot was removed in favor of dance and spectacle. Diarist Samuel Pepys saw this version and called it "the most insipid, ridiculous play that I ever saw." Pepys adds, however, "I saw, I confess, some good dancing and some handsome women, which was all my pleasure." Dancing and women on the stage—*A Midsummer Night's Dream* had, indeed, been truly transformed. *Dream* was also transmogrified into an opera entitled *The Fairy Queen* with music by the composer Henry Purcell. Among the added characters are Night, Mystery, Secrecy, Sleep, the four seasons, Juno, "a Grand dance of 24 *Chineses,*" and a dance of six monkeys—an operatic experience with something for everyone.

Throughout the nineteenth century, the play was presented with more and more scenic display and spectacle. Felix Mendelssohn's music for the play, first the Overture and then the complete incidental music, became de rigueur in the theater. Director Charles Kean's 1856 production ran for 150 performances, with 800 of Shakespeare's lines removed to make room for song, ballet, and splendor. About 220,000 people attended the elaborate 1900 production of *Dream,* directed by Herbert Beerbohm Tree, that included real rabbits.

Modern Stage Productions

In the twentieth century, director Harley Granville Barker attempted to return to the simplicity and intimacy of Shakespeare's original theater, using a nearly complete text of *Dream* when he staged it in 1914. Barker required clear and rapid presentation of lines from his actors, and employed only two sets: Oberon's palace, and the forest. Although his approach to *Dream* received mixed responses from audiences and critics at the time, Barker pointed the way toward the play's treatment on the stage into the twenty-first century.

Perhaps the most important production of *A Midsummer Night's Dream* in modern times took place in 1970, directed by Peter Brook for the Royal Shakespeare Company at Stratford. Brook rejected everything traditional about the staging of the play; instead, he had his cast and designers totally rethink the play in terms of a magical celebration of the theatrical experience. Sally Jacobs designed a stark white box with a hammock made of scarlet ostrich feathers and trapezes for the set. Richard Peaslee prepared a score of "organized noise" with unusual instruments and sounds. Actors juggled and flew in on swings; those not on "stage" watched the proceedings from above. During extensive rehearsals, Brook required the cast members to find their own truth for their

Midsummer Music

In 1826 in Germany, after reading *A Midsummer Night's Dream,* the 17-year-old Felix Mendelssohn was inspired to compose music based on what he had read. Sixteen years later, he wrote incidental music for the play, and used his early composition as the Overture. His music for Shakespeare's play also included the famous "Wedding March."

BELOW: *This German production in 2007, in Salzburg, featured British-style school uniforms as costumes for the two pairs of young lovers. Here Demetrius (Patrick Gueldenberg) and a miserable Hermia (Mavie Hoerbiger) are urged to marry.*

RIGHT: *Fourteen-year-old Mickey Rooney bounded on screen as a young, impish Puck in Max Reinhardt and William Dieterle's 1935 film version of* A Midsummer Night's Dream. *The* New York Times *called Rooney's performance "one of the most memorable juvenile performances in film history."*

lines. For those who experienced it, Brook's *Dream* was a revolutionary approach to a familiar play. As critic Clive Barnes predicted in his review in the *New York Times,* the production was "going to exert a major influence on the contemporary stage."

A Dream on Screen

The magic of *A Midsummer Night's Dream* makes it a natural for a range of cinematic treatments. As early as 1909, Vitagraph filmed a single-reel, silent version of *Dream*—with forest scenes filmed in Brooklyn, New York. Two decades later, in 1935, Warner Brothers produced an opulent black-and-white film version of *Dream.* Directing were Max Reinhardt and William Dieterle. Reinhardt had left Germany when Hitler came to power. He directed *Dream* in Oxford and then brought his outdoor production to the Hollywood Bowl with popular success. But Reinhardt had no movie experience; however, Dieterle had worked with Reinhardt in Berlin, and provided the directorial know-how.

Hoping to appeal to a mass audience seeking escape during the Depression, they cast popular personalities such as Olivia de Havilland and a young Mickey Rooney, who had performed the role of Puck in the stage version; crooner Dick Powell, beautiful Anita Louise, tough James Cagney, comic Joe E. Brown, and virile Victor Jory were all acting in their first (and last) Shakespeare play. Sets and costumes were rich, but roughly half of Shakespeare's original text was abandoned. The results are at times very charming, and at other times simply annoying.

A Midsummer Night's Dream inspired Swedish director Ingmar Bergman's *Sommarnattens Leende (Smiles of a Summer Night)* in 1955. In the United States, Bergman's film then inspired Stephen Sondheim's musical *A Little Night Music* (1973), and the film *A Midsummer Night's Sex Comedy* (1982) directed by Woody Allen. New York City Ballet's George Balanchine even produced a wordless dance adaptation of *Dream* in 1962, with a score using Felix Mendelssohn's original music for the play and other selected works by the composer.

No matter how we encounter the spectacle of *A Midsummer Night's Dream,* we watch the confusion of the lovers and the theatrical attempts of Bottom and the amateur thespians, and exclaim with Puck, "Shall we their fond pageant see? / Lord, what fools these mortals be!" (Act 3, Scene 2, lines 114–15).

Sensual Descriptions

I know a bank where the wild thyme blows,
Where oxlips and the nodding violet grows,
Quite over-canopied with luscious woodbine,
With sweet musk-roses and with eglantine;
There sleeps Titania sometime of the night,
Lull'd in these flowers with dances and delight[.]
—*Oberon* (ACT 2, SCENE 1, LINES 249–54)

Be kind and courteous to this gentleman,
Hop in his walks and gambol in his eyes;
Feed him with apricocks and dewberries,
With purple grapes, green figs, and mulberries;
The honey-bags steal from the humble-bees,
And for night-tapers crop their waxen thighs,
And light them at the fiery glow-worm's eyes,
To have my love to bed and to arise;
And pluck the wings from painted butterflies,
To fan the moonbeams from his sleeping eyes.
—*Titania* (ACT 3, SCENE 1, LINES 164–73)

The Merchant of Venice

Dramatis Personae

The Duke of Venice
The Prince of Morocco, the Prince of Arragon, *suitors to Portia*
Antonio, *a merchant of Venice*
Bassanio, *his friend, suitor to Portia*
Solanio, Gratiano, Salerio, *friends to Antonio and Bassanio*
Lorenzo, *in love with Jessica*
Shylock, *a rich Jew*
Tubal, *a Jew, his friend*
Launcelot Gobbo, *a clown, servant to Shylock*
Old Gobbo, *father to Launcelot*
Leonardo, *servant to Bassanio*
Balthazar, Stephano, *servants to Portia*
Portia, *a rich heiress, of Belmont*
Nerissa, *her waiting-gentlewoman*
Jessica, *daughter to Shylock*
Magnificoes of Venice, Officers of the Court of Justice, Jailer, Servants to Portia, and other Attendants

WRITTEN
c. 1596–97
SETTING AND PERIOD
Venice and Belmont, sixteenth century
CHARACTERS 24
ACTS 5
SCENES 20
LINES 2,701

THE PLOT: *Bassanio, needing money to woo Portia, entreats his friend Antonio for a loan. His wealth invested in ships, Antonio borrows from Shylock, a Jewish moneylender who hates him. Shylock proposes that, if the loan is unpaid in three months, he can exact a pound of Antonio's flesh. Antonio agrees. Suitors beset Portia in Belmont. Her father's will requires them to choose from among three caskets, one of which contains her portrait. Several princes fail and depart. Choosing correctly, Bassanio marries Portia. Lorenzo elopes with Jessica, the daughter of Shylock. Antonio's ships are reported to have foundered and Shylock claims the forfeiture of his bond. Learning of Antonio's predicament, Bassanio returns to Venice. Portia, disguised as Balthazar, a lawyer, follows with her maid Nerissa as clerk. Bassanio offers many times the loan amount to Shylock, who demands revenge. Portia awards Shylock Antonio's flesh, but no blood. And, since taking his flesh would kill Antonio, Shylock forfeits his wealth (and his loan): half to Venice, half to Antonio. Antonio foregoes his half if Shylock bequeaths it to Jessica and converts to Christianity. Portia tests her new husband's devotion by requesting Bassanio's wedding ring as payment; he yields it at Antonio's behest. Portia charges Bassanio with unfaithfulness; he renews his wedding vows and is accepted back. Antonio hears his ships are safe.*

BELOW: *Venice in the sixteenth century was one of Europe's great mercantile centers. The painter Vittore Carpaccio depicts the city's busy waterways in his work,* Healing of the Madman *(c. 1496).*

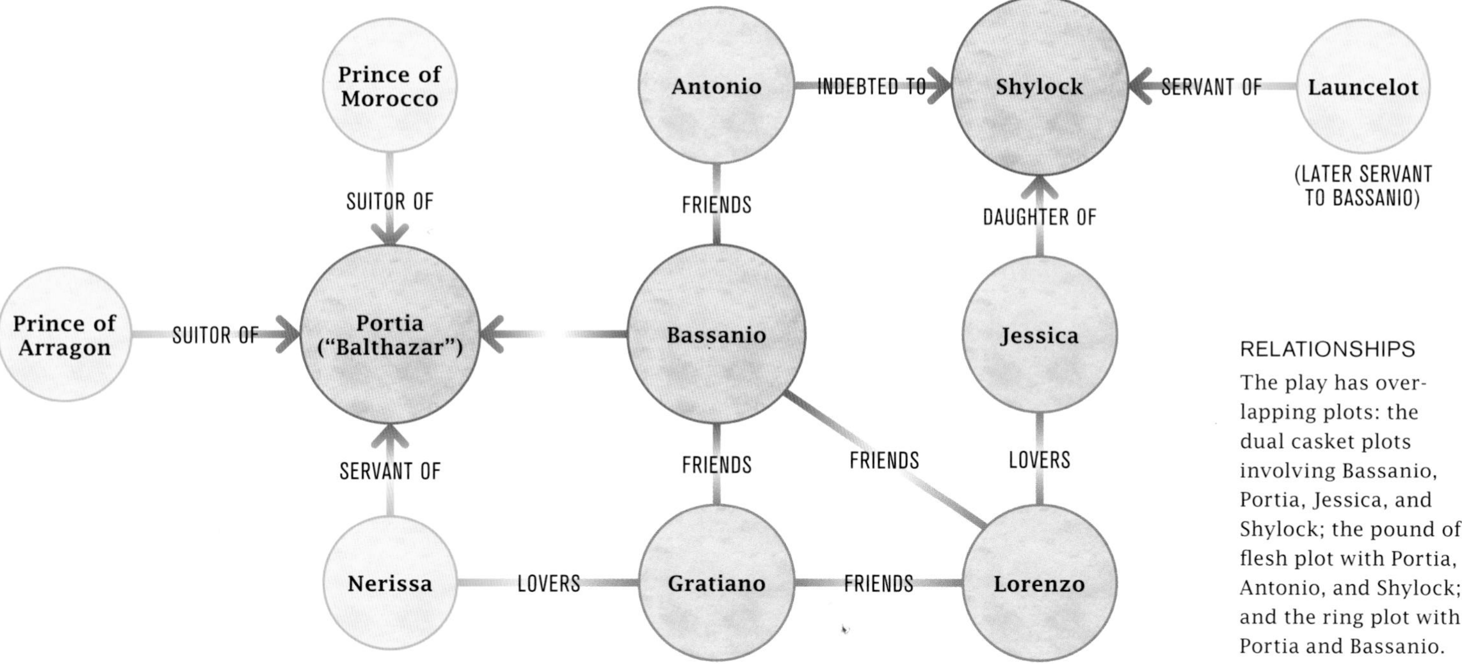

RELATIONSHIPS
The play has overlapping plots: the dual casket plots involving Bassanio, Portia, Jessica, and Shylock; the pound of flesh plot with Portia, Antonio, and Shylock; and the ring plot with Portia and Bassanio.

The Merchant of Venice is one of Shakespeare's most problematic plays. First, its genre is dubious: it was originally called *The Most Excellent Historie of the Merchant of Venice*. Classified as a comedy in the First Folio, it was viewed as a tragedy in the nineteenth century, and now it is usually deemed a tragicomedy or problem play. As with *Othello* (racism) and *The Taming of the Shrew* (misogyny), a highly charged cultural issue (in this instance, anti-Semitism) dominates the play's discussion and analysis, even though Shylock, the Jewish moneylender and the play's most famous character, appears in just five of the 20 scenes and speaks only 14 percent of its words.

Merchant is also a problematic play because of its unique structure: it has a dual setting (like *A Midsummer Night's Dream, As You Like It,* and *Antony and Cleopatra*), but it is the only play by Shakespeare with three sequential, if overlapping, plots: the romantic love plot (Act 1, Scene 1 to Act 3, Scene 2); the pound of flesh plot (Act 1, Scene 3 to Act 4, Scene 1); and, finally, the ring plot (Act 4, Scene 1 to Act 5, Scene 1). What links them is Antonio, the merchant of the title, who has increasingly been seen as a major character, perhaps even the protagonist, in recent decades.

Shakespeare's Sources

Shakespeare's likely sources include a collection of tales—*Il Pecorone* (*The Simpleton, c.* 1378), by Italian writer Ser Giovanni Fiorentino—one of which contains the bond story, the heroine who is disguised as a lawyer, and the ring plot. The casket story came from the *Gesta Romanorum,* a collection of tales that appeared in English in 1577.

Other possible sources are *The Jew* (1579), an anonymous, lost play about a greedy usurer that included both the bond and the casket stories, and Christopher Marlowe's *The Jew of Malta* (1590), though the latter play, which depicts a Jew named Barabas as a savage murderer, differs greatly in plot and characterization. Shylock also emerged from the Vice character in morality plays and the stereotypical representations of Jews with a hooked nose and wielding a knife, a figure susceptible to treatment as comic and villainous.

World Weariness

In sooth, I know not why I am so sad[.]
—*Antonio* (ACT 1, SCENE 1, LINE 1)

By my troth, Nerissa, my little body is a-weary
of this great world.
—*Portia* (ACT 1, SCENE 2, LINES 1–2)

The curse never fell upon our nation till now,
I never felt it till now.
—*Shylock* (ACT 3, SCENE 1, LINES 85–86)

I am a tainted wether of the flock,
Meetest for death; the weakest kind of fruit
Drops earliest to the ground, and so let me.
—*Antonio* (ACT 4, SCENE 1, LINES 114–16)

I pray you give me leave to go from hence,
I am not well ...
—*Shylock* (ACT 4, SCENE 1, LINES 395–96)

The Business of Venice

Imagery of Venice's greatness as a trading state occurs throughout the play. Trying to explain Antonio's melancholy, Salerio says that "Your mind is tossing on the ocean" (Act 1, Scene 1, line 8). Antonio replies that he has risked only some of his estate and that his fortune is safe. Bassanio outfits a ship to carry him over the sea that connects and separates Venice and Belmont, to Portia, a romantic figure to whom "the four winds blow in from every coast/ Renowned suitors ... many Jasons" (Act 1, Scene 1, lines 168–72). For Shylock, the sea represents danger: "ships are but boards, sailors but men; there be land-rats and water-rats, water-thieves and land-thieves, I mean pirates, and then there is the peril of waters, winds, and rocks" (Act 1, Scene 3, lines 22–25). Gratiano announces Bassanio's and his successful romantic quest with: "We are the Jasons, we have won the fleece" (Act 3, Scene 2, line 241). And at the play's end Antonio is restored to "life and living" by the news his ships have returned safely.

Two Worlds

Merchant is set in sixteenth-century Venice, which at that time was a rich commercial and banking center that financed many of Europe's ventures and was its main port of trade with Asia. It is also set in Belmont, a wealthy fictional kingdom presumably sited on Italy's mainland. In addition to commerce, Venice was a place of great scientific and technical innovation, learning, printing, artistic patronage, and manufacturing. The city welcomed foreigners, although they could live in designated locations only. Jews, who were proscribed and persecuted elsewhere in Europe, had their place in the city (the first "ghetto"), which became a center of commerce and learning.

The play takes place in ostensibly contrasting worlds: commercial, contractual Venice and the romantic, fairy-tale Belmont. The water between them connects as well as divides them, and shared themes and imagery of love, wealth, law and legal documents, music, and food subverts their opposition and renders their boundaries fluid.

"If You Do Love Me"

Love is represented variously throughout the play: as wealth, a quest object, what one confesses to under torture, a bond, a marriage ring. Upon first appearing, for all their wealth and privilege, both Antonio—"In sooth, I know not why I am so sad" (Act 1, Scene 1, line 1)—and Portia—"By my troth, Nerissa, my little body is a-weary of this great world" (Act 1, Scene 2, lines 1–2)—sound the same melancholy note, then happily consider Bassanio, for whose love they seem to be in sad competition. Solanio says of Antonio: "I think he only loves the world for him" (Act 2, Scene 8, line 50), and Antonio, en route to jail, says "Pray God Bassanio come / To see me pay his debt; and then I care not!" (Act 3, Scene 3, lines 35–36). In the casket scene, Portio tells Bassanio that "I could teach you / How to choose right, but then I am forsworn"; she contemplates revealing the truth anyway, but then says "If you do love me, you will find me out" (Act 3, Scene 2, lines 10–11, 41). Yet Bassanio, having journeyed from Antonio to Portia and wisely, and advisedly, chosen the lead casket, betrays that choice by opting for Antonio over Portia in the courtroom scene:

> *I am married to a wife*
> *Which is as dear to me as life itself,*
> *But life itself, my wife, and all the world,*
> *Are not with me esteem'd above thy life.*
> *I would lose all, ay, sacrifice them all*
> *Here to this devil, to deliver you.*
> (ACT 4, SCENE 1, LINES 282–87)

Noting Bassanio's implicit betrayal—"Your wife would give you little thanks for that / If she were by to hear you make the offer" (Act 4, Scene 1, lines 288–89)—the disguised Portia initiates the ring plot that ultimately reaffirms their marriage. The bawdy Gratiano, who tries to dismiss the marriage jewel as "a hoop of gold, a paltry ring" (Act 5, Scene 1, line 147) gets the play's last word, punningly equating wealth with both marriage and his new wife's genitals: "while I live I'll fear no other thing / So sore, as keeping safe Nerissa's ring" (lines 306–7).

"All that Glisters"

Venice, a place with few natural resources, was nonetheless the richest city in Renaissance Europe. It is unsurprising that Bassanio, initiating his love quest, seems to be little more than a fortune-hunter who embodies the sumptuousness of both Venice and Belmont, valuing Portia for her wealth ("a lady richly left"), her beauty ("she is fair"), and her virtue ("Of wondrous virtues"), in that order (Act 1, Scene 1, lines 161–63).

Yet, if he is to prove worthy of Portia, Bassanio must learn the lesson of the golden casket—"All that glisters is not gold" (Act 2, Scene 7, line 65): appearances are not to be trusted. Paradoxically, in choosing the lead casket that contains "Fair Portia's counterfeit" (Act 3, Scene 2, line 115), Bassanio wins his love and reprises Jessica's theft of Shylock's casket, which is full of material wealth. But in yielding his wedding ring at the end of the courtroom scene, Bassanio debases the commitment and virtue it represents. So Antonio, who "once did lend my body for his wealth," must again "be his surety," for higher stakes: "My soul upon the forfeit" (Act 5, Scene 1, lines 249, 254, and 252).

Wealth also largely defines Shylock. He repeats his first words, "Three thousand ducats," five times in his first scene (Act 1, Scene 3, lines 1, 9, 56, 65, 103, and 122). After Jessica's elopement, he seems less concerned with her loss than with that of his ducats and "precious jewels." After failing to gain revenge against Antonio or repayment of his debt, he is desperate to retain as much wealth as possible. His despairing plea enables him to do so:

You take my house when you do take the prop
That doth sustain my house; you take my life
When you do take the means whereby I live.
(ACT 4, SCENE 1, LINES 375–77)

Antonio makes a similar equation at the end of the play when he tells Portia:

you have given me life and living,
For here I read for certain that my ships
Are safely come to road.
(ACT 5, SCENE 1, LINES 286–88)

The quality of mercy is not strain'd,/It droppeth as the gentle rain from heaven/Upon the place beneath .../It is enthroned in the hearts of kings,/It is an attribute to God himself;/And earthly power doth then show likest God's/When mercy seasons justice ...

—*Portia* (ACT 4, SCENE 1, LINES 184–86, 194–97)

Having initially embodied riches, Portia restores Antonio's wealth and also informs an amazed Lorenzo, who receives it like manna, of Shylock's bequest to him and Jessica.

Justice Versus Mercy

Antonio willingly enters into a legal bond with Shylock even as Portia complains, "the will of a living daughter [is] curb'd by the will of a dead father" (Act 1, Scene 2, lines 24–25). Shylock, knowing that Venice lives by its inviolable legal contracts, insists his claim is just and that the Duke must grant it. Antonio, his intended victim, agrees: "The Duke cannot deny the course of law" (Act 3, Scene 3, line 26). And having pleaded in

BELOW: *The deep bond between Antonio and Bassanio—played by Jeremy Irons (left) and Joseph Fiennes in the 2004 film directed by Michael Radford—jeopardizes the love of Portia and Bassanio.*

Anti-Semitism in Shakespeare's England

Jews were banished from England by Edward I in 1290, a time of rampant anti-Semitism. Therefore, Shakespeare probably never met a Jew, though he would have known of the scandal in 1594 concerning Roderigo Lopez, a Jewish–Portuguese physician who converted to Christianity and was hanged for his supposed role in a plot on Queen Elizabeth's life. Shakespeare emphasizes Shylock's Jewishness by having him cite the Hebrew Bible, complain of anti-Semitism, and refer to his eating of kosher food, plus having him called by his own name only 11 times but by "Jew" 57 times throughout the play.

vain with Shylock to show mercy while embodying justice in her lawyer's disguise, Portia concurs: "there is no power in Venice / Can alter a decree established" (Act 4, Scene 1, lines 218–19).

At the end of the courtroom scene, Antonio grants Shylock his "life and living" if he converts to Christianity and bequeaths his wealth to Jessica and Lorenzo. Shylock has no option and accedes, exiting with some dignity by refusing to sign the "deed of gift" to Jessica and Lorenzo—"Send the deed after me, / And I will sign it" (Act 4, Scene 1, lines 396–97)—which he presumably does since Nerissa produces it at the end of the play (Act 5, Scene 1, line 292). But whether Shylock's sentence enacts justice or mercy depends on how it is interpreted and performed.

"Mark the Music"

One of Shakespeare's richest passages on music is Jessica and Lorenzo's dialogue beginning Act 5. Lorenzo describes "the moonlight [that] sleeps upon this bank," and explains that "Soft stillness and the night / Become the touches of sweet harmony" (Scene 1, lines 54–57). He discusses the stars, each in its separate "orb," or sphere, contributing to the heavenly music angels sing but that humans, clothed in earthly, decaying bodies, cannot hear. Jessica is unknowingly attuned, however—"your spirits are attentive" (line 70), Lorenzo says—to the music of the spheres. In contrast, Lorenzo concludes,

The man that hath no music in himself,
Nor is not moved with concord of sweet sounds,
Is fit for treasons, stratagems, and spoils;
. . . .
Let no such man be trusted. Mark the music.
(ACT 5, SCENE 1, LINES 83–88)

Lorenzo may unwittingly reference Shylock who, disturbed by musical masques in the street the night he is invited out, tells Jessica to lock up the house "when you hear the drum / And the vile squealing of the wry-neck'd fife" (Act 2, Scene 5, lines 29–30). Jessica, however, defiantly opens the casements and escapes with much of Shylock's wealth. Subsequently, Shylock may be alluding

BELOW: *"In which predicament I say thou stand'st" (Act 4, Scene 1, line 357), the disguised Portia says to Shylock in the courtroom scene, illustrated here by the nineteenth-century artist James Linton.*

to himself when he cites those who, "when the bagpipe sings i' th' nose / Cannot contain their urine" (Act 4, Scene 1, lines 49–50).

Music also marks Bassanio's transition from fortune-seeker to romantic lover. Portia summons "music [to] sound while he doth make his choice," and "if he lose he makes a swan-like end, / Fading in music" (Act 3, Scene 2, lines 43–45). She then underscores its significance:

> *such it is*
> *As are those dulcet sounds in break of day*
> *That creep into the dreaming bridegroom's ear,*
> *And summon him to marriage . . .*
> (ACT 3, SCENE 2, LINES 50–53)

Having seen inside the caskets, Portia commands a song whose key words rhyme with "lead," which "ring[s] fancy's knell," and whose last word, "bell," was a lead product (Act 3, Scene 2, lines 63–72). Music gives Portia to Bassanio, and music brings her home to reunite with him in Act 5.

Images of Food

Another motif is food. Mocking her pampered mistress and her languorous melancholy, Nerissa says that overfed people are as malnourished as starving people: "they are as sick that surfeit with too much as they that starve with nothing" (Act 1, Scene 2, lines 5–7). Shylock rejects the dinner invitation of Bassanio:

> *to smell pork, to eat of the habitation which your prophet the Nazarite conjur'd the devil into. I will buy with you, sell with you, talk with you, walk with you . . . but I will not eat with you, drink with you, nor pray with you.*
> (ACT 1, SCENE 3, LINES 33–38)

Yet he subsequently, and inexplicably, changes his mind: "I'll go in hate, to feed upon / The prodigal Christian" (Act 2, Scene 5, lines 14–15). Shylock's going affords Jessica the opportunity to elope. Launcelot later mocks Jessica's conversion to Christianity, saying it will raise the price of pork.

Antonio, anticipating his own death, speaks of being eaten rather than eating: "the weakest kind of fruit / Drops earliest to the ground" (Act 4, Scene 1, lines 115–16). And Lorenzo, learning of Shylock's bequest, echoes Nerissa's food image: "Fair ladies, you drop manna in the way / Of starved people" (Act 5, Scene 1, lines 294–95).

Playing Shylock

The Merchant of Venice is one of Shakespeare's most performed plays, attracting top actors. Taking Shylock's sufferings seriously, Charles Macklin in the 1740s humanized him. The nineteenth-century Shylock of Edmund Kean was a sacrificial hero; Henry Irving's achieved tragic dignity and pathos. In notable twentieth-century portrayals, Peter O'Toole's Shylock in the 1960 production directed by Michael Langham was effortlessly superior to Christians, and Laurence Olivier's assimilated Jew underwent a moral and spiritual reversion in a 1973 television production.

In two Royal Shakespeare Company productions directed by John Barton, the Shylock of Patrick Stewart in 1978 emerged undefeated, and David Suchet depicted an outsider defeated by anti-Semites in 1981. In a 1984 RSC production, Nazis beset Ian McDiarmid's Shylock. The 2001 British National Theatre's television production shows Christian nastiness overcoming Henry Goodman's powerful, self-blinded Shylock.

ABOVE: *In the 1989 Peter Hall-directed production, Dustin Hoffman played Shylock as a modest, genial man driven to revenge by the bestial behavior of Christians toward him.*

> *Hath not a Jew eyes? Hath not a Jew hands, organs, dimensions, senses, affections, passions . . . If you prick us, do we not bleed? If you tickle us, do we not laugh? If you poison us, do we not die? And if you wrong us, shall we not revenge?*

—*Shylock* (ACT 3, SCENE 1, LINES 59–67)

The Merry Wives of Windsor

WRITTEN c. 1597 or 1600
SETTING AND PERIOD Windsor, England, late 1590s
CHARACTERS 22
ACTS 5
SCENES 23
LINES 2,891

THE PLOT: *Sir John Falstaff and his men have been doing mischief in the village of Windsor. Justice Robert Shallow accuses Falstaff of theft, threatening to bring him before the authorities. Falstaff denies the accusation, and he sets his amorous sights on Mistresses Page and Ford, the "merry" wives of the play's title. The women see through Falstaff's attempts to take advantage of them, and together they subject him to a series of humiliations.*

But Mistress Ford's husband is jealous and conspires with Falstaff to catch his wife in the act of adultery. She proves her goodness, and her husband learns that his suspicions are false. The Pages' daughter, Anne, is sought by three suitors: Robert Shallow's cousin, Slender; Doctor Caius, a French physician; and Fenton, a young gentleman. Each suitor is supported by a different member of the family or community, and Fenton, with whom Anne is in love, wins her by stratagem. In the final scene of the play, when Falstaff is given his just punishment for his bad behavior, Anne and Fenton fool her parents and sneak off together.

ABOVE: *The sharp-witted wives—Mistress Page and Mistress Ford—deflate the ego of Falstaff in a rollicking production of* The Merry Wives of Windsor *at the new Globe theater in London in 2008.*

Dramatis Personae

Sir John Falstaff
Fenton, *a gentleman*
Robert Shallow, *a country justice*
Abraham Slender, *cousin to Shallow*
Francis Ford, George Page, *gentlemen of Windsor*
William Page, *a boy, son to Page*
Sir Hugh Evans, *a Welsh parson*
Doctor Caius, *a French physician*
Host of the Garter Inn
Bardolph, Pistol, Nym, *followers of Falstaff*
Robin, *page to Falstaff*
Peter Simple, *servant to Slender*
John Rugby, *servant to Doctor Caius*
Mistress Alice Ford
Mistress Margaret Page
Mistress Anne Page, *her daughter*
Mistress Quickly, *servant to Doctor Caius*
Servants to Page, Ford, etc.

Probably written in either early 1597 or in early 1600, *The Merry Wives of Windsor* is the sole contribution of Shakespeare to the genre known as "citizen comedy." Being his only comedy set in England, and with a relatively contemporary setting, the play deserves special attention as a representation, however oblique, of the Elizabethan middle class.

The play's characters—from Sir John Falstaff (the knight), to Evans (the Welsh parson), to the Host of the Garter Inn—are not the stuff of myth, fantasy, history, or far-off lands. If Shakespeare ever intended to hold the mirror up to nature, he did so in this comedy.

The realism that offers us English characters in an English setting gives way, in the plot, to a rather silly set of goings-on. With its insistence on comedic bumbling, coincidence, near misses, and overblown characters (pomposity, funny accents, outrageous rhetoric), the action of *The Merry Wives* does lend to the whole enterprise a rather farcical quality. Although serious subjects do arise—such as jealousy, enforced marriage, robbery, beatings, humiliation, and adultery—they are leavened by the infectious comic tone.

The Queen's Entertainment

English critic and playwright John Dennis claimed in 1702 that Queen Elizabeth I had specifically asked Shakespeare to write a comedy that showed Falstaff in love, and gave him two weeks in which to do it. (Sir John Falstaff is a character in the two *Henry IV* plays and is mentioned in *Henry V*.) Although many scholars doubt the truth of this anecdote, *The Merry Wives of Windsor* does have topical resonances that place it firmly in its late 1590s milieu. Some date the first performance of the play to April 23, 1597 (St. George's Day). On this day an Order of the Garter festival was held at Whitehall Palace to celebrate the newly elected knights. The patron of the Lord Chamberlain's Men, Shakespeare's company, was George Carey, Lord Hunsdon, who was one of those honored: it is possible he was responsible for the production of a play to mark the festivities.

There are several textual markers that point to this possible first performance in *The Merry Wives*. One example is the inn where Falstaff resides, which is called the Garter. Another occurs when

The Humiliations of Falstaff

I suffer'd the pangs of three several deaths: first, an intolerable fright, to be detected with a jealious rotten bell-wether; next, to compass'd like a good bilbo in the circumference of a peck, hilt to point, heel to head; and then to be stopp'd in like a strong distillation with stinking clothes that fretted in their own grease. Think of that—a man of my kidney. Think of that—that am as subject to heat as butter; a man of continual dissolution and thaw. It was a miracle to scape suffocation.

(ACT 3, SCENE 5, LINES 107–117)

I would all the world might be cozen'd, for I have been cozen'd and beaten too. If it should come to the ear of the court, how I have been transform'd, and how my transformation hath been wash'd and cudgell'd, they would melt me out of my fat drop by drop, and liquor fishermen's boots with me. I warrant they would whip me with their fine wits till I were as crestfall'n as a dried pear.

(ACT 4, SCENE 5, LINES 93–100)

RELATIONSHIPS

The comedy is built around deception and jealousy: deception employed by Falstaff to seduce Mistresses Page and Ford, who use the situation to teach their husbands a lesson. In contrast, Anne Page is genuinely in love.

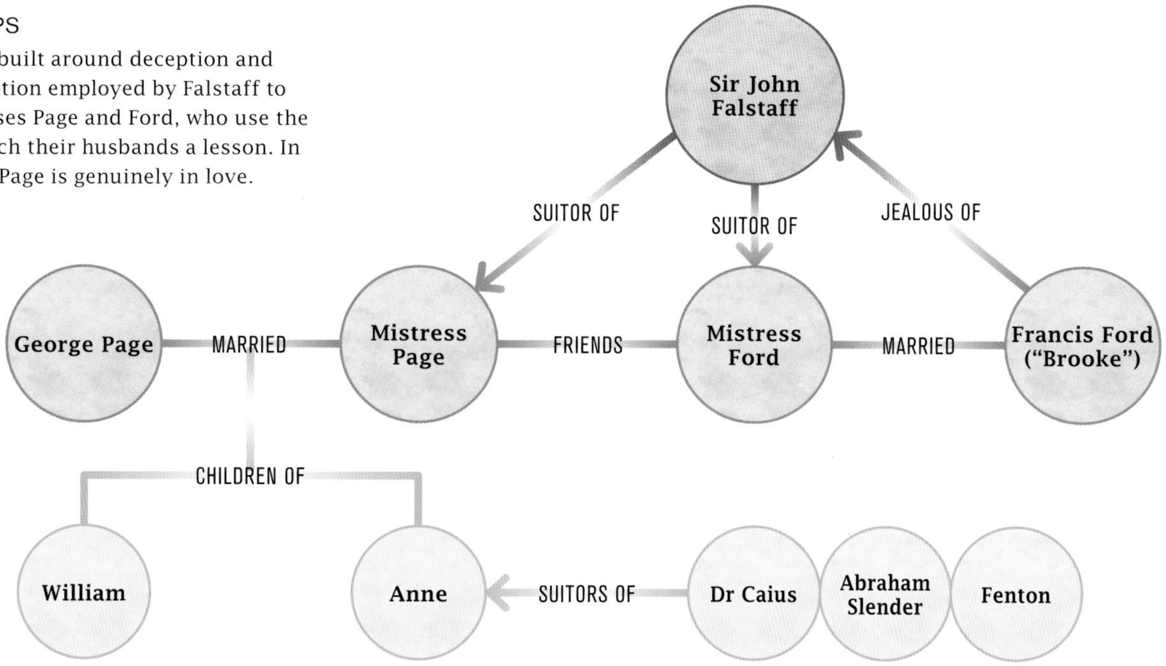

Sir John Falstaff
SUITOR OF
SUITOR OF
JEALOUS OF
George Page
MARRIED
Mistress Page
FRIENDS
Mistress Ford
MARRIED
Francis Ford ("Brooke")
CHILDREN OF
William
Anne
SUITORS OF
Dr Caius
Abraham Slender
Fenton

ABOVE: *Ellen Terry played Mistress Page in the famous 1902 Herbert Beerbohm Tree production of* The Merry Wives of Windsor, *which ran for 56 performances at Her Majesty's Theatre, London.*

Mistress Quickly, conducting the masque near the end of the play, says:

> *And nightly, meadow-fairies, look you sing,*
> *Like to the Garter's compass, in a ring.*
> *Th' expressure that it bears, green let it be,*
> *More fertile-fresh than all the field to see;*
> *And* "Honi soit qui mal y pense" *write[.]*
> (ACT 5, SCENE 5, LINES 65–69)

The Middle French phrase *Honi soit qui mal y pense* is the Order of the Garter's motto ("Shame to he who thinks evil of it").

Others note that the play we have come to know might not be the entertainment played in 1597, since there is no direct evidence for this.

> *We'll leave a proof, by that which we will do,/*
> *Wives may be merry, and yet honest too:/*
> *We do not act that often jest and laugh;/*
> *'Tis old, but true: still swine eats all the draff.*

—*Mistress Page* (ACT 4, SCENE 2, LINES 104–7)

Rather, it may well be from late 1599 or early 1600, composed after the history-play cycle that concludes with *Henry V*. This is suggested by some characters from those plays appearing in *The Merry Wives* (such as Justice Shallow, Pistol, and Nym).

Laugh and "Be Reveng'd"

It is typical of Shakespeare's comedic style that a character such as Falstaff can function as both the subject and object of humor. Falstaff is the motive force of wit in the two *Henry IV* plays. As he says, "I am not only witty in myself, but the cause that wit is in other men" (*Henry IV, Part 2*, Act 1, Scene 2, lines 9–10). What makes the merry wives merry is their ability to outfox Falstaff in order to control the means of comic production.

Despite the generic necessity for a happy ending and orderly resolution at the end of a comedy, in Shakespeare's contributions to the genre there are certainly winners and losers. An important theme of the play is the way in which characters are either in control of the joke (or the strategy or plot) or not. If so, they expect to have the last laugh and to avoid being outmaneuvered; if not, they are likely to fail to accomplish this by some characteristic that defines them. Mistresses Ford and Page understand immediately that Falstaff is up to something, and their plotting shows us how the play will function. Mistress Page suggests:

> *Let's be reveng'd on him: let's appoint him*
> *a meeting, give him a show of comfort in his*
> *suit, and lead him on with a fine-baited delay,*
> *till he hath pawn'd his horses to mine host*
> *of the Garter.*
> (ACT 2, SCENE 1, LINES 93–97)

The reason the female characters are "merry" is not because they are silly or even happy. The jealousy of her husband is a real threat to Mistress Ford's contentment and safety, for example. Only through their skills in reading situations correctly, and acting decisively, do the wives maintain their reputations and preserve the respect they deserve. Master Ford must learn a hard lesson about his assumptions and about his wife's true character.

Even the Pages, who have no marital issues, are forced to admit that their attempts to coerce their daughter into marrying someone she does not love violate an important thematic principle. This also happens to coincide with one of the definitions of comedy—you cannot stop desire. This is articulated wonderfully at the end of *The Merry Wives* when Master Page learns Anne and Fenton have tricked him: "Well, what remedy? Fenton, heaven give thee joy! / What cannot be eschew'd must be embrac'd" (Act 5, Scene 5, lines 236–37).

The Comic Language of Deception

Deception and disguise figure prominently in the play's action and in its language. Ford disguises himself as "Brooke" to fool Falstaff and to test his wife: "I have a disguise to sound Falstaff. If I find her honest, I lose not my labor; if she be otherwise, 'tis labor well bestow'd" (Act 2, Scene 1, lines 237–40). Caius and Evans plot revenge on the Host of the Garter, who has deceived them into fighting one another. Pistol and Nym resolve to be revenged on Falstaff. Greatest of all, Falstaff attempts, by deception, to sleep with Mistresses Ford and Page, and make money doing so, all the while being the object of the wives' deceptions. This latter thread leads Falstaff to deploy disguise to get out of his own deceptions, with comical and painful results for him. Thrown into the river with the laundry and beaten while disguised as an old lady, he presents a lasting image of the wages of sin:

> *Have I liv'd to be carried in a basket like a barrow of butcher's offal? and to be thrown in the Thames? Well, [and] I be serv'd such another trick, I'll have my brains ta'en out and butter'd, and give them to a dog for a new-year's gift. The rogues slighted me into the river with as little remorse as they would have drown'd a blind bitch's puppies, fifteen i' th' litter; and you may know by my size that I have a kind of alacrity in sinking[.]*
> (ACT 3, SCENE 5, LINES 4–13)

At the end, the play brings together deception and disguise for a climactic revenge scene that is humorous to all but Falstaff, its target. He is fooled into meeting the wives for an assignation for the final time, late at night in Windsor forest, and is to disguise himself as the legendary Herne the hunter. He does so, but the joke is on him because he is set upon by the children of Windsor disguised as "urchins, ouphes, and fairies" (Act 4, Scene 4, line 50), who pinch and burn him in a final act of humiliation.

A Character Larger Than Life

Like the history plays in which Falstaff also appears, *The Merry Wives* has enjoyed lasting stage popularity due to this larger-than-life character. During the eighteenth century, it was played nearly as much as *Henry IV, Part 1*. In the twentieth century, the play found its voice through modern-dress adaptations and major international productions, in Russia (1957) and in Rome (1980), for example, and a 1991 version in Tokyo translated Falstaff into the *Braggart Samurai*. Two notable comic operas center on Falstaff: Giuseppe Verdi's *Falstaff* (1893) and Ralph Vaughan Williams's *Sir John in Love* (1933).

Herbert Beerbohm Tree

Early in his career, the British actor–director Herbert Beerbohm Tree played what contemporaries called "the best Falstaff of all." In 1902, he played Falstaff again in a production in the wake of Queen Victoria's death. The production coincided with the crowning of a lecherous fat man (Edward VII), and Tree played his Falstaff in remembrance of the widow of Windsor. Tree presented the play as more than farce: his Falstaff and the whole production emphasized the human element exhibited by these English characters of the middling class.

BELOW: *The cover of* Illustrazione Italiana *features the opera* Falstaff *by Giuseppe Verdi. The three-act* commedia lirica *had a libretto by Arrigo Boito, who adapted* Merry Wives *and incorporated scenes from* Henry IV.

As You Like It

THE PLOT: *Duke Frederick has usurped his brother, Duke Senior, who is now living exiled in the Forest of Arden. Oliver, the eldest son of a disgraced knight, plots to kill his youngest brother, Orlando. After defeating Frederick's champion in a court wrestling match, Orlando attracts the attention of Duke Senior's daughter Rosalind, cousin and childhood friend of Celia, Frederick's daughter.*

Frederick banishes Rosalind from court. Celia and Rosalind escape to the forest with the clown, Touchstone. Celia becomes "Aliena," while Rosalind disguises herself as a boy, Ganymed. Orlando also escapes to the forest with his old servant, Adam. All meet Duke Senior, whose followers in the forest include the world-weary Jaques. Rosalind, as Ganymed, befriends Orlando and offers to pretend to be his beloved Rosalind. Local shepherds and shepherdesses mirror the love antics of their forest interlopers.

Orlando saves Oliver's life and they are reconciled. Rosalind reveals her identity and, at a pagan forest ceremony, promises to marry Orlando. Duke Senior is restored to his dukedom.

ABOVE RIGHT: *For his 2005 staging of* As You Like It *at Wyndham's Theatre in London, director David Lan transplanted his court exiles—including Celia (Sienna Miller) and Rosalind (Helen McCrory)—to 1940s France.*

Dramatis Personae

Duke Senior, *living in banishment*
Duke Frederick, *his brother, and usurper of his dominions*
Amiens, Jaques, *lords attending on the banished Duke*
Le Beau, *a courtier attending upon Duke Frederick*
Charles, *wrestler to Duke Frederick*
Oliver, Jaques, Orlando, *sons of Sir Rowland de Boys*
Adam, *servant to Orlando*
Dennis, *servant to Oliver*
Touchstone, *a clown*
Sir Oliver Martext, *a vicar*
Corin, Silvius, *shepherds*
William, *a country fellow, in love with Audrey*
A person representing **Hymen**
Rosalind, *daughter to the banished Duke*
Celia, *daughter to Duke Frederick*
Phebe, *a shepherdess*
Audrey, *a country wench*
Lords, Pages, Foresters, and Attendants

WRITTEN
c. 1598

SETTING AND PERIOD
France, *c.* sixteenth century

CHARACTERS 25

ACTS 5

SCENES 22

LINES 2,810

As You Like It is a fascinating mixture of English medieval folklore, European courtly romance, and Classical Greek and Roman mythology, all packaged as a lively tale set in a fanciful, forest-bound French dukedom. It is crammed with poems and songs—in fact, it has more songs than any other play by Shakespeare—as well as puns and wordplay that highlight its writer's skill and Classical knowledge.

Set in an idyllic pastoral world ("pastoral" offers an idealized portrayal of shepherds and country life), *As You Like It* questions how far hardship and the encroachment of urban city-dwellers affect the well-being of those who, through their innocence or lack of education, suffer exploitation in their rural retreat. The play also questions the merit of excessive romantic love, as encouraged by the fourteenth-century Italian Renaissance poets such as Petrarch, which advocated the selfless, self-destructive adoration of aloof and unobtainable young women by love-struck young men.

In the process, the play introduces the themes of destructive all-consuming love, changeability, falsehood, disguise, and a longed-for but ultimately impossible return to a "golden world" (Act 1, Scene 1, lines 118–19) of pastoral peace and prosperity. Bittersweet as it might seem, *As You Like It*

Inspired By ...

Shakespeare took elements for his story from Thomas Lodge's *Rosalynde* (1590), a pastoral romance that follows the adventures of Rosalynd and her friend, Alinda, who disguise themselves as "Ganimede" and "Aliena." Based on a medieval English Robin Hood tale, Lodge's story is relocated to an Italian-inspired French rural idyll complete with innocent shepherds and shepherdesses, as in Shakespeare's play.

ends—like all good comedies—with multiple betrothals and marriage vows, all exchanged during its nighttime pagan forest festivity.

As They Liked It ...

Like so many of Shakespeare's plays, *As You Like It* was first published in the Folio of 1623, although reference is made to it in official documents dating back to 1600. As well as in Shakespeare's public playhouse in London, the Globe, it was most likely performed privately for Queen Elizabeth, possibly at Richmond Palace as part of the February 1599 Shrove Tuesday celebrations. Shakespeare scholars argue that this "Pancake Day" performance would account for Touchstone's seemingly topical though otherwise inexplicable jokes about pancakes in Act 1, Scene 2. Less convincing is the fanciful idea that Shakespeare himself played Orlando's faithful old servant, Adam.

Politically, *As You Like It* depicts a world of usurpation and escape from oppression. It refers to "the old Robin Hood of England" (Act 1, Scene 1, line 116), a myth well known among Shakespeare's contemporaries and associated with radical popular resistance against tyrannical and oppressive ruling regimes. The references to forest deer and hunting, a sport reserved only for the monarch, was also of topical significance. Deer poaching was considered to be a crime against the queen, but following several years of bad harvests in the 1590s, for the rural poor it became not only their sole means of survival, but also an act of defiance against the perceived injustices imposed by an uncompromising urban courtly elite.

Courtly Love

The theme of courtly love, and its debilitating effect on those who foolishly allow themselves to suffer its pains, is explored in *As You Like It*. Responding to a European romance tradition, Shakespeare makes several references to the Italian poet Francesco Petrarca (Petrarch), who, having caught sight of a woman named Laura, wrote no less than 366 heartrending poems dedicated to his enigmatic love-object. It is in this spirit that the outlawed Orlando indulges his new passion for Rosalind, admitting that he is "overthrown" by love (Act 1, Scene 2, line 259), and deciding, like Petrarch, to compose poem after tortured poem dedicated to Rosalind's beauty and his own pain. Unlike Laura, who died oblivious of her lover's plight, Rosalind (as Ganymed) is fully aware of Orlando's obsession. As she declares:

> *Love is merely a madness, and I tell you, deserves as well a dark house and a whip as madmen do; and the reason why they are not so punish'd and cur'd is, that the lunacy is so ordinary that the whippers are in love too.*
> (ACT 3, SCENE 2, LINES 400–404)

[M]en are April when they woo, December when they wed; maids are May when they are maids, but the sky changes when they are wives.

—*Rosalind* (ACT 4, SCENE 1, LINES 147–49)

Orlando's later comment that he will "die" if his advances are rejected receives Rosalind's equally mocking response, "men have died from time to time, and worms have eaten them, but not for love" (Act 4, Scene 1, lines 106–8). Even the shepherd Silvius, explaining his love for the cold-hearted shepherdess Phebe, expresses his passion with courtly anxiety worthy of a Petrarchan poet:

O, thou didst then never love so heartily!
If thou rememb'rest not the slightest folly
That ever love did make thee run into,
Thou hast not loved[.]
(ACT 2, SCENE 4, LINES 33–36)

BELOW: *Katharine Hepburn put in a star turn as Rosalind, seen here in her Ganymed disguise, in a 1950 Broadway production of* As You Like It, *with William Prince as Orlando. The wooing scenes between the hoodwinked Orlando and Ganymed are some of the liveliest in the play.*

Poor Silvius, tricked into acting as unwilling go-between between Phebe and her newfound object of desire—the equally unobtainable youth Ganymed—suffers the madness of unrequited love. Phebe's later command for Silvius to "tell this youth [Ganymed] what 'tis to love" (Act 5, Scene 2, line 83) appears as poignant as it does self-indulgent in its innocent pain; as Silvius perceptively observes, "It is to be all made of sighs and tears" (Act 5, Scene 2, line 84).

Country versus City

Throughout *As You Like It,* Shakespeare explores the theme of city versus country life. The city-dwellers, exiled from court, reside among their rural counterparts with little likelihood of truly integrating with them. To these exiles, the country represents an idyllic utopian world: a place of freedom and escape from political duplicity and social display. As the usurped Duke Senior asks of his followers:

Now, my co-mates and brothers in exile,
Hath not old custom made this life more sweet
Than that of painted pomp? Are not these woods
More free from peril than the envious court?
(ACT 2, SCENE 1, LINES 1–4)

Duke Senior's response to his forest haven—finding "tongues in trees, books in the running brooks, / Sermons in stones, and good in every thing" (Act 2, Scene 1, lines 16–17)—is as romantically idealized as it is blind to the cold hardship of rural existence. It is Jaques who, with bitter perception, recognizes the truth

Melancholy Jaques

I can suck melancholy out of a song, as a weasel sucks eggs.
(ACT 2, SCENE 5, LINES 12–13)

I do not desire you to please me, I do desire you to sing.
(ACT 2, SCENE 5, LINES 17–18)

I'll go sleep, if I can; if I cannot, I'll rail against all the first-born of Egypt.
(ACT 2, SCENE 5, LINES 60–61)

A fool, a fool! I met a fool i' th' forest,
A motley fool. A miserable world!
(ACT 2, SCENE 7, LINES 12–13)

And so from hour to hour, we ripe and ripe,
And then from hour to hour, we rot and rot;
And thereby hangs a tale ...
(ACT 2, SCENE 7, LINES 26–28)

My lungs began to crow like chanticleer,
That fools should be so deep contemplative;
And I did laugh sans intermission
An hour by his dial. O noble fool!
A worthy fool! Motley's the only wear.
(ACT 2, SCENE 7, LINES 30–34)

"Sweet Ganymed!"

Rosalind's choice of name for her boy's disguise—Ganymed—would have had particular significance for Shakespeare's audience, not least because Rosalind's character would be played by a boy pretending to be a girl pretending to be a boy! According to Greek mythology, Ganymed (or Ganymede) was a beautiful Trojan boy who was abducted by Zeus, the king of the gods, to serve as an immortal cupbearer. Homer's *Iliad* refers to the myth, as does the Roman poet Ovid in his *Metamorphoses,* a highly erotic book also known by Shakespeare and many of his contemporaries.

The name "Ganymed" was therefore synonymous with youth–adult male love. When Rosalind becomes Ganymed, Shakespeare's contemporaries would have recognized the Classical irony of her choice of name, as well as the homoerotic implication of her boyish disguise.

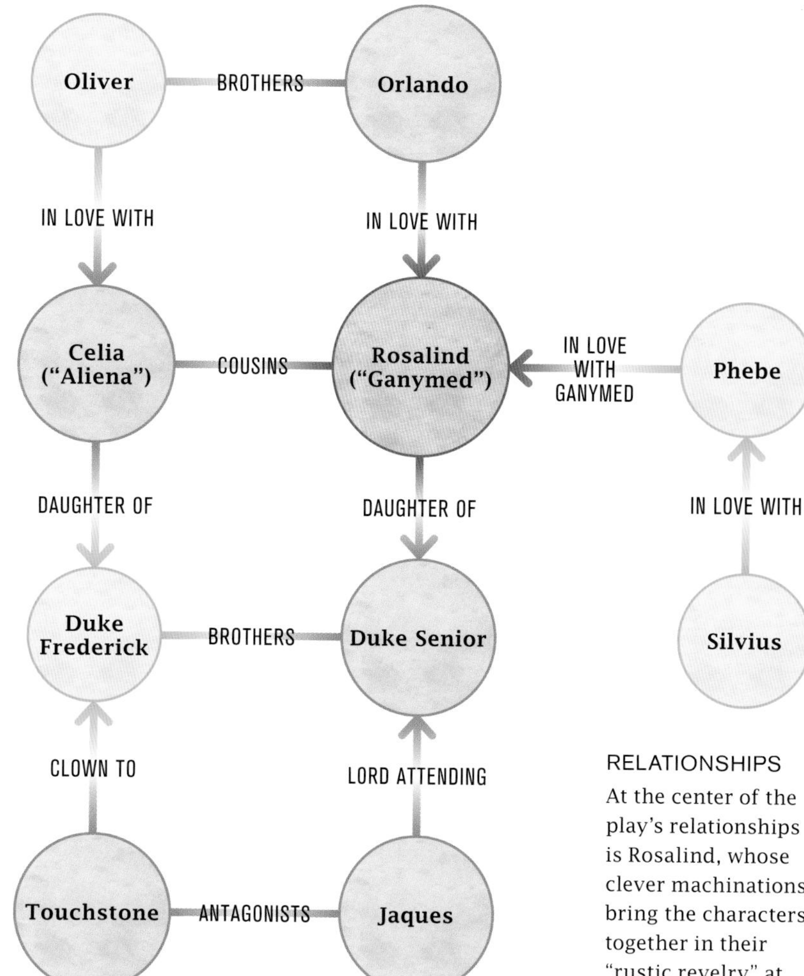

RELATIONSHIPS

At the center of the play's relationships is Rosalind, whose clever machinations bring the characters together in their "rustic revelry" at the end of the play.

that the Duke and his followers are little more than "mere usurpers, tyrants" (Act 2, Scene 1, line 61) in the forest. Later, when the shepherd Corin asks Touchstone what he thinks of "this shepherd's life," the court-fool replies:

> *[I]n respect of itself, it is a good life; but in respect that it is a shepherd's life, it is naught. In respect that it is solitary, I like it very well; but in respect that it is private, it is a very vild life. Now in respect it is in the fields, it pleaseth me well; but in respect it is not in the court, it is tedious.*
>
> (ACT 3, SCENE 2, LINES 13–19)

Touchstone's caustic humor is not lost on the shepherd, who observes astutely that "Those that are good manners at the court are as ridiculous in the country as the behavior of the country is most mockable at the court" (Act 3, Scene 2, lines 45–48). Corin's uneducated commonsense as a "natural philosopher" (Act 3, Scene 2, line 32) relies on an understanding and an acceptance of his role in society: "I am a true laborer: I earn that I eat, get that I wear, owe no man hate, envy no man's happiness" (Act 3, Scene 2, lines 73–75). How different from the city-dwellers, who can only fully enjoy "rustic revelry" (Act 5, Scene 4, line 177) when they are assured of a safe return to their urban existence.

Horns and the Cuckold

If a recurring theme is the conflict between an idealized rural world and the harsh realities of country existence, then a recurring image is that of the cuckold—the married man who is not aware that his wife is seeking sexual satisfaction elsewhere. The traditional imagery for a cuckold was a man with horns or antlers growing out of his forehead, symbolizing that all his friends and neighbors know of his plight long before he does. Where better to explore this imagery than in the Forest of Arden, whose woodland teems with antlered deer? When the Lords and Foresters return celebrating their successful kill, Jaques invokes the cuckold by suggesting that "it would do well to set the deer's horns upon his [Duke Senior's] head, for a branch of victory" (Act 4, Scene 2, lines 4–5). In response to this jocular proposal, the Lords and Foresters sing:

> *Take thou no scorn to wear the horn,*
> *It was a crest ere thou wast born;*
> *Thy father's father wore it,*
> *And thy father bore it.*
> *The horn, the horn, the lusty horn*
> *Is not a thing to laugh to scorn.*
>
> (ACT 4, SCENE 2, LINES 13–18)

Not just the subject of ridicule, the figure of the cuckolded husband also held a deep significance for

Shakespeare's contemporaries, who relied on their faithful wives to guarantee purity of blood for their children. A cuckold, like the cuckoo from which the word is anciently derived, might play host to another's offspring. Such fears are expressed by Touchstone, who notes the regularity with which married men are made cuckolds:

> *As horns are odious, they are necessary. It is said, "Many a man knows no end of his goods." Right! many a man has good horns, and knows no end of them. Well, that is the dowry of his wife, 'tis none of his own getting.*
> (ACT 3, SCENE 3, LINES 51–56)

Touchstone's harsh and offensive opinion—that wives (and women in general) are sexually promiscuous and unfaithful—is one that is typical of Shakespeare's age. Touchstone's belief that the horns of the cuckold were not worn by "Poor men alone," but that even "the noblest deer hath them as huge as the rascal" (Act 3, Scene 3, lines 56–58), also shows that male anxiety crossed social boundaries. It is with bitter irony that Touchstone notes that:

> *[As] a wall'd town is more worthier than a village, so is the forehead of a married man more honorable than the bare brow of a bachelor[.]*
> (ACT 3, SCENE 3, LINES 59–61)

Apparently based solely on the biased male assumption that women represented a weaker, susceptible sex, the image of the cuckold as the prevailing plight of husbands throughout the land demonstrates how common this belief was, and how important Shakespeare deemed it for a play that explores the ease with which people change according to the circumstances in which they find themselves.

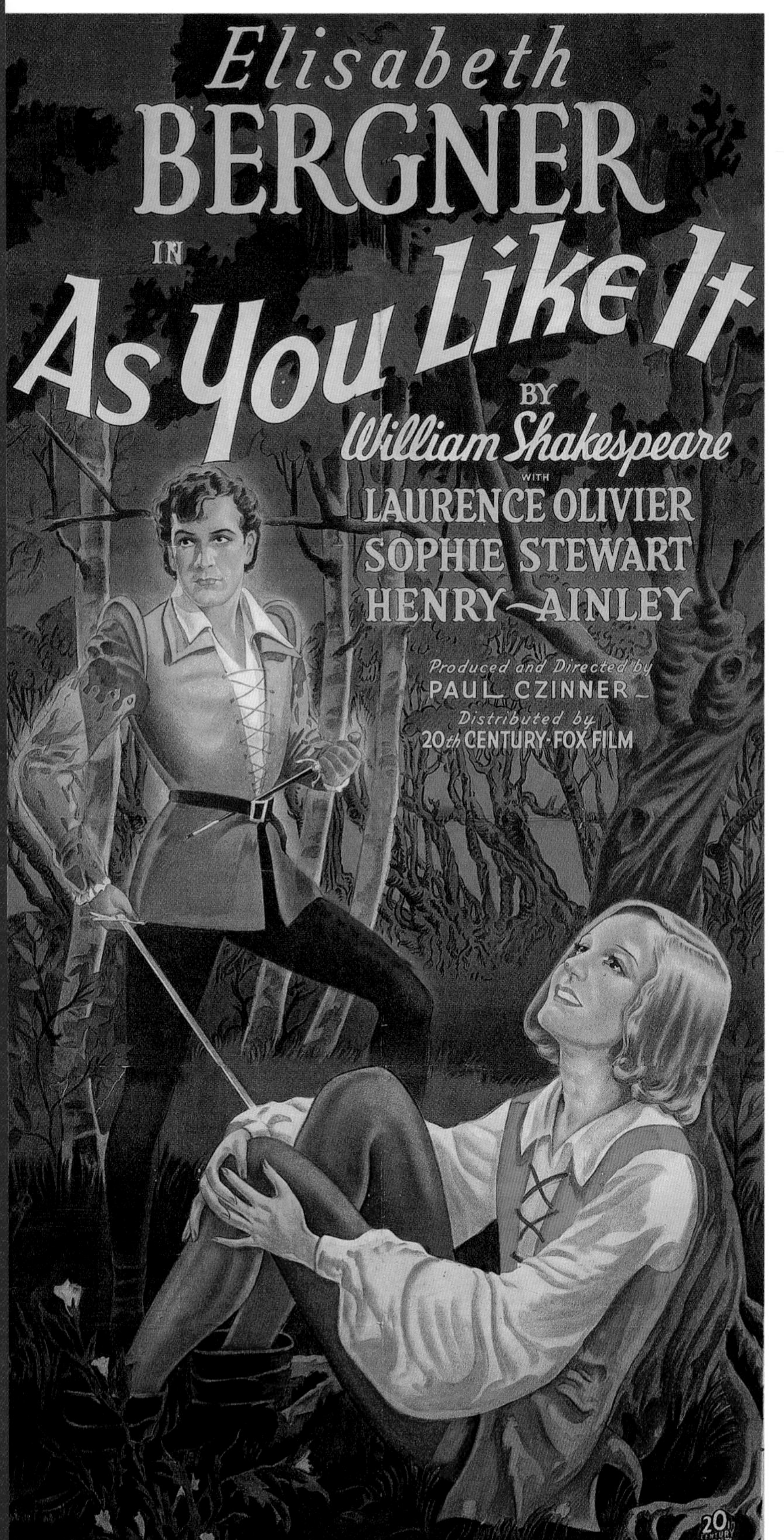

LEFT: *A poster for the 1936 film, starring Laurence Olivier as Orlando, suggests as much about the gender ideals of its time as it does about the play: Orlando strikes an assertive pose, while a feminine Rosalind smiles softly.*

Early Adaptations

Like so many of Shakespeare's plays, little is known about the early stagings of *As You Like It,* or how many times it was performed on the seventeenth-century stage. In 1723, however, Charles Johnson adapted the play for London's Drury Lane Theatre, renaming it *Love in a Forest*. Starring Colley Cibber as Jaques, *Love in a Forest* was written without Oliver and Touchstone, and missing Silvius, Audrey, Corin, and any other pastoral characters, leaving Jaques free to woo Celia. Celia's betrothal to Jaques was repeated

RIGHT: *Director Kenneth Branagh's lively, Japanese-inspired film version of the play (2006) featured a fresh and versatile cast. Here Alfred Molina, as the mischievous and much-hairsprayed Touchstone, teases Romola Garai's Celia in a scene at court.*

in the 1856 French adaptation by George Sands, *Comme il vous plaira*. In the twentieth century, the most radical staging was the 1991 Cheek by Jowl production, directed by the company's co-founder, Declan Donnellan, which toured internationally and which featured a multiracial, all-male cast.

Later Revivals

On film, the 1936 version, starring Laurence Olivier as Orlando and directed by Paul Czinner, received lackluster reviews despite the literary involvement of J.M. Barrie and William Walton's musical score. For the twenty-first century, the Golden Globe–nominated 2006 film, directed by Kenneth Branagh and starring David Oyelowo and Bryce Dallas Howard, relocated Shakespeare's play to nineteenth-century Japan. The court exiles become English traders settling in Japan just as it was transforming itself from an agricultural to an industrial nation. Japan was, by opening the country to foreign influences, mirroring those vulnerable rural communities of Shakespeare's day that accepted urban interlopers in their midst, without realizing what difficulties might result from such a clash of cultures.

> *All the world's a stage,/ And all the men and women merely players;/ They have their exits and their entrances,/ And one man in his time plays many parts,/ His acts being seven ages ...*

—*Jaques* (ACT 2, SCENE 7, LINES 139–43)

Much Ado about Nothing

WRITTEN
c. 1598

SETTING AND PERIOD
Messina, Sicily,
c. sixteenth century

CHARACTERS 16

ACTS 5

SCENES 17

LINES 2,787

THE PLOT: *Don Pedro, victorious in a recent war, comes to stay with Leonato, governor of Messina. His retinue includes Benedick, another regular visitor, who resumes his verbal sparring with Beatrice, Leonato's niece, and Claudio, who falls in love with Leonato's daughter, Hero. Don Pedro woos Hero on Claudio's behalf, and instigates a plot to make Beatrice and Benedick admit their love for each other. Don Pedro's illegitimate half-brother, Don John, resents Claudio's preferment and uses Borachio to convince Claudio and Don Pedro that Hero is promiscuous. As a result, Claudio denounces Hero at the altar, she swoons, and Friar Francis advises her family to pretend that she is dead until Claudio comes to his senses. To prove his love for Beatrice, Benedick challenges Claudio to a duel. When, despite Dogberry's bumbling, Borachio confesses his slander, Claudio agrees, as penance for his misapprehension, to marry a niece of Leonato's the next day. Beatrice and Benedick also decide to wed, and the "niece" reveals herself as Hero. Finally, the two couples marry.*

Dramatis Personae

Don Pedro, *Prince of Arragon*
Don John, *his bastard brother*
Claudio, *a young lord of Florence*
Benedick, *a young lord of Padua*
Leonato, *governor of Messina*
Antonio, *his brother*
Balthasar, *attendant on Don Pedro*
Conrade, Borachio, *followers of Don John*
Friar Francis
Dogberry, *a constable*
Verges, *a headborough*
Sexton
Boy
Hero, *daughter to Leonato*
Beatrice, *niece to Leonato*
Margaret, Ursula, *gentlewomen attending on Hero*
Messengers, Watch, Lord, Attendants, etc.

Much Ado about Nothing is not a romantic comedy as such, but a sophisticated play about romantic love, largely represented by the characters of Beatrice and Benedick, who display a clear distaste for the unselfknowing romanticism of Hero and Claudio, mainly because of their own anxieties about loss of freedom in marriage. To regard the play as a straightforward comedy is also to do it a disservice. There are dark elements in the Claudio–Hero story, hinted at in the punning title of the play, which are central to its meaning and help define the nature of the dramatic experience it offers.

Shakespeare's treatment of this story is very different from that of his probable source, a large collection of short stories by the Italian author Matteo Bandello, *La prima parte de le novelle* (1554), a work that was highly influential in western Europe. The most straightforward borrowing is the setting of the play in Messina.

RIGHT: *Diana Wynyard played Beatrice and John Gielgud took the part of Benedick in a 1952 production of* Much Ado about Nothing *at the Phoenix Theatre in London. A young Paul Scofield was Don Pedro.*

Nothing and Noting

The title of *Much Ado about Nothing* puns on the word "nothing," which was pronounced like "noting" in Shakespeare's day. This is evident in Act 2, Scene 3, in the dialogue between Don Pedro and Balthasar:

> BALTHASAR *Note this before my notes:*
> *There's not a note of mine that's worth the noting.*
> DON PEDRO *Why, these are very crotchets that he speaks—*
> *Note notes, forsooth, and nothing.*
> (LINES 54–57)

It is possible that the title also makes a lewd pun on "no thing," referring to either the male or female sexual organ, in relation to the slander of Hero and the sexual tensions in the relationship between Beatrice and Benedick. But primarily it points to the way in which the play deals with deception, a failure to *note* qualities, and a failure to communicate successfully.

Social Death

The potentially tragic element in the play—the effect on Hero of Claudio's brutal denunciation—means that we might well see it as tragicomedy. More specifically, the play might be seen as located midway between the comedy of forgiveness, as represented by *The Two Gentlemen of Verona* (where the heroine revives and pardons the former lover who rejects her), and the more edgily tragicomic "problem plays," *All's Well That Ends Well* and *Measure for Measure*.

Claudio's renunciation is a form of social death for Hero—she can only be rehabilitated if Claudio marries her in the end. This is dramatized by her swoon, following which the audience is left unsure whether she is alive and her father hopes that she has died because "Death is the fairest cover for her shame" (Act 4, Scene 1, line 116). Although the audience is subsequently privy to Hero's survival and the friar's conspiracy, the nature of the trauma is fully felt. Even when Borachio's plot is discovered, we have no confidence in Dogberry's ability to convey the essential facts, and are left wondering how things will turn out until near the end of the play.

This potentially tragic situation is often discounted because the Beatrice–Benedick part of the plot has for so long been the play's most popular element, but it should be remembered that Beatrice's affection for her cousin Hero and her demand that Benedick "Kill Claudio" (Act 4, Scene 1, line 289) to prove his love for her, connect the two parts of the plot closely.

Honor and Marriage

Together, the idea of "noting" and the tragicomic suspense focus the audience's attention on two important and topical issues of the time in middle- and upper-class circles: male and female versions of honor, and arranged marriages. The prevailing notion that young men should win personal and family honor by martial pursuits is reflected in Claudio's confiding to Don Pedro that he suspended his interest in Hero until he had won military honor (Act 1, Scene 1, lines 296–305).

Beatrice and Benedick

The Beatrice and Benedick story has been the most popular part of the play's plot since at least 1613, when the play was called *Benedicte and Betteris* in the Lord Treasurer's accounts. The role of Beatrice has challenged actors since the first performances, when male apprentices played the female roles.

As in his history plays, Shakespeare explores through subsequent actions the question of whether the fighting man is truly honorable.

The female equivalent of honor, in the Renaissance view, is chastity: virginity before marriage, followed by marital fidelity. This is at the heart of Claudio's going beyond a sense of deeply felt betrayal to self-righteous public denunciation of Hero, after he thinks he has seen her with another man the night before their wedding. In this period, upper-class marriages were arranged by the respective fathers or other patriarchal authorities, in order to ensure congruence of property, family honor, and the production of male heirs to carry on the line. Love was expected to follow marriage, rather than necessarily precede it, although, if the arranging fathers were liberal-minded, they might take account of their children's wishes. Thus Claudio inquires whether Hero is Leonato's heir (Act 1, Scene 1, line 294) before deciding he wants to marry her, and Don Pedro undertakes to arrange the match. So, too, Don Pedro sees himself as having the right to arrange a marriage between Beatrice and Benedick by tricking them into giving their consent. In both cases, he is acting as princely patriarch: Beatrice's father is dead, and the fathers of Claudio and Benedick are also absent.

[W]hat we have we prize not to the worth / Whiles we enjoy it, but being lack'd and lost, / Why then we rack the value; then we find / The virtue that possession would not show us / Whiles it was ours ...

—*Friar* (ACT 4, SCENE 1, LINES 218–22)

Beatrice's social, and especially verbal, freedom comes partly from her fatherlessness, but also partly from her own nature, which her uncles regard as shrewish—"shrewd of ... tongue" and "curst" (Act 2, Scene 1, lines 19–20)—and therefore potentially subversive of male authority. In Elizabethan times, it was widely believed that the best way to tame a shrew was to marry her off to a man who was capable of "handling" her, and Shakespeare had dealt with such a situation, though not without qualifying ironies, in his earlier play, *The Taming of the Shrew*. In *Much Ado*, the issue of gender roles is explored more fully, and Beatrice's attitude is more obviously related to specific anxieties about loss of freedom.

BELOW: *English actor Ellen Terry formed a famous partnership with Henry Irving at the Lyceum Theatre in London. Beginning in 1882, she several times played Beatrice opposite Irving in the role of Benedick.*

Beatrice on Marriage

Lord, I could not endure a husband with a beard on his face, I had rather lie in the woollen!
(ACT 2, SCENE 1, LINES 29–31)

Would it not grieve a woman to be over-master'd with a piece of valiant dust? to make an account of her life to a clod of wayward marl?
(ACT 2, SCENE 1, LINES 60–63)

[W]ooing, wedding, and repenting, is as a Scotch jig, a measure, and a cinquepace; the first suit is hot and hasty, like a Scotch jig, and full as fantastical; the wedding, mannerly-modest, as a measure, full of state and ancientry; and then comes repentance, and with his bad legs falls into the cinquepace faster and faster, till he sink into his grave.
(ACT 2, SCENE 1, LINES 73–80)

"Dying for Love"

The principal themes of the play derive from its overall concern with "noting," but it is also illuminating to approach them from the perspective of the love-death nexus that is such a prominent feature of the Claudio–Hero strand of the story. The notion of "dying for love" is applied not only to Hero, but also, more figuratively, to Beatrice and Benedick.

Before both sets of lovers are ready for marriage, they must undergo a period of testing, during which the marriage of Claudio and Hero is deferred. Beatrice is also subconsciously "dying for love" in the colloquial sense, though she is anxious about trusting a man and losing her independence. She implies to Don Pedro that she has formerly been more forthcoming with Benedick, and has suffered for it:

> *Indeed, my lord, he lent it me awhile, and I gave him use for it, a double heart for his single one. Marry, once before he won it of me with false dice, therefore your Grace may well say I have lost it.*
>
> (ACT 2, SCENE 1, LINES 278–82)

Benedick, a self-declared "profess'd tyrant to [the female] sex" (Act 1, Scene 1, line 169), is sometimes regarded by commentators as a witty misogynist, but it is possible that he simply shares Beatrice's anxieties about trust—also a major issue for Claudio and Hero. In dialogue, Benedick evinces a Renaissance male anxiety about being cuckolded:

ABOVE: *The influential English actor and impresario David Garrick (1717–79) played Benedick several times between 1748 and 1776. Benedick's witticisms and air of superiority fail to conceal his lack of self-knowledge.*

Beatrice — NIECE OF → Leonato
Leonato — BROTHERS — Antonio
Benedick — FALLS IN LOVE WITH → Beatrice
Hero — DAUGHTER OF → Leonato
Benedick — COMPANIONS — Claudio
Claudio — SUITOR OF → Hero
Margaret — ATTENDANT OF → Hero
Benedick — LORD ATTENDING → Don Pedro
Claudio — LORD ATTENDING → Don Pedro
Conrade — FOLLOWER OF → Don John
Borachio — POSES AS SUITOR OF → Margaret
Don Pedro — HALF-BROTHERS — Don John
Borachio — FOLLOWER OF → Don John

RELATIONSHIPS

The rivalry between the half-brothers, Don Pedro and the malcontent Don John, is a vital plot strand. While Don Pedro helps Claudio woo Hero, Don John does all he can to undermine his efforts.

RIGHT: *In a drama replete with pretence and deceit, Hero's unmasking, in Act 5, Scene 4, is a fitting denouement. Olivia Darnley played the role of Hero in a 2005 production at the Theatre Royal in Bath, England.*

> DON PEDRO *Well, as time shall try: "In time the savage bull doth bear the yoke."*
> BENEDICK *The savage bull may, but if ever the sensible Benedick bear it, pluck off the bull's horns, and set them in my forehead, and let me be vildly painted, and in such great letters as they write "Here is good horse to hire," let them signify under my sign, "Here you may see Benedick, the married man."*
> (ACT 1, SCENE 1, LINES 260–68)

Rallying to Hero's Defense

Although Claudio has won honor in war, the manner in which he rejects Hero suggests that he is not honorable in a broader sense. Ironically, he behaves in this way from a sense of affronted honor, but Beatrice has no doubt that Claudio is dishonorable:

> *Is 'a not approv'd in the height a villain, that hath slander'd, scorn'd, dishonor'd my kinswoman? O that I were a man! What, bear her in hand until they come to take hands, and then with public accusation, uncover'd slander, unmitigated rancor—O God, that I were a man! I would eat his heart in the market-place.*
> (ACT 4, SCENE 1, LINES 301–7)

By contrast, Benedick, who also "hath done good service" in the wars (Act 1, Scene 1, line 48) as well as conducting a "merry war" with many a "skirmish of wit" with Beatrice (Act 1, Scene 1, lines 62–63), can be prevailed upon to defend Hero by challenging his friend Claudio.

Friar Francis becomes convinced of Hero's innocence "By noting of the lady" (Act 4, Scene 1, line 158), and sets about restoring love by illusion, just as it has been destroyed by "mistaking"; he changes "slander to remorse" (Act 4, Scene 1, line 211). Soon Claudio and Don Pedro are isolated as a consequence of their misreading. Claudio must do penance before the play can end in a dance, and he asks Leonato to impose that penance: an epitaph at the family tomb, and a promise to marry Hero's supposed cousin, who is not only her spitting image, but also the heir to both Leonato and Antonio. Given the tragicomic tendency of the play, we might have expected something more testing. But the theatrical representation of penitence is always a problem, since it must necessarily be brief, and Valentine's remark in *The Two Gentlemen of Verona* is salutary: "Who by repentance is not satisfied / Is nor of heaven nor earth" (Act 5, Scene 4, lines 79–80).

Role-playing and Sincerity

It is to be hoped that Claudio plays the role of penitent sincerely, but the issue of role-playing and sincerity is widely explored in the play in relation to the themes of deceit and self-deceit. Both Beatrice and Benedick role-play indifference out of distrust (see Act 1, Scene 1, lines 166–69, 189–94), before Benedick succumbs to his friends' trickery and plays the role of a conventional courtly lover; this role in turn becomes a kind of caricature because he is so earnestly inverting his former pose. When Don Pedro woos Hero on Claudio's behalf, and his role is widely misinterpreted, neither he nor Claudio learns anything, and they are easily deceived by Don John, whose malevolent trickery contrasts with his half-brother's well-intentioned trickery of Beatrice and Benedick. Don John's villainy looks like role-playing because it is so predictably conventional, the resentful deceptions of the illegitimate (indeed, the quarto often calls him "Bastard" in speech prefixes and stage directions); he is a "plain-dealing villain" (Act 1, Scene 3, line 32) who tries to destroy love, just as Don Pedro tries to create it.

In this context, investigation of motive is vital—Dogberry's cowardly counsel to the Watch in Act 3, Scene 3, to let difficult situations alone, is seen as both absurd and dangerous. As it turns out, the Watch does arrest the malefactors, however incompetent Dogberry's subsequent examination of them may be, and Borachio points out to Don Pedro that "What your wisdoms could not discover, these shallow fools have brought to light" (Act 5, Scene 1, lines 232–34).

Kemp and Cowley

In the 1600 quarto, the speech prefixes in Act 4, Scene 2 substitute the name of the famous comic actor Will Kemp for Dogberry, and that of Dick Cowley for Verges. This suggests that Shakespeare wrote the parts for these actors, or they first played the roles, or both.

Marry, sir, they have committed false report; moreover they have spoken untruths; secondarily, they are slanders; sixt and lastly, they have belied a lady; thirdly, they have verified unjust things; and to conclude, they are lying knaves.

—*Dogberry* (ACT 5, SCENE 1, LINES 215–19)

BELOW: Dogberry's Charge to the Watch *(1859), by English artist Henry Stacey Marks, depicts the malapropian constable organizing his bumbling but ultimately successful citizen-police force.*

Manipulating Expectations

Given the extensive use of prose in the play, it is not surprising that there is limited "poetic" imagery. In keeping with the play's date and its punning title, much of its imagery is subservient to the witty wordplay in the dialogue, which is courtly in style, with plentiful use of rhetorical devices, Classical references, sexual innuendo, and allusions to courtly pursuits such as hunting.

Shakespeare often manipulates our expectations through his characters' imagery. Beatrice mockingly calls Benedick "Signior Mountanto" (Act 1, Scene 1, line 30), after the fencing term for a thrust, and has offered to eat those he kills in the war (Act 1, Scene 1, lines 44–45). Yet, when he comically transforms himself into a stage image of a conventional lover—washed, perfumed, made up, with his beard shaved off (Act 3, Scene 2)—Beatrice demands that he "Kill Claudio" (Act 4, Scene 1, line 289) to prove his love.

Borachio calls Don John "the devil my master" (Act 3, Scene 3, line 155) and speaks of his possessing Claudio and Don Pedro (line 156), but in the end we see him not as demonic, but as comic: dependent on Borachio, cowardly enough to run away, and slow enough to be caught. Dogberry's malapropisms give comic vitality to the play, but they make Leonato decline an examination that would prevent Claudio's denunciation of Hero:

> DOGBERRY *Our watch, sir, have indeed comprehended two aspicious persons, and we would have them this morning examin'd before your worship.*
> LEONATO *Take their examination yourself, and bring it me. I am now in great haste ...*
> (ACT 3, SCENE 5, LINES 45–50)

Consequently, at the play's climactic moment, Claudio continues to misread Hero, and uses a

RIGHT: *Claudio's sincere repentance rescues Hero from her feigned demise and from social obliteration. Robert Sean Leonard and Kate Beckinsale play the lovers in director Kenneth Branagh's 1993 film adaptation.*

striking verbal image directly related to the stage image he forms of a self-righteous young man mistakenly rejecting purity and fidelity at the altar:

There, Leonato, take her back again.
Give not this rotten orange to your friend,
She's but the sign and semblance of her honor.
(ACT 4, SCENE 1, LINES 31–33)

The rotten orange image is emblematic: oranges can keep up appearances while going bad on the inside. Hero's ambivalent blush, tending toward orange, is "guiltiness, not modesty", claims Claudio (line 42), but the audience knows better, and we may recall Beatrice's earlier comment that Claudio is "civil as an orange, and something of that jealous complexion" (Act 2, Scene 1, lines 294–95). Beatrice's pun on the word "Seville" suggests a parallel between Claudio and those yellowish and bitter oranges that is puzzling when she makes it, but seems apt at this later point in the play. In this instance, Shakespeare's use of imagery in relation to characterization is *poetically* complex and subtle.

Changing Ideals of Womanhood

Much Ado about Nothing has been a popular stage play from the beginning, except during the Restoration period, when it was displaced by William Davenant's adaptation, *The Law Against Lovers* (which combines elements of *Much Ado* and *Measure for Measure*). Although versions of the Claudio–Hero plot were popular during the Renaissance, it became clear early in the play's stage life that the Beatrice and Benedick story was its most appealing element. While Beatrice's assertive wit was well received in the eighteenth century (Hannah Pritchard and, later, Jane Pope and Frances Abington were especially well matched with David Garrick's Benedick), its "masculine" quality, which had of course suited the male apprentice actor who originally played the part, was problematic for Victorian audiences, culturally conditioned to expect idealized images of "tender" womanhood. Thus, in the nineteenth century, the most admired Beatrices were actors who managed to balance wit with feeling and a light touch: Ellen Tree and, later, Ellen Terry were acclaimed on both sides of the Atlantic, and Helena Modjeska was a great hit in New York and on the American circuit toward the end of the century.

Beatrice has been played very differently since the second half of the twentieth century, as the popularization of feminist principles has changed preconceptions about female behavior, and directors have emphasized the play's gender politics. An early example of the modern dominant Beatrice was Katharine Hepburn in Stratford, Connecticut, in 1957; other memorable Beatrices in modern English productions have included Maggie Smith in director Franco Zeffirelli's London production of 1965, which emphasized the patriarchal Sicilian setting; Janet Suzman in director Trevor Nunn's 1968 Stratford, England, staging, which drew attention to the dark elements in the Claudio–Hero story; and Judi Dench as a middle-aged spinster, beautifully matched with Donald Sinden in the 1976–77 Stratford, England, production directed by John Barton, using an Indian Raj setting. More recently, Yolanda Vasquez played Beatrice opposite Josie Lawrence as Benedick in an all-female production directed by Tamara Harvey at the Globe, London, in 2004.

The play has been successfully adapted for film and television, initially in the United States, with a Hollywood silent film in 1926 (directed by Arthur Rosson). There was a BBC television version of Zeffirelli's stage production in 1967 and a *Much Ado* in a BBC/Time-Life series of Shakespeare plays, directed by Stuart Burge in 1984 and starring Cherie Lunghi and Robert Lindsay. But the 1993 Hollywood film, directed by Kenneth Branagh, who also played Benedick, and with Emma Thompson as Beatrice and a constellation of film stars in other parts (Kate Beckinsale as Hero, Robert Sean Leonard as Claudio, Denzel Washington as Don Pedro, Keanu Reeves as Don John, and Michael Keaton as Dogberry), has had more impact than any other production. It is both energetic and sensuous, and does justice to the more disturbing elements in the Claudio–Hero story, if at the expense of Beatrice and Benedick's verbal jousting and the subtler comic elements in the Dogberry part of the plot.

Pseudo-death and "Resurrection"

In this play, as in *Romeo and Juliet*, a friar devises a pseudo-death and "resurrection," with the intention of preserving love. This is appropriate, not only because of the religious role of friars (to preach Christ's death and resurrection as manifestations of divine love) but also because they have a degree of social autonomy, since their direct ministry to the people bypasses issues of local authority. In *Romeo and Juliet*, simulated death and resurrection represent the hopefulness of love but cannot prevent a tragic ending. In *Much Ado*, a simpler love-death nexus has a happy outcome, although the pretense of death after swooning underlines the serious social and emotional consequences of Claudio's denunciation of Hero. Friar Francis is helpfully articulate about the social symbolism involved in Hero's playing dead: her life in society has been killed by slander, and her only hope is "resurrection" into a reconstructed relationship with Claudio (Act 4, Scene 1, lines 210–43).

Twelfth Night

THE PLOT: *In Illyria, Duke Orsino courts the Countess Olivia, who, in mourning for her brother, refuses to pay heed to him. Olivia's uncle, Sir Toby, meanwhile, tries to match her with the pitiful Sir Andrew Aguecheek, although the two men spend most of their time drinking with Feste, the clown. Into this topsy-turvy world enters Viola, survivor of a shipwreck. Viola, to protect herself until she can establish her identity, disguises herself as a boy (Cesario). She falls in love with Duke Orsino, and, unwittingly, becomes the object of Olivia's desires. In a subplot, Olivia's steward, Malvolio, is gulled into thinking that Olivia loves him. Meanwhile, Viola's twin brother, Sebastian, thought lost in the same shipwreck, arrives in Illyria. Chaos ensues. Sebastian marries Olivia and is then reunited with his twin. Once Viola has revealed that she is a woman, Orsino declares he will marry her. The final moment is marred when the wronged Malvolio calls out for revenge, and then exits.*

Dramatis Personae

Orsino, *Duke of Illyria*
Sebastian, *brother to Viola*
Antonio, *a sea captain, friend to Sebastian*
Sea Captain, *friend to Viola*
Valentine, Curio, *gentlemen attending on the Duke*
Sir Toby Belch, *uncle to Olivia*
Sir Andrew Aguecheek
Malvolio, *steward to Olivia*
Fabian, Feste *(a clown), servants to Olivia*
Olivia, *a rich countess*
Vlola, *sister to Sebastian*
Maria, *Olivia's gentlewoman*
Lords, Priests, Sailors, Officers, Musicians, Gentlewoman, Servant, and other Attendants

WRITTEN
c. 1601–2

SETTING AND PERIOD
Illyria, a semifictional country, *c.* 1600

CHARACTERS 18

ACTS 5

SCENES 18

LINES 2,591

BELOW: *In Act 3, Scene 4, the steward Malvolio, played here by Richard Cordery at the Royal Shakespeare Theatre in Stratford in 2005, is deceived into believing that Olivia (Aislin McGuckin) wants him to wear yellow stockings and cross-garters—which really she abhors—and smile a lot.*

The offhand double title, *Twelfth Night, or What You Will* (the only double title in the Shakespeare canon), might lead us to take a casual stance toward the play. Here, we might think, is something the Bard quickly tossed off: a piece of comic fluff for us to enjoy and forget. Certainly, *Twelfth Night* possesses frantic comic energy, as well as an intricate plot, tireless wordplay, and characters who, rather like billiard balls, encounter each other only to set off on new trajectories.

Illyria, furthermore, a semifictional land with a seacoast, might be seen as no more than a place of fantasy, another land of Cockaigne—it certainly doesn't resemble the Illyria of Classical antiquity, the northwestern part of the Balkan Peninsula. At its core, however, the play deals with profound themes: identity, mortality, and madness. These are dealt with in far greater depth than in the principal source for *Twelfth Night,* the story of "Apollonius and Silla," contained in *Riche His Farewell to Militarie Profession*, by English author and soldier Barnabe Riche (1581).

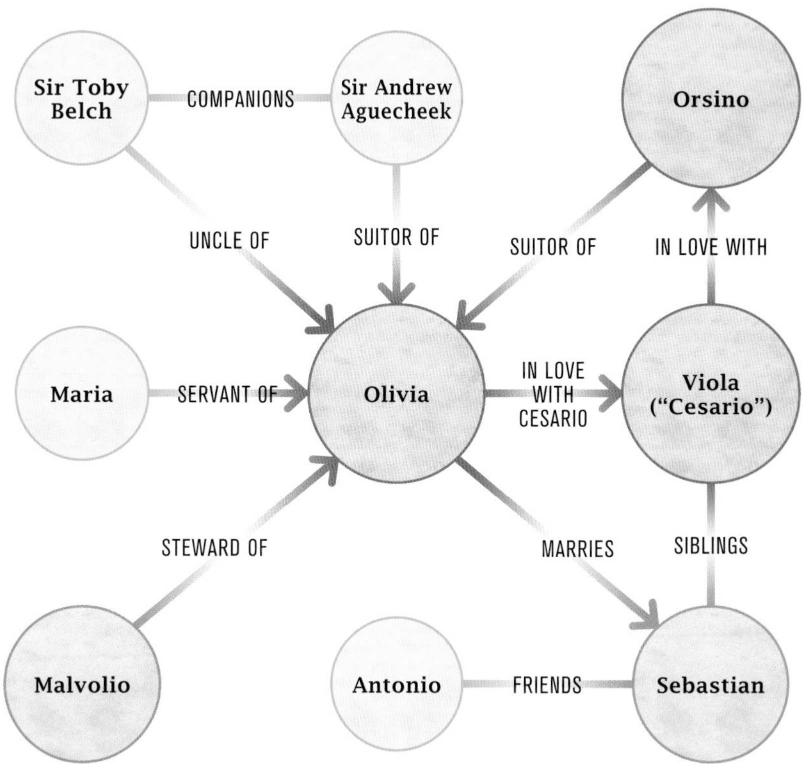

RELATIONSHIPS
Characters and events revolve around the Countess Olivia, who is not only adored in turn by Duke Orsino and Viola's brother, Sebastian, but also, in an entertaining subplot, by her steward, Malvolio.

Identities Transformed

The central characters in Illyria, apparently a stagnant place, are, like Malvolio, "sick of self-love" (Act 1, Scene 5, line 90), and their identities seem closed off from the possibilities of change. Viola's arrival, as Cesario, throws this into sharp relief. Out of the tangle of their vanities, she transforms two of the characters: Orsino and Olivia. As they become attracted to Viola/Cesario as if by the gravity of a star, these two become somewhat manic, but they also begin to take an energetic interest in the world outside of themselves.

Orsino, for example, who in his first speech spends much time extolling music and love (without ever mentioning his beloved's name), comes to notice Viola/Cesario as a particular and unique human being:

> *Diana's lip*
> *Is not more smooth and rubious; thy small pipe*
> *Is as the maiden's organ, shrill and sound,*
> *And all is semblative a woman's part.*
> (ACT 1, SCENE 4, LINES 31–34)

The homoerotic moment may startle Orsino (surely it startles Viola), but the point is that his attention has been drawn away from himself. If only for a moment, he completely forgets his obsessive, rather tired, love of the distant Olivia—and it is Viola who, later, must return him to the plot at hand: "Sir, shall I to this lady?" she asks (Act 2, Scene 4, line 122). Orsino, as if he had lost his train of thought, replies, "Ay, that's the theme" (Act 2, Scene 4, line 122). The real theme, of course, is the unselfish affection Orsino has begun to feel for Viola. The restrictions placed on them by their seemingly same-sex gender only add a kind of titillating spice to the situation—as does the wooing of Viola/Cesario by Olivia.

A Startling Metamorphosis

Olivia, perhaps, undergoes the most startling metamorphosis when she meets Viola/Cesario. She quickly begins asking questions, directing her interest outward, and, within a shamefully small number of lines, draws her mourning veil aside and invites Viola/Cesario to inspect her beauty, stating,

> *I will give out divers schedules of my beauty. It shall be inventoried, and every particle and utensil labell'd to my will: as,* item, *two lips, indifferent red;* item, *two grey eyes, with lids to them;* item, *one neck, one chin, and so forth.*
> (ACT 1, SCENE 5, LINES 244–49)

She flirts and she banters. That she flirts with another woman adds to the absurdity of the plot. That in Shakespeare's time these parts were usually played by two male actors only added to the sexual tension. Instead of weeping for her brother, Olivia finds herself caught in the toils of love. It is not necessarily a pleasant sensation: Olivia likens it to catching the plague.

It is Viola, however, one of Shakespeare's most beloved heroines, who has the greatest need to

ABOVE: *With Helen Hayes and Maurice Evans in the lead roles,* Twelfth Night *had a strong run in 1940 at the St. James Theatre, Broadway, New York.*

establish her self. Viola loses her identity to circumstance, not to love, moments after her arrival on the beaches of Illyria. As she states to Olivia, "What I am, and what I would, are as secret as maidenhead" (Act 1, Scene 5, lines 215–16). It is Sebastian who eventually proves himself the anchor to Viola's identity: in his face, the reflection of her own, Viola finds, at the end of the play, an assurance of her past.

Deep Shadows

Twelfth Night is far from being too objectionably light, bright, and sparkling. This seemingly light comedy casts deep shadows, and airy motifs of misconstrued identity and love triumphant intertwine with themes of death and madness. *Twelfth Night* strains the very nature of the comic genre—which may not surprise, given its close proximity to the composition of *Hamlet*.

Mortality is central to the play, both in theme and imagery. Despite the practical jokes, the lively wordplay, and the air of the ridiculous, *Twelfth Night* reminds us that we are all mortal, most poignantly in Feste's songs of the brevity of youth and the inevitability of death:

In delay there lies no plenty,
Then come kiss me sweet and twenty;
Youth's a stuff will not endure.
(ACT 2, SCENE 3, LINES 50–52)

The play, moreover, is framed with instances of the fragility of life: it commences with the contemplation of the death of Olivia's brother, and it ends with the wounds of Sir Toby and a threat of murder. Life is brief and fraught with peril; if this is to be a comedy, the characters need to find their marriage partners quickly.

Shakespeare also invites us to see that the characters in Illyria are all a little unstable. Sebastian's reaction to the population is to ask, "Are all the people mad?" (Act 4, Scene 1, line 27). Yet Sebastian is willing to marry a woman he has just met: "I am mad," he states, "Or else the lady's

Words of Love

If music be the food of love, play on,
Give me excess of it; that surfeiting,
The appetite may sicken, and so die.
That strain again, it had a dying fall;
O, it came o'er my ear like the sweet sound
That breathes upon a bank of violets,
Stealing and giving odor …
—*Orsino* (ACT 1, SCENE 1, LINES 1–7)

Come away, come away, death,
And in sad cypress let me be laid.
[Fly] away, [fly] away, breath,
I am slain by a fair cruel maid.
—*Feste* (ACT 2, SCENE 4, LINES 51–54)

she never told her love,
But let concealment like a worm i' th' bud
Feed on her damask cheek; she pin'd in thought,
And with a green and yellow melancholy
She sate like Patience on a monument,
Smiling at grief …
—*Viola* (ACT 2, SCENE 4, LINES 110–15)

mad" (Act 4, Scene 3, lines 15–16). Orsino wishes to marry a woman he has, up until the last moments of the play, thought to be a man. And, as we follow the frantic pace of the plot of *Twelfth Night*, perhaps we might be accused of madness ourselves—the kind of madness that comes when theater starts working its magic. The words of the Cheshire Cat in Lewis Carroll's *Alice's Adventures in Wonderland* come to mind: "We're all mad here. You're mad. I'm mad." Illyria is not Wonderland, but it is not far from it.

Water Everywhere

Shakespeare may have set his play in Illyria because that ancient place was known to be surrounded by water. *Twelfth Night* opens with a brush with death from drowning, and from that moment on imagery of drowning floods the play: characters are awash with ale, or tears, or sea-water. Sir Toby drinks so much that Olivia remarks that "he's in the third degree of drink, he's drown'd" (Act 1, Scene 5, line 135). Indeed, drunkenness mars the happy ending of the play: when Sir Toby and Sir Andrew need their wounds dressed, they find that the surgeon is drunk "an hour agone; his eyes were set at eight i' th' morning" (Act 5, Scene 1, lines 198–99). The play's drunkards remain, disturbingly, unhealed at the end of the final act.

Tears, too, are associated with drowning. Sebastian begins to weep as he describes his sister, Viola, to Antonio:

> *[S]he bore a mind that envy could not but call fair. She is drown'd already, sir, with salt water, though I seem to drown her remembrance again with more.*
> (ACT 2, SCENE 1, LINES 29–32)

Sebastian's tears threaten to cut off his description of Viola—salt tears are in this case, like salt water,

As I am man,/My state is desperate for my master's love;/ As I am woman (now alas the day!),/What thriftless sighs shall poor Olivia breathe!/O time, thou must untangle this, not I,/ It is too hard a knot for me t' untie.

—*Viola* (ACT 2, SCENE 2, LINES 36–41)

BELOW: *Directed by Peter Hall, Dorothy Tutin (right) played Viola and Geraldine McEwan appeared as Olivia in the Royal Shakespeare Company's 1960 production of* Twelfth Night *at the Aldwych Theatre in London.*

Breeches Parts

In Shakespeare's time, the female roles were usually played by men. So, in *Twelfth Night*, a boy actor would don a dress to play Viola and then change to breeches when Viola disguised herself as a boy. As a result, in the eighteenth and nineteenth centuries, when women began to play the female characters, the kinds of roles in which women would put on male garb became known as "breeches parts." Some found such exhibitions of the female leg improper, but the plot device enjoyed considerable popularity.

dangerous. They render Sebastian momentarily dumb, his memorial to Viola unspoken. Even Olivia's tears, meant to keep the memory of her brother alive, are "eye-offending", unsalutary, and described, rather unromantically, as "brine" (Act 1, Scene 1, line 29)—and thus linked to the salt water of the sea.

Seawater can drown, but it can also be benevolent. Both Viola and Sebastian, for example, narrowly escape drowning. And when Viola is cast up on the shores of Illyria, she, in a parallel to baptism, takes a new name: Cesario. Sebastian, when he comes to the coast of Illyria, becomes Rodorigo. It is not going too far to see this imagery of water as providing characters with new life, new hope, new possibilities. As Viola suggests, "Tempests are kind and salt waves fresh in love" (Act 3, Scene 4, line 384).

A Night of Revelry

Twelfth Night, January 6, is the Eve of the Epiphany, the day on which the Magi visited the infant Jesus, and concludes the Twelve Days of Christmas. In Shakespeare's time, it involved misrule, revelry, and carnival, when "cakes and ale" weighed down the tables, and ginger was "hot i' th' mouth" (Act 2, Scene 3, lines 116–18). This atmosphere pervades the play.

BELOW: *The title of Dutch painter Jan Havicksz Steen's painting* The Feast of Kings *(1660) is another name for the Twelfth Night festival, the kings being the Three Wise Men, or Magi.*

"The Food of Love"

More disturbing, perhaps, is the imagery of love as an act of appetite and digestion. Duke Orsino opens the play by juxtaposing love and hunger: "If music be the food of love, play on" (Act 1, Scene 1, line 1). Orsino gives love sway to feed, until he envisions "surfeiting" (Act 1, Scene 1, line 2). Orsino's desire is a monster. It is "as hungry as the sea, / And can digest as much" (Act 2, Scene 4, lines 100–101). Such is the nature of male obsession—as Orsino explains to the (probably) taken-aback Viola/Cesario. He accuses women, on the other hand, of lust:

> *Alas, their love may be call'd appetite,*
> *No motion of the liver, but the palate,*
> *That suffer surfeit, cloyment, and revolt[.]*
> (ACT 2, SCENE 4, LINES 97–99)

Women fill up with love and get sick—much as, ironically, Orsino sickened of music in Act 1, Scene 1. Despite his capacious hunger for love, Orsino knows very little about loving at the beginning of the play.

Willing a Happy Ending

Twelfth Night is a comedy that fights against time to remain a comedy. The characters mourn, court, drink, dance, and love, but, at the end, they teeter on the verge of sending the play into a spiral of murder and revenge. Just as *The Winter's Tale* ends happily largely through the last-minute machinations of Paulina, *Twelfth Night* remains a comedy only through Orsino's final optimism. Near the end, after all, Sir Toby is wounded and livid with rage; Sir Andrew is wounded and betrayed; Orsino muses about killing Viola/Cesario; and Malvolio seeks vengeance.

Orsino and Viola, when they acknowledge their love for each other, do not even have an onstage hug. Duke Orsino does promise to embrace Viola once she puts on her dress, but that moment may be deferred indefinitely—the ship's captain who has Viola's clothes is in "durance, at Malvolio's suit" (Act 5, Scene 1, line 276), and so unavailable to retrieve the garments. Revenge is in the air—as Feste notes, "the whirligig of time brings in his

LEFT: *In Trevor Nunn's film* Twelfth Night *(1996), English actor Ben Kingsley played Feste as an enigmatic loner who knows more than he will say.*

revenges" (Act 5, Scene 1, lines 376–77)—and Malvolio threatens to bring it down on them, ranting that he'll "be reveng'd on the whole pack of you" (Act 5, Scene 1, line 378).

Orsino, however, looks into the future, beyond the confines of the text, for his happy ending:

Pursue him [Malvolio], and entreat him to a
peace;
He hath not told us of the captain yet.
When that is known, and golden time convents,
A solemn combination shall be made
Of our dear souls. Mean time, sweet sister,
We will not part from hence. Cesario, come—
For so you shall be while you are a man;
But when in other habits you are seen,
Orsino's mistress, and his fancy's queen.
(ACT 5, SCENE 1, LINES 380–88)

Completion remains in the future. The action of the play moves to the "mean time," where the audience cannot follow.

Feste remains a moment to leave us with another song about the trials of life: "For the rain it raineth every day" (Act 5, Scene 1, line 392). In the sacred community of the playhouse, however, players and playgoers will gather again, to enjoy another moment when misery gives way onstage to comic good fortune, and a glimpse of a future that holds something inestimably bright.

Sophisticated Clowning

It is fitting that the enigmatic Feste has the last word. Around 1600, Will Kemp, who usually played Shakespeare's lower-class bumbling clowns, was replaced by the witty Robert Armin, who played Feste in *Twelfth Night*. With the advent of Armin, Shakespeare was able to write parts for fools that were filled with sophisticated wordplay. The difference between Kemp and Armin was like the difference between the comedy of the Three Stooges and that of the Marx Brothers.

In director Trevor Nunn's 1996 film version, set in the nineteenth century, Ben Kingsley plays Feste as a figure set apart. This fine, sometimes dark, film deserves more general acclaim, but has been overshadowed by more pyrotechnical movie adaptations of some of Shakespeare's other plays.

O mistress mine, where are you roaming?/ O, stay and hear, your true-love's coming,/ That can sing both high and low./Trip no further, pretty sweeting;/Journeys end in lovers meeting,/Every wise man's son doth know.

—*Feste* (ACT 2, SCENE 3, LINES 39–44)

All's Well That Ends Well

RIGHT: *Helena (Zoe Caldwell) enlists the help of the Widow (Angela Baddeley) in her quest for Bertram's affection in Tyrone Guthrie's 1959 production in Stratford. Helena is supported by a group of female characters who believe in her intrinsic worth.*

THE PLOT: *Helena, the orphan of a physician, has fallen in love with Bertram, the Count of Rossillion. After curing the gravely ill King of France, she asks to marry Bertram as reward. The King forces the reluctant Count to accept this lowborn wife. Bertram immediately leaves for war in Italy with his companion Parolles. In an elaborate prank, Parolles is fooled into believing he has been captured by the enemy and betrays Bertram. In a letter to Helena, Bertram declares that he will only accept the marriage if she obtains a ring from his finger and bears his child. With the help of Diana, whom Bertram has been wooing, Helena is able to trick the Count into sleeping with her. The play concludes when Helena appears at court, pregnant and wearing Bertram's ring. Providing Helena can fully explain herself, the humbled Count agrees to love her "dearly."*

WRITTEN
c. 1604–5

SETTING AND PERIOD
Rossillion, Paris, Marseilles, and Florence, *c.* sixteenth century

CHARACTERS 16

ACTS 5

SCENES 23 plus Epilogue

LINES 3,013

Dramatis Personae

King of France
Duke of Florence
Bertram, *Count of Rossillion*
Lafew, *an old lord*
Parolles, *a parasitical follower of Bertram*
Two French Lords, *in the Florentine service*
Rinaldo, *a steward, servant to the Countess of Rossillion*
Lavatch, *a clown, servant to the Countess of Rossillion*
Page, *servant to the Countess of Rossillion*
Countess of Rossillion, *mother to Bertram*
Helena, *a gentlewoman protected by the Countess*
An old Widow of Florence
Diana, *daughter to the Widow*
Violenta, Mariana, *neighbors and friends to the Widow*
Lords, Officers, Soldiers, etc., French and Florentine

All's Well That Ends Well dates from around 1604–5, a period in which Shakespeare wrote plays featuring dark themes, unsettling endings, and anguished characters as well as lighter, comic moments. These "problem plays," as they are generally known, mark the beginning of Shakespeare's experimentation with genre, culminating in the sophisticated mix of comedy and tragedy that characterizes his late writing.

Jacobean Parallels

The King of France shapes the plot of the play by allowing and then enforcing the marriage between Helena and Bertram; this may reflect Shakespeare's perception of the recently crowned King James I. After his father's death, Bertram becomes the King's ward and so must accept his command. Jacobean England employed a similar system: James I controlled the state of any nobleman who inherited his family's estate before the age of twenty-one. In 1604, the potential abuses of the wards and guardian system were debated in Parliament. The King's ability to decide that Bertram should marry Helena may have been an oblique commentary on this same debate.

Age and Youth

In *All's Well,* an older generation of characters (the Countess, the King, Lafew, the Widow) provide nostalgic commentaries alongside the present events of the play. This strong sense of the past gives the play a depth beyond the momentum of the plot. Observing lovelorn Helena, the Countess comments: "Even so it was with me when I was young" (Act 1, Scene 3, line 112). During Act 1, Scene 2, the King longingly eulogizes his friendship with Bertram's dead father:

He lasted long,
But on us both did haggish age steal on,
And wore us out of act. It much repairs me
To talk of your good father …
(ACT 1, SCENE 2, LINES 28–31)

The younger characters provide the plot's momentum, but rely on the insightful support of their elders; age and youth work together. In particular, the older characters' support of Helena serves to dissipate potential antagonism toward the "upwardly mobile" daughter of a physician. The older characters, in fact, facilitate Helena's rapid social advancement on the basis of her worthiness: the Countess admiringly refers to Helena as her daughter—"I say I am your mother" (Act 1, Scene 3, line 142). The play is a complex depiction of life in transition between the old and the new generations.

Inspired By ...

All's Well That Ends Well is a complex version of a story in William Painter's *The Palace of Pleasure* (1566), a translation of Italian poet Giovanni Boccaccio's *Decameron.* At the end of Boccaccio's tale, Giletta (Helena's character) is embraced by her husband because she has secretly raised his twin sons and managed his estate while he was at war.

Class Division

Helena is acutely aware of her social inferiority to Bertram. She laments her situation:

That I should love a bright particular star
And think to wed it, he is so above me.
In his bright radiance and collateral light
Must I be comforted, not in his sphere.
(ACT 1, SCENE 1, LINES 86–89)

BELOW: *The Countess (Judi Dench) looks kindly on Helena (Claudie Blakley), with Bertram (Jamie Glover) and Lafew (Charles Kay), in a scene from the 2003 Royal Shakespeare Company production in Stratford.*

Bertram is equally mindful. His response to her proposal of marriage is incredulous snobbery: "A poor physician's daughter my wife!" (Act 2, Scene 3, line 115). Their marriage is probably the most socially mixed in Shakespeare's canon and may have shocked his audience. *All's Well* forces audiences to question the status afforded by class. Bertram's family name entitles him to the status of an honorable man, but his behavior toward Helena is distinctly dishonorable. Helena, on the other hand, exhibits the moral judgment, courtesy, and wisdom traditionally associated with nobility. She is intrinsically honorable. As the King notes:

She is young, wise, fair,
In these to nature she's immediate heir;
And these breed honor …
(ACT 2, SCENE 3, LINES 131–33)

Another contrast to Helena's virtue is established in Parolles, who pursues social advancement with arrogance and without merit. As Lord Lafew rails at him: "You are more saucy with lords and honorable personages than the commission of your birth and virtue gives you heraldry" (Act 2, Scene 3, lines 260–62).

Sexual Politics, Romance, and Realism

All's Well reverses the traditional gender roles by foregrounding the assertive actions of a woman. From the opening scene, Helena reveals her progressive thinking when she suggests that a woman should be able to lose her virginity "to her own liking" (Act 1, Scene 1, line 151). Controversially for a woman on Shakespeare's stage, Helena explicitly expresses sexual pleasure, mentioning Bertram's "sweet use" (Act 4, Scene 4, line 22) in bed. But Helena does not work alone; she achieves her aims through a network of female support. The Countess, for instance, threatens to disown Bertram because of his behavior, while the Widow and Diana help Helena to perform the bed-trick.

The narratives of many fairy tales describe the arrival of a lowborn young man at court, who completes a demanding task and wins the hand of a virtuous princess. Bertram's initial rejection of Helena is a rejection of this fairy tale narrative. Romance conflicts with the realities of gender and social inequality. While "happy ever after" seems to have been achieved at the end of the play, the title *All's Well That Ends Well* is nevertheless a provocative invitation to interrogate this very ending. Helena has won Bertram, but his behavior, and particularly his desperate lying in the final scene, lead us to question whether he is worthy of his wife. Does it really "end well" for Helena?

BERTRAM *If she, my liege, can make me know this clearly,*
I'll love her dearly, ever, ever dearly.
HELENA *If it appear not plain and prove untrue,*
Deadly divorce step between me and you!
(ACT 5, SCENE 3, LINES 315–18)

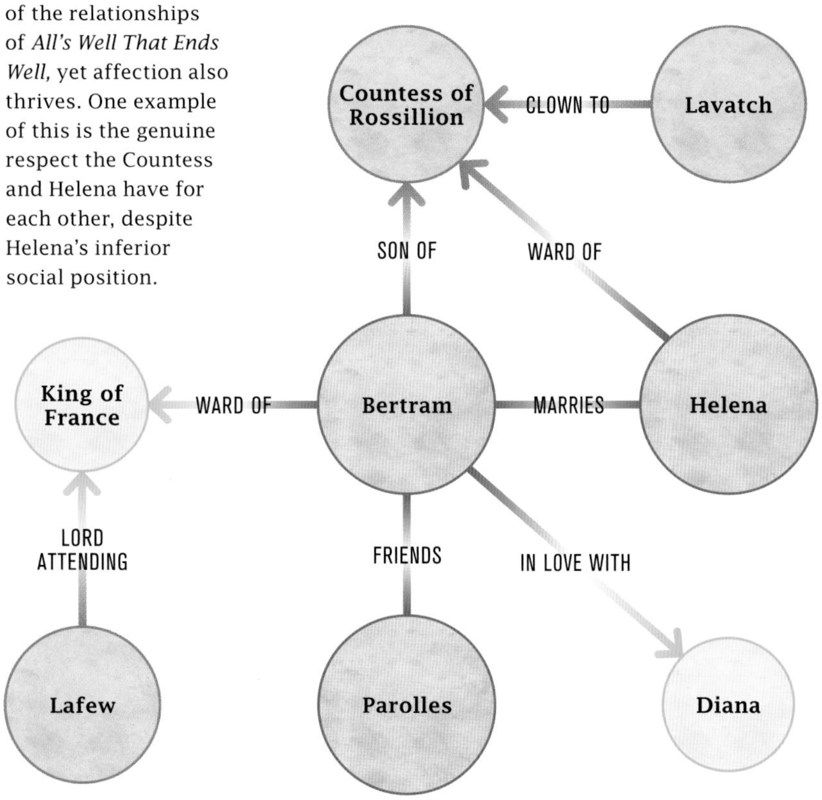

RELATIONSHIPS
Obligation and duty characterize many of the relationships of *All's Well That Ends Well,* yet affection also thrives. One example of this is the genuine respect the Countess and Helena have for each other, despite Helena's inferior social position.

Countess of Rossillion
CLOWN TO
Lavatch
SON OF
WARD OF
King of France
WARD OF
Bertram
MARRIES
Helena
LORD ATTENDING
FRIENDS
IN LOVE WITH
Lafew
Parolles
Diana

Quotable Helena

Our remedies oft in ourselves do lie,
Which we ascribe to heaven …
(ACT 1, SCENE 1, LINES 216–17)

Dear sir, to my endeavors give consent,
Of heaven, not me, make an experiment.
(ACT 2, SCENE 1, LINES 153–54)

Let us assay our plot, which if it speed,
Is wicked meaning in a lawful deed,
And lawful meaning in a lawful act,
Where both not sin, and yet a sinful fact.
(ACT 3, SCENE 7, LINES 44–47)

All's well that ends well! still the fine's the crown;
What e'er the course, the end is the renown.
(ACT 4, SCENE 4, LINES 35–36)

All's well that ends well yet,
Though time seem so adverse and means unfit.
(ACT 5, SCENE 1, LINES 25–26)

ABOVE: *Esteemed English actress Peggy Ashcroft appeared as the Countess of Rossillion in Trevor Nunn's production of* All's Well *for the Royal Shakespeare Company, 1981. Nunn described the play as "Shakespeare's most Chekhovian."*

Bertram, directing his comments to the King, states he will love Helena only if she can verify the events of the play; Helena offers him the possibility of divorce. There is the chance the marriage may not be resolved, leaving the prospect that we have not witnessed the story's "end."

Reiterating Imagery

All's Well That Ends Well stages a battle of the sexes, in which male courting is figured as sexual warfare. Similar imagery appears in *Troilus and Cressida,* written around the same time. In the opening scene, Helena notes how men aggressively pursue women, and asks Parolles how women can resist: "But he assails, and our virginity though valiant, in the defense yet is weak. Unfold to us some warlike resistance" (Act 1, Scene 1, lines 115–17). Helena's image of men as aggressive attackers of female honor is realized later by Bertram's courting of Diana. The Widow again employs the image of female resistance: "But she is arm'd for him, and keeps her guard / In honestest defense" (Act 3, Scene 5, lines 73–74).

> *The web of our life is of a mingled yarn, good and ill together.*
>
> 
>
> —First Lord (ACT 4, SCENE 3, LINES 71–72)

Bertram's ring is central to the plot but also represents the themes of the play. He describes the ring as "an honor 'longing to our house / Bequeathed down from many ancestors" (Act 4, Scene 2, lines 42–43), a physical manifestation of his noble family name. Using this ring to woo Diana compounds Bertram's dishonoring of this name. However, at the end of the play, Helena perhaps wishes that the ring represented what it is traditionally supposed to: marriage, faith, and love.

A Heroine for Modern Times?

Scholars and audiences have had mixed responses to *All's Well That Ends Well,* in particular the character of Helena. In the eighteenth century, Helena's speeches were edited to reduce her assertiveness; for instance, her bawdy conversation with Parolles about virginity (Act 1, Scene 1, lines 106–86) was completely cut. In an 1894 adaptation of the play (entitled *Priyaradhana or Propitiation of a Lover*) in Poona, India, Helena bewails her misery in song and attributes her bad luck to her misdeeds in a past life. Even in the early twentieth century, playwright George Bernard Shaw argued that Helena was "too modern" for audiences. However, the number of performances has since increased. Director Tyrone Guthrie launched the first Stratford Ontario Shakespeare Festival in 1953 with a critically acclaimed production of the play. The success of seminal productions by directors Trevor Nunn in 1981–83 (Stratford, London, New York), and Gregory Doran at the Royal Shakespeare Company (Stratford) in 2003, show that the play's depiction of the realities of sexual and class politics resonates with modern audiences.

WRITTEN	c. 1604
SETTING AND PERIOD	Vienna, c. sixteenth century
CHARACTERS	23
ACTS	5
SCENES	17
LINES	2,891

Measure for Measure

THE PLOT: *Vincentio, Duke of Vienna, embarks on a journey, leaving the upright Angelo as his deputy, but secretly returns disguised as Friar Lodowick. Angelo imposes strict penalties against sexual misconduct, and on finding that Claudio has made his betrothed, Juliet, pregnant, sentences him to death. Claudio's sister, Isabella, a trainee nun, pleads for her brother. Consumed by lust, Angelo offers Isabella the choice of sleeping with him in exchange for Claudio's life. Isabella refuses. Vincentio, as Friar Lodowick, convinces Isabella to trick Angelo by offering sex, but then arranges for Angelo's ex-fiancée, Mariana, to take her place. Despite his promises, Angelo still orders Claudio's death. He is then shown the head of a dead prisoner, which he takes to be that of Claudio. Vincentio abandons his disguise, and Angelo is denounced as a hypocrite and murderer; Mariana and Isabella, however, plead for leniency on his behalf. Claudio is shown to be alive, Angelo is forgiven and married to Mariana, and Vincentio surprisingly offers to marry Isabella.*

RIGHT: *King James I of England (reigned 1603–25) and VI of Scotland (reigned 1567–1625) was an enthusiastic patron of the company of actors to which Shakespeare belonged, which in turn came to be known as the King's Men. This portrait of James, by the Flemish artist Paul Van Somer, dates from* c. *1610.*

Like over half the works printed in the 1623 Folio edition of Shakespeare's plays, no version of *Measure for Measure* has survived from prior to that date. Scholars are therefore unsure how far the play represents Shakespeare's original intentions or how much it was adapted by another playwright, Thomas Middleton. We do know that it was presented on December 26, 1604, at the Banqueting Hall in Whitehall, London, in a royal performance for Shakespeare's patron, King James I. After that, however, the play appears to disappear from favor, possibly because of the dubious sexual behavior of many of its characters, and the overt references to prostitution and sexual disease, which so offended later critics. A twentieth-century reawakening of interest in the social implications of the play's engagement with problems of power, justice, sexuality, and the role of women in society has ensured that *Measure for Measure* continues to foster topical debate and controversy.

Matters of Life and Death

Shakespeare's play was written and performed following a time of great political uncertainty and apprehension. After the death of Queen Elizabeth I in 1603, the political vacuum created as a result of her dying childless was filled by the nation's new Scottish monarch, King James. Unfortunately, James's arrival in London coincided with a virulent outbreak of the plague, a disease that killed one in three Londoners that year. Nobody knew its cause or how it was spread, but all recognized the danger of people gathering in large numbers, especially to see plays, so the playhouses were forcibly closed. Many believed that the plague was a punishment of God. The vice districts of London, the "suburbs" or "stews" as they were known, came under particular attack, with "houses of ill repute" forcibly closed

Dramatis Personae

Vincentio, *the Duke*
Angelo, *the Deputy*
Escalus, *an ancient lord*
Claudio, *a young gentleman*
Lucio, *a fantastic*
Two other like Gentlemen
Provost
Thomas, Peter, *two friars*
Justice
Varrius
Elbow, *a simple constable*
Froth, *a foolish gentleman*
Pompey, *clown, servant to Mistress Overdone*
Abhorson, *an executioner*
Barnardine, *a dissolute prisoner*
Servant
Isabella, *sister to Claudio*
Mariana, *betrothed to Angelo*
Juliet, *beloved of Claudio*
Francisca, *a nun*
Mistress Overdone, *a bawd*
Lords, Officers, Citizens, Boy, and Attendants

Inspired By ...

The plot derives from a story in the *Ecatommiti* (*Hundred Tales*, 1565) by Italian dramatist and poet Giambattista Giraldi, also adapted as a play by English dramatist George Whetstone (1578) and Giraldi himself (1583). In the story, Juriste offers Epitia, sister of Vico (jailed for raping a virgin), her brother's life if she sleeps with him. Epitia accepts. Juriste beheads Vico anyway, and Epitia appeals to the Emperor. Juriste is ordered to marry Epitia before being executed, but Epitia pleads successfully for her husband's life.

LEFT: *The Stratford-upon-Avon staging of* Measure for Measure *in 1950, with John Gielgud as Angelo and Barbara Jefford as Isabella, is seen as a milestone for its use of simple sets and restoration of the full text after centuries of truncated versions.*

and demolished. Prostitution and venereal disease, as well as the nation's morality, were subjects that many believed, quite literally, were matters of life and death. Shakespeare's *Measure for Measure* taps into this moral paranoia, at the same time making fascinating comment on the concepts of blame and guilt, good and evil.

Why Shakespeare chose to relocate his topical play to faraway Vienna remains a mystery. Was he, as some believe, shielding his social comments behind a thin veneer of foreignness, or might "Vienna," as others have argued, be a later alteration for the Folio, the play originally being set in Italy? It is unlikely we will ever know.

Justice and Mercy

The balance between justice and mercy is fundamental to *Measure for Measure*. Even the play's title alludes to a passage from the New Testament: "Judge not, that ye be not judged. For with that judgment ye judge, ye shall be judged, and with that measure you mete, it shall be measured to you again" (Matthew 7: 1–2). It is with this in mind that Isabella, when first pleading on behalf of her brother, asks of the intransigent Angelo:

> *How would you be*
> *If He, which is the top of judgment, should*
> *But judge you as you are? O, think on that,*
> *And mercy then will breathe within your lips,*
> *Like man new made.*
> (ACT 2, SCENE 2, LINES 75–79)

Isabella, by calling on Angelo to judge his own actions as God would judge him, supposes that such self-questioning will lead to mercy and forgiveness of Claudio's sins. Unfortunately, Angelo has accepted the Duke's command to "be thou at full ourself," and for "Mortality and mercy in Vienna [to] / Live in thy tongue and heart" (Act 1, Scene 1, lines 43–45), in its literal sense, meting out justice and punishment as he deems fit. Angelo's devotion to the "strict statutes and most biting laws" that the Duke had for so long "let slip"

ABOVE: *English artist William Holman Hunt's* Claudio and Isabella *(1850) shows the siblings reflecting on their predicament in Act 3, Scene 1.*

> *Ay, but to die, and go we know not where;/To lie in cold obstruction, and to rot.*
>
> 
>
> —*Claudio* (ACT 3, SCENE 1, LINES 117–18)

(Act 1, Scene 3, lines 19–21), and his enthusiasm for imposing the death sentence rather than showing mercy, leads Isabella into Angelo's gaze. Of course, Angelo's lust is awakened, and his subsequent sins become far greater than those he condemns. No hypocrite when forced finally to confess, Angelo calls for his own "Immediate sentence" and "sequent death" (Act 5, Scene 1, line 373). Mariana and Isabella might plead for Angelo's life, but his crimes are only forgiven after the Duke has implied another biblical reference to Jesus Christ's Sermon on the Mount:

"An Angelo for Claudio, death for death!"
Haste still pays haste, and leisure answers
leisure;
Like doth quit like, and Measure *still* for
Measure.
(ACT 5, SCENE 1, LINES 409–11)

The Duke's "eye-for-an-eye" sentence is only revoked when he shows that Claudio is still alive. Having secretly observed Angelo's wrongdoings "like pow'r divine" (Act 5, Scene 1, line 369), the Duke opts to show mercy—to all except Lucio, whose punishment, of marrying a prostitute by whom he has an illegitimate child, seems as much for his slanderous outbursts as for his undoubtedly immoral behavior.

Power and Authority

Angelo's description of the all-seeing Duke as "like pow'r divine" would have reminded contemporary audiences of King James's own perception of kingship as divinely ordained. The abuse of authority by those in ultimate power is an ever-present theme in the play. Within its first few lines, Duke Vincentio admits that the old lord Escalus is well versed in the "properties" of "government"—the "nature of our people, / Our city's institutions, and the terms / For common justice"—making him the ideal man for the job (Act 1, Scene 1, lines 3–11). Nevertheless, the Duke still places the junior Angelo in control of Vienna. Why should he do this? When later donning a friar's habit—a disguise that replaces political authority with religious authority—the Duke admits his own lax administration, adding:

Sith 'twas my fault to give the people scope,
'Twould be my tyranny to strike and gall them
For what I bid them do …
(ACT 1, SCENE 3, LINES 35–37)

To deflect blame from himself and to prevent accusations of "tyranny" for reimposing laws that he himself had allowed to lie dormant, the Duke has "on Angelo impos'd the office, / Who may, in th' ambush of my name, strike home" (Act 1, Scene 3, lines 40–41). The Duke's duplicity appears self-serving, although his final remark—"hence shall we see / If power change purpose: what our seemers be" (Act 1, Scene 3, lines 53–54)—betrays his personal doubts about Angelo's true character. When Angelo's power does indeed "change purpose," Isabella notes "it is excellent / To have a giant's strength; but it is tyrannous / To use it like a giant" (Act 2, Scene 2, lines 107–9), adding that it should not be "every pelting, petty officer" (line 112) who passes judgment, only the supreme authority, God:

but man, proud man,
Dress'd in a little brief authority,
Most ignorant of what he's most assur'd
(His glassy essence), like an angry ape
Plays such fantastic tricks before high heaven
As makes the angels weep …
(ACT 2, SCENE 2, LINES 117–22)

Women and Sexuality

The abuse of power is most evident in Angelo's monstrous offer to Isabella: the ransom of her brother's life in exchange for sex. Isabella's plight demonstrates attitudes toward women at the time.

Legal Measures

We must not make a scarecrow of the
law,
Setting it up to fear the birds of prey,
And let it keep one shape, till custom
make it
Their perch and not their terror.
—*Angelo* (ACT 2, SCENE 1, LINES 1–4)

The jury, passing on the prisoner's life,
May in the sworn twelve have a thief or
two
Guiltier than him they try …
—*Angelo* (ACT 2, SCENE 1, LINES 19–21)

[E]very true man's apparel fits your thief.
—*Abhorson* (ACT 4, SCENE 2, LINES 46–47)

I have seen corruption boil and bubble,
Till it o'errun the stew; laws for all faults,
But faults so countenanc'd that the strong
statutes
Stand like the forfeits in a barber's shop,
As much in mock as mark.
—*Duke* (ACT 5, SCENE 1, LINES 318–22)

Contracts of Marriage

The plot of *Measure for Measure* hinges on Claudio's "crime" of having made his young lover Juliet pregnant. As the Duke observes, Juliet's "most offenseful act/Was mutually committed" (Act 2, Scene 3, lines 26–27), with no suggestion that Claudio forced himself on her. Claudio, indeed, claims to have slept with Juliet "upon a true contract" (Act 1, Scene 2, line 145). Although condemned by moralists, such a "contract," whereby the man and woman vowed "I marry you" rather than "I will marry you," was, for many in Shakespeare's day, sufficient to be called a "marriage"—all that was lacking was an official religious service. Claudio is therefore charged and ordered to pay the ultimate price for a "crime" that some in Shakespeare's audience might themselves have committed. However, whether Shakespeare saw Claudio as guilty or innocent is less than clear.

Isabella is certainly no fool. As her brother admits, "she hath prosperous art / When she will play with reason and discourse, / And well she can persuade" (Act 1, Scene 2, lines 184–86). Even the lecherous Lucio appears genuinely in awe of her:

> *I hold you as a thing enskied, and sainted,*
> *By your renouncement an immortal spirit,*
> *And to be talk'd with in sincerity,*
> *As with a saint.*
> (ACT 1, SCENE 4, LINES 34–37)

As for Angelo's opinion of Claudio's sister, he might view Isabella as "enskied" or placed among the clouds of heaven, but her angelic purity only adds to her sexual appeal. Isabella's religious fervor might be attractive to Angelo, but it makes his proposal intolerable to the novice nun. Isabella refuses to sleep with him even if this might save her brother's life.

To what extent Isabella's intransigence represents the character's own harsh and unforgiving nature has been a matter of debate for generations of Shakespeare scholars. The Duke appears, however, to voice an awareness of a woman's status that reveals the precise nature of Isabella's predicament. When he mock-interrogates Mariana after she has slept with Angelo, he asks if she is "married," "a maid," "A widow then?" (Act 5, Scene 1, lines 171–75). Mariana responds to all these questions in the negative, which prompts the Duke's response, "Why, you are nothing then[!]" (Act 5, Scene 1, line 177).

Isabella, if she were to sleep with Angelo, would likewise be not wife, widow, or virginal "maid"—she would indeed become "nothing," in her own and in society's eyes—perhaps no better than the prostitutes who in Shakespeare's time touted for business in the alleyways of London's debauched "suburbs."

RIGHT: *In a German-language version of* Measure for Measure, Maß für Maß, *staged at the Burgtheater in Vienna, Austria, in 2007, Christiane von Poelnitz played Isabella and Nicholas Ofczarek was Angelo.*

Coins of the Realm

The predominant imagery of *Measure for Measure*, one that troubled the sensitivity of nineteenth-century critics of the play, is that of sex and its resultant diseases, both of the individual and of the state. Shakespeare uses punning and double entendres, especially in Act 1, Scene 2, and Act 2, Scene 1, to describe the horrific effects of syphilis on a vice-ridden population that mirrored London's own.

There is, however, another less contentious image that touches not on those engaged in the sex industry, but on those who rule the land: the stamping of the ruler's image on coins. As Duke Vincentio asks of Escalus, at the start of the play, before he has announced his decision to appoint Angelo deputy, "What figure of us think you he will bear?" (Act 1, Scene 1, line 16). The Duke is inquiring to what extent Angelo's regime will correspond to the Duke's own "figure" or stamped image. When given his commission, Angelo protests:

> *Let there be some more test made of my mettle*
> *Before so noble and so great a figure*
> *Be stamp'd upon it.*
> (ACT 1, SCENE 1, LINES 48–50)

Angelo pleads to be tested like a coin of gold to ensure its purity before he accepts the impression of the Duke's royal stamp of office. Shakespeare even puns within this imagery, a "noble" being the old name for an "angel," a gold coin originally worth one third of an English pound and still in use in Shakespeare's day, which depicted the Angel Michael slaying the dragon and from which Angelo's name is probably derived.

Similarly, when Claudio asks Lucio to approach Isabella so she can plead mercy from Angelo, he suggests that she "assay him" like a gold coin (Act 1, Scene 2, line 181). Shakespeare is thus likening Angelo to a counterfeit coin whose precious metal is debased with inferior metal. Only the Duke, by returning to power, can restore the true value of good rule—can stamp the image of moral virtue on the metaphorical coins of his dukedom.

The Political Message

Like many of Shakespeare's plays, *Measure for Measure* was adapted by the poet and dramatist William Davenant, whose 1662 Restoration version (renamed *The Law Against Lovers*) removed all the low-life sexual material, leaving only the Claudio–Angelo–Isabella plot. He also added Beatrice and Benedick from *Much Ado about Nothing*, splicing whole sections of the two plays together. Richard Wagner even wrote an opera, *Das Liebesverbot* (1836), based on Isabella's plight. Wagner's political opera, complete with rebel-leading Isabella, was threatened with closure until the local police were assured it was based on Shakespeare.

The political message of the play was also significant for twentieth-century Europeans responding to post–World War II suffering and Cold War uncertainty. German director Bertolt Brecht's 1951 adaptation represented a critique of the totalitarianism of capitalist societies, whereas director Krystyna Skuszanka's 1956 production at the Rapsodyczny Theatre in Cracow, Poland, made Communism its target. Not until the 2004 National Theatre, London, coproduction with the Complicite theater company, directed by Simon McBurney, was the sexual depravity of the play given equal weight to its political significance.

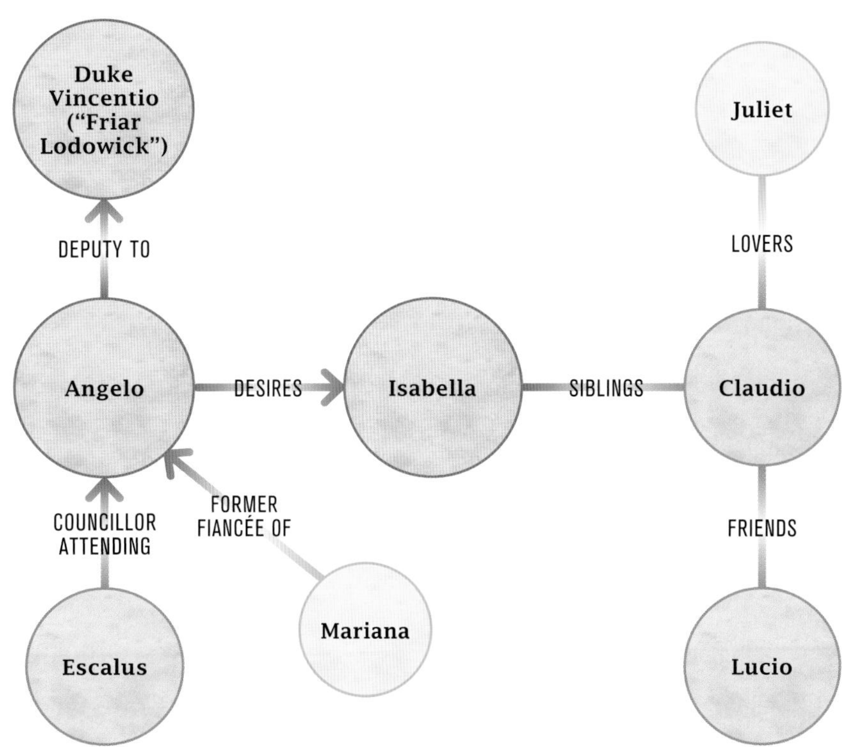

RELATIONSHIPS
As a result of the Duke's abdication of temporal power in favor of Angelo, the unworldly Isabella comes to hold her brother's, and ultimately Angelo's, life in her hands.

> *Be absolute for death:*
> *either death or life/*
> *Shall thereby be the sweeter.*
> *Reason thus with life:/*
> *If I do lose thee, I do lose*
> *a thing/That none but*
> *fools would keep ...*

—*Duke* (ACT 3, SCENE 1, LINES 5–8)

The Tragedies

The tragedies are Shakespeare's most celebrated and consistently performed works; some are among the greatest dramatic masterpieces of all time. Their themes and plots are dark and often shocking, and their conflicted, flawed heroes endure—and inflict—great suffering. Of all his plays, it is in these somber works that Shakespeare seems to come closest to touching the essence of humanity.

Titus Andronicus

THE PLOT: *Titus Andronicus, a Roman general, returns to Rome after achieving a great victory against the Goths. To mark his triumph, he sacrifices Alarbus, the eldest son of Tamora, queen of the defeated Goths. However, Tamora soon marries Saturninus, the Emperor of Rome, and, in her new position of power, starts the engines of revenge. Her two sons, Chiron and Demetrius, capture Lavinia, Titus's daughter, rape her, cut off her hands, and cut out her tongue. Eventually, Lavinia manages to reveal to Titus who perpetrated the crime. Titus entraps Chiron and Demetrius and cuts their throats while Lavinia catches their blood in a basin. He then plans a banquet during which he ends Lavinia's grief by killing her, feeds Chiron and Demetrius (now baked in a pie) to Tamora, and then stabs her. Saturninus stabs Titus. Titus's son, Lucius, stabs the emperor. Backed by the army of the Goths, Lucius becomes emperor.*

Dramatis Personae

Saturninus, *son to the late Emperor of Rome, afterward Emperor*
Bassianus, *brother to Saturninus*
Titus Andronicus, *a noble Roman, general against the Goths*
Marcus Andronicus, *tribune of the people, brother to Titus*
Lucius, Quintus, Martius, Mutius, *sons to Titus Andronicus*
Young Lucius, *a boy, son to Lucius*
Aemilius, *a noble Roman*
Publius, *son to Marcus Andronicus*
Sempronius, Caius, Valentine, *kinsmen to Titus*
Alarbus, Demetrius, Chiron, *sons to Tamora*
Aaron, *a Moor, beloved by Tamora*
Captain
Messenger
Tribune
Clown
Tamora, *Queen of the Goths*
Lavinia, *daughter to Titus Andronicus*
Nurse, *and a black* **Child**
Romans and Goths, Senators, Tribunes, Officers, Soldiers, and Attendants

WRITTEN c. 1593–94
SETTING AND PERIOD Ancient Rome, c. fourth century CE
CHARACTERS 28
ACTS 5
SCENES 14
LINES 2,538

Titus Andronicus has held a shaky position in the Shakespeare canon. While now accepted as one of his plays, it was, until recently, at the best, politely ignored or branded as an early effort of the Bard. Early it is: *Titus* is the first of Shakespeare's tragedies, but we disregard it at our peril. The Elizabethans loved this revenge play, with its blood and rape and mayhem and cannibalism. True, *Titus* lacks subtlety; but, as revenge tragedy, it excels.

Shakespeare had no main source for *Titus*, but material from the gruesome story of Progne and Philomela (culled from Roman poet Ovid's *Metamorphoses*) permeates the play.

A Tragedy of Revenge

Revenge is the key theme in *Titus*, although the text contains other themes: the limits of language, desensitization to violence, the role of a military leader in a time of peace. When Titus Andronicus returns triumphantly from the wars with the Goths, he finds, once he has refused the role of emperor, that his life has little meaning. What he does best from that point on is learn to suffer—the extravagant violence done to his family, and especially to Lavinia, his daughter, touches him in a way that the wartime deaths of 21 out of his 25 sons did not.

In seeking to understand the mutilated Lavinia and discover her assailants, Titus, the martial automaton, actually sheds tears. When he is told by Tamora's evil lover that he can save two of his remaining sons by chopping off a hand—as a sign of goodwill to the emperor—Titus does so. But Titus's sons do not receive a reprieve, and a messenger delivers their heads to Titus. This leads to a notorious scene in the play as he instructs the remainder of his family:

> *Come, brother, take a head,*
> *And in this hand the other will I bear;*
> *And, Lavinia, thou shalt be employ'd;*
> *Bear thou my hand, sweet wench, between thy teeth.*
>
> (ACT 3, SCENE 1, LINES 279–82)

The grotesque assemblage proceeds offstage: it is no wonder that this play has so often been considered over-the-top. Titus, however, through

Speak, gentle niece: what stern ungentle hands/Hath lopp'd and hew'd, and made thy body bare/Of her two branches, those sweet ornaments/Whose circling shadows kings have sought to sleep in,/And might not gain so great a happiness/As half thy love?

—*Marcus* (ACT 2, SCENE 4, LINES 16–21)

suffering, learns not only that "Rome is but a wilderness of tigers" (Act 3, Scene 1, line 54), but that grief can drive one into madness.

The Limits of Language

Revenge drives this play, and to have revenge Titus must find out who ravished and mutilated his daughter. While an audience might be able to think of numerous ways in which the mute and handless Lavinia could convey the information, Titus is, well, stumped. Without language, he can only try to "wrest an alphabet" (Act 3, Scene 2, line 44) from his mutilated daughter and to "interpret all her martyr'd signs" (Act 3, Scene 2, line 36). This reveals the inherent limits of communication: words fail to ease the suffering of the characters, and words cannot be found to convey the horrors of this play.

Titus finds his only respite in violent action. He captures Tamora's sons, grinds their bones to flour, and mixes it with their flesh and blood to make a pie that he serves to Tamora. She thus finds herself "Eating the flesh that she herself hath bred" (Act 5, Scene 3, line 62). It is hard to imagine a more

Lopped Parts

O, that delightful engine of her thoughts,
That blabb'd them with such pleasing
eloquence,
Is torn from forth that pretty hollow cage,
Where like a sweet melodious bird it sung
Sweet varied notes, enchanting every ear!
—*Marcus* (ACT 3, SCENE 1, LINES 82–86)

Then which way shall I find Revenge's cave?
For these two heads do seem to speak to me,
And threat me I shall never come to bliss
Till all these mischiefs be return'd again,
Even in their throats that hath committed them.
—*Titus* (ACT 3, SCENE 1, LINES 270–74)

Hark, villains, I will grind your bones to dust,
And with your blood and it I'll make a paste,
And of the paste a coffin I will rear,
And make two pasties of your shameful heads[.]
—*Titus* (ACT 5, SCENE 2, LINES 186–89)

BELOW: *In this scene from a Royal Shakespeare Company production at the Barbican in London in 1988, a horrified Marcus, played by Donald Sumpter, finds his mutilated niece, Lavinia, acted by Sonia Ritter.*

ABOVE: *Laurence Olivier was a suitably imperious Titus, while his wife, Vivien Leigh, appeared as Lavinia, in director Peter Brook's mid-1950s production, seen here at the Théâtre de la Ville in Paris.*

thorough vengeance, but, of course, like all acts of vengeance, the deed restores nothing. In the bloodbath, revenge, which has become a kind of character in the play, consumes the revenger.

Three Heads, Two Hands, a Tongue

Body parts cascade through *Titus Andronicus,* both literally and in imagery. At the opening of the play, Marcus invites Titus to "set a head on headless Rome" (Act 1, Scene 1, line 186); Titus, declining, answers that "A better head her glorious body fits / Than his that shakes for age and feebleness" (Act 1, Scene 1, lines 187–88). Already we see the state as fragmented, and the image disturbs: not only is Rome a headless trunk, but also Marcus offers to join a male head to a female body. Something is seriously out of joint.

The rising number of references to body parts throughout the play only serves to reinforce this image of a torn country. Lavinia, just before her rape and mutilation, cryptically asks Tamora for something that "womanhood denies my tongue to tell" (Act 2, Scene 3, line 174). Lavinia's modesty keeps us from knowing what she wants, but it's worth noting this sudden reference to the tongue as an organ of communication. We do not really tell things by tongue alone—it is a figure of speech—but that figure occurs at least ten more times. The text will not release us from the image of Lavinia's lost tongue, any more than it will cease to iterate the image of the hand.

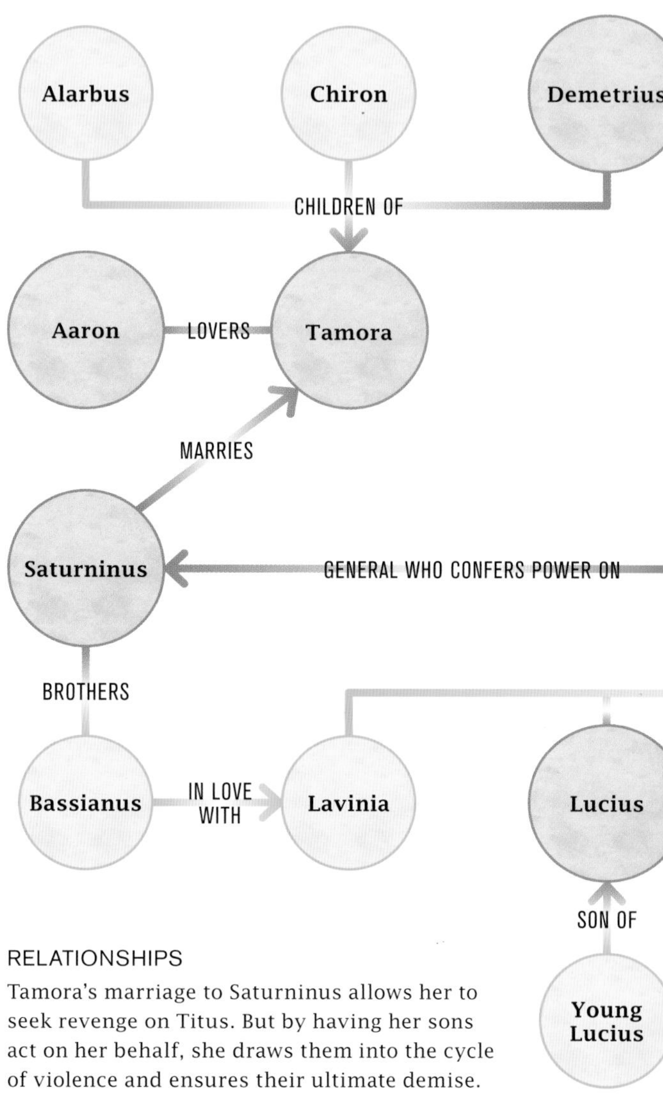

RELATIONSHIPS
Tamora's marriage to Saturninus allows her to seek revenge on Titus. But by having her sons act on her behalf, she draws them into the cycle of violence and ensures their ultimate demise.

More than tongues, or even heads, the hand figures as the predominant image in this play—not merely because three hands are lopped off, but because so many characters use turns of phrase that employ the word "hand." We might well understand Titus's exclamation after Marcus (rather tactlessly) speaks of the handless Lavinia laying "violent hands upon her tender life":

What violent hands can she lay on her life?
Ah, wherefore dost thou urge the name of hands,
. . . .
O, handle not the theme, to talk of hands,
Lest we remember still that we have none.
Fie, fie, how franticly I square my talk,
As if we should forget we had no hands,
If Marcus did not name the word of hands!
(ACT 3, SCENE 2, LINES 25–26, 29–33)

Both literal and figurative hands interlace like fingers. And throughout the play, with imagery working on both these levels, we are never far from the realization that the political body of Rome has begun to come apart. While at the beginning Rome seems to have lost its head, throughout the play we see the "lopp'd and hew'd" (Act 2, Scene 4, line 17) individual bodies that make up the body politic. The whole world of *Titus Andronicus* is one of both literal and figurative violent dismemberment.

At the end of the play, after the carnage of the banquet, when Marcus and Lucius are the only adult Andronici remaining, Marcus, at least, seems to realize the fragmented state of Rome. He says to the people:

O, let me teach you how to knit again
This scattered corn into one mutual sheaf,
These broken limbs again into one body.
(ACT 5, SCENE 3, LINES 70–72)

His metaphors suggest a great heaping together of the body parts that have gone missing in this play. It may be too late, however, for us to have a sanguine vision of the future of this world.

Horrors that Never Cease

Although it seems to belong to another world and time, *Titus Andronicus* has much relevance to our own. Titus's helplessness after his return to Rome reveals the plight of all soldiers who, desensitized by war, must try to reintegrate into peacetime life. Lavinia's silence stands for the failures of language: words cannot convey depths of suffering or heal a sick country. At the end of the play, moreover, we are left with the raving of the evil character Aaron: the violence will never cease. It is not surprising, perhaps, that the play found modern favor: notable productions include the 1955 staging starring Vivien Leigh and Laurence Olivier, and director Julie Taymor's 1999 film adaptation, *Titus*.

Bloody Props

The text of *Titus Andronicus* calls for one hand, two heads, and a great deal of blood. While other Renaissance plays refer to false heads, and a fake hand could be easily constructed, the probable use of animal blood conjures to mind a lurid (and smelly) spectacle.

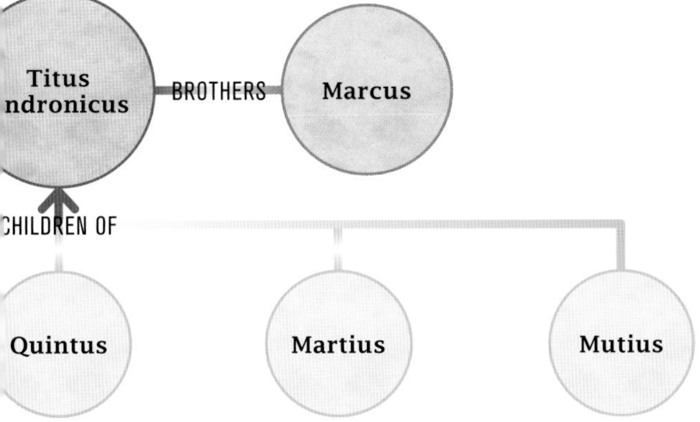

BELOW: *In Julie Taymor's arresting film* Titus *(1999), the lead role is played by Anthony Hopkins, seen here at right alongside Alan Cumming in the role of Saturninus.*

Romeo and Juliet

THE PLOT: *The play opens with a brawl between two feuding families, the Montagues and the Capulets. Soon after, Romeo, a Montague, attends a ball at the Capulet house in disguise, where he falls in love with the daughter of the house, Juliet. Later that night, he encounters Juliet at her window and they exchange vows of love. The next day, they are secretly married, but before they can consummate the relationship, Juliet's cousin, Tybalt, challenges Romeo to a duel. In the ensuing fray, Romeo's friend, Mercutio, is killed. Romeo takes revenge by killing Tybalt and is banished from Verona.*

Meanwhile, Juliet's parents prepare to marry her off to a young nobleman, Paris, but she drinks a potion so that on the morning of the wedding she is discovered apparently dead and taken to the Capulet tomb. Believing that Juliet is truly dead, Romeo arrives at the tomb with the intention of committing suicide (though he first gets into a fight with Paris, whom he kills). Alone with Juliet, Romeo drinks poison and dies. Juliet wakes, discovers his body and stabs herself to death. Confronted by the bodies of their children, the Montagues and Capulets are finally reconciled.

Dramatis Personae

Chorus
Escalus, *Prince of Verona*
Paris, *a young nobleman, kinsman to the Prince*
Montague, Capulet, *heads of two houses at variance with each other*
An Old Man, *of the Capulet family*
Romeo, *son to Montague*
Mercutio, *kinsman to the Prince, and friend to Romeo*
Benvolio, *nephew to Montague, and friend to Romeo*
Tybalt, *nephew to Lady Capulet*
Petruchio, *a (mute) follower of Tybalt*
Friar Lawrence, Friar John, *Franciscans*
Balthasar, *servant to Romeo*
Abram, *servant to Montague*
Sampson, Gregory, Clown, *servants to Capulet*
Peter, *servant to Juliet's nurse*
Page to Paris
Apothecary
Three Musicians
Lady Montague, *wife to Montague*
Lady Capulet, *wife to Capulet*
Juliet, *daughter to Capulet*
Nurse to Juliet
Citizens of Verona; several Gentlemen and Gentlewomen of both houses; Maskers, Torch-bearers, Pages, Guards, Watchmen, Servants, and Attendants

RIGHT: *For George Cukor's 1936 film version of* Romeo and Juliet, *with Leslie Howard and Norma Shearer in the title roles, a historically accurate re-creation of an Italian Renaissance town was built on a Hollywood studio lot, at vast expense.*

Romeo and Juliet has defined many of the ways in which we think about romantic love and those who engage most passionately with it. In writing the play, Shakespeare responded to the love conventions of his own time, even as he proceeded to rewrite them.

The legend of Romeo and Juliet was known in Italy from the fifteenth century, subsequently taking shape through the prose fiction collections of Luigi da Porto, Matteo Bandello, and Pierre Boaistuau (published in 1530, 1554, and 1559, respectively). In England, it was rewritten as a narrative poem by Arthur Brooke, called *The Tragicall Historye of Romeus and Juliet* (1562), which was probably Shakespeare's immediate source.

Brooke's poem reveals its own conflicts on the subject of love. On the one hand, the prose address, "To the Reader," insists that the point of the narrative is to present

> *a couple of unfortunate lovers, thralling themselves to unhonest desire, neglecting the authority and advice of parents and friends ... abusing the name of lawful marriage ... [and] by all means of unhonest life, hasting to meet most unhappy death.*

However, the poem itself is considerably more sympathetic, with the narrator desiring to preserve "the memory of so perfect, sound, and so approved love." In part, Brooke was responding to a larger cultural ambivalence. From the 1560s onward, Italian *novelle* had become hugely popular with English readers, who relished the tales of adultery and of tragic desire most often to be found there. At the same time, English Protestants were pressing Elizabeth for stricter religious and moral controls over the country: the insistence on the uncontrollability of desire and its fatal consequences in Brooke's preface is clearly informed by the latter.

For Shakespeare, the narrative is an opportunity to question the value of erotic love, as voiced in the exchanges between Friar Lawrence and the young protagonists. It also encouraged him to challenge a style of love poetry that had been popular throughout the 1580s and early 1590s in England, mainly through the work of Francesco Petrarca, known in the English-speaking world as Petrarch. Although Shakespeare draws upon many of Petrarch's poetic conceits (fire and ice, the beloved as a star, desire as death), he also moves away from the nature of Petrarchan love in which the male suitor languishes in unrequited passion for a distant, chaste beloved. Rather, Shakespeare brings Romeo into intoxicating physical intimacy with Juliet, who returns his love with equal fervor.

WRITTEN
c. 1594–95

SETTING AND PERIOD
Verona and Mantua, fourteenth century

CHARACTERS 32, including a Chorus

ACTS 5

SCENES 22

LINES 3,099

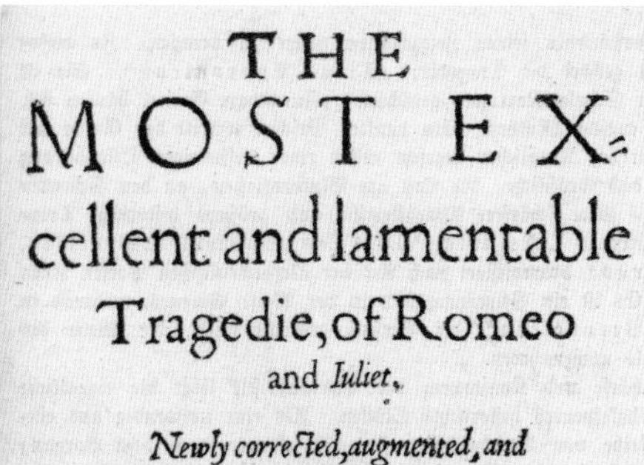

THE MOST EX-cellent and lamentable Tragedie, of Romeo and Iuliet.

Newly corrected, augmented, and amended:

As it hath bene sundry times publiquely acted, by the right Honourable the Lord Chamberlaine his Seruants.

LONDON
Printed by Thomas Creede, for Cuthbert Burby, and are to be sold at his shop neare the Exchange.
1599.

ABOVE: *The first edition of the play, probably written down by actors, appeared in 1597. This "corrected, augmented, and amended" quarto, likely based on Shakespeare's draft, dates from 1599.*

It is the fascination of this mutual passion, its intensity (which does not fade or become mundane), and the affecting spectacle of its destruction that have made *Romeo and Juliet* one of Shakespeare's best-loved plays.

Not Quite a Tragedy

The tragic destiny that shapes Romeo and Juliet's end initially appears quite self-explanatory. The Prologue tells us that they are a pair of "star-cross'd lovers" (line 6), while Romeo prophesies that "Some consequence yet hanging in the stars" will end with his "untimely death" (Act 1, Scene 4, lines 107, 111). But if the play maintains an atmosphere of doom (not least in the fact that the protagonists' deaths are already written), critics have been less satisfied with the tragic necessity of their demise. For example, it might be argued that it is the feud into which they are born—that is, the social context in which they fall in love—that makes their passion fatal, not anything in the nature of that desire or any flaw in the protagonists themselves. Some critics have felt that the tragedy is a matter of mere accident and mischance, such as the delay that prevents Romeo from receiving the letter telling him that Juliet is still alive. (This perception is heightened in those productions, such as director Baz Luhrmann's 1996 film *Romeo + Juliet*, where Juliet wakes just as Romeo draws his last breath.)

Equally, the cathartic power of the ending may be diminished by the fact that Romeo and Juliet's deaths are providential, ensuring civic harmony and reconciliation between the families. The Prince brings out this ambiguity nicely when he tells the Capulets and Montagues: "See what a scourge is laid upon your hate, / That heaven finds means to kill your joys with love" (Act 5, Scene 3, lines 292–93). The difficulty of deciding on what basis Romeo and Juliet must die is one of the reasons that the play has been adjudged a lesser tragedy than the four heavy-hitters: *Hamlet, Othello, King Lear,* and *Macbeth*. Further reasons are that it has two tragic protagonists instead of one, and that its subject matter is mainly love rather than the political destiny of a kingdom. Although Shakespeare's play did much to change this perception, love was often considered an unsuitable subject for tragedy.

The Generation Gap

One of the play's strongest themes is the innate hostility it describes, not between Capulets and Montagues, but between the generations. Partly because we are never told the specific nature of the "ancient grudge" that keeps the lovers apart, it is the generational conflict that perhaps emerges most strongly in the play. Although we do not know the precise age of Romeo, Juliet is specified as just under 14, and the rest of the dramatis personae are fairly easily divided into young characters—Paris, Tybalt, Mercutio—and their older parents and guardians. This difference is consistently understood in terms of speed: both physical quickness and emotional volatility. For example, while Juliet waits for news from Romeo, she declares that

> *Love's heralds should be thoughts,*
> *Which ten times faster glides than the sun's beams,*
> *Driving back shadows over low'ring hills;*
> *Therefore do nimble-pinion'd doves draw Love,*
> *And therefore hath the wind-swift Cupid wings.*
> (ACT 2, SCENE 5, LINES 4–8)

Yet she is reliant upon the Nurse, and "old folks—many feign as they were dead, / Unwieldy, slow, heavy, and pale as lead" (Act 2, Scene 5, lines 16–17). Friar Lawrence's first scene with Romeo also emphasizes such difference. He upbraids Romeo for the alacrity with which he has abandoned love of Rosaline in favor of Juliet. But the argument shifts to the physical distinction in their movements when Romeo urges that they hurry to make arrangements for the wedding: "O, let us hence, I stand on sudden haste," and the Friar responds: "Wisely and slow, they stumble that run fast" (Act 2, Scene 3, lines 93–94).

Although the play's representation of the young recognizes their self-absorption and lack of ability to empathize with their elders, it is the latter's failure to understand the deep passions and miseries of their offspring that largely contributes to the children's destruction. The most obvious example is Capulet and his wife forcing Juliet to marry Paris at a time when she is in great distress (they believe she is grieving for Tybalt; in fact, it is for Romeo's banishment).

> *My only love sprung from my only hate!/*
> *Too early seen unknown, and known too late!/*
> *Prodigious birth of love it is to me/*
> *That I must love a loathed enemy.*

—*Juliet* (ACT 1, SCENE 5, LINES 138–141)

More serious failures are incurred by the Nurse and the Friar, both of whom have greater intimacy with their charges. For example, the Nurse fatally underestimates Juliet's love for Romeo. By endorsing bigamy, she loses Juliet's confidence, thereby leaving her to her own tragic devices. (Comic characters such as the Nurse and Mercutio significantly fall away in the course of the tragedy.) Friar Lawrence retains the lovers' trust but he, too, lets them down. It is not just that he arrives at the tomb too late to save Romeo (in the tardy manner that characterizes the old in this play), but that he refuses to linger with Juliet when he hears the Prince's men approaching. This has usually been seen as an act of self-preservation on the Friar's part. However, it may also be that he fails to appreciate Juliet's despair or the fact that she will immediately kill herself if left alone. One of the simplest but most poignant lines in the play is Romeo's remonstrance to the Friar: "Thou canst not speak of that thou dost not feel" (Act 3, Scene 3, line 64). The play extends this invitation of greater empathy to the audience at large.

Masculine Violence

Another source of tragedy in the play is the perception of masculinity as inveterately linked with violence. In the opening scene, the Capulet servants, Gregory and Sampson, appear bearing heavy swords and shields. These are evidently unnecessary for their domestic duties, and suggest the extent to which the feud has affected different social levels in Verona. At the same time, being a servant in the Renaissance period was often viewed as a state of immaturity: it required you to be passive and subordinate within a family, much like a child. Hence, the appearance of Gregory and Sampson and their eagerness to engage in fighting with the Montagues may be suggestive of their ambition to act "like men." More disturbing is the sexual violence by which they promise to achieve this, which blurs the distinction between murder, rape, and consensual sex:

> SAMPSON *'Tis all one; I will show myself a tyrant: when I have fought with the men, I will be civil with the maids; I will cut off their heads.*
> GREGORY *The heads of the maids?*
> SAMPSON *Ay, the heads of the maids, or their maidenheads, take it in what sense thou wilt.*
> (ACT 1, SCENE 1, LINES 21–26)

Where this association between masculinity and violence proves dangerous for Romeo is in his encounter with Tybalt. The latter will not be denied, and when Romeo fails to meet his challenge other men are drawn into the fighting in

Feuds Close to Home

Shakespeare's patron, Henry Wriothesley, Earl of Southampton, had experience of feuding and fugitives. In 1594, he helped his friends Henry and Charles Danvers to escape from England after they had killed a man in a duel. Possibly Shakespeare was present at the earl's estate, Titchfield, when the fugitives were hiding out there.

LEFT: *Convention compels Romeo, played here by Matthew Rhys (left), in Peter Gill's 2004 Royal Shakesepeare Company production at Stratford, to avenge the death of Mercutio by killing Tybalt (right, Tam Mutu).*

order to defend Romeo's honor. When Mercutio is killed, Romeo succumbs to the pressure to "be a man" and takes his revenge. More disturbingly, his passion for Juliet now looks like a kind of weakness against which he must defend himself:

O sweet Juliet,
Thy beauty hath made me effeminate,
And in my temper soft'ned valor's steel!
(ACT 3, SCENE 1, LINES 113–15)

For some critics, it is Romeo's prioritizing of hatred over love (where the play's couplets have consistently put him on the other side of that equation) and his reversion to an aggressive, patriarchal, unloving form of masculinity that seals his doom.

Holy Love

A common convention of Elizabethan poetry (inherited from the troubadours, Dante, and others) was to elevate erotic love by describing it in religious terms: for example, by making the beloved into a kind of saint toward whom the lover performs acts of worship. *Romeo and Juliet* is full of such imagery. On first meeting Juliet, Romeo says:

If I profane with my unworthiest hand
This holy shrine, the gentle sin is this,
My lips, two blushing pilgrims, ready stand
To smooth that rough touch with a tender kiss.
(ACT 1, SCENE 5, LINES 93–96)

In fact, in Italian the word *Romeo* originally meant "a pilgrim traveling to Rome," and Romeo's words and Juliet's response on seeing him suggest he may even have worn the costume of a pilgrim to the Capulet ball. Similarly, as the object of his devotion, Juliet is likened to a "bright angel" (Act 2, Scene 1, line 68), and she is dressed as such in the 1996 Baz Lurhmann film.

Though this imagery was conventional, it has an added resonance in the play, for two reasons. First, it suggests the extent to which Romeo and Juliet's love has replaced their passion for God. Juliet refers to her lover as "the god of my idolatry" (Act 2, Scene 2, line 113) in a manner that comes perilously close to blasphemy and that might be thought to require divine chastisement. Second, these references remind an audience that the lovers are presumably both Catholic, given the narrative's Italian setting, at a time when English Catholics were being persecuted for their faith. This fact is registered in a curious extended metaphor, where Romeo insists that his tears for Juliet are real:

When the devout religion of mine eye
Maintains such falsehood, then turn tears to
[fires];

RIGHT: *The quasi-religious ardor of the lovers is underlined by the costumes they don for the Capulet ball in Baz Luhrmann's 1996 film* Romeo + Juliet. *Juliet (Claire Danes) wears the wings of an angel, Romeo (Leonardo DiCaprio) the shining armor of a crusading knight.*

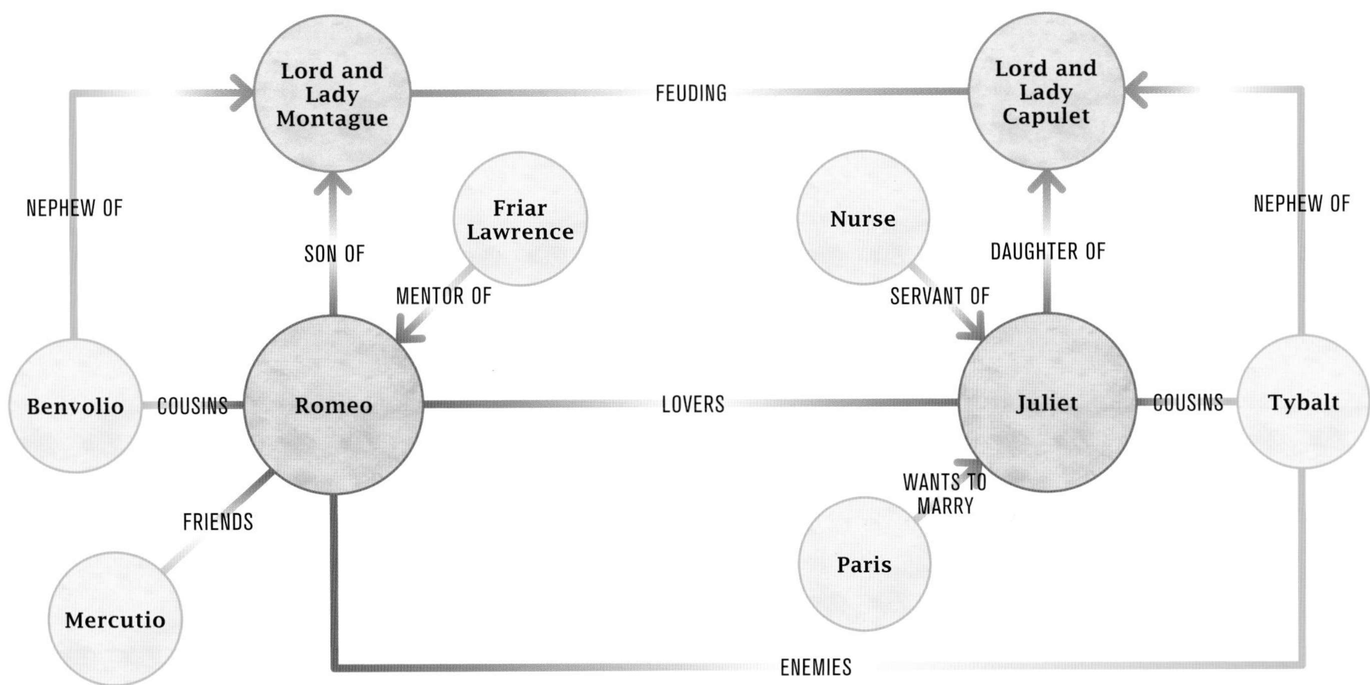

RELATIONSHIPS
All the characters are members of or closely associated with the Montague and Capulet families, feuding dynasties of Renaissance Verona.

And these, who, often drown'd, could never die,
Transparent heretics, be burnt for liars!
(ACT 1, SCENE 2, LINES 88–91)

Not only the fidelity associated with the Catholic martyr, but also the fact that Romeo sees himself in their position might suggest an unusual degree of sympathy for Catholics in Shakespeare's play. Equally, although the Friar has often been understood as a negative representative of that faith (he abuses confession by using it to plot against authority), Shakespeare's portrayal of a Catholic cleric is considerably more sympathetic than that of his contemporaries. This may have been in Shakespeare's interests, not just because his father, John, may have maintained his Catholic faith, but also because one of the playwright's patrons, Henry Wriothesley, Earl of Southampton, was Catholic.

Fatal Attraction

Two households, both alike in dignity,
In fair Verona, where we lay our scene,
From ancient grudge break to new mutiny,
Where civil blood makes civil hands unclean.
From forth the fatal loins of these two foes
A pair of star-cross'd lovers take their life[.]
(PROLOGUE, LINES 1–6)

How oft when men are at the point of death
Have they been merry, which their keepers call
A lightning before death! O how may I
Call this a lightning? O my love, my wife,
Death, that hath suck'd the honey of thy breath,
Hath had no power yet upon thy beauty[.]
—*Romeo* (ACT 5, SCENE 3, LINES 88–93)

For never was a story of more woe
Than this of Juliet and her Romeo.
—*Prince* (ACT 5, SCENE 3, LINES 309–10)

Opposites and Equals

Another significant image pattern in the play is that of sweetness and bitterness. Again, "sweet" and "sweetest" were familiar terms from Elizabethan love poetry, and they recur straightforwardly as terms of endearment in *Romeo and Juliet*. However, the play also explores the possibility that this sweetness might not be what it seems.

During the balcony scene, Romeo cannot believe his luck and wonders whether this dream is "Too flattering-sweet to be substantial" (Act 2, Scene 2, line 141). More dangerous is the possibility that love will turn into its opposite. It is Tybalt who first refers to the flip-side of sweetness when he anticipates that Romeo's intrusion into the ball "shall, / Now seeming sweet, convert to bitt'rest gall" (Act 1, Scene 5, lines 91–92). The idea is later taken up by those who discourse on love. The Friar warns the lovers at their wedding that

The sweetest honey
Is loathsome in his own deliciousness,
And in the taste confounds the appetite.
Therefore love moderately …
(ACT 2, SCENE 6, LINES 11–14)

ABOVE: *The Montague and Capulet families reconcile over the bodies of Romeo and Juliet in this 1853 painting by English artist Lord Frederic Leighton.*

Speeding up the Action

One of Shakespeare's most significant changes to his narrative source, English poet Arthur Brooke's poem *The Tragicall Historye of Romeus and Juliet* (1562), is its abbreviated timescale. In the poem, the action takes place over a number of months, but Shakespeare has telescoped it to just five days: from Sunday to Thursday morning.

The perception of opposites resolving into equals is a more general pattern throughout the play. Most famously, love becomes death: the marriage-bed for which Capulet is preparing his daughter turns out to be a deathbed, while Paris as bridegroom is usurped by Death himself (Act 4, Scene 5). In the final scene in the tomb, this imagery is replayed, with Romeo gazing on an apparently dead Juliet and likening her to Death's "paramour" (Act 5, Scene 3, line 105). Juliet's act of kissing Romeo's lips becomes not merely amorous but a way in which to end her life. This relentless identification between love and death is part of a larger theme in Renaissance culture, reflected in the language itself, where the term for orgasm is also the same for mortal expiration, namely "to die." But in Shakespeare's play, this image pattern also recalls the more specific fate that awaits the lovers, and for which the Chorus has prepared us from the very first speech.

A Rich Cultural Legacy

Romeo and Juliet has such cultural familiarity in the West that its terms are often used by people who have never read the play. For example, not only is an amorous male sometimes referred to as a "Romeo," but teenagers who love in defiance of parental opposition become "Romeo and Juliet" figures, perhaps prompted to do so by what psychologists have referred to as a "Romeo and Juliet effect."

While the play continues to be popular on all kinds of stages—in schools, universities, and prisons, as well as in professional theaters—it is also adapted for a wide range of media, from advertisements to rap music, from opera and ballet to pornography, novels, poetry, and films. It has had a particularly strong presence in the cinema, with seminal productions by directors George

Cukor (1936), Franco Zeffirelli (1968), and Baz Luhrmann, whose *Romeo + Juliet* (1996) was a huge international success.

The play's adaptability seems to originate in the vagueness with which the conflict is defined, so that a range of historical and social divisions can be substituted for this "ancient grudge" (Prologue, line 3). For example, in the musical *West Side Story,* by Leonard Bernstein and Stephen Sondheim (1957, film 1961), the conflict is between two rival gangs in 1950s Manhattan: white Americans versus Puerto Ricans. More recently, productions have located the love plot within the context of the Israeli-Palestinian conflict and of the apartheid era in South Africa. However, sexual prejudices have also been explored. Director Joe Calarco's play *Shakespeare's R&J*, first produced in New York in 1998 and revived in London in 2003, focuses on four schoolboys in a repressive Catholic boarding school who read Shakespeare's play secretly while becoming aware of their own homosexuality.

Fictional Conjectures

A more mainstream adaptation for the cinema, *Shakespeare in Love* (1998), directed by John Madden, linked *Romeo and Juliet* to Shakespeare's own life. We see the play evolve from comic origins (its working title is *Romeo and Ethel, the Pirate's Daughter*) into a tragedy in response to Shakespeare's thwarted relationship with Lady Viola de Lesseps. Among the many fictional conjectures the film makes about Shakespeare's relationship to his play is the idea that his later success as a playwright depended upon *Romeo and Juliet*'s ability to represent the truth about love. While the ways in which the play continues to be adapted for different audiences suggest that its version of love includes considerable flexibility and variation, *Romeo and Juliet* does seem to capture at least an essence of what we would like love to be.

Emulating the Italians

Romeo and Juliet makes use of a number of popular Italian stereotypes, such as the Italians having a passionate and hot-blooded nature, and being prone to violent love, jealousy, and quarreling. In 1570, English scholar and traveler Roger Ascham also observed the Italians' "private contention in many families" as well as "open factions in every city." Romeo's visit to the Apothecary in order to procure poison would have reminded an audience of the Italians' admired (and feared) skill in the art of poisoning. Finally, the play's allusions to dueling reflect the Italian manuals on that art that were eagerly read by Elizabethan aristocrats, though the violence that breaks out in Verona's streets follows few of the established rules.

These violent delights have violent ends,/And in their triumph die, like fire and powder,/Which as they kiss consume ...

—*Friar Lawrence* (ACT 2, SCENE 6, LINES 9–11)

LEFT: *The Broadway musical* West Side Story, *an adaptation of* Romeo and Juliet, *was made into a movie in 1961. George Chakiris (left) played Bernardo, leader of the Puerto Rican gang, the Sharks, and the counterpart of Shakespeare's Tybalt.*

Julius Caesar

THE PLOT: *Julius Caesar returns triumphantly to Rome, having defeated the forces of Pompey. At the festival of the Lupercal, while Brutus and Cassius debate the implications of Caesar's rise in power, Caesar refuses the offer of a crown. This rejection of absolute power only increases the popularity of Caesar, but it is unconvincing to many prominent Romans. Cassius plots to kill Caesar, and he enlists the help of several others, most importantly Caesar's close friend, Brutus. On the ides of March, the conspirators succeed, stabbing Caesar to death in the Senate in Rome. The Roman citizens are outraged but Brutus calms them with his explanation of the murder. Then Mark Antony delivers a powerful speech that manipulates the crowd and turns the people against the conspirators, who are forced to flee from Rome. Mark Antony and Caesar's nephew, Octavius, who have assumed command, lead a Roman army against the forces of Brutus and Cassius, and win a decisive victory. Separately—in defeat and in remorse—Cassius and Brutus stab themselves to death.*

Dramatis Personae

Julius Caesar
Octavius Caesar, Mark Antony, M. Aemilius Lepidus, *triumvirs after the death of Julius Caesar*
Cicero, Publius, Popilius Lena, *senators*
Marcus Brutus, Cassius, Casca, Trebonius, Caius Ligarius, Decius Brutus, Metellus Cimber, Cinna, *conspirators against Julius Caesar*
Flavius, Murellus, *tribunes*
Artemidorus of Cnidos, *a teacher of rhetoric*
Soothsayer
Cinna, *a poet*
Another Poet
Lucilius, Titinius, Messala, Young Cato, Volumnius, Flavius, *friends to Brutus and Cassius*
Varrus, Clitus, Claudio, Strato, Lucius, Dardanius, *servants to Brutus*
Pindarus, *servant to Cassius*
Calphurnia, *wife to Caesar*
Portia, *wife to Brutus*
Senators, Citizens, Guards, Attendants, etc.

WRITTEN
c. 1599
SETTING AND PERIOD
Rome, Sardis, and Philippi, 44–42 ABD
CHARACTERS 52
ACTS 5
SCENES 17
LINES 2,591

BELOW: *A modern-dress* Julius Caesar *at the Barbican, London, in 2005 directed by Deborah Warner emphasized the tensions between democracy and autocracy in today's world. Here Mark Antony (Ralph Fiennes) discovers the bloody body of Caesar (John Shrapnel).*

Julius Caesar is a play concerned with turning points. It is set in a crumbling republic, as Rome seems about to face either the tyrannical reign of Julius Caesar or the dangerous mob rule of its citizens.

It was first staged in late Elizabethan London, in which concerns over the ageing queen and the imminent possibility of regime change coincided with thoughts of rebellion and revolution. More simply, though, *Julius Caesar* is a turning point for Shakespeare himself. The playwright is roughly halfway through his writing life, and behind him are plays that, though wonderful and promising, are not defining. Ahead of him, however, lie the great tragedies, the subtlest comedies, and the autumnal flourish of the romances. More simply still, *Julius Caesar* marks the clearest turning point in the playwright's career, because this is almost certainly the first play to be performed at the new playhouse, the Globe theater.

The success of the Globe, which was sited on London's Bankside, was crucial to Shakespeare as a shareholder; its structure invited experimentation and encouraged his development as a playwright. This play was the first result of these catalysts.

Caesar's Rome

Shakespeare's success as a playwright up to 1599 was based largely on his history plays, the last of which (until the much later *Henry VIII*) was *Henry V*, written immediately before *Julius Caesar*.

Whereas the English histories work mainly in sequence, Shakespeare's Roman works are stand-alone plays. *Titus Andronicus* was completed much earlier than *Julius Caesar*, and *Antony and Cleopatra* and *Coriolanus* much later. Rather than telling the entire story of a republic and empire, Shakespeare was more interested in the Roman setting to create drama out of a set of strict societal values, and throughout *Julius Caesar* the name of Rome itself is used to allude to those values. Brutus insists of Messala, "Now as you are a Roman tell me true," to which the response is, "Then like a Roman bear the truth I tell" (Act 4, Scene 3, lines 187–88). When the conspirators have finally decided on murder, Brutus reminds them of the ability of Rome's thespians:

Good gentlemen, look fresh and merrily;
Let not our looks put on our purposes,
But bear it as our Roman actors do,
With untir'd spirits and formal constancy.
(ACT 2, SCENE 1, LINES 224–27)

Julius Caesar sees Shakespeare, for the first time, use the writings of Greek philospher Plutarch, whose *Lives of the Noble Grecians and Romans* became the playwright's chief source for his dramas set in the Classical world. Plutarch's work, written about 150 years after the assassination of Julius Caesar, is arranged in alternating biographies of notable Greeks and Romans, drawing comparison between the lives of each pair. It was translated into English by Thomas North in 1579 and revised in 1595.

The plot of *Julius Caesar* is based on Plutarch's account of the lives of Caesar, Marcus Brutus, and Marcus Antonius, with some details from the life of Cicero included. The biographies of Plutarch are lengthy; in terms of plot, Shakespeare includes only the last few pages of the life of Caesar. Much of the rest of the source, however, is alluded to throughout the play.

Staging the Storm

The stage directions of Act 1, Scene 3 call for *"Thunder and lightning"* throughout the scene and reappear in Act 2, Scene 2. In the original productions at the Globe theater, these special effects were achieved with a combination of techniques: fireworks for lightning, and drums, an explosive device called a maroon, and rolled cannonballs to imitate thunder.

BELOW: *In an 1898 production at His Majesty's Theatre, London, Herbert Beerbohm Tree directed a* Julius Caesar *that combined scenic realism with a modern reading of the play, underlining the importance of Mark Antony and of the Roman mob. Charles Fulton (right) played the title role.*

And therefore think him as a serpent's egg,/ Which, hatch'd, would as his kind grow mischievous,/ And kill him in the shell.

—*Brutus* (ACT 2, SCENE 1, LINES 32–34)

The Humors

The Elizabethans believed that the human body, and psyche, was governed by a system of fluids, known as the humors. These four fluids, when in perfect balance, constitute a healthy person, with a level personality. But if one particular humor dominates, the body and the character are affected.

Of the four main male characters in *Julius Caesar*, it is notable that each embodies one of these humors. Most clearly, Brutus exemplifies a predominance of black bile (or melancholy), which is recognizable in his gloominess and his sleeplessness. Similarly, Cassius displays the irascible nature of the influence of yellow bile, or choler. Julius Caesar himself has the type of philosophical indifference that we still identify as phlegmatic—that is, a predominance of phlegm. Mark Antony, passionate and optimistic, typifies the sanguine: one influenced by blood. Thus, the four leading roles are assigned one humor each—which would have been obvious to the original audience. This is not simply a matter of balancing out the play in terms of Elizabethan psychology; it also shows that Shakespeare's company of actors had a cast capable of representing every human nuance. *Julius Caesar* had a new playhouse, and displayed the ability of the company playing there.

THE HISTORY BEHIND THE PLAY

c. 100 BCE	Birth of Julius Caesar
84 BCE	Marries Cornelia
80 BCE	Military service in Asia
78 BCE	Embarks on a political career in Rome
74 BCE	Raises a private army to fight Mithradates, King of Pontus
c. 68 BCE	Death of Cornelia; marries Pompeia; obtains a seat in the Senate
63 BCE	Elected *pontifex maximus* (chief priest)
62 BCE	Divorces Pompeia
61 BCE	Becomes governor of Farther Spain (modern Andalusia and Portugal)
59 BCE	Elected consul; forms a coalition (the first triumvirate) with Pompey and the general Crassus; marries Calphurnia
58 BCE	Begins the conquest of Gaul
55 BCE	Leads a raid on Britain; a second raid follows a year later
53 BCE	Death of Crassus
51 BCE	Completes the conquest of Gaul; a split develops between Caesar and Pompey
49 BCE	Leads an army across the Rubicon into Italy; outbreak of civil war between Caesar and Pompey
48 BCE	Defeats Pompey at the Battle of Pharsalus; Pompey flees to Egypt and is assassinated there; Caesar occupies Alexandria, where he and Cleopatra become lovers
47 BCE	Cleopatra gives birth to a son, Ptolemy Caesar (Caesarion), possibly fathered by Caesar
46 BCE	Appointed dictator for ten years
44 BCE	Appointed dictator for life; assassination of Caesar (March 15)
43 BCE	Formation of the second triumvirate—Mark Antony, Octavius Caesar, and Lepidus
42 BCE	Antony and Octavius defeat Caesar's assassins at the Battle of Philippi

Honor and Power

Like all of Shakespeare's tragedies, *Julius Caesar* addresses many themes that are instantly recognizable: revenge, betrayal, and murder, for example. As with the other Roman plays, honor and power are especially closely examined. It is concern over Caesar's growing power that initiates the events of the play, Cassius claiming that Caesar "doth bestride the narrow world / Like a Colossus" (Act 1, Scene 2, lines 135–36). Against the image of this superhuman power is set the Roman ideal of honor. Brutus makes this declaration early on:

> *Set honor in one eye and death i' th' other,*
> *And I will look on both indifferently;*
> *For let the gods so speed me as I love*
> *The name of honor more than I fear death.*
> (ACT 1, SCENE 2, LINES 86–89)

By the end of the play, this assertion is proven: when he wants to kill himself, he chooses Strato, a man with "some smatch of honor," to hold his sword and calmly runs on to it (Act 5, Scene 5, line 46). Strato has understood the significance of Brutus's act, and reports to the Roman army: "Brutus only overcame himself, / And no man else hath honor by his death" (lines 56–57).

The concept of honor also serves a function in the plot itself. The epithet "honorable men" is used by Antony to syncopate the rhythm of his speech to the Roman crowd, gradually turning them against the conspirators, so that he maintains his own honor by not overtly questioning theirs.

Into the Future

Another dominant theme in *Julius Caesar* is prediction. At every stage, the characters display concern for the future.

Antony Turns the Crowd

Friends, Romans, countrymen, lend me your ears!
I come to bury Caesar, not to praise him.
(ACT 3, SCENE 2, LINES 73–74)

When that the poor have cried, Caesar hath wept;
Ambition should be made of sterner stuff:
Yet Brutus says he was ambitious,
And Brutus is an honorable man.
(LINES 91–94)

Let but the commons hear this testament—
Which, pardon me, I do not mean to read—
And they would go and kiss dead Caesar's wounds[.]
(LINES 130–32)

I fear I wrong the honorable men
Whose daggers have stabb'd Caesar; I do fear it.
(LINES 151–52)

If you have tears, prepare to shed them now.
(LINES 169)

For Brutus, as you know, was Caesar's angel.
Judge, O you gods, how dearly Caesar lov'd him!
This was the most unkindest cut of all[.]
(LINES 181–83)

For I have neither [wit], nor words, nor worth,
Action, nor utterance, nor the power of speech
To stir men's blood[...]
(LINES 221–23)

ABOVE: *Marlon Brando's performance as Mark Antony in the 1953 film* Julius Caesar, *directed by Joseph L. Mankiewicz, was widely praised. He played Antony as an intense idealist, swaying the crowd with his eloquence—but most of all with his passion.*

The Soothsayer repeatedly warns Caesar to "Beware the ides of March" (Act 1, Scene 2, lines 18 and 23). Brutus acknowledges in his detailed soliloquy that Caesar does not deserve to die for what he is, but for what he may become—his acceptance of the "dictator for life" role would have changed republican Rome forever:

to speak truth of Caesar,
I have not known when his affections sway'd
More than his reason. But 'tis a common proof
That lowliness is young ambition's ladder,
Whereto the climber-upward turns his face;
But when he once attains the upmost round,
He then unto the ladder turns his back,
Looks in the clouds, scorning the base degrees
By which he did ascend. So Caesar may;
Then lest he may, prevent ...
(ACT 2, SCENE 1, LINES 19–28)

During the dramatic spectacle of a storm, Casca lists the terrible omens he has seen, and determines that "they are portentous things / Unto the climate that they point upon" (Act 1, Scene 3, lines 31–32). Perhaps most startlingly, when the conspirators have murdered Caesar, Cassius recognizes the historical nature of the moment, and its inherent theatricality: "How many ages hence / Shall this our lofty scene be acted over / In [states] unborn and accents yet unknown!" (Act 3, Scene 1, lines 111–13).

Against this forward-looking prevalence, and the notion of unborn countries and languages, the final words of Caesar, in Latin and describing the present, seem all the more stark and memorable. Ironically, this is the line of the play—and in the minds of many, of Julius Caesar, the historical figure—to last the ages: "*Et tu Brute?*—Then fall Caesar!" (Act 3, Scene 1, line 77).

ABOVE: *Orson Welles directed a famous version of* Julius Caesar *in 1937, the longest-running production of the play on Broadway. Welles subtitled it "Death of a Dictator," dressed the actors in fascist uniforms and modern everyday clothes, and cut the text to concentrate on Caesar, Brutus, and the crowd.*

"Death but Once"

In the maximum security prison on Robben Island, South Africa, Sonny Venkatrathnam kept a copy of the complete works of Shakespeare. In order to keep the guards from confiscating the book, it was disguised as a religious text. Over the course of several years, the sonnets and plays were circulated by Venkatrathnam to his fellow political prisoners, so each inmate could autograph his favorite passages. Thus, in one way, a community was maintained between the single çells and the tiniest respite gained from the daily atrocities suffered.

On December 16, 1977, a famous phrase of Shakespeare's was given a new intensity and level of meaning: "Cowards die many times before their deaths,/The valiant never taste of death but once" (Act 2, Scene 2, lines 32–33). Next to these lines, spoken by Julius Caesar, Nelson Mandela signed his name.

"Did Run Pure Blood"

In terms of metaphor, the most persistent image in *Julius Caesar* is that of blood. Again and again, the word and its derivatives are spoken: fittingly, it is a pulse throughout the play, consistently reminding the audience of the human cost of tyranny, or the stakes of revolution.

The impact of this symbolic corporeality is not lost on Brutus. When the conspirators are planning Caesar's murder, Cassius suggests that Mark Antony should also be slain. Brutus rejects the notion because, as he says, it "will seem too bloody," and he goes on to develop the point carefully:

For Antony is but a limb of Caesar.
Let's be sacrificers, but not butchers, Caius.
We all stand up against the spirit of Caesar,
And in the spirit of men there is no blood;
O that we then could come by Caesar's spirit,
And not dismember Caesar! But, alas,
Caesar must bleed for it! ...
(ACT 2, SCENE 1, LINES 165–71)

Brutus's own diction is used by Antony as he grieves over Caesar's corpse—"O, pardon me, thou bleeding piece of earth, / That I am meek and gentle with these butchers!" (Act 3, Scene 1, lines 254–55)—thus reminding the audience that Brutus's idealism is paid for with a cruel price.

Before the ides of March, Calphurnia dreams that the statue of Caesar "like a fountain with an hundred spouts, / Did run pure blood," in which the Romans "bathe their hands" (Act 2, Scene 2, lines 77–79). Decius Brutus, the conspirator sent to fetch Caesar to the Senate, convinces Caesar that Calphurnia's dream signifies Caesar will revive Rome. In this way, the flexibility of the symbol is used to further the plot. The image is revived by Marcus Brutus after Caesar's death, and this time is literally staged:

Stoop, Romans, stoop,
And let us bathe our hands in Caesar's blood
Up to the elbows, and besmear our swords;
Then walk we forth, even to the market-place,
And waving our red weapons o'er our heads,
Let's all cry, "Peace, freedom, and liberty!"
(ACT 3, SCENE 1, LINES 105–10)

As the conspirators cover themselves in the blood of Caesar, the play's central image becomes visual. Simultaneously, it stands for brutality and peace, distrust and hope, expurgation and freedom.

A Political Play

Julius Caesar has almost always been popular in the theater, but in recent history it has been a favorite of directors seeking to make a political point:"why should Caesar be a tyrant then?" (Act 1, Scene 3, line 102). In the twentieth century there were a great many antifascist productions.

Although the text of the play may seem to be fit for this purpose, the removal of all the moral ambiguity from Caesar's characterization renders Brutus's self-questioning at best redundant, at worst ridiculous. Nonetheless, the director's stance has often focused on a particular figure, and, with dictatorship a prevalent theme, Caesar has been variously aligned with Benito Mussolini, Adolf Hitler, Fidel Castro, Nicolae Ceausescu, and others. In 1993, at the Baron's Court Theatre in London, a female Caesar offered a retrospective take on Margaret Thatcher.

Just as Cicero says to Casca during the storm, "men may construe things after their fashion, / Clean from the purpose of the things themselves" (Act 1, Scene 3, lines 34–35), *Julius Caesar* is clearly tempting to politically minded directors; however, no adapting is necessary for the modern audience. If Shakespeare's play is performed well,

Cry "Havoc!" and let slip the dogs of war, / That this foul deed shall smell above the earth / With carrion men, groaning for burial.

—*Mark Antony* (ACT 3, SCENE 1, LINES 273–75)

its nuances prompt reflection on contemporary life, whether the actors are dressed in togas or in more politically charged blackshirts.

On screen—"In [states] unborn and accents yet unknown!" (Act 3, Scene 1, line 113)—the most successful version, in every sense, is the 1953 film directed by Joseph L. Mankiewicz. As Mark Antony, Marlon Brando was a revelation, and John Gielgud and James Mason shined as Cassius and Brutus, respectively. Previous US film productions of Shakespeare's plays had been box-office failures, and Hollywood had seemed wary of further ventures, but Mankiewicz's film made a great profit. On film, there are possibilities not available to most theater companies, and this is most evident in this version as Brutus and Antony give their orations to a crowd of twelve hundred Romans. The film makes clear that this is a play for an all-star cast, and it is fitting to remember that the original cast—the Lord Chamberlain's Men—was just that, and, furthermore, that for the first productions of *Julius Caesar*, twelve hundred Londoners could have stood listening to the play in the yard of the newly built Globe.

BELOW: *The 1953 Hollywood film of* Julius Caesar *was directed by Joseph L. Mankiewicz, and had a star-studded cast led by Marlon Brando as Mark Antony, and James Mason and John Gielgud as the main conspirators.*

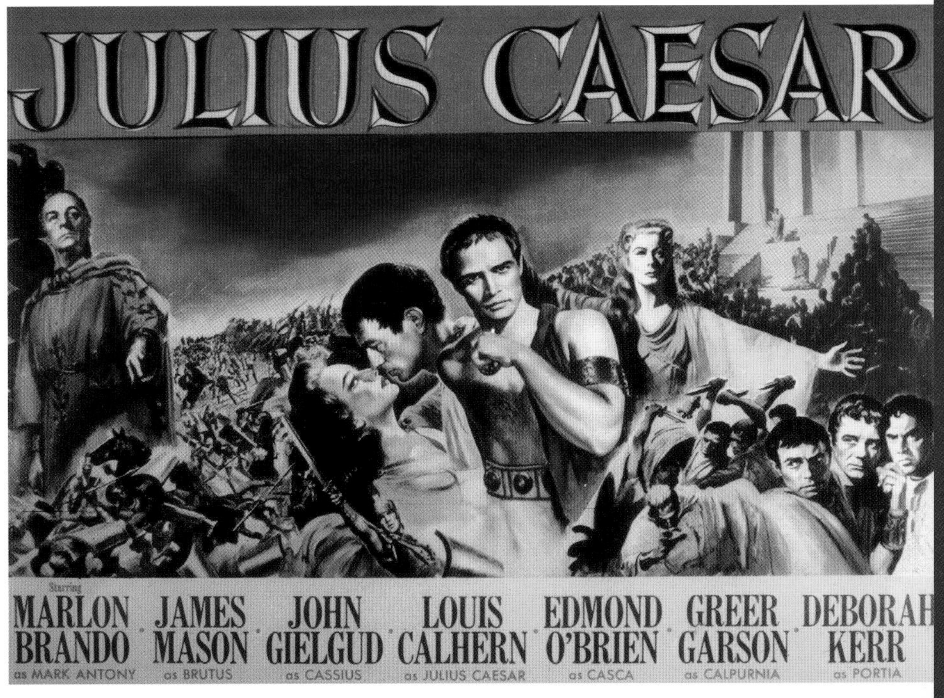

Hamlet

THE PLOT: *Just after midnight, the Ghost of the former King of Denmark appears on the battlements of Elsinore Castle. He reveals to his son, Hamlet, that he was murdered by Claudius, the brother who now wears the crown and has married his widow, Gertrude. Hamlet swears to avenge his father's murder.*

To avoid suspicion, Hamlet pretends to be mad. He arranges for actors to perform a play featuring the murder of his father in order to prove Claudius's guilt. But before he can act upon this evidence, he is arrested for killing the king's chief adviser, Polonius. Hamlet is put on a ship to England, where Claudius has arranged for him to be executed, but he escapes and returns to Denmark.

In the meantime, Polonius's son, Laertes, has come to court to avenge his father's murder. His sister, Ophelia, once Hamlet's beloved, is mad with grief and subsequently drowns. Claudius and Laertes now hatch a plot against Hamlet. In a fencing match, both Hamlet and Laertes are mortally wounded, Gertrude is accidentally poisoned, and Hamlet finally kills Claudius. Before the prince dies, he begs his friend, Horatio, to tell his story.

Dramatis Personae

Claudius, *King of Denmark*
Hamlet, *son to the late King Hamlet, and nephew to the present king*
Polonius, *Lord Chamberlain*
Horatio, *friend to Hamlet*
Laertes, *son to Polonius*
Voltemand, Cornelius, Rosencrantz, Guildenstern, Osric, Gentleman, *courtiers*
Marcellus, Barnardo, *officers*
Francisco, *a soldier*
Reynaldo, *servant to Polonius*
Fortinbras, *Prince of Norway*
Norwegian Captain
Doctor of Divinity
Players
Two Clowns, *gravediggers*
English Ambassadors
Gertrude, *Queen of Denmark, and mother to Hamlet*
Ophelia, *daughter to Polonius*
Ghost of Hamlet's Father
Lords, Ladies, Officers, Soldiers, Sailors, Messengers, and Attendants

Hamlet is probably the most celebrated tragedy in the English language. Its fame is attributable to a thrilling mix of ghost story and murder mystery; powerful stage images (not least a man contemplating a skull in a graveyard); an abundance of memorable lines—"To be or not to be," "Alas, poor Yorick"—but above all to the enigmatic nature of the protagonist himself. The characters' desire to "pluck out the heart of [Hamlet's] mystery" (Act 3, Scene 2, line 366) has extended to generations of audiences, readers, and critics. Among the questions that the play poses are the nature of Hamlet's madness (is it real or fake?), how much Hamlet's mother knows, the reliability of the Ghost, and, above all, why Hamlet delays in taking revenge for his father's death. It is what Shakespeare left unexplained that has contributed to *Hamlet*'s continuing popularity.

WRITTEN
c. 1600
SETTING AND PERIOD
Elsinore Castle, Denmark, Middle Ages/Renaissance
CHARACTERS 30
ACTS 5
SCENES 20
LINES 4,042

The Legend of Amleth

Shakespeare did not invent the plot of *Hamlet*. The narrative originates in the *Historiae Danicae*, a twelfth-century Latin history of Denmark by Danish scholar Saxo Grammaticus (Saxo the Grammarian), which was retold by French author François de Belleforest in his *Histoires Tragiques* (1570). There are significant differences between Shakespeare's version and the Danish legend of Amleth. In the latter, the murder of Amleth's father is performed openly by his brother, Feng, who seizes the throne while Amleth is still a child. But in Shakespeare's play, the murder is carried out in secret and is only revealed to Hamlet by the Ghost, thus placing the protagonist under greater pressure and heightening his sense of isolation. The consequences are also different. In the Danish chronicle, Amleth kills Feng, brings all the nobles together to explain his actions, and is then proclaimed king. Hamlet's revenge concludes not only with his own death and the installation of a foreign monarch on the throne of Denmark, but

Different Texts

Hamlet exists in three very different early texts. The First Quarto, which dates from 1603, is the shortest and seems to have been based on an actor's recollection of the play. The Second Quarto, dated to 1604, is almost twice as long. The last is that included in the First Folio of 1623, which shows strong evidence of having been revised by Shakespeare himself.

RIGHT: *Crown askew, David Tennant plays a feisty Hamlet in the Royal Shakespeare Company production of 2008. More than 400 years after it was first performed,* Hamlet *continues to fascinate audiences and readers alike.*

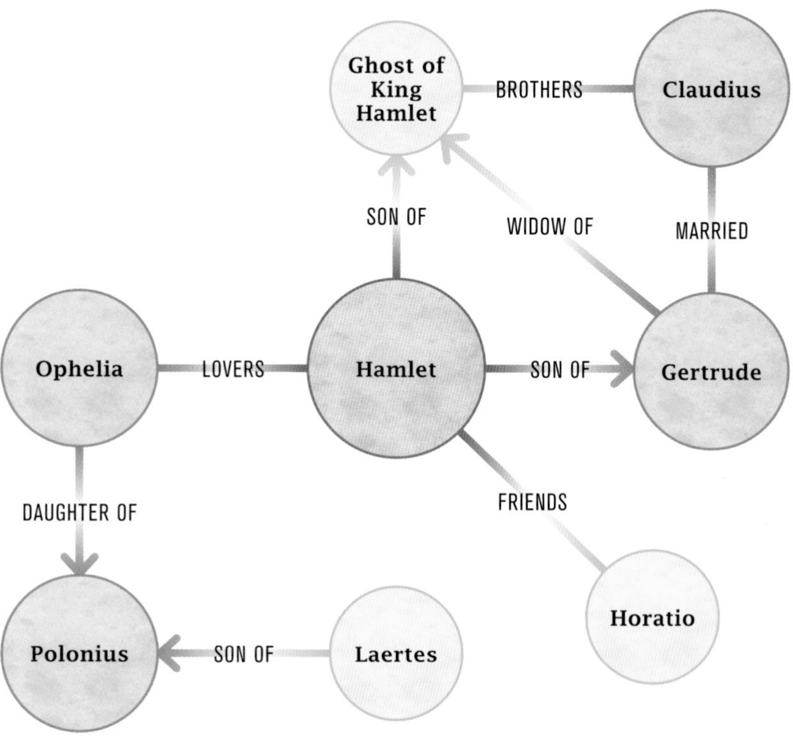

RELATIONSHIPS
Most of the main characters belong to two families—the royal family, of which Hamlet is a member, and Polonius's. Hamlet's actions lead to the destruction of both.

with intense anxiety about the "wounded name" (Act 5, Scene 2, line 344) he leaves behind him.

This old Danish legend might have piqued Shakespeare's interest because of its contemporary relevance to England at the end of the 1590s. Hamlet's frustration as prince-in-waiting reflects the situation of many young aristocrats under the ageing Elizabeth I. Hamlet may also have something in common with James VI of Scotland, the future King of England. Not only was James waiting for the English succession to be decided, he was the product of a similarly violent past. His mother, Mary, Queen of Scots, had been accused of adultery and of plotting the murder of James's father, Henry Stuart, Lord Darnley, who died, like Hamlet's father, in an orchard. Moreover, although James never took revenge himself, in a painting entitled *The Memorial of Lord Darnley* (*c.* 1567), by Livinus de Vogelaare, he was depicted as a child praying: "Arise, O Lord, and avenge the innocent blood of the King."

A Fashion for Revenge

Shakespeare's attraction to the Hamlet story was also informed by what was fashionable in the theater. Since the early 1560s, revenge tragedy had been popular at court and in the law schools, and then in the public playhouses. Indeed, there seems to have been another *Hamlet* play in the repertoire (often called the *Ur-Hamlet* by scholars) as early as 1589, perhaps by Shakespeare's contemporary, Thomas Kyd. Revenge tragedies usually focused on a terrible crime perpetrated against the protagonist. He attempts to gain justice through appeals to the law and to a pagan or Christian divinity, but in the end he is forced to take action for himself, resulting in a spiral of violence that claims more and more lives, including that of the revenger himself.

Shakespeare's *Hamlet* follows many of the conventions of contemporary revenge tragedy. While none of the prose versions of the story included a ghost, on the stage (partly through the influence of Roman playwright Seneca) this figure had become an important agent of revenge. In 1596, dramatist Thomas Lodge recalled a production in which the ghost "cried so miserably … like an oyster wife, *Hamlet, revenge*." Madness is another recurrent feature of revenge tragedy: the terrible suffering and frustration of the protagonist often see him deranged by the end of the play, performing acts of self-mutilation and/or committing suicide. Finally, the play-within-the-play was a means by which the revenger could get close to his intended victim, either by having him as an audience member or casting him in the play whose violence is then performed for real.

Rewriting Conventions

What is fascinating about *Hamlet* is the way in which Shakespeare rewrites these conventions to create a much more ambiguous tragedy. For example, since the play is set in a Christian society, the injunction to commit murder is highly

Hamlet Plots Revenge

Remember thee!
Ay, thou poor ghost, whiles memory holds a seat
In this distracted globe …
(ACT 1, SCENE 5, LINES 95–97)

When he is drunk asleep, or in his rage,
Or in th' incestious pleasure of his bed,
At game a-swearing, or about some act
That has no relish of salvation in't—
Then trip him, that his heels may kick at heaven,
And that his soul may be as damn'd and black
As hell, whereto it goes …
(ACT 3, SCENE 3, LINES 89–95)

Does it not, think thee, stand me now upon—
He that hath kill'd my king and whor'd my
mother,
Popp'd in between th' election and my hopes,
Thrown out his angle for my proper life,
And with such coz'nage—is't not perfect
conscience
To quit him with this arm? …
(ACT 5, SCENE 2, LINES 63–68)

questionable. Shakespeare's audience would have been keenly aware that revenge was prohibited by law, recalling also the biblical prohibition: "Vengeance is mine; I will repay, said the Lord" (Romans 12:19). Shakespeare's Ghost is also a curiously unreliable figure, reflecting the transitional religious moment in which Shakespeare wrote. England had abandoned Catholicism and was now officially Protestant. Yet *Hamlet* initially seems to adhere to the old faith. For example, the Ghost reveals that he is

> *confin'd to fast in fires,*
> *Till the foul crimes done in my days of nature*
> *Are burnt and purg'd away …*
> (ACT 1, SCENE 5, LINES 11–13)

This suggests that he is in purgatory—a staple feature of the Catholic afterlife. The possibility that the dead might appear to their survivors, either to ask for prayers or to give them secret information, was also a Catholic belief. Yet, not only is Shakespeare's audience supposed to be Protestant, but Hamlet, we are told, has come from Wittenberg, the university where Protestant reformer Martin Luther taught. Protestantism not only denied the existence of purgatory but insisted that the dead could not come back to life: ghosts were more likely to be evil spirits who tempted the bereaved to suicide—a fate that Horatio explicitly fears for Hamlet (Act 1, Scene 4, lines 69–74). Thus, Hamlet cannot straightforwardly trust the Ghost's word.

Other ways in which Shakespeare has complicated the revenge tragedy form are the use of madness, the play-within-the-play, and the characterization of the villain. Madness in revenge tragedies could be either genuine or affected, but its end result was to lull the villain into a false sense of security (in Saxo's Danish tale, Amleth pretends to be a lunatic and is therefore viewed by the other characters as harmless). In Shakespeare's play, however, Hamlet only succeeds in drawing attention to himself by appearing to be mad. There is something about his performance that does not convince Claudius, that makes him actively suspicious of the prince.

The play-within-the-play was usually a means of committing revenge, but it might also be used to discover the spectator's guilt (Act 2, Scene 2, lines 588–94). In the anonymous tragedy *A Warning for Fair Women* (dating from 1599), which was performed by Shakespeare's company, reference is made to a woman from Norfolk who confessed to the murder of her husband after watching a similar action performed in the theater. But the response of Claudius to *The Mousetrap* is not so straightforward. He may react as much to Hamlet's aggressive behavior as to the play's subject matter, and the play itself seems to be more concerned with Gertrude's remarriage than with regicide. It is also significant that the murderer, Lucianus, is

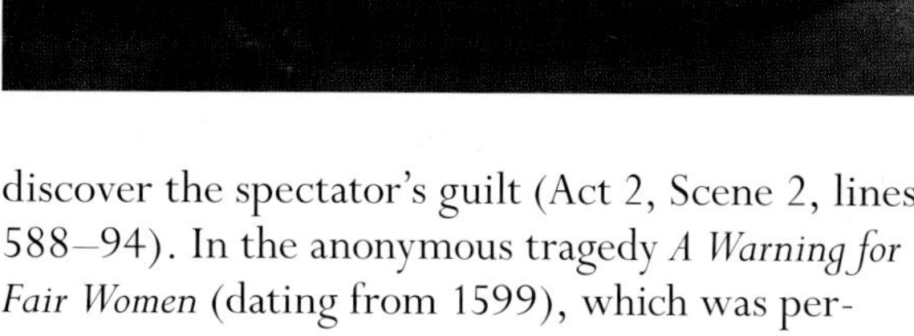

Thus was I, sleeping, by a brother's hand/Of life, of crown, of queen, at once dispatch'd,/…/O, horrible, O, horrible, most horrible!/If thou hast nature in thee, bear it not.

—*Ghost* (ACT 1, SCENE 5, LINES 74–75, 80–81)

ABOVE: *Having first appeared in Act 1 to demand revenge, the Ghost reappears in Act 3, Scene 4 to "whet [Hamlet's] almost blunted purpose" (line 111). This painting of the scene, from the 1750s, also shows Gertrude, who interprets Hamlet's reactions as proof of his madness.*

identified as "nephew to the king" (Act 3, Scene 2, line 244). Thus, Hamlet has staged a play about murdering his uncle.

Finally, Claudius is a more psychologically realized and sympathetic character than was characteristic of the revenge villain. He clearly has a conscience, since he attempts to pray for forgiveness for his crime, and his act of fratricide seems partly to have been motivated by love. He confesses that Gertrude is

> *so [conjunctive] to my life and soul,*
> *That, as the star moves not but in his sphere,*
> *I could not but by her . . .*
> (ACT 4, SCENE 7, LINES 14–16)

Hamlet and Filial Duty

A recurrent theme in Shakespeare's histories and tragedies is the pressure on sons to live up to the reputation of their fathers, and this is a pressure that Hamlet feels keenly. Though he shares his father's name, he doubts that he has inherited the former king's virtues. In fact, he seems to identify more strongly with the flawed brother, Claudius. It is partly on this basis that British psychoanalyst Ernest Jones developed his famous Oedipal theory of Hamlet, based on Sigmund Freud's *The Interpretation of Dreams* (1900). In an essay published in 1910, Jones theorized that Hamlet cannot kill Claudius because the latter has acted out Hamlet's own subconscious desire to murder his father and then marry his mother.

But if Hamlet's feelings about his father are singularly conflicted—a combination of hero-worship, resentment, guilt, and aggression—he is certainly not alone in the play in feeling a duty to take revenge. Laertes plays the role of avenging son while Hamlet is absent in England, and what is at stake is usefully clarified by the dialogue between him and Claudius. Where Claudius makes it a matter of proving filial affection (Act 4, Scene 7, lines 107–9), Laertes is more concerned with proving his paternity:

> *That drop of blood that's calm proclaims me*
> *bastard,*
> *Cries cuckold to my father, brands the harlot*
> *Even here between the chaste unsmirched brow*
> *Of my true mother.*
> (ACT 4, SCENE 5, LINES 118–21)

This same question of legitimacy also deeply affects Hamlet: if his mother has committed adultery before, then his whole relationship to his father is potentially cast into doubt. Other Hamlet doubles in the play are young Fortinbras, heir to

Father and Son

Shakespeare's only son was Hamnet (also written "Hamlet"), who died of unknown causes in 1596, aged only 11. In conceiving a play that begins and ends with the deaths of a father and a son so named, Shakespeare must have recalled his own personal loss. He may also have been anticipating the death of his father, John, in 1601. Hamlet's compulsion to help the Ghost has sometimes been read as indicative of the playwright's guilt regarding his father, whom he had left behind in Stratford and far surpassed in education (evidence suggests that John Shakespeare may have been illiterate).

Even in performance, the play seems to inspire belated confrontations between fathers and sons. In 1989, while playing the role at the National Theatre in London, Daniel Day-Lewis claimed to have seen the ghost of his father, Cecil. He quit the role in the middle of the run.

BELOW: *Does Hamlet subconsciously want to marry his mother? Laurence Olivier, the star and director of the 1948 film version, certainly thought so, giving emphasis to an Oedipal interpretation in his scenes with Gertrude (played by Eileen Herlie).*

Melancholy Hamlet

How [weary], stale, flat, and unprofitable
Seem to me all the uses of this world!
Fie on't, ah fie! 'tis an unweeded garden
That grows to seed, things rank and gross in
nature
Possess it merely ...
(ACT 1, SCENE 2, LINES 133–37)

The time is out of joint—O cursed spite,
That ever I was born to set it right!
(ACT 1, SCENE 5, LINES 188–89)

What [a] piece of work is a man, how noble in reason, how infinite in faculties, in form and moving, how express and admirable in action, how like an angel in apprehension, how like a god! the beauty of the world; the paragon of animals; and yet to me what is this quintessence of dust?
(ACT 2, SCENE 2, LINES 303–8)

the throne of Norway, whose father was killed by King Hamlet, and the Greek warrior Pyrrhus, son of Achilles, who avenges the death of his father at the fall of Troy (as recounted by the player's speech in Act 2, Scene 2). Both men are capable of bloody and wasteful action in pursuit of revenge; they are what Hamlet desires and partly fears to become.

Madness, Real and Otherwise

Another recurrent theme in the play is madness, its causes and effects. During the period in which Shakespeare wrote, bereavement was considered by physicians to be a real danger to a person's mental stability. Hence, when in Act 1, Scene 2 Gertrude and Claudius warn Hamlet against taking the death of his father to heart, there might be those in the audience who recognized this as sound advice. Certainly, before the appearance of the Ghost, Hamlet is suffering from a depression so severe that he contemplates suicide ("O that this too too sallied flesh would melt"; "To be, or not to be," Act 1, Scene 2, line 129; Act 3, Scene 1, lines 55 and following), and his subsequent "antic disposition" is easily interpreted as a manifestation of true mental disturbance.

There is a special providence in the fall of a sparrow. If it be [now], 'tis not to come; if it be not to come, it [will] be now; if it be not now, yet it will come—the readiness is all.

—*Hamlet* (ACT 5, SCENE 2, LINES 219–22)

ABOVE: *Ophelia's descent into madness mirrors Hamlet's apparent "antic disposition." Shown here are Kenneth Branagh (Hamlet) and Kate Winslet (Ophelia) in Branagh's 1996 film version.*

The madness experienced by Ophelia is more obviously attributable to the death of her father, Polonius. In some productions, she puts on his bloodstained clothes, and in her "mad" scenes refers to the fact that he has not been properly buried, and endorses the need for vengeance. At the same time, the play examines the possibility that one might run mad for love. This is initially thought to be the cause of Hamlet's insanity, but it has more obviously contributed toward Ophelia's plight. In one of her ballads, she identifies with a maiden who gives in to the sexual demands of her beloved only to be jilted by him:

Ophelia's Drowning

The image of Ophelia, floating in the water, wearing garlands of flowers, has become one of the play's most iconic images, reproduced in a famous painting (1851–52) by English artist John Everett Millais. It has been read as emphasizing the symbolic relationship between the feminine and fluidity, through the physical association of women's bodies with tears, blood, amniotic fluid, and milk. Its floral attributes have suggested both Ophelia's innocent "blossoming" sexuality and (when she gives the flowers away) her own deflowering. However, this aspect of Shakespeare's plot may also have been taken from real life. In December 1579, a girl called Katherine Hamlett drowned in the Avon River near Shakespeare's home. A verdict of accidental death was given, but the dramatist may also have heard the rumors that she was suffering from a broken heart and had committed suicide, inspiring the ambiguity that surrounds Ophelia's death.

ABOVE: *"Her clothes spread wide, / And mermaid-like:" John Everett Millais took great pains to re-create Gertrude's description (Act 4, Scene 7, lines 166–83) of Ophelia's death, right down to the species of flowers in Ophelia's garland.*

"Quoth she, 'Before you tumbled me,
You promis'd me to wed.'"
(He answers.)
"'So would I 'a' done, by yonder sun,
And thou hadst not come to my bed.'"
(ACT 4, SCENE 5, LINES 62–66)

Madness also affords Shakespeare's characters the possibility of saying the unsayable. Hamlet's condition, whether real or fake, is characterized by his contempt for authority. He is rude about old men, such as Polonius, at a time when respect for one's elders was strongly drilled into Elizabethan children, and he disputes the fact that there is any essential difference between a king and a beggar since they are both food for worms (Act 4, Scene 3, lines 19–25), which is treasonable.

The same kind of transgression characterizes Ophelia's mad speech in Act 4, Scene 5, though hers relates to questions of gender rather than of politics. The main duty of Ophelia, as far as her father and brother are concerned, is to keep her virginity intact and unsuspected until she can be married. To appear chaste, she must pretend not even to understand Hamlet's innuendo when he asks to "lie in her lap" (Act 3, Scene 2, line 112). However, in her madness Ophelia is able to express some knowledge of sexual relationships and even to use bawdy language herself in the form of oaths: "By Gis, and by Saint Charity … / By Cock, [men] are to blame" (Act 4, Scene 5, lines 58, 61). Also, one of the flowers that she bears when she goes to her watery death is associated with male genitalia:

long purples,
That liberal shepherds give a grosser name,
But our cull-cold maids do dead men's fingers
call them.
(ACT 4, SCENE 7, LINES 169–71)

RIGHT: *"Not one now to mock your own grinning[?]" (Act 5, Scene 1, lines 191–92) asks Hamlet (Innokenti Smoktunovsky) of Yorick's skull, as the gravedigger looks on, in this scene from the Russian film version made in 1964.*

Again, we have the sense that unmarried women cannot afford to give things their right names.

Serious Laughter

Finally, *Hamlet* is famous for its deft mingling of comedy and tragedy. From the beginning of the play, the festive and carnivalesque have existed in parallel with the tragic perspective on life. Thus, the celebration of Claudius and Gertrude's wedding acknowledges the death that made it possible. As Hamlet acerbically remarks: "The funeral bak'd-meats / Did coldly furnish forth the marriage tables" (Act 1, Scene 2, lines 180–81). But if Hamlet appears here to be an enemy to the carnivalesque, exhibiting a particular distaste for excessive eating and drinking, he also brings the worlds of comedy and tragedy together. Describing himself as a "jig-maker," and playing the role of court jester or "antic" to the king, he punctures men's pretensions to greatness by reducing them to the condition of decaying and vermiculated flesh. Polonius becomes no more than a malodorous corpse whose "guts" must be "lug[ged]" into the other room (Act 3, Scene 4, line 212).

The gravediggers who appear in Act 5 (and seem to have been Shakespeare's own invention) expand on Hamlet's role. As ordinary, laboring men, digging in the earth, they represent an expansion of the narrow, claustrophobic world characterized by the Danish court. Moreover, their comic disrespect for death as they toss skulls out of graves is matched by a similar contempt for the distinctions conveyed by class and wealth (Act 5, Scene 1, lines 26–31). It is this spectacle that gets Hamlet meditating on the skull, and he too finds comedy in the fact that Yorick, the man who was paid to tell jokes at his father's court, should have been reduced to such a hideous object. Although this scene is often taken as an image of high seriousness and philosophical contemplation, as a *memento mori* (a reminder of one's mortality), it is also a comic epiphany of the absurdity of death (and life). The entrance of Ophelia's funeral procession, with all the assembled court, shifts our attention back to the play's tragic viewpoint. It may be significant, however, that Shakespeare has not given the gravedigger an exit line, allowing him to remain on stage throughout the scene, an amused spectator of these great ones and their tribulations.

"Brief Let Me Be"

Hamlet is the longest play in the Shakespearean canon, with 4,042 lines and more than 29,000 words, making for a lengthy evening at the theater or cineplex. The 1996 film version, directed by and starring Kenneth Branagh, clocks in at just under four hours.

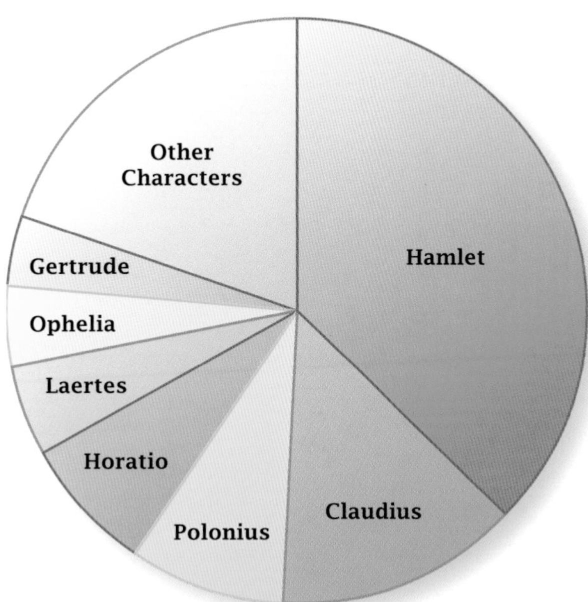

MAJOR ROLES
Hamlet dominates the play, as this pie chart of the percentages of lines spoken by major characters shows. In fact, his is the largest speaking part in Shakespeare, with nearly 40 percent of the play's lines.

Images of Poison and Deceit

Poison is not just an important plot device in the play; it is also a metaphor for emotional and political corruption. For example, Hamlet's grief at the death of his father ruins his pleasure in the world, so that the very air has become no more than "a foul and pestilent congregation of vapors" (Act 2, Scene 2, lines 302–3). For some critics, Hamlet himself is a kind of poison or blight,

ABOVE: *Rosencrantz (Gary Oldman, left) and Guildenstern (Tim Roth, center), minor characters in* Hamlet, *take center stage in Tom Stoppard's play* Rosencrantz and Guildenstern Are Dead. *Also shown in this scene from the film version of 1990 is the Player (Richard Dreyfuss), leader of an acting troupe.*

destroying the kingdom of Denmark from within, with Claudius describing him as "a foul disease" (Act 4, Scene 1, line 21). Yet Claudius is equally viewed as the source of political contamination. As a murdering and usurping king, he infects the whole of his kingdom: "Something is rotten in the state of Denmark" (Act 1, Scene 4, line 90).

Another frequent image (related to this) is that of the deceitful woman whose beauty belies her moral ugliness. This originates in Hamlet's disgust with his mother—Gertrude seemed a devoted wife but has remarried with abhorrent speed, and there is even some question as to whether she knew of the murder. However, Hamlet also extends his sense of female treachery to Ophelia. In Act 3, Scene 1, he accuses her of creating a deceptively alluring exterior through cosmetics and false gestures: "God hath given you one face, and you make yourselves another. You jig and amble, and you [lisp] ..." (lines 143–44). Where this image coincides with the fear of sexuality that pervades the play is in the image of the prostitute. When Hamlet tells Ophelia to "Get thee to a nunn'ry" (Act 3, Scene 1, lines 136–37), he is trying to prevent her from having sex, but he is also condemning her to a life of prostitution, since the word "nunn'ry" could mean "brothel" at this time. Male characters also use the image of the whore and her false beauty to condemn themselves. Thus, Claudius insists that

> *The harlot's cheek, beautied with plast'ring art,*
> *Is not more ugly to the thing that helps it*
> *Than is my deed to my most painted word.*
> (ACT 3, SCENE 1, LINES 50–52)

Hamlet also blames himself for his inaction by likening himself to the whore who "unpack[s her] heart with words" (Act 2, Scene 2, line 585).

Performance and Adaptation

Hamlet continues to thrive on the stage, with productions tending to emphasize either the psychological or the political aspects of the play.

For example, in 1937, Laurence Olivier played the role for director Tyrone Guthrie at the Old Vic theater, London, with a strong sense of Hamlet's Oedipal conflict. In the subsequent film (released in 1948), the arrangement of the bed-hangings in Gertrude's closet was implicitly vaginal, and the appeal of the actress playing Hamlet's mother, Eileen Herlie, was enhanced by the fact that she was 12 years younger than Olivier.

Now cracks a noble heart. Good night, sweet prince,/ And flights of angels sing thee to thy rest!

—*Horatio* (ACT 5, SCENE 2, LINES 359–60)

The political reading of *Hamlet*—derived partly from Hamlet's assertion that "Denmark's a prison" (Act 2, Scene 2, line 243)—has been most popular in European countries with communist regimes. German dramatist Heiner Müller's play *Hamletmachine* (1977, performed in Paris, 1979) is made up of two monologues by Hamlet and Ophelia exploring the fate of intellectuals in East Germany. More recently, *Hamlet* has been found relevant to the present-day conflict in the Middle East, with Ophelia appearing as a suicide bomber in Kuwaiti writer and director Sulayman Al-Bassam's Arabic *The Al-Hamlet Summit* at the Riverside Studios, London, in 2004.

Hamlet remains one of the Shakespearean plays most often adapted for the cinema. Some notable productions include the Russian version by Grigori Kozintsev (1964), British adaptations by Laurence Olivier (1948) and Kenneth Branagh (1996), and, in Hollywood, films by Franco Zeffirelli (1990, starring Mel Gibson), and Michael Almereyda (2000, starring Ethan Hawke).

Shakespeare's play has also inspired some fascinating cultural spin-offs, from *Wilhelm Meister's Apprenticeship* (1795–96), by German author Johann Wolfgang von Goethe, to *The Lion King* (1994), a Disney animated film. A characteristically modern approach has been to retell the *Hamlet* story from the perspective of the more marginal characters. British playwright Tom Stoppard's play *Rosencrantz and Guildenstern Are Dead* (1966, directed by him as a film in 1990) focuses on this pair whom Hamlet sends, unwittingly, to their deaths.

Elsewhere, the unease that feminist critics have often felt with *Hamlet* is registered in the expansion of Ophelia's and Gertrude's roles. For example, *Gertrude and Claudius* (2000), by US novelist John Updike, suggests that the former was unhappily married to Hamlet's father and found real passion only with his brother. While Updike exonerates the queen from any knowledge of her husband's death, in the short story "Gertrude Talks Back" (in Canadian author Margaret Atwood's collection, *Good Bones*, 1992) she confesses: "It wasn't Claudius, darling, it was me." The frequency with which *Hamlet* is not only performed and adapted but also alluded to in brief verbal or visual quotations demonstrates its ongoing relevance for the twenty-first century.

Women Playing Hamlet

Hamlet has long been a popular role for women, with some intriguing consequences for the play's meaning. In the silent German film *Hamlet* (1921), directed by Sven Gade and Heinz Schall, Danish star Asta Nielsen played Hamlet as a girl brought up as a boy. This was thought to explain not only Hamlet's lacking the stomach for murder but his/her complicated relationships with both Ophelia and Horatio. Other female performances of the role have maintained Hamlet's gender but explored the androgynous effect thereby created. Angela Winkler, for example, played Hamlet in a 1999 production directed by Peter Zadek in the newly reunified Germany. Her combination of masculinity and femininity was intended to suggest an image of reconciliation and peace.

ABOVE: *Angela Winkler (left) continued a long tradition of women playing Hamlet, in Peter Zadek's 1999 production, with Eva Mattes (Gertrude) and Hermann Lause (Ghost).*

Troilus and Cressida

WRITTEN
c. 1601

SETTING AND PERIOD
Troy, thirteenth century BCE

CHARACTERS 26

ACTS 5

SCENES
24 plus Prologue

LINES 3,531

THE PLOT: *The play begins seven years after the Trojan prince Paris abducted Helen from her husband, Menelaus of Sparta, that is, in the stalemate between the Greeks and the Trojans, with the Greeks camped outside the walls of Troy. The warriors quarrel among themselves about necessary action and the ethics of war. Pandarus brings together his niece, Cressida, with Paris's brother, Troilus, but after just one night Cressida is exchanged for the Trojan commander, Antenor, and turns to a new lover, Diomedes.*

The play has two chorus figures. Cassandra (daughter of Priam, and sister to Paris, Hector, and Troilus) predicts the death of Hector, one of the more moral-minded of the warriors, while Thersites criticizes the actions of the supposedly heroic warriors. The play ends with Troilus's anger at the death of his brother, and determination for revenge, and Pandarus's speech full of images of diseases and prostitution.

Dramatis Personae

Priam, *King of Troy*
Hector, Troilus, Paris, Deiphobus, Helenus, *his sons*
Margarelon, *a bastard son of Priam*
Aeneas, Antenor, *Trojan commanders*
Calchas, *a Trojan priest, taking part with the Greeks*
Pandarus, *uncle to Cressida*
Alexander, *servant to Cressida*
Servant and Boy to Troilus
Servant to Paris
Agamemnon, *the Greek general*
Menelaus, *his brother*
Nestor, Ulysses, Achilles, Ajax, Diomedes, Patroclus, *Greek commanders*
Thersites, *a deformed and scurrilous Greek*
Servant to Diomedes
Helen, *wife to Menelaus*
Andromache, *wife to Hector*
Cassandra, *daughter to Priam, a prophetess*
Cressida, *daughter to Calchas*
Trojan and Greek Soldiers, and Attendants

LEFT: *The play casts a skeptical eye on the legends of the Trojan War. While Helen (Marianne Oldham, with Greek warriors, in a 2008 London production) is undeniably beautiful, the Greeks debate whether she is worth fighting for. Diomedes says: "For every false drop in her bawdy veins, / A Grecian's life hath sunk" (Act 4, Scene 1, lines 70-71).*

Troilus and Cressida is regarded as one of the more difficult of Shakespeare's plays to read, and watch, and is less often performed than are many of the others in the canon. While the play's title bears the names of the two lovers, the love between them is short lived, and, for most audiences, their story is far less well known than that of Paris's abduction of Helen, which precipitated the Trojan War:

In Troy there lies the scene. From isles of Greece
The princes orgillous [proud], their high blood chaf'd,
Have to the port of Athens sent their ships
Fraught with the ministers and instruments
Of cruel war ...
(PROLOGUE, LINES 1–5)

The play begins in the middle of the Trojan War, but the war's most famous event, the scheme to take Troy by stealth, by means of the "Trojan horse," is not mentioned. Shakespeare's emphasis is not on battle and heroic deeds by great men, but on the disarray and disillusion that are the effects of a long, drawn-out, and inconclusive campaign.

BELOW: *What the male characters interpret as Cressida's fickle nature is for them confirmed in Act 5, Scene 2, when Ulysses and Troilus secretly watch as Diomedes and Cressida kiss and wrestle with Troilus's love token. The scene is captured in this 1850s engraving.*

Troy and New Troy

London in the sixteenth century was sometimes thought of as New Troy (Troynovant), based on the idea that the city was founded by a refugee from Troy, Brutus. In this light it is perhaps not surprising that the play does not focus on the fall of Troy. An account of the Trojans being seduced into taking a wooden horse inside their gates, only to be surprised by the enemy within, might have been seen as implicit criticism of the powers that be.

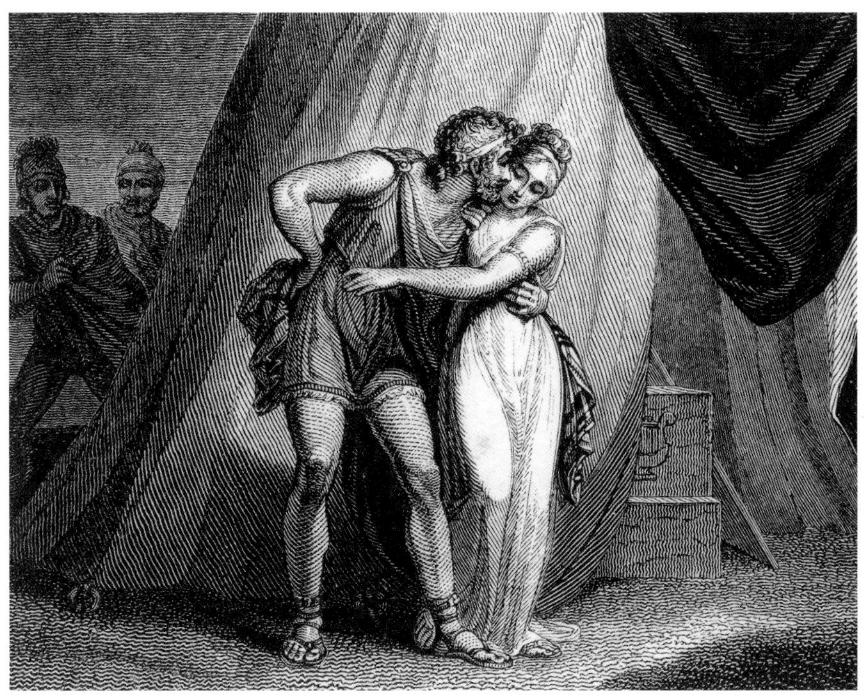

Proportion Is Preferable to Excess

The heavens themselves, the planets, and this centre
Observe degree, priority, and place,
Insisture, course, proportion, season, form,
Office, and custom, in all line of order;
....
But when the planets
In evil mixture to disorder wander,
What plagues and what portents, what mutiny!
What raging of the sea, shaking of earth!
—*Ulysses* (ACT 1, SCENE 3, LINES 85–88, 94–97)

'Tis mad idolatry
To make the service greater than the god,
And the will dotes that is attributive
To what infectiously itself affects,
Without some image of th' affected merit.
—*Hector* (ACT 2, SCENE 2, LINES 56–60)

She was belov'd, [she lov'd]; she is, and doth:
But still sweet love is food for fortune's tooth.
—*Troilus* (ACT 4, SCENE 5, LINES 292–93)

Instead, the play's core is the destruction that the seizing of Helen has brought, paralleled with the fleeting passion between Troilus and Cressida; the latter becomes a byword for inconsistency. Here the figure of Ulysses appears less than heroic or chivalrous when, in Act 4, Scene 5, he sees Cressida talking to Diomedes, and immediately assumes her infidelity to Troilus, and goes from there to compare her with prostitutes, "daughters of the game" (Act 4, Scene 5, line 63).

What Kind of Play Is This?

Troilus and Cressida has attracted considerable debate among critics about its nature, or genre. Sometimes listed as a tragedy, it is also a romance. More important, its strongest elements are comedy and satire, particularly in the characterizations of Ulysses and Achilles.

Central themes in the play link ideas about moral order, the need for social stability, and what constitutes bravery. Ulysses' long speech in Act 1, Scene 3 is full of imagery of the necessity for order, hierarchy, and the proper exercise of power. It is an impressive speech of some 70 lines, but the moment is undercut by its final sentence, which reveals the short moral, "To end a tale of length, / Troy in our weakness stands, not in her strength" (Act 1, Scene 3, lines 136–37). This two-line summary undermines the dignity of the

Women are angels, wooing:/Things won are done, joy's soul lies in the doing./That she belov'd knows nought that knows not this:/ Men prize the thing ungain'd more than it is.

—*Cressida* (ACT 1, SCENE 2, LINES 286–89)

previous words, and contributes to the characterizations of key figures in the play—such as Ulysses, Priam, and Agamemnon—as old and out of touch. Throughout the play, words take the place of actions, and key heroic figures such as Achilles and Hector seem ineffectual.

One source of the play's difficulty lies in the fact that while many other plays have characters through whom the action is focused, such as Lear, Hamlet, or Macbeth, or even Rosalind in *As You Like It* and Portia in *The Merchant of Venice*, there are no clear central characters in *Troilus and Cressida*. The action shifts between camps, and between characters, and this means that an audience or reader cannot find an easy path to follow in interpreting the play. In general, no one character is more sympathetically treated than another.

Another source of difficulty is the play's pace. The early acts have a uniform structure of three scenes of between 100 and 400 lines. The final two acts, however, consist of many very short scenes, and here the action picks up. This contributes to the sense of a play in two parts: in the first, the politicians pontificate; in the second, the consequences of their decisions occur. The disjunction that this suggests between words and deeds is unsettling.

MAJOR ROLES
The play lacks a dominant figure or figures, with most of the main characters having a similar number of lines, as this pie chart shows.

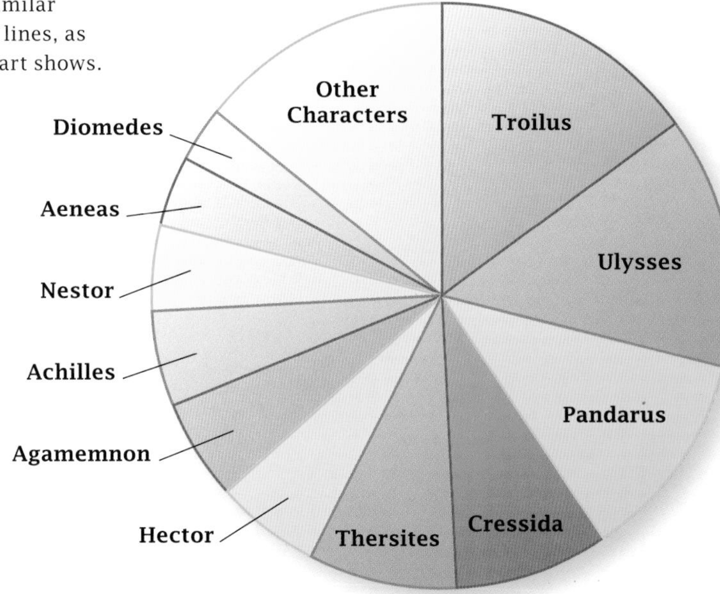

Love and War

A sense of futility pervades the play. Act 2, Scene 2 contains important exchanges between Priam and his three sons, Hector, Troilus, and Paris, about whether keeping Helen is worth the trouble. Hector at one point argues, "Let Helen go" (Act 2, Scene 2, line 17), and again later, "she is not worth what she doth cost / The keeping" (Act 2, Scene 2, lines 51–52), yet the scene ends with his complete change of heart. And the play ends with his death, with little to show for his sacrifice.

There is also no clear sense of difference between the Greeks and the Trojans, so it is difficult for an audience to feel sympathy for one side over the other. The numerous debates on whether the war is justified, and the presentation of both sides of any argument, add to the sense of pointlessness. Debate, it seems, is often mere bombast. Those who look for heroic images and figures in the play will be disappointed—there are none.

Gender and Action

Much of the play revolves around the notion that action is masculine and inaction is feminine. The first lines after the Prologue focus on the rejection of fighting and battle because of love. The taking of Helen by Paris from Menelaus is suggested to render Menelaus effeminate. Similarly, the love of Achilles for Polyxena turns him into an "effeminate man" (Act 3, Scene 3, line 218), and Troilus, too, sees his own inability to fight as "womanish" (Act 1, Scene 1, line 107), overcome as he is by his love of Cressida. Love of women unmans men in this play, rendering them inactive and lacking in bravery. Action in the end is taken when men are stirred by events occurring to other men, in particular in reaction to the death of Hector.

Another of the play's themes involves the difference between public causes and private interests, where the public domain of battle is masculine and the private domain feminine. For example, Achilles' entourage of warriors, the Myrmidons, operates as a separate army serving Achilles rather than the common good. Achilles' retreat into his own private world with his own entourage is part of an equation that sees action as public and masculine, and inaction as private and feminine:

the proud lord
... bastes his arrogance with his own seam [fat],
And never suffers matter of the world

ABOVE: *Achilles is exposed as anything but heroic when in Act 5, Scene 8 he orders his followers, the Myrmidons, to kill the unarmed Hector. In this 2008 London production, he administers the coup de grâce.*

Unheroic Heroes

Troilus and Cressida does not portray the soldiers of the Trojan War as heroes, as they seem in Homer's epic poem, *The Iliad*. Some of them are pompous, some foolish. Achilles, for example, is love-sick for Polyxena, a woman we never see, and spends most of his time lounging around, avoiding battle.

Enter his thoughts, save such as doth revolve
And ruminate [concern] himself . . .
(ACT 2, SCENE 3, LINES 184–88)

To get Achilles back into action, Ulysses promotes Ajax in order to goad Achilles, and much of the play explores how individuals are affected by circumstances of love, power, and war.

A Play for Our Times

Given that most of the characters seem uncertain about why they are fighting and whether fighting is worthwhile anyway, the play can be seen as opposed to war. Some modern critics and directors have seen the play's treatment of war as being especially in tune with our times. In the 1970s, for example, US critic R.A. Yoder in the essay "'Sons and Daughters of the Game'" suggested that the play has special relevance in relation to the world wars of the twentieth century, and to the United States and the war in Vietnam, arguing that "Of all Shakespeare, *Troilus and Cressida* is our play."

Thersites provides a perspective that undercuts the long speeches on the necessity of war. Some of the play's sharpest lines belong to him. This "slave whose gall coins slanders like a mint" (Act 1, Scene 3, line 193) stands outside the main action and criticizes everyone. For him, status means nothing, and the behavior of

those crafty swearing rascals, that stale old
mouse-eaten dry cheese, Nestor, and that
same dog-fox, Ulysses, is not prov'd worth
a blackberry.
(ACT 5, SCENE 4, LINES 9–12)

While he is not a sympathetic character, he is a means by which the play includes a critique of its key historical characters.

The imagery used by Thersites is dark and cynical; the emphasis is on the ability of words to persuade people to actions that may not in themselves be moral. *Troilus and Cressida* is a profoundly provocative play in its exploration of the gaps between words and deeds, and the morality of war.

The power of the play has attracted fine actors, particularly in the title roles—Ian Holm, Ralph Fiennes, and Helen Mirren among them—and for the role of Thersites, including Peter O'Toole. In the United States, a notable production was director Joseph Papp's 1965 New York staging, in which Cressida was portrayed as a victim of male violence. The play has been performed in continental Europe since the late nineteenth century. Italian director Luchino Visconti's production of 1949, in Florence, was memorable for its stage design by Franco Zeffirelli.

Othello

THE PLOT: *It is night in Venice. Roderigo is angry; Iago has been taking money from him to help him marry Desdemona, but she has secretly married Othello. Iago is jealous because Othello has promoted Cassio over him. Othello and Brabantio (Desdemona's father) are summoned to the council; the Turks are about to launch an attack on Cyprus, a Venetian colony, and Othello is to command the Venetian defense. At the council, Brabantio complains that Othello has used witchcraft to bewitch his daughter. Desdemona is sent for and requests permission to accompany Othello to Cyprus.*

Iago plans to undermine Othello. Once they arrive in Cyprus, he gets Cassio drunk on duty, and Cassio is cashiered. Iago tells him to ask Desdemona to persuade Othello to give him back his job. Emilia picks up Desdemona's handkerchief and gives it to Iago. He leaves it in Cassio's lodging, and convinces Othello of Desdemona's adultery. Othello orders Iago to murder Cassio, and smothers Desdemona in her bed.

Dramatis Personae

Duke of Venice
Brabantio, *a senator, father to Desdemona*
Other Senators
Gratiano, *brother to Brabantio, a noble Venetian*
Lodovico, *kinsman to Brabantio, a noble Venetian*
Othello, *the Moor, in the military service of Venice*
Cassio, *an honorable lieutenant*
Iago, *an ensign, a villain*
Roderigo, *a gull'd gentleman*
Montano, *governor of Cyprus before Othello*
Clown, *servant to Othello*
Desdemona, *daughter to Brabantio and wife to Othello*
Emilia, *wife to Iago*
Bianca, *a courtezan*
Gentlemen of Cyprus, Sailors, Officers, Messenger, Herald, Musicians, and Attendants

LEFT: *This sixteenth-century painting,* The Piazzetta di San Marco, *depicts St. Mark's Square in the heart of Venice. The Square, containing St. Mark's Basilica and the Doge's Palace, was the base of Venetian power for centuries.*

WRITTEN c. 1603

SETTING AND PERIOD Venice and Cyprus, c. 1500

CHARACTERS 15

ACTS 5

SCENES 15

LINES 3,551

Shakespeare found the source story for his play in Italian poet and dramatist Giambattista Giraldi's *Ecatommiti* (1565). This book presents a group of noblemen and ladies, who, while fleeing the rampaging forces of the Holy Roman Emperor after the sack of Rome in 1527, entertain each other on board ship by swapping stories about the various types of love. An opening dialogue argues the necessity for reason in love and suggests that like should marry like. The book contains 110 stories, arranged in themed decades, or groups of ten.

All the characters in Giraldi's story except for "Disdemona" (whose name is identified as meaning "unlucky") are known simply by their status: Ensign; Corporal; Moor. Shakespeare followed this rather sordid tale of domestic violence remarkably closely, and yet he managed to transform it into one of the greatest and most enduring of his plays. To begin to understand how he managed this, we must look at what he changed. Shakespeare provides the characters with names, identities, and back stories. We hear how Desdemona would listen enraptured to Othello as he recounted the events of his life; we meet her father and learn that his tolerance of a black man only goes so far. And most important, Shakespeare provides a military and political backdrop to the play—the expansion of the Turkish Ottoman Empire—and we learn that Othello and Iago have fought together in wars many times in the past, "At Rhodes, at Cyprus, and on [other] grounds" (Act 1, Scene 1, line 29). As a result they have seemingly developed the strong bond of trust and interdependence essential for effective fighting units. Othello trusts him implicitly, as do all the other professional soldiers in the play; "honest, honest Iago" is a refrain that runs throughout *Othello*.

Turks and Christians

The mention of recent military engagements in Rhodes and Cyprus sets the play in the past for an Elizabethan audience, before these places were

A Visit from the Moors

Ambassadors from the King of Barbary (Morocco) visited London in 1600. Elizabethan historian John Stow tells us they were "bountifully entertained" by the queen, but he is resistant to their Islamic dietary practices, and suspicious that they "diligently observed the manner of our weights and measures, and all things else that might avail their native merchants, and prejudice the English Nation" (*Chronicles*, 1618).

The Moor and Disdemona

Shakespeare's source for *Othello* is Giambattista Giraldi's *Ecatommiti,* Decade 3, story 7. In it, the Moor and Disdemona fall in love with each other's good qualities and live happily together in Venice. The Senate appoints him governor of Cyprus and she eagerly accompanies him there. His trusted Ensign falls in love with Disdemona, although she has eyes only for the Moor. This makes the Ensign think that she must love the Moor's friend, the Corporal. He decides to take his revenge by persuading the Moor of this too, stealing her handkerchief and leaving it in the Corporal's lodging. Later he attacks the Corporal as he leaves his mistress's house. The Moor and the Ensign together batter Disdemona to death with a sandbag, pulling down the roof on top of her body to make it look like an accident. The Moor is banished and later murdered by Disdemona's relatives. The Ensign eventually dies after being tortured for another offense; thus God avenges Disdemona's innocence.

captured by the Turks. Rhodes had belonged to a religious military order, the Knights Hospitaller; it withstood a Turkish siege in 1480, but finally fell to Sultan Süleyman the Magnificent in 1522. Famagusta, the main fortified port on the Venetian island of Cyprus, had surrendered after a siege in August 1571 on the promise of safe evacuation to Crete. Following a misunderstanding, the entire garrison had been taken prisoner and the governor flayed alive. This horrific event is described in a number of late sixteenth-century books, among them Hakluyt's *Voyages*, which Shakespeare is known to have read. Two months later, combined Spanish, Venetian, and Genoese Christian forces under Don John of Austria won an astonishing victory at the Battle of Lepanto, a naval engagement that resulted in the loss of half the Turkish fleet. This, however, did nothing to halt the spread of the Ottoman Empire, which by the time Shakespeare was writing stretched almost as far as Vienna in the north, and encompassed all the North African Berber kingdoms bordering the Mediterranean. Contemporary writers moralized on this frightening success, attributing it to the schism within Christianity. Hubert Folieta of Genoa, in *The Mahumetane or Turkish Historie* (1600), wrote:

> *[W]e are desperately diseased, even to the death, our soldiers being mutinous, factious, disobedient, who fashioned by no rules of discipline, contained in duty by no regard of punishment ... for the most part work more mischief than what at any time they receive from the weapons of the enemy ... a number of whom studying their particular revenge, their private ambition or (than which with men of war there is naught more odious) their servile gain, betray their country, neglect their prince's command, and without executing aught worthy their trust and employment, cause often impediments though malicious envy of another's glory[.]*

As a young man, the Scottish king, James VI, had written an epic poem on the Battle of Lepanto. He became James I of England in 1603—and his poem reprinted in London—the year Shakespeare was probably writing his play. The king explains in his introduction that the Turks in his poem were intended to represent the evils of Catholicism. It is therefore perhaps not accidental that the Turks in Shakespeare's play are defeated by a great storm, which was also the fate of the Spanish Armada that had sailed against England in 1588.

BELOW: *A Spanish-led Christian fleet of more than two hundred galleys defeated the Ottoman navy at Lepanto in 1571, a feat depicted in this contemporary painting by an unknown Venetian artist. An estimated eight thousand Christians and twenty-five thousand Turks died.*

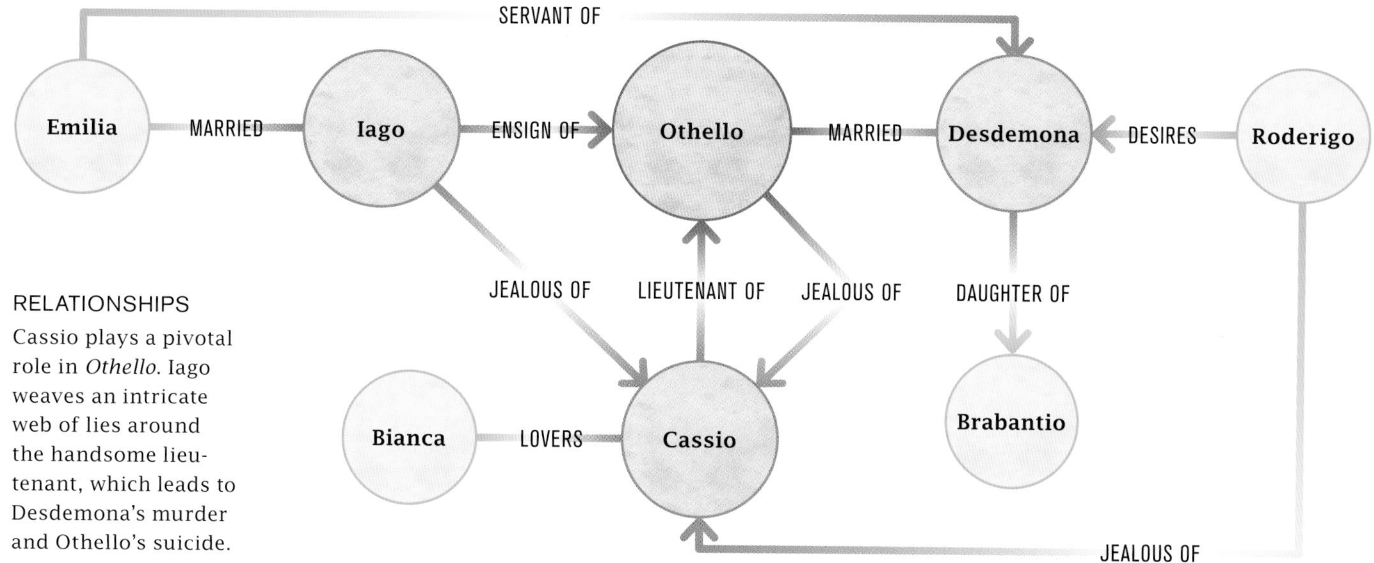

RELATIONSHIPS
Cassio plays a pivotal role in *Othello*. Iago weaves an intricate web of lies around the handsome lieutenant, which leads to Desdemona's murder and Othello's suicide.

Opposites and Harmony

Cyprus lies at the very eastern extremity of the Mediterranean on the boundary between East and West, Christianity and Islam. The seas off Cyprus were said to be the birthplace of the goddess of love, Venus, whose marriage to Mars, the god of war, had resulted in the birth of a child, Harmony. Such uniting of opposites is both an ideal and a threat to the status quo: love might effeminize or emasculate the war hero and make him too soft to fight. Botticelli's painting *Venus and Mars* (c. 1485), for example, shows a serene Venus, with not a hair out of place, smiling gently while cupids play mischievously with Mars's lance and helmet as he lies sprawled and vulnerable in postcoital exhaustion.

Throughout the play's first half, Othello is able to balance the demands of his public and private lives. He talks of Desdemona and of his military role in the same breath, and denies that he will "scant" the business of the state if she accompanies him into a war zone. When they meet again on Cyprus, they greet each other in terms that continue this mingling of love and war. He terms her his "fair warrior," and she him, her "dear Othello" (Act 2, Scene 1, line 182). But while Cassio sees Desdemona as Othello's inspiration, "our great captain's captain" (Act 2, Scene 1, line 74), Iago sees the hen-pecked husband: "Our general's wife is now the general" (Act 2, Scene 3, lines 314–15).

Thus, Desdemona and Othello represent love and war, female and male, young and old, public and private, as well as white and black. Critics have tended to concentrate on the last of these pairings at the expense of the others. But this is not *just* a play about race. It is a play in which social norms are threatened in a variety of ways by two individuals who offer their society a whole set of different approaches to life. The cancellation of those hopes represents not just their tragedy, but also ours.

ABOVE: *An engraving of 1883 depicts Othello as he tells the "story of his life" (Act 1, Scene 3, line 129) to Brabantio and Desdemona. The scene is recounted by Othello before the Venetian Senate, using rhetorically dazzling language.*

Language, Race, and Class

Although Othello claims that his speech is "rude" and "unvarnish'd" (Act 1, Scene 3, lines 81, 90), his language is more exotic, even more educated, than that spoken by the Venetians who surround him in the play; he uses a large number of unusual words with Latin roots, and employs melodic patterns of repetition and antithesis.

Wherein I spoke of most disastrous chances:
Of moving accidents by flood and field,
Of hair-breadth scapes i' th' imminent deadly breach,
Of being taken by the insolent foe
And sold to slavery, of my redemption thence
And portance in my [travel's] history[.]
(ACT 1, SCENE 3, LINES 134–39)

ABOVE: *Played by Ewan McGregor, Iago stands menacingly over Chiwetel Ejiofor's Othello in a 2007 production at the Donmar Warehouse, London. Iago is driven by class, racial, and sexual resentment to bring down his commanding officer.*

This wonderful way with words is not uncommon in those who acquire their second language from books rather than native speakers. This and the stories of a multicultural life of travel and adventure seem to have been inspired by *A Geographical History of Africa* (published in English in 1600), by John Leo (Leo Africanus), identified by the translator John Pory on the title page as "a Moor, born in Granada and brought up in Barbary." Pory's introduction describes Leo as "extraordinarily learned," skilled in rhetoric, and an accomplished poet. He notes that he "seemeth not to have bin ignoble," and marvels on his many escapes from "thousands of imminent dangers ... how many desolate cold mountains, and huge dry, and barren deserts passed he? How often was he in hazard to have been captived ...?" (compare this description with Othello's in Act 1, Scene 2, line 22, and Act 1, Scene 3, lines 135–45). Leo himself describes two types of Africans: "negroes or black moors"; and "white or tawny moors," or Berbers, concentrating on the latter and repeatedly remarking on the "jealousy" or perhaps pride of those fellow North Africans:

> *The Moors are a people of great fidelity ... they had rather die then break promise. No nation in the world is so subject unto jealousy; for they will rather lose their lives, then put up any disgrace in the behalf of their women.*

Similarly, not just through color but also through life experience, Othello is conscious of his difference from the "curled darlings" of Venice. This makes him vulnerable to the racism and misogyny of Iago. As the play progresses, he begins to see his color and his age as impediments, and begins to refer to himself repeatedly in the third person as "Othello"; it is as if his former secure identity as a proud African and a soldier starts to belong to someone else. Eventually this overwhelms both language and consciousness and he collapses, mouthing a string of words for disconnected body parts; love and war becomes mere sex and dismemberment.

But Iago, too, is concerned about his status. Unlike Othello, he cannot claim that he fetches his parentage from men of "royal siege." He is a senior noncommissioned officer, the equivalent

Iago: "Motiveless Malignity"?

And I ([God] bless the mark!) his Moorship's
ancient.

(ACT 1, SCENE 1, LINE 33)

I follow him to serve my turn upon him.

(ACT 1, SCENE 1, LINE 42)

I hate the Moor,
And it is thought abroad that 'twixt my sheets
[H'as] done my office. I know not if't be true,
But I, for mere suspicion in that kind,
Will do as if for surety ...

(ACT 1, SCENE 3, LINES 386–90)

I do suspect the lusty Moor
Hath leap'd into my seat ...
....
(For I fear Cassio with my night-cap too)[.]

(ACT 2, SCENE 1, LINES 295–96, 307)

in the modern army of a sergeant major, and he might suspect that it is his class that is holding him back from promotion. His speech varies depending on the person to whom he is speaking. He is the active, bluff, and "honest" soldier with Othello, "I had thought t' have yerk'd him here under the ribs" (Act 1, Scene 2, line 5); engages in "jokingly" misogynist banter with Desdemona (Act 2, Scene 1, lines 100–164); but becomes the cold, dismissive husband with Emilia, "what do you here alone?" (Act 3, Scene 3, line 300). Having stage-managed the brawl between Cassio and Roderigo, he pretends to be reluctant to say what has happened for fear of incriminating Cassio, while dropping his name no less than six times into his 26-line account of events. His artful tentativeness works, and what Othello hears is an attempt to cover up Cassio's guilt, "Thy honesty and love doth mince this matter, / Making it light to Cassio" (Act 2, Scene 3, lines 247–48). Once Cassio has been deprived of his rank, however, Iago adopts the tone of solicitous comrade—"Reputation is an idle and most false imposition; oft got without merit, and lost without deserving," although he cannot resist putting the boot in, and addresses Cassio by the title he has lost, "What, are you hurt, lieutenant?" (Act 2, Scene 3, lines 268–70, 259).

Far from the pure evil or "motiveless malignity" of English poet and critic Samuel Taylor Coleridge's famous description of him, Iago is an embodiment of the conventional prejudices of the society in which he lives. He is an everyman, and each successive facet of his language betrays the chips on his shoulder.

Music, Harmony, and Disharmony

English Shakespeare critic G. Wilson Knight in his book *The Wheel of Fire* (1930) used the term "the Othello music" to denote the extraordinary quality of Othello's poetry. But there is more actual music in this play than in any other tragedy by Shakespeare, and this music is manifested in all the forms known to Renaissance music theory: the perfect music of the heavenly spheres, inaudible to fallen man; the "loud" music of drums and trumpets; the "soft" domestic or courtly music of lutes and keyboards; and the coarse earthy music of the tavern. Ironically, the concept of perfect harmony is first introduced into the language of the play by Iago in an aside as he watches Othello and Desdemona embrace:

O, you are well tun'd now!
But I'll set down the pegs that make this music,
As honest as I am.
(ACT 2, SCENE 1, LINES 199–201)

The Ensign and the Mathematician

Iago describes Cassio disparagingly as an "arithmetician" (Act 1, Scene 1, line 19), but Othello's decision to promote him reflects the demands of early modern siege warfare. He does not need another officer who knows how to "set a squadron in the field" (line 22), but someone with the mathematical capability to improve fortifications, and plan the direction of the mines that would be dug to lay explosives beneath any besieging army.

Iago is Othello's ensign or standard bearer. The person specified for this difficult and dangerous role in William Garrard's *The Arte of Warre* (1591) is a man "of able courage to advance and bear up the ensign in all extremities, secret, silent, and zealous, able often to comfort, animate and encourage the company." Iago exhibits all these qualities while undermining the integrity and safety of the entire garrison.

ABOVE: *Disaster results when Othello (Laurence Fishburne in the 1995 film) overlooks Iago (left, Kenneth Branagh) in favor of Cassio (Nathaniel Parker).*

Significantly, he sets about his plot to destroy them by singing two low-class songs: the drinking song "And let me the cannikin clink" enables Shakespeare to achieve the sleight of hand of getting Cassio realistically drunk in a minimum of stage time; while the old folk song "King Stephen" is an expression of Iago's own social

Let her have your voice./Vouch with me, heaven, I therefore beg it not/To please the palate of my appetite,/Nor to comply with heat (the young affects/ In [me] defunct) and proper satisfaction;/But to be free and bounteous to her mind.

—*Othello* (ACT 1, SCENE 3, LINES 260–65)

ambition. Cassio enjoys that music, yet his own social and moral insecurity makes him wary of it, and he suggests that singing is "unworthy" of a soldier (Act 2, Scene 3, lines 69–102).

Having been undone in music, Cassio tries to make amends by supplying the traditional musical aubade that should greet a newly wedded couple on the morning after the wedding night. Perhaps through his own ineptness, or perhaps because there is nothing else available on Cyprus, Cassio is unfortunate in his choice of instruments. He comes on stage with musicians playing a selection of double reed instruments which "speak i' th' nose"—bagpipes, and perhaps crumhorns, with their distinctively phallic, upturned ends—allowing the Clown to make jokes about syphilis, wind instruments, and farts, as he conveys the message that Cassio and the musicians should go away. Othello, he says, needs "music that cannot be heard"—either silence, or the divine music of the spheres (Act 3, Scene 1, lines 1–20).

Desdemona, of course, "sings, plays, and dances [well]"; indeed she can "sing the savageness out of a bear" (Act 3, Scene 3, line 185; Act 4, Scene 1, line 189). As Othello is aware, however, and as Iago keeps affirming, there have always been people who will say that this musicality rather denotes waywardness, or the power to emasculate. As that belief takes hold in Othello too, any notion of harmony is replaced by murder, so that when in Act 5 he learns that his order for Cassio's death has misfired, he complains that "murther's out of tune, / And sweet revenge grows harsh" (Act 5, Scene 2, lines 115–16).

Even Desdemona's musical powers are affected by Iago's false tune. She remarks to Cassio that her "advocation is not now in tune" (Act 3, Scene 4, line 123), and when it comes to the singing of the willow song, she muddles the order of verses and finally breaks off in distress (Act 4, Scene 3, lines 40–59). But her struggle to sing this very beautiful and affecting song is, for us who see and hear her, an expression of truth and love stronger than Iago's insinuations.

Desdemona: Feisty or Submissive?

Brabantio may have an idea of his daughter as "never bold," but the character presented to us in the play asserts her demands in front of the entire Venetian Senate, and is unfazed by Iago's bawdy jokes when he greets her on Cyprus. Both these examples of her feistiness were an embarrassment to earlier critics, and the dialogue with Iago is still regularly cut in performance. This has the effect of making her appear more consistent with Brabantio's view of her, but it can make her later actions seem weaker and even irritating. In the play as written, she displays a strong sense of duty and a determination to do whatever it takes to improve the situation, resisting social norms: "[God] me such uses send,/Not to pick bad from bad, but by bad mend" (Act 4, Scene 3, lines 104–5). She will never succumb as Emilia suggests to adultery, but nor will she be Brabantio's good, quiet girl.

LEFT: *In this painting of 1849, Desdemona is shown, with Emilia in attendance, having sung the poignant willow song (in Act 4, Scene 3), which foreshadows her death.*

ABOVE: *A large white bed dominates the stage of a 1921 Berlin production of* Othello, *directed by Leopold Jessner. Desdemona's bed, made up with her wedding sheets in Act 4, Scene 2, and with symbolic echoes of the handkerchief, becomes her death-bed in the final scene.*

"Ocular Proof"

Shakespeare's problem is to make it credible to us that his characters believe something we know to be impossible. He does this, famously, through his use of a double time scheme in which, although the *story* time must take several weeks at least, since Bianca complains that Cassio has kept "a week away" (Act 4, Scene 1, line 168), the *plot* time is apparently accomplished in three consecutive nights, thus leaving no time for adultery. Unusually, more than half the play takes place at night—the whole of Act 1; Act 2, Scenes 2 and 3; and then from supper time at the end of Act 4, Scene 2, right through to the end. The characters frequently cannot quite see, either factually or metaphorically, what is clearly before our eyes. Even in daytime scenes, vision is obscured—by the storm in Act 2, Scene 1—or distorted, as when Iago tells Othello to "encave" himself, within sight but out of ear-shot of the dialogue between Iago and Cassio concerning the handkerchief, which for us truly defines what is being shown (Act 4, Scene 1, line 81). In such dim conditions it is particularly unwise to call for "ocular proof" (Act 3, Scene 3, line 360), as Othello does. Characters see what they expect to see. This even extends to Iago, who confidently, but mistakenly, announces the arrival of Brabantio and his household in pursuit of Othello in the second scene, because that is what he has arranged to happen.

> *That I [did] love the Moor to live with him,/My downright violence, and storm of fortunes,/May trumpet to the world. My heart's subdu'd/Even to the very quality of my lord./I saw Othello's visage in his mind.*
>
> —*Desdemona* (ACT 1, SCENE 3, LINES 248–52)

Handkerchief and Bed

As so often, Shakespeare creates a sense of the verisimilitude or worldview of his play by making a single word slide between verbal image, metaphor, and stage prop. The play makes use of two such words: "handkerchief" and "bed," signifying "sex,"

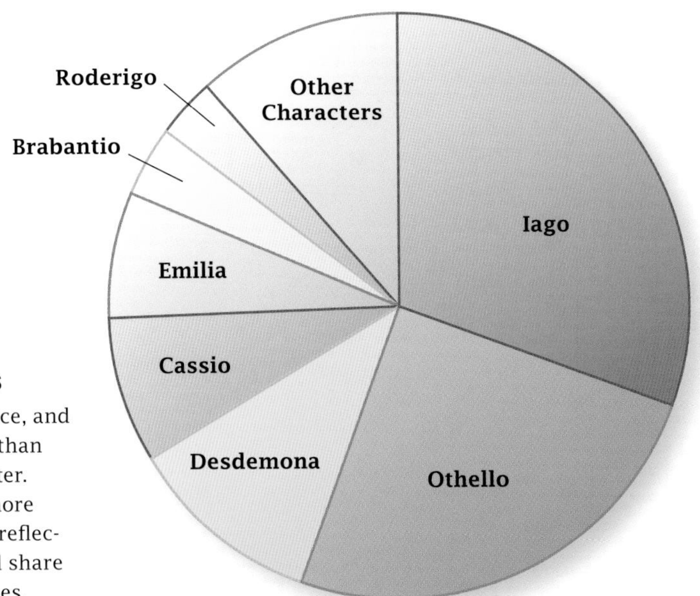

MAJOR ROLES
Iago sets the pace, and has more lines than the title character. Desdemona's more reactive role is reflected in her small share of the play's lines.

and often represented by the word "sheets." This image of woven cloth is a tangible representation of the weaving of Iago's plot, which he describes as a "net / That shall enmesh them all" (Act 2, Scene 3, lines 361–62). The handkerchief passes between the three pairs of sexual partners in the play—Othello and Desdemona; Iago and Emilia; Cassio and his mistress, Bianca—and each time, it causes an argument. There is indeed "magic in the web" (Act 3, Scene 4, line 69), but not so much in the spells of the Egyptian enchantress who first gave it to Othello's mother, as in the way each character who holds the handkerchief sees in it some aspect of their deepest desire or fear; in this way, an apparently tangible object of proof becomes the epitome of irrationality.

This culminates in Othello's "I'll not expostulate with her, lest her body and beauty unprovide my mind" (Act 4, Scene 1, lines 204–6). But ironically it is not her beauty that might stop him killing her; he demonstrates that by the way he kisses her, again and again, in the final scene, as she lies sleeping (Act 5, Scene 2, lines 10–20). Rather, it is her words he fears, the expression of her mind, to which he once wanted to be so "bounteous": "expostulate" means to argue or remonstrate with. The terrible irony of the play, and the cause of its tragedy, is that, despite their sense that their love is a meeting of minds, there is not one scene in which they are shown communicating clearly with each other. Indeed, the play has been designed in such a way that there is no time for them to get to know one another as husband and wife. Their wedding night is interrupted twice—once in Venice by the summons to the Senate and once on Cyprus by Iago's staged disturbance on the court of guard. Thereafter, urged on by Cassio on the one hand and Iago on the other, the subjects that they might be talking about are skewed by the demands of others. Desdemona is confident, both of their love and of her status, and promises Cassio she will talk her husband into reinstating him:

My lord shall never rest,
I'll watch him tame, and talk him out of patience;
His bed shall seem a school, his board a shrift,
I'll intermingle every thing he does
With Cassio's suit . . .

(ACT 3, SCENE 3, LINES 22–26)

Othello, perhaps fearful of criticism that his wife is interfering in matters that do not concern her, refuses to talk, and subsequently, on the occasions they are together, he talks *at* her rather than *to* her.

Continuing Impact

The aspects of the play that have most concerned modern critics are race and gender; it is taking a long time to emerge from nineteenth-century prejudices and preconceptions, epitomized by John Quincy Adams, US president 1825–29, who was appalled by the idea of a "negro" touching a white woman. As a result, it has recently seemed racist to some people to argue that Shakespeare probably had a "tawny moor" like John Leo in mind. But there were no nation states in the world when he was writing; class and religion were more

The Moor is of a free and open nature, / That thinks men honest that but seem to be so, / And will as tenderly be led by th' nose / As asses are.

—*Iago* (ACT 1, SCENE 3, LINES 399–402)

Willard White on Othello

In 1989, Jamaican-born opera singer Willard White played Othello on the British stage. He told the *Independent* newspaper: "A play that's so overwhelmingly about male–female relationships needs a physical relationship between Othello and Desdemona. And with a white actor in black make-up that's the one thing you can't have. If they touch each other, Othello comes off on Desdemona."

Husbands and Wives

if I be left behind,
A moth of peace, and he go to the war,
The rites for why I love him are bereft me[.]
—*Desdemona* (ACT 1 SCENE 3, LINES 255–57)

And heaven defend your good souls, that you
think
I will your serious and great business scant
[For] she is with me …
—*Othello* (ACT 1, SCENE 3, LINES 266–68)

In Venice they do let [God] see the pranks
They dare not show their husbands …
—*Iago* (ACT 3, SCENE 3, LINES 202–3)

O curse of marriage!
That we can call these delicate creatures ours,
And not their appetites! …
—*Othello* (ACT 3, SCENE 3, LINES 268–70)

It is a common thing— …
To have a foolish wife.
—*Iago* (ACT 3, SCENE 3, LINES 302–4)

Let husbands know
Their wives have sense like them; they see, and
smell,
And have their palates both for sweet and sour,
As husbands have …
—*Emilia* (ACT 4, SCENE 3, LINES 93–96)

ABOVE: *A scene from* Otello, *Giuseppe Verdi's operatic retelling of* Othello, *is shown on the cover of Italian weekly magazine* Illustrazione Italiana. *The classic opera was first performed in 1887 in Milan, Italy.*

important than race, and the Elizabethans could be fascinated by princes of any color. The play undoubtedly contains some racist comments, but this does not mean that it carries a racist message. Roderigo's reference to Othello as "thick lips" (Act 1, Scene 1, line 66) signals his prejudice and inability to distinguish between different physical characteristics in dark-skinned people. But then, Roderigo is a fool with a grudge.

The first black actor to play Othello was the American Ira Aldridge in 1833 in London, a part he played all over Europe, as far as Russia, for the next 30 years. Other notable black Othellos have been the singers Paul Robeson (London 1930, New York 1943, Stratford 1959) and Willard White (Royal Shakespeare Company, Stratford, 1989; filmed for TV in 1990), although until nearly the end of the twentieth century, when it finally became inconceivable, the role remained the preserve of blacked-up white actors. A notable variation was director Jude Kelly's "photonegative" production, staged in Washington, D.C. in 1998, which featured an African-American cast and Patrick Stewart as a white Othello.

The play has been filmed a number of times. Orson Welles directed and played the lead in 1952; Laurence Olivier starred in the 1965 version; and, in 1995, Laurence Fishburne played Othello and Kenneth Branagh Iago. Perhaps the most moving and successful version, partly because it was made in apartheid-era South Africa, was director Janet Suzman's 1987 production for the Market Theatre, Johannesburg, later filmed for TV.

Adaptations include the opera *Otello* (1887), by Italian composer Giuseppe Verdi, the film *O* (2001), directed by Tim Blake Nelson, set in a US high school, and *Desdemona: A Play about a Handkerchief* (1979), by US playwright Paula Vogel, which reimagines *Othello* from Desdemona's perspective.

The act of wife-killing has resulted in continuing glib attempts to equate O.J. Simpson's actions with Othello's. In psychiatry, the term "Othello syndrome" is sometimes attached to someone who exhibits intense and irrational jealousy.

King Lear

THE PLOT: *King Lear elects to retire. Choosing to divide his kingdom among his daughters, Lear asks for public expressions of love. Goneril and Regan flatter their father. Lear's favorite daughter, Cordelia, refuses and is disinherited. She marries the French king and becomes his queen. Lear's ally, Kent, is then banished for defending Cordelia; he returns in disguise.*

Meanwhile, Gloucester is duped by his illegitimate son Edmund into believing Edgar plans to kill him. Edgar escapes, disguising himself as Poor Tom, a mad beggar. Edmund seduces Goneril and Regan, who then turn on their father. In his grief and rage, Lear is driven mad. Gloucester is blinded by Regan's husband, Cornwall, for defending Lear. Cordelia returns with a French force, which is defeated. Lear, although reunited with Cordelia, is captured by Edmund's army. Cordelia is hanged. Edmund is exposed and killed by Edgar. Goneril kills herself, having poisoned Regan. Lear dies of a broken heart. Albany, Goneril's husband, assumes control of the kingdom.

Dramatis Personae

Lear, *King of Britain*
King of France
Duke of Burgundy
Duke of Cornwall, *husband to Regan*
Duke of Albany, *husband to Goneril*
Earl of Kent
Earl of Gloucester
Edgar, *son to Gloucester*
Edmund, *bastard son to Gloucester*
Curan, *a courtier*
Oswald, *steward to Goneril*
Old Man, *tenant to Gloucester*
Doctor
Fool, *to Lear*
Captain *employed by Edmund*
Gentleman *attendant on Cordelia*
Herald
Servants *to Cornwall*
Goneril, Regan, Cordelia, *daughters to Lear*
Knights of Lear's train, Gentlemen, Officers, Messengers, Soldiers, and Attendants

WRITTEN
c. 1604–5

SETTING AND PERIOD
Ancient Britain, *c.* eighth century BCE

CHARACTERS 25

ACTS 5

SCENES 26

LINES 3,487

BELOW: *An engraving of the coronation of King James I in 1603 shows the coats of arms of England (left) and Scotland. By depicting the turmoil resulting from Lear's division of his realm, Shakespeare may be commenting favorably on James I's plans for a unified kingdom.*

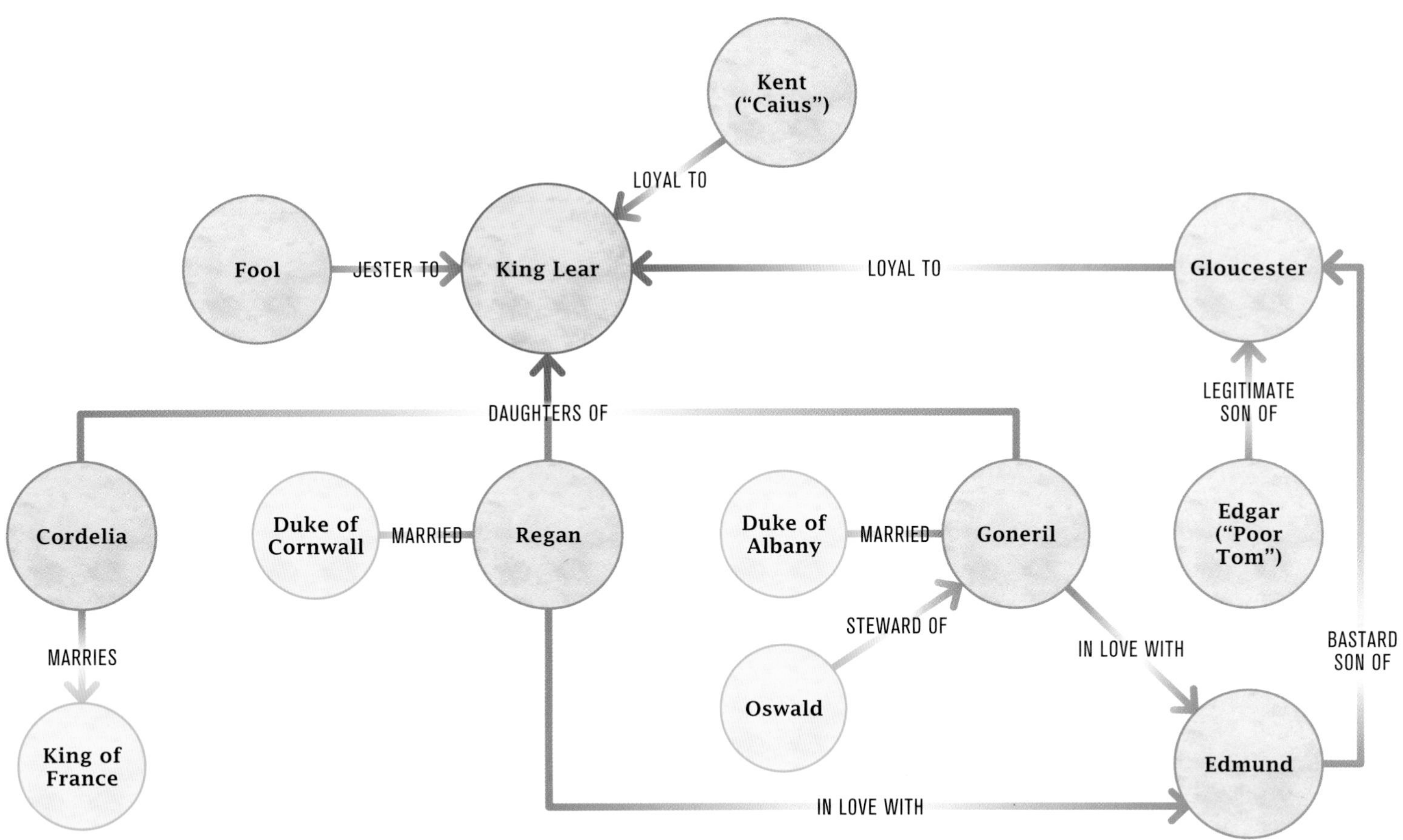

RELATIONSHIPS
Family bonds are no match for greed and evil in *King Lear*, as Goneril and Regan turn on their father, Lear vilifies Cordelia, while Edmund betrays his family and anyone who stands in his way.

When *King Lear* was first performed remains a mystery, although what is certain is that King James I was entertained by a performance of the play on December 26, 1606, during the Christmas Court Revels. There are three distinct versions of the play: a quarto published when Shakespeare was still alive, dating from 1608; another quarto of 1619; and the First Folio of 1623 (the latter two appeared after his death). The 1623 Folio has approximately 100 lines which do not appear in the play's 1608 quarto counterpart. The 1608 quarto, however, has nearly 300 lines which are not reproduced in the Folio, lines which many would recognize from modern performances of the play. This is because directors of Shakespeare productions, following the lead of Shakespeare scholars and editors, have traditionally conflated, or combined, the quarto and Folio texts to make one long version of *King Lear*. What follows is a discussion of this "conflated" version of *King Lear,* a play which was, perhaps, never actually seen on the Jacobean stage but which incorporates some of the most vivid and exciting dramatic writing of Shakespeare's career.

A Divided Kingdom

Shakespeare's depiction of an ageing monarch dividing his kingdom among his daughters, so leading to internal strife and a nation susceptible to invasion, will have reminded many in his audience of the uncertainty surrounding the final years of Queen Elizabeth I. Without any direct heirs to secure the succession, Elizabeth had led her nation into dangerous times, with the threat of Spanish invasion a very real possibility. The arrival of King James VI of Scotland as James I of England in 1603, however, seemed to settle such problems. Eager to forge peace between England and Spain, James strove for stability rather than continued conflict. He also strove to fulfill a personal vision for his island state—the uniting of Scotland and England into one Great Britain, similar to the ancient realm of the fictitious King Lear.

Although the English Parliament opposed such measures, James unilaterally issued a Proclamation in 1604 announcing his new title as "King of Great

Inspired By ...

Shakespeare used Geoffrey of Monmouth's work of mythological fiction, *Historia Regum Britanniae* (*History of the Kings of Britain, c.* 1136), for the basis of his *King Lear* story. Beginning with the founding of "Britain" by the Trojan Brutus, Monmouth's *History* covers 2,000 years and tells of one King Leir, son of Bladud, who divided Britain among his three daughters.

OPPOSITE: *Laurence Olivier, one of the many revered actors of stage and screen to have portrayed Shakespeare's iconic king, took on the role for a 1983 television production of* King Lear, *directed by Michael Elliott.*

Britain, France, and Ireland." When Lear first produces the "map" of his land and announces he has "divided / In three our kingdom" (Act 1, Scene 1, lines 37–38), his actions are directly opposite to those of Shakespeare's monarch. For many, this suggests that Shakespeare was flattering the new royal patron of the King's Men by highlighting the tragic consequences of a divided rather than united nation. Certainly, it would have struck a chord with those who recognized the benefit of a united Great Britain, even if James's dream was not to be fully realized until 1707, more than 100 years after *King Lear* was privately performed before Shakespeare's king.

How sharper than a serpent's tooth it is/ To have a thankless child ...

—*Lear* (ACT 1, SCENE 4, LINES 288–89)

Recurring Themes

Shakespeare re-creates the decline of an elderly ruler into senile forgetfulness and despair with uncanny observation and stark realism. The play's overriding theme seems to be that of uncertainty and chaos—what appears natural collides with the unnatural, and good and evil people suffer in equal measure. Traditionally viewed as a very nihilistic work that argues for the pointlessness of trust, virtue, hope, and existence, *King Lear* presents a vision of a world that is "cheerless, dark, and deadly" (Act 5, Scene 3, line 291). It is a tragic and chaotic place in which folly and wisdom are constantly swapping places. The king acts like a fool—"Dost thou call me fool, boy?" he asks his Fool (Act 1, Scene 4, line 148)—while the Fool appears wise, his perceptive jibes highlighting the absurdity of authority and power in a world ruled not by reason, but by uncontrollable uncertainty.

"Jesters Do Oft Prove Prophets"

Have more than thou showest,
Speak less than thou knowest[.]
—*Fool* (ACT 1, SCENE 4, LINES 118–19)

The hedge-sparrow fed the cuckoo so long,
That [it] had it head bit off by it young.
—*Fool* (ACT 1, SCENE 4, LINES 215–16)

May not an ass know when the cart draws the horse?
—*Fool* (ACT 1, SCENE 4, LINE 224)

Let go thy hold when a great wheel runs down a hill, lest it break thy neck with following; but the great one that goes upward, let him draw thee after.
— *Fool* (ACT 2, SCENE 4, LINES 71–74)

He that has and a little tine wit–
With heigh-ho, the wind and the rain–
Must make content with his fortunes fit,
Though the rain it raineth every day.
—*Fool* (ACT 3, SCENE 2, LINES 74–77)

Justice and Authority

The final chaotic state of Lear's nation stems from his initial decision to "shake all cares and business from our age," and to then "Unburthen'd crawl toward death" (Act 1, Scene 1, lines 39, 41). In an apparent effort to prevent his children from fighting over their inheritances, Lear seems intent that "future strife / May be prevented now" (Act 1, Scene 1, lines 44–45). In return, Lear promises to "divest" himself "both of rule, / Interest of territory, cares of state" (Act 1, Scene 1, lines 49–50). Unfortunately, he also wishes to hold on to all the honors due to him as the king. A king in name but not in authority? No wonder his conniving and power-hungry daughters turn on their weakened father. Having handed over power, Lear, through age and mental infirmity, soon finds himself powerless to reclaim it.

Lear's fault is to trust his judgment and react so proudly and violently to the honest expressions of duty and filial affection expressed by his one-time favorite daughter, Cordelia. It is Cordelia who, alone among her sisters, answers her father honestly when declaring:

> *You have begot me, bred me, lov'd me: I*
> *Return those duties back as are right fit,*
> *Obey you, love you, and most honor you.*
> (ACT 1, SCENE 1, LINES 96–98)

The injustice of Lear's subsequent outburst—"Here I disclaim all my paternal care" (Act 1, Scene 1, line 113)—leads inexorably to him being metaphorically bound "Upon a wheel of fire, that mine own tears / Do scald like molten lead" (Act 4, Scene 7, lines 46–47). He suffers the consequences of his rash decisions, which result in the near-destruction of his nation and, ultimately, a succession of terrible deaths, including his own and those of his daughters.

Edgar in Disguise

Pillicock sat on Pillicock-Hill, alow! alow, loo, loo!
(ACT 3, SCENE 4, LINES 76–77)

Poor Tom, that eats the swimming frog, the toad, the todpole, the wall-newt, and the water; that in the fury of his heart, when the foul fiend rages, eats cow-dung for sallets; swallows the old rat and the ditch-dog; drinks the green mantle of the standing pool[.]
(ACT 3, SCENE 4, LINES 129–34)

But mice and rats, and such small deer,
Have been Tom's food for seven long year.
(ACT 3, SCENE 4, LINES 138–39)

The prince of darkness is a gentleman ...
(ACT 3, SCENE 4, LINE 143)

Fie, foh, and fum,
I smell the blood of a British man.
(ACT 3, SCENE 4, LINES 183–84)

The foul fiend bites my back.
(ACT 3, SCENE 6, LINE 17)

ABOVE: *Actor Joseph George Holman portrayed Edgar in a late eighteenth-century London production of* King Lear. *This portrait, painted by Gainsborough Dupont, captures Holman in the role.*

Betrayal and Reconciliation

The theme of betrayal is foregrounded in Lear's uncompromising rejection of Cordelia as one "Unfriended, new adopted to our hate" (Act 1, Scene 1, line 203). Reconciliation comes only when Cordelia has returned to Britain as Queen of France, leading a French invasion force, so facing the irreversible decline in her father's mental health. Despite all she has suffered, Cordelia is still compassionate and forgiving:

O my dear father, restoration hang
Thy medicine on my lips, and let this kiss
Repair those violent harms that my two sisters
Have in thy reverence made ...
(ACT 4, SCENE 7, LINES 25–28)

Cordelia's dutiful love for the father who rejected her is echoed in the parallel plot of Gloucester rejecting his legitimate son Edgar. Believing the false statements of the illegitimate Edmund, Gloucester exhibits poor judgment in his gullible belief in Edgar's guilt. Expressing the chaos of the times, Gloucester complains that:

Love cools, friendship falls off, brothers divide: in cities, mutinies; in countries, discord; in palaces, treason; and the bond crack'd 'twixt son and father. This villain of mine comes under the prediction; there's son against father[.]
(ACT 1, SCENE 2, LINES 106–110)

It is, however, Edgar who comes to his father's aid when, alone and blind, Gloucester wanders through the land, seeking his own death and a release from his pain. Although Edgar seems to rebuke his father, protesting that "Men must endure / Their going hence even as their coming hither" (Act 5, Scene 2, lines 9–10), Edgar still describes his final reconciliation with his father with deep emotional sincerity, describing how he asked for his father's "blessing, and from first to last / Told him our pilgrimage" (Act 5, Scene 3, lines 196–97). Edgar's desire for "blessing" from the father who violently and unwisely rejected him reminds us of Cordelia's loyal care for her father, even after he vehemently spurns her. Gloucester's "blessing," however, comes at an awful price, as Edgar narrates the devastating effect of the truth on his ailing father:

But his flaw'd heart
(Alack, too weak the conflict to support!)
'Twixt two extremes of passion, joy and grief,
Burst smilingly ...
(ACT 5, SCENE 3, LINES 197–200)

RIGHT: *Director Peter Brook's 1971 film of* King Lear *starred Paul Scofield (right) in an acclaimed performance. Here he is watched by the perspicacious Fool (Jack McGowran), who recognizes the danger of the king's actions, yet remains loyal.*

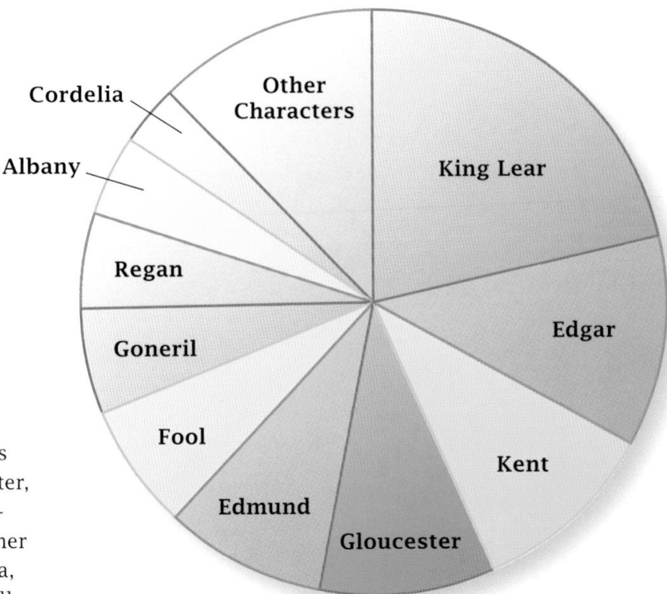

MAJOR ROLES
As befits his status as the title character, Lear has more dialogue than any other character. Cordelia, while a symbolically central character, spends much time offstage, which is reflected in her small proportion of lines.

Like Lear, Gloucester dies knowing the depth of his worthiest child's love and devotion. Unlike Lear, however, Gloucester will lose only one of his children. Edgar survives to recount the tale of "this sad time," observing sorrowfully that "we that are young / Shall never see so much, nor live so long" (Act 5, Scene 3, lines 324, 326–27).

Old Age and Madness

Edgar's reference to "we that are young" comes as a final reminder of the play's unrelenting concern with old age and senility. Lear might be driven mad by the consequences of his folly and by his exposure to the elemental forces of nature, but there is little doubt that his daughters had already considered his abdication from power as an act of age-related madness. Almost as soon as Lear relinquishes power, Regan describes "the infirmity of his age," and Goneril "the unruly waywardness that infirm and choleric years bring with them" (Act 1, Scene 1, lines 293, 298–99), adding later that "Old fools are babes again" (Act 1, Scene 3, line 19). Lear's Fool also recognizes his master's folly, complaining to him that "thou hast par'd thy wit o' both sides, and left nothing i' th' middle" (Act 1, Scene 4, lines 187–88). Even so, the most expressive description of age-related dementia comes from Lear himself, when he is finally reunited with Cordelia:

I fear I am not in my perfect mind.
Methinks I should know you, and know this man,
Yet I am doubtful: for I am mainly ignorant
What place this is, and all the skill I have
Remembers not these garments; nor I know not
Where I did lodge last night ...
(ACT 4, SCENE 7, LINES 62–67)

Throughout the play, Lear expresses his ultimate fear—that of going mad. Whether frantically pounding his forehead, exclaiming "Beat at this gate, that let thy folly in, / And thy dear judgment out!" (Act 1, Scene 4, lines 271–72), or shouting impotently, "O, let me not be mad, not mad, sweet heaven!" (Act 1, Scene 5, line 46), Lear voices the dreadful reality of his predicament. Unconsciously aware of his own decline, Lear's frantic request to "Let me have surgeons, / I am cut to th' brains" (Act 4, Scene 6, lines 192–93) only confirms how far his mental state has declined. It is, however, the return to second childhood that haunts Lear's actions, even when he reminds us all that "When we are born, we cry that we are come / To this great stage of fools" (Act 4, Scene 6, lines 182–83). Old age, folly, and madness all threaten the welfare of nation and family alike. In his depiction of Lear's madness, Shakespeare is able to express a universal fear as timeless in its theme as it is frightening in its debilitating effects.

*And my poor fool is hang'd! No, no, no life!/
Why should a dog, a horse, a rat, have life,/
And thou no breath at all?
Thou'lt come no more,/
Never, never, never, never, never.*

—*Lear* (ACT 5, SCENE 3, LINES 306–9)

The Image of the Storm

Shakespeare uses the natural image of the storm to depict inner turmoil. When finally rejected by Regan and Goneril, Lear frantically calls on the heavens for "patience" (Act 2, Scene 4, line 271), adding a disjointed curse against those "unnatural hags," his daughters:

*I will have such revenges on you both
That all the world shall—I will do such
things—
What they are yet I know not ...*
(ACT 2, SCENE 4, LINES 279–81)

Lear's maddened outburst coincides with the stage direction *"Storm and tempest."* While Goneril and Regan scurry to avoid the "wild night" (Act 2, Scene 4, line 308), Lear is left to suffer the physical and mental torture of his storm-tossed body and mind. Meanwhile, the disguised Kent wanders through the storm and, stopping to ask a passing gentleman of Lear's whereabouts, learns that the tormented king is:

*Contending with the fretful elements;
Bids the wind blow the earth into the sea,
Or swell the curled waters 'bove the main,
That things might change or cease, [tears his
white hair,
Which the impetuous blasts with eyeless rage
Catch in their fury, and make nothing of,
Strives in his little world of man to outscorn
The to-and-fro-conflicting wind and rain.]*
(ACT 3, SCENE 1, LINES 4–11)

Kent's later concern that the weather is too violent for humans to bear is countered by Lear's own appraisal of the storm's effect on his physical and mental state:

*Thou think'st 'tis much that this contentious
storm
Invades us to the skin; so 'tis to thee;
But where the greater malady is fix'd,
The lesser is scarce felt ...*
(ACT 3, SCENE 4, LINES 6–9)

Although suffering the discomfort of bodily exposure to the wind and rain, Lear recognizes that it is not the physical storm raging all around him that he fears most, but the "tempest in my mind" that "Doth from my senses take all feeling else, / Save what beats there" (Act 3, Scene 4,

Kurosawa's Reimagining

Akira Kurosawa, the Japanese writer and director, loosely based the story for his 1985 film *Ran* (*"Chaos"*) on *King Lear*. The last major epic that Kurosawa directed, and costing an astonishing US$12 million, *Ran* depicts the downfall of Hidetora Ichimonji, an ageing Sengoku warlord from late sixteenth-century Japan who divides his nation among his three sons—Taro, Jiro, and Saburo. Saburo, like Cordelia, is banished for questioning his father's wisdom. Urged by their wives, Taro and Jiro turn violently against Hidetora, and the resulting conflict finds Saburo returning to aid his father. As in Shakespeare's tragedy, the entire family perish at the last. Unlike Shakespeare's Lear, Hidetora is himself violent and murderous; some years before, he had ordered the gouging out of lord Tsurumaru's eyes, in a plot that mirrors the blinding of Gloucester. Kurosawa also developed the Fool's role, creating the sexually ambiguous Kyoami, who accompanies Hidetora on his journey through madness.

ABOVE: *In Kurosawa's epic film* Ran, *Hidetora's sons—including Jiro (Jinpachi Nezu), pictured here—defy their father, just as Lear is defied by his daughters.*

ABOVE: *Blindness is not only a metaphor but a shocking reality in* King Lear; *the blinding of Gloucester is the most violent scene in the play. In this 2008 production at the Globe, London, Regan (Kellie Bright) takes her revenge on the earl (Joseph Mydell).*

lines 12–14). Lear's inner tempest is hauntingly echoed in the thunderous imagery of Shakespeare's staged tempest, which evokes the futility of out-scorning not only nature's wrath, but also the mind's irreparable ageing and decline.

Blindness

Lear's "eyeless rage" (Act 3, Scene 1, line 8) at the relentless storm suggests another image that dominates *King Lear*—that of blindness. When cursing Regan, Lear calls on the lightning to strike its "blinding flames" into her eyes (Act 2, Scene 4, line 165). Similarly, Lear's original angry response to Cordelia—"Hence, and avoid my sight!" (Act 1, Scene 1, line 124)—symbolizes the blindness of this foolish father toward his loving child.

By far the most horrific representation of blindness comes, however, during Gloucester's trial at the hands of Cornwall and Regan. After secretly going to Lear's aid and offering him shelter, Gloucester falls prey to Goneril's wrath and her vicious desire to "Pluck out his eyes" (Act 3, Scene 7, line 5). Cornwall and Regan act accordingly, binding the helpless Gloucester to a chair. In response to their angry questioning about why he helped the king, Gloucester replies, "Because I would not see thy cruel nails / Pluck out his poor old eyes" (Act 3, Scene 7, lines 56–57). Gloucester's metaphorical description of Lear's plight and his daughters' cruel intentions

Half-blooded Edmund

Why bastard? Wherefore base?
When my dimensions are as well compact,
My mind as generous, and my shape as true,
As honest madam's issue? Why brand they us
With base? with baseness? bastardy? base,
base?
(ACT 1, SCENE 2, LINES 6–10)

Now, gods, stand up for bastards!
(ACT 1, SCENE 2, LINE 22)

I should have been that I am, had the maidenl'est star in the firmament twinkled on my bastardizing.
(ACT 1, SCENE 2, LINES 131–33)

That which my father loses: no less than all.
The younger rises when the old doth fall.
(ACT 3, SCENE 3, LINES 24–25)

To both these sisters have I sworn my love;
Each jealous of the other, as the stung
Are of the adder. Which of them shall I take?
Both? one? or neither? Neither can be enjoy'd
If both remain alive …
(ACT 5, SCENE 1, LINES 55–59)

is answered by the sickening reality of Cornwall's response: "See 't shalt thou never. Fellows, hold the chair, / Upon these eyes of thine I'll set my foot" (Act 3, Scene 7, lines 67–68).

Blinded in both eyes, Gloucester is ejected from Regan's castle with all the dignity of an old, sightless dog: "Go thrust him out at gates, and let him smell / His way to Dover" (Act 3, Scene 7, lines 93–94). Eventually, with the aid of his disguised son Edgar, Gloucester is reunited with Lear and discovers the king's madness. When Gloucester asks if the king recognizes him, Lear ironically replies, "I remember thine eyes well enough" (Act 4, Scene 6, line 136). Explaining how he sees the world "feelingly," Gloucester is greeted with Lear's bitter response: "What, art mad? A man may see how this world goes with no eyes. Look with thine ears" (Act 4, Scene 6, lines 150–51). Lear's only advice to the nobleman is to feign his sight:

> *Get thee glass eyes,*
> *And like a scurvy politician, seem*
> *To see the things thou dost not ...*
> (ACT 4, SCENE 6, LINES 170–72)

Lear is blind to Cordelia's worth, just as he is blind to Goneril's and Regan's self-serving flattery. Gloucester is blind to Edgar's honesty, just as he is blind to Edmund's villainy. Lear equates such blindness with the art of politics, in which outward show is all, and the politician, although appearing to see all, actually turns a blind eye to much.

Productions for Changing Times

As with so many of Shakespeare's plays, *King Lear* was adapted to accommodate the taste of the age in which it was performed. In 1681, the playwright Nahum Tate substantially rewrote the play to give it a happy ending. Edgar and Cordelia were allowed to marry, Lear was restored to the throne, and all trace of the Fool was removed. Apart from a period between the 1780s and 1820, when the British government suppressed *King Lear* for political reasons (the mentally ill King George III was the reigning monarch), Tate's version dominated the stage until 1838, when William Charles Macready restored Shakespeare's original tragic ending to a revived, though shortened, version of *King Lear.*

Lear Stripped Bare

Ian McKellen famously stripped naked for his Royal Shakespeare Company portrayal of Lear in 2007, but when touring the production to Singapore was obliged to cover up—a strictly enforced Singaporean law bans minors from seeing onstage nudity. The televised version for the US Public Broadcasting Service was likewise edited to guarantee the actor's (imposed) modesty.

BELOW: *"But now her price is fallen" (Act 1, Scene 1, line 197): King Lear (Ian McKellen) contemplates Cordelia (Romola Garai) and her mercenary suitor the Duke of Burgundy (Peter Hinton), who rejects her when Lear reveals that she has been disinherited.*

ABOVE: *Director Bill Alexander, in a 2005 production for the Royal Shakespeare Company, portrayed Cordelia (Siân Brooke) as a younger, favored half-sister to Goneril and Regan, sharing a father but a different mother. This added an extra dimension to Goneril and Regan's resentment of her.*

Even in the twentieth century, Shakespeare's tragedy was often drastically cut. For his 1953 live televised portrayal of the maddened king, Orson Welles and his director, Peter Brook, reduced the play to 90 minutes, most noticeably by removing Edgar and Edmund's rivalry from the plot. Nine years later, Brook directed Paul Scofield as Lear for the 1962 Royal Shakespeare Company season in London. Brook directed the film of this production in 1971, transporting his actors to a wintry, windswept Denmark, so creating what for many is a masterpiece of cinema and Scofield's finest role.

Despite its checkered past, *King Lear* has a history of attracting the finest stage actors, with famous performances from the likes of Laurence Olivier, John Gielgud, Lee J. Cobb, James Earl Jones, and Ian Holm. As if confirming the play's relevance to a twenty-first-century audience, the 2004 production of *King Lear* at New York's Vivian Beaumont Theater, directed by Jonathan Miller, earned its star, Christopher Plummer, a nomination for a coveted Tony Award.

Blow, winds, and crack your cheeks! rage, blow!/ You cataracts and hurricanoes, spout/ Till you have drench'd our steeples, [drown'd] the cocks!

—*Lear* (ACT 3, SCENE 2, LINES 1–3)

A Soviet Setting

At the height of the Cold War between the USSR and the United States, Ukrainian-born director Grigori Kozintsev created his black-and-white adaptation of *King Lear,* called *Korol' Lir* (1971). Based on a translation of Shakespeare's play by Russian writer Boris Pasternak, *Korol' Lir* was underscored with music by Dmitri Shostakovich. Kozintsev cast Jüri Järvet to play the mad king, filming on location in Järvet's native Estonia.

Korol' Lir focuses less on the individual tragedy of Lear and more on the collective suffering of his impoverished subjects. The film ends with a long, lingering image of the nation's destruction, while the Fool sits among the ashes, plaintively playing his pipe. Kozintsev's filmic expression of "socialist realism," which combined an awareness of shared human suffering with the director's own reaction to the World War II horrors of Hiroshima and Auschwitz, presents a world in which death and destruction can ultimately lead to progress and positive social change—as long as humanity as a whole makes the conscious choice to transform the world for the better.

A "New Asian" Lear

Premiering in Tokyo, Japan, in 1997, the *King Lear* adaptation *LEAR* by Singaporean director Ong Keng Sen created a radical vision of "new Asia." Written by feminist Japanese playwright Rio Kishida, *LEAR* incorporated several Asian dramatic forms: Chinese opera, Japanese Noh theater, traditional music from Indonesia and Japan, and choreography based on Indonesian martial arts, all performed by a diverse group of artists from China, Japan, Malaysia, Thailand, Indonesia, and Singapore.

"New Asia" was represented by the Older Daughter, a Chinese-opera "Goneril" (played, like the Thai Younger Daughter, by a male actor), who usurps and murders her father, the Noh-speaking Old Man ("Lear"). Watching over the Younger Daughter ("Cordelia"), the ghost of her Mother provides a maternal image of "old Asia." In killing the Old Man, the Older Daughter embraces a male violence that eventually destroys her too. Ong Keng Sen's adaptation provided a harsh appraisal of "new Asia" as it approached the twenty-first century.

Macbeth

WRITTEN
c. 1606
SETTING AND PERIOD
Scotland and England, mid-eleventh century
CHARACTERS 36
ACTS 5
SCENES 31
LINES 2,349

THE PLOT: *Three Witches plan to meet Macbeth and Banquo, whose military prowess prevents a Norwegian invasion of Scotland. The Witches inform Macbeth that he will become King of Scotland, although Banquo's heirs will also rule. Hearing the prediction, Lady Macbeth urges her husband to murder King Duncan, which he does. Duncan's sons escape, Malcolm to England and Donalbain to Ireland. Fearing his friend, Macbeth orders Banquo's murder, although Banquo's son Fleance escapes. Guilt-ridden, Macbeth sees Banquo's ghost at a banquet.*

Macbeth's murderous tyranny forces many lords, including Macduff, to seek refuge in England. There they join Malcolm, who unites with the English to invade Scotland. The Witches warn Macbeth to beware Macduff, whose wife and children are killed on Macbeth's orders. Maddened by her guilt, Lady Macbeth kills herself. Macbeth fights his enemies, the Witches having assured him he could not be killed by any born of woman. Their ironic prediction comes true when Macduff, who had been delivered by Caesarean section, kills Macbeth. Malcolm is hailed King of Scotland.

RIGHT: *The bloody ghost of Banquo haunts Macbeth in the banquet scene, as imagined by artist Théodore Chassériau in the nineteenth century. Ghosts and the supernatural are recurring motifs in the play.*

Dramatis Personae

Duncan, *King of Scotland*
Malcolm, Donalbain, *his sons*
Macbeth, Banquo, *generals of the king's army*
Macduff, Lennox, Rosse, Menteth, Angus, Cathness, *noblemen of Scotland*
Fleance, *son to Banquo*
Siward, *Earl of Northumberland, general of the English forces*
Young Siward, *his son*
Seyton, *an officer attending on Macbeth*
Boy, *son to Macduff*
English Doctor
Scots Doctor
Sergeant
Porter
Old Man
Three Murderers
Lady Macbeth
Lady Macduff
Gentlewoman *attending on Lady Macbeth*
Three Witches, *the Weird Sisters*
Three other Witches
Hecat
Apparitions
Lords, Gentlemen, Officers, Soldiers, Attendants, and Messengers

Macbeth is a bloody, violent, and exciting play, full of supernatural conjurings and events. Its exploration of power, fear, and anger, as well as the forceful and homicidal determination of its principal female character, Lady Macbeth, have thrilled and troubled audiences and actors over the four centuries since it was first performed. *Macbeth* remains a favorite with those who enjoy the spectacle of witches and bloody knives, gory ghosts, and fast-paced battle scenes, and the final lifting of the severed head of the murderous tyrant, Macbeth.

Flattering a New King

Although Shakespeare based his play on characters and events recorded by writers such as Raphael Holinshed, whose quasi-historical *Chronicles* (1577, revised 1587) traced the royal ancestry of English, Scottish, and Irish rulers, and which pandered to a Tudor fascination with genealogy, Shakespeare was also reacting to a number of contemporary political and social events. Most important, *Macbeth* appears to have been written in direct response to the arrival in England of its new Scottish monarch, King James. In 1603, Queen Elizabeth had died. Despite the political uncertainty and danger of the

The King's Evil

Malcolm's asylum in the English court of King Edward the Confessor (reigned 1042–66) introduces the Anglo-Saxon king as saint and healer (Act 4, Scene 3). Tradition stated that since Edward's reign, the rulers of England and France had been blessed with the ability to cure the "King's Evil" or scrofula, a painful tuberculosis of the neck. As Malcolm says, "people, / All swoll'n and ulcerous" are cured by the touch of the king (Act 4, Scene 3, lines 150–53). Confirming that, to "succeeding royalty," Edward "leaves / The healing benediction" of this magical cure (Act 4, Scene 3, lines 155–56), Malcolm's observations effectively flattered Shakespeare's own "succeeding" royal, James I, who regularly conducted the ceremony of "Touching for the King's Evil" in the royal Banqueting House, London, pronouncing *"Le Roy te touche, et Dieu te guérit"* (The King touches you, and God heals you).

childless (and heirless) Elizabeth's final years, England experienced a peaceful transition when James VI of Scotland became James I of England, so uniting the two nations for the first time.

England's new Protestant king came complete with a ready-made royal family and, best of all, sons and heirs. Many Shakespearean scholars view *Macbeth* as decidedly supportive of the new regime, especially in the way the play highlights the survival of Fleance, Banquo's son. Ever since the 1590s, and following a particularly skillful rewriting of Scottish history, James had consolidated his hold on Scotland's crown by stressing his Stuart family's ancestral links to Banquo, a character who (although actually fictional) was believed to have partnered Macbeth in his murderous deeds. Shakespeare now flattered his new king and patron—Shakespeare's company of actors, the Lord Chamberlain's Men, had, on James's arrival in 1603, been awarded the royal title King's Men—by altering the known facts about Macbeth's rule and presenting Banquo as the founder of a great and legitimate royal line.

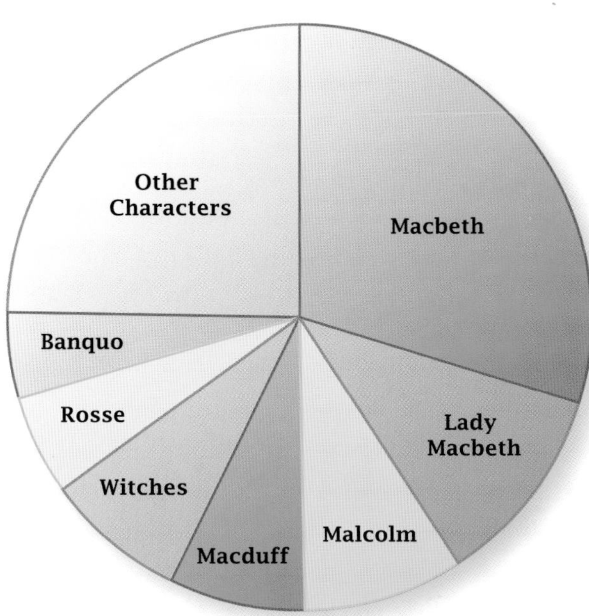

MAJOR ROLES
Shakespeare keeps the Macbeths at the center of the play, giving some 30 percent of the total dialogue to Macbeth and about 11 percent to Lady Macbeth.

Gunpowder and Fear

Shakespeare's portrayal of murder, first of King Duncan and then of Banquo, ancestral founder of the royal Stuart line, had another topical relevance, one fraught with recent memories of danger and intrigue. If, as is generally believed, *Macbeth* was written and produced in 1606, its appearance followed close on the heels of an abortive coup against the crown and the state. In November 1605, a group of dissidents—led by Robert Catesby and including the infamous Guy Fawkes—unhappy with continued intolerance toward England's Roman Catholics, hatched a plot to explode barrels of gunpowder beneath the Houses of Parliament during the annual State Opening of Parliament, when James

ABOVE: *Evil presents itself to Macbeth (Simon Russell Beale in a 2005 London production) in the form of the Witches, who touch on his deep-seated ambition. Belief in the existence and power of witches was widespread in Shakespeare's day.*

and the entire English government were inside. But the plot was foiled and the perpetrators arrested, tried, and executed. For *Macbeth*'s audiences in 1606, the portrayal of a murdered king and the subsequent evil tyranny of his usurping counterpart must have seemed particularly frightening in view of the topical immediacy of its message.

Demons and Witches

There is little doubt that *Macbeth* also catered to King James's particular interest in the supernatural. In 1597, James published *Demonology*, in which he demonstrated his faith in superstition and witchcraft. James's beliefs stemmed from an uncomfortable and near-fatal voyage to Denmark in 1589 to meet his bride, Anne, the daughter of the King of Denmark. As storms and tempests lashed his ship, James became convinced that witches were secretly escorting his fleet, traveling in magical vessels made out of kitchen sieves, as alluded to by the First Witch:

But in a sieve I'll thither sail,
And, like a rat without a tail,
I'll do, I'll do, and I'll do.
(ACT 1, SCENE 3, LINES 8–10)

A year after his arrival in London, James legislated *An Act against conjuration, witchcraft and dealing with evil and wicked spirits* (1604), which demanded that "lawfully convicted" witches "shall suffer pains of death." What better way to acknowledge his new patron's obsession with witches than for Shakespeare to present in a play these "secret, black, and midnight hags" (Act 4, Scene 1, line 48) as malevolent creatures who equivocate and quibble, leaving destruction and death in their wake?

Fate, Prophecy, and the Status of Women

The theme of witchcraft has, understandably, branded *Macbeth* as a play primarily about the occult. Even so, Shakespeare explores several

Witches' Conjuring Spells

When shall we three meet again?
In thunder, lightning, or in rain?
(ACT 1, SCENE 1, LINES 1–2)

Fair is foul, and foul is fair,
Hover through the fog and filthy air.
(ACT 1, SCENE 1, LINES 11–12)

Double, double, toil and trouble;
Fire burn, and cauldron bubble.
(ACT 4, SCENE 1, LINES 10–11)

Eye of newt and toe of frog,
Wool of bat and tongue of dog,
Adder's fork and blind-worm's sting,
Lizard's leg and howlet's wing,
For a charm of pow'rful trouble,
Like a hell-broth boil and bubble.
(ACT 4, SCENE 1, LINES 14–19)

By the pricking of my thumbs,
Something wicked this way comes.
(ACT 4, SCENE 1, LINES 44–45)

other themes that also connect to the Witches in unexpected ways. Among the most important of them is the role of fate and prophecy in people's lives, especially when prophecy is linked to equivocation—the art of meaning one thing and saying another. Even the drunken Porter at Dunsinane is aware of the "equivocator, that could swear in both the scales against either scale" (Act 2, Scene 3, lines 8–9), a comment that many scholars believe refers to the Jesuit priest Henry Garnet, executed in 1606 for his role in the Gunpowder Plot (Father Garnet had written a treatise on equivocation, published secretly *c.* 1595). The equivocating Witches are as dangerous as this potential assassin; they also symbolize, for the play's male-dominated society, the subversion of a seventeenth-century woman's traditional duty,

To-morrow, and to-morrow, and to-morrow,/Creeps in this petty pace from day to day,/To the last syllable of recorded time;/And all our yesterdays have lighted fools/The way to dusty death ...

— *Macbeth* (ACT 5, SCENE 5, LINES 19–23)

whether as nurturer of children or as homemaker and food-provider. It seems no coincidence that Malcolm should describe Macbeth and his wife as "this dead butcher and his fiend-like queen" (Act 5, Scene 9, line 35). Macbeth himself recognized the Witches as double-dealing fiends:

I pull in resolution, and begin
To doubt th' equivocation of the fiend
That lies like truth ...
(ACT 5, SCENE 5, LINES 41–43)

For Malcolm, the "fiend-like" Lady Macbeth seems no different from the "midnight hags" who haunt the "blasted heath" (Act 1, Scene 3, line 77). Shakespeare certainly strengthens such an opinion. Although Macduff initially and mistakenly describes Lady Macbeth as a "gentle lady," for whom "repetition" of Duncan's death, "in a woman's ear / Would murther as it fell" (Act 2, Scene 3, lines 85–86), Lady Macbeth's lust for power makes her far from "gentle." Shakespeare's audiences might have expected their women to be meek and humble, but Lady Macbeth flies in the face of convention when she calls on those "spirits" that "tend on mortal thoughts" to

unsex me here,
And fill me from the crown to the toe topful
Of direst cruelty! ...
(ACT 1, SCENE 5, LINES 41–43)

Her call for evil spirits to "Come to my woman's breasts, / And take my milk for gall" (Act 1, Scene 5, lines 47–48) adds to the sense that Lady Macbeth has more in common with the Witches who prophesy her husband's rise to ultimate power than to those playgoers who would find her cruelty far from comfortable.

Heredity, Tyranny, and Politics

Important to all who hear the prophecies of the Witches is the fear of failed succession, of barrenness, and the insecure hereditary rights of those who die childless. Such a message, too unpalatable to be staged in Elizabeth's reign, now flatters James and his family. To Macbeth's dismay, the Witches foretell not only of his kingly success in this life, but also of his failure to found an everlasting dynasty. It is Banquo who is hailed as "father to a line of kings," whereas Macbeth complains that:

Upon my head they plac'd a fruitless crown,
And put a barren sceptre in my gripe,
Thence to be wrench'd with an unlineal hand,
No son of mine succeeding ...
(ACT 3, SCENE 1, LINES 60–63)

Quotable Macbeth

Bring forth men-children only!
For thy undaunted mettle should compose
Nothing but males ...
(ACT 1, SCENE 7, LINES 72–74)

Away, and mock the time with fairest show:
False face must hide what the false heart doth know.
(ACT 1, SCENE 7, LINES 81–82)

Hang out our banners on the outward walls,
The cry is still "They come!" ...
(ACT 5, SCENE 5, LINES 1–2)

They have tied me to a stake; I cannot fly,
But bear-like I must fight the course ...
(ACT 5, SCENE 7, LINES 1–2)

Lay on, Macduff,
And damn'd be him that first cries, "Hold, enough!"
(ACT 5, SCENE 8, LINES 33–34)

ABOVE: *Macbeth (Patrick Stewart in a 2007 stage production), schooled in duplicity by his wife, presents himself to the world as a loyal general, caring host, and good king—all that he is not.*

Macbeth and Lady Macbeth have no heirs. The resulting political uncertainty feeds Macbeth's lust for power and for murder. His only recourse is, as he sees it, systematically to eliminate all who pose a threat to his personal rise to the throne. Duncan and Banquo, Lady Macduff and her children, all are killed to ensure that as much as possible of the Witches' prophecy is fulfilled. On a political level, the villainous actions of Macbeth serve to highlight other universal themes. Tyranny and political expediency, those corrupt forces that destroy the integrity of leaders the world over, become the focus for those rebelling against Macbeth. Malcolm describes how "This tyrant" Macbeth, "whose sole name blisters our tongues, / Was once thought honest" (Act 4, Scene 3, lines 12–13). Unfortunately for Scotland, Macbeth has followed the advice of his wife, who, having complained that her husband's "face" is as open "as a book where men / May read strange matters," explains the importance of political duplicity:

To beguile the time,
Look like the time; bear welcome in your eye,
Your hand, your tongue; look like th' innocent flower,
But be the serpent under't ...
(ACT 1, SCENE 5, LINES 63–66)

> *Is this a dagger which I see before me,/The handle toward my hand? Come, let me clutch thee:/I have thee not, and yet I see thee still.*
>
> 
>
> —Macbeth (ACT 2, SCENE 1, LINES 33–35)

Like the traditional image of the beguilingly devilish serpent, Macbeth's outward show of innocence must mask the true extent of his evil intentions. Ultimately, it is Macbeth's rejection of the "king-becoming graces"—described by Malcolm as "justice, verity, temp'rance, stableness, / Bounty, perseverance, mercy, lowliness, / Devotion, patience, courage, fortitude" (Act 4, Scene 3, lines 91–94)—which leads to his downfall, so upholding the play's prevailing theme of good rule by the just and upright monarch.

Sleeplessness, Guilt, and Madness

The theme of sleeplessness, with a murderer's guilty conscience leading to loss of restful sleep, recurs throughout the play. Sleeplessness and guilt combined, according to Shakespeare, can also result in madness. The Witches first describe sleeplessness when discussing the poor captain of the *Tiger* for whom "Sleep shall neither night nor day / Hang upon his penthouse [eye] lid" (Act 1, Scene 3, lines 19–20). It is Macbeth, however, who best describes the horror of this theme:

Methought I heard a voice cry, "Sleep no more!
Macbeth does murther sleep"—the innocent sleep,
Sleep that knits up the ravell'd sleave of care,
The death of each day's life, sore labor's bath,
Balm of hurt minds, great nature's second course,
Chief nourisher in life's feast.
(ACT 2, SCENE 2, LINES 32–37)

For Macbeth, guilt at having killed Duncan translates into the loss of soothing sleep. Lady Macbeth's response, that "You do unbend your noble strength, to think / So brain-sickly of things" (Act 2, Scene 2, lines 42–43), hints at the slow and inexorable spiral into madness that such sleeplessness will bring to her and her husband. The ultimate expression of sleeplessness comes, however, with Lady Macbeth's guilty sleepwalking—her "slumb'ry agitation" (Act 5, Scene 1, line 11)—which is the precursor to her eventual suicide. As Lady Macbeth's Doctor informs Macbeth, "she is troubled with thick-coming fancies, / That keep her from her rest" (Act 5, Scene 3, lines 38–39). To Macbeth's command to "Cure [her] of that," and his question, "Canst thou not minister to a mind diseas'd[?]" (Act 5, Scene 3, lines 39–40), the Doctor pleads his powerlessness and inability. "This disease is beyond my practice," the Doctor had earlier admitted (Act 5, Scene 1, line 59). The Macbeths' longing for "downy sleep, death's counterfeit" (Act 2, Scene 3, line 76) will be satisfied only upon their own violent deaths.

Sinister Imagery

Shakespeare's imagery focuses on the dark and sinister aspects of the play. His language matches the overwhelming sense of despair and anguish that Macbeth's regime causes his Scottish subjects. Whether on the field of battle or in the supposed safety of a castle banquet, blood in all its vividly disturbing color is ever present.

The time for nightmares and murderous deeds is, by convention of course, the night. The overwhelming darkness that pervades the play has led some scholars to believe that *Macbeth* was written specifically for an indoor venue, where candles could be trimmed and ghostly figures emerge from darkened corners. Blood and darkness are also linked to the imagery of childbirth. That which

Inspired By ...

Chronicler Raphael Holinshed, in the revised edition of his *Chronicles of England, Scotland and Ireland* (1587), describes Macbeth killing Duncan in battle and claiming the Scottish throne in 1040. Shakespeare added Macbeth's guilty mental anguish, itself inspired by another Holinshed account about King Kenneth, who had slaughtered his nephew, Malcolm Duff, some 70 years before Macbeth's reign.

BELOW: *Lady Macbeth's vaunting ambition was symbolized in an 1880s production when Ellen Terry, playing Lady Macbeth in a spectacular costume, raised Duncan's crown to her head—a scene portrayed in this 1889 painting, by John Singer Sargent.*

LEFT: *"My hands are of your color," says Lady Macbeth (Helen Baxendale) to her husband (Jason Connery) in a made-for-TV version of the play. Shakespeare refers to blood no less than 38 times in the course of* Macbeth, *with many characters appearing onstage covered with gore.*

is most natural to humankind is transformed into something strangely unnatural and alien. Similarly, Shakespeare employs imagery based on the bird and animal kingdoms, with nature turned upside down symbolically to represent the political turmoil of Macbeth's rule. *Macbeth* is a play full of imagery of inversion and pain.

Blood

Following the short and enigmatic 11-line opening scene with the Witches, Duncan's query about the Captain, "What bloody man is that?" (Act 1, Scene 2, line 1), announces the first onstage appearance of a blood-spattered actor. From then on, blood becomes an oft-repeated image. The metaphorical blood-staining that cannot be washed from murderous hands signifies the mental anguish of those weighed down with guilt. Having stabbed Duncan in his sleep, Macbeth stares down in disbelief, exclaiming "What hands are here?":

Will all great Neptune's ocean wash this blood
Clean from my hand? No; this my hand will
rather
The multitudinous seas incarnadine,
Making the green one red.
(ACT 2, SCENE 2, LINES 57–60)

The deed is so appalling that even if Macbeth were to wash his hands in the seas of the world, the green waters would become "one red" bloody mass. On returning from Duncan's room, Lady Macbeth also proudly proclaims, "My hands are of your color" (Act 2, Scene 2, line 61). Her callous suggestion that "A little water clears us of this deed" (Act 2, Scene 2, line 64) will, however, prove bitterly ironic. Later, when sleepwalking in her madness, she rubs her hands obsessively as if washing away invisible blood. "Out, damn'd spot! out, I say!" she complains in desperate annoyance, adding, "Yet who would have thought the old man to have had so much blood in him?" (Act 5, Scene 1, lines 35–40). Macbeth's initial reaction might be one of frantic disbelief, especially when the bloody ghost of Banquo gatecrashes the royal banquet, but he still acknowledges that "blood will have blood" (Act 3, Scene 4, line 121). Ever more hardened by his murderous resolve, Macbeth recognizes that he is

in blood
Stepp'd in so far that, should I wade no more,
Returning were as tedious as go o'er.
(ACT 3, SCENE 4, LINES 135–37)

Blood, and the imagery of blood, symbolically oozes from the souls of the play's guilty couple.

Darkness and Night

Murderous and villainous deeds are, it was thought in Shakespeare's time, best performed at night, that "unruly" time when "strange screams of death" foretell of "confus'd events" (Act 2, Scene 3, lines 54–58), and when "Good things of day begin to droop and drowse, / Whiles night's black agents

Middleton's Macbeth?

The 2007 *Oxford Collected Works of Thomas Middleton* includes *Macbeth.* Sixteen years Shakespeare's junior, Middleton was a prolific playwright, famous for gruesome tragedies and sexual comedies. Scholars believe nearly 11 percent of *Macbeth* is by Middleton. The witch leader Hecat's dialogue surrounding the song references, "Come away, come away" (Act 3, Scene 5, after line 33) and "Black spirits" (Act 4, Scene 1, after line 43), was most likely added the year of Shakespeare's death (1616). The complete songs (and Hecat) had already appeared in Middleton's play *The Witch* (*c.* 1616), most likely performed by the King's Men at their Blackfriars venue. Often removed from modern staged versions of *Macbeth*, Hecat and her songs add that all-singing, all-dancing element which early adapters of Shakespeare's play found so appealing.

to their preys do rouse" (Act 3, Scene 2, lines 52–53). When Macbeth hears Duncan naming Malcolm heir to the Scottish throne, he calls on the "Stars" to "hide your fires, / Let not light see my black and deep desires" (Act 1, Scene 4, lines 50–51). Likewise, when Lady Macbeth first plots to assassinate Duncan, she calls on night and darkness to shield her wicked plans:

> *Come, thick night,*
> *And pall thee in the dunnest smoke of hell,*
> *That my keen knife see not the wound it makes,*
> *Nor heaven peep through the blanket of the dark*
> *To cry, "Hold, hold!"*
> (ACT 1, SCENE 5, LINES 50–54)

By calling upon the night to "pall" or envelop itself in the "dunnest" or darkest smoke of hell, Lady Macbeth is conjuring imagery of darkness and evil that highlights her devilish resolve. She is immediately united with those whom Banquo describes as the "instruments of darkness"—the equivocating Witches—who appear to "tell us truths," but really only trick us "In deepest consequence" (Act 1, Scene 3, lines 124–26). For Macbeth, faced with the duplicitous truth of the Witches' predictions, night and darkness figuratively represent his own doom. As he laments in the play's final act, "I gin to be a-weary of the sun" (Act 5, Scene 5, line 48), the dreadful darkness of that ultimate night—death—becomes his only world-weary hope.

THE HISTORY BEHIND THE PLAY

The historical Macbeth succeeded to the Scottish throne after killing his predecessor, but unlike his fictional counterpart, he seems to have been a conscientious monarch, at least by the standards of the time.

Born	Possibly 1005
Father	Findlaech, the Mormaer (Earl) of Moray
Mother	Possibly Donada, daughter of King Malcolm II (reigned 1005–34)
Married	Gruoch, granddaughter of King Kenneth III (reigned 997–1005)
Children	Lulach, a stepson
Came to the throne	August 14, 1040, after killing King Duncan I (reigned 1034–40) in battle
Died	August 15, 1057, killed in battle by Malcolm III Canmore (reigned 1058–93), son of Duncan I
Succeeded by	Lulach (reigned 1057–58)
Buried	Island of Iona

Animals and Birds

The animals and birds that, even if only in allusion, frequent the play's nighttime world add to its sense of gloom and despondency. Rhinos and tigers, scorpions, bats and beetles, dogs, wolves, toads, and violently cannibalistic horses that "eat each other" (Act 2, Scene 4, line 18), all reside within Shakespeare's menagerie of animal imagery. Of the birds, Shakespeare employs sparrows, eagles, ravens, falcons, vultures, kites, magpies,

LEFT: *The play likens the secret wrongdoings of the Macbeths to darkness and night, a fact directors take full advantage of. Here, Macbeth (Paul Scofield), carrying a sword, strides a dimly lit stage in director Peter Hall's Stratford production of 1967.*

Out, out, brief candle!/Life's but a walking shadow, a poor player,/That struts and frets his hour upon the stage,/And then is heard no more. It is a tale/Told by an idiot, full of sound and fury,/Signifying nothing.

— *Macbeth* (ACT 5, SCENE 5, LINES 23–28)

rooks, choughs, and wrens, in fact a virtual aviary of feathered creatures with which to comment on nature's ills. The owl, however, is most frequently mentioned as a sign of foreboding. Since the ancient Greek epic poetry of Homer's *Iliad* and *Odyssey*, owls have been thought of as birds of ill-omen, their calls signifying impending death. Lady Macbeth, startled at the noise of "the owl that shriek'd," also recognizes the bird as "the fatal bellman" announcing her husband's murder of Duncan (Act 2, Scene 2, line 3).

Motherhood and Children

Shakespeare's most disturbing imagery is that connected with the natural function of child-bearing and -rearing. Lady Macbeth's lack of maternal instinct shockingly highlights her spiritual decline. When goading her husband to murder Duncan, she proves her resolve by describing her own, presumably dead, child:

> *I have given suck, and know*
> *How tender 'tis to love the babe that milks me;*
> *I would, while it was smiling in my face,*
> *Have pluck'd my nipple from his boneless gums,*
> *And dash'd the brains out, had I so sworn as you*
> *Have done to this.*
> (ACT 1, SCENE 7, LINES 54–59)

Lady Macbeth's horrific description of infanticide is in contrast to Lady Macduff's care for her own children, and her dismay at being left alone to fend for their safety. About her husband's escape to England, Lady Macduff comments that "He loves us not," accusingly describing how Macduff "wants the natural touch" as a caring father (Act 4, Scene 2, lines 8–9). There is now little the unfortunate mother and children can do to save themselves from the murderous plans of Macbeth, who, in an attempt to counter the Witches' warning to "beware Macduff," had already given orders to "give to th' edge o' th' sword" Macduff's "wife, his babes, and all unfortunate souls / That trace him in his line" (Act 4, Scene 1, lines 151–53). Lady Macduff and her family will die at the murderers' hands, an act so appalling in its merciless tyranny that the man who "was from his mother's womb / Untimely ripp'd" (Act 5, Scene 8, lines 15–16) is driven to avenge his family, and the nation of Scotland, for the bloody rule of Macbeth.

On Stage

From the 1660s, until actor–producer David Garrick's revised production in 1774, *Macbeth* was performed using poet and dramatist William Davenant's spectacularly rewritten version of Shakespeare's play, *MacBeth*, complete with flying

Peter O'Toole

Peter O'Toole's 1980 *Macbeth* at London's Old Vic (directed by Bryan Forbes) is hailed the worst production ever staged, with audiences guffawing at its gallons of artificial blood. Following universal panning by the critics—Michael Billington of *The Guardian* wrote that "O'Toole delivers every line with a monotonous tenor bark as if addressing an audience of Eskimos"—it also became a box-office hit.

RIGHT: *Director Roman Polanski adjusts the cloak of Francesca Annis (Lady Macbeth) on the set of his 1971 film version. Although criticized at the time for its violence and nudity, the film is now widely admired.*

Throne of Blood

Definitely not a translation of Shakespeare's play, but a spin-off that adapts the plot and themes of *Macbeth*, Japanese director Akira Kurosawa's film *Throne of Blood* (1957) combines artistic elements of Japanese Noh theater with the Samurai warrior film genre. A literal translation of the film's Japanese title, *The Castle of the Spider's Web*, suggests Kurosawa's fascination with power and deceit, and with an oriental feudal authority undermined by military violence and greed. Set in sixteenth-century Japan, *Throne of Blood* abandons Shakespeare's text, focusing instead on the universal nature of honor, trust, and betrayal. The Witches are replaced by a single malevolent spirit who lives in the forest and symbolically spins wool on a wheel of fortune. Macduff and his family are absent from the film. In the end, Washizu, Kurosawa's Macbeth, dies in a hail of arrows, his death signifying less the return to good rule and more the inevitable decline of an ill-fated feudal system, which mirrors anxieties within Japanese society in the immediate post–World War II period.

ABOVE: *A Japanese poster shows the film's stars: Toshiro Mifune (Washizu) and Isuzu Yamada (Lady Asaji).*

witches, songs and dances, and extravagant special effects. Garrick was not averse to incorporating such melodramatic material, but it was actor–manager John Philip Kemble and his sister, Sarah Siddons, who added a chorus of more than 50 singing and dancing comedy witches to their 1790s London stagings. By the 1840s, *Macbeth* was established in the United States, where William Charles Macready appeared in Boston opposite Charlotte Cushman. Cushman developed her own uniquely violent portrayal of Lady Macbeth. Cushman's radical reinterpretation was later matched by Italy's Adelaide Ristori, who traveled to London in 1857 to perform an Italian adaptation called *Macbetto*. In the 1880s, Ristori played Lady Macbeth in New York and Philadelphia alongside Edwin Booth.

In April 1936, at the Lafayette Theater, Harlem, 20-year-old Orson Welles directed his New York debut of Shakespeare's tragedy, later referred to as the "Voodoo" *Macbeth*. Set in the postcolonial court of the Haitian King Henri Christophe, the "Voodoo" *Macbeth* saw Welles employing a cast of African-American actors with little experience of classical theater. Welles replaced the three Witches with voodoo witch doctors, adding the beat of drums and chanting to heighten the play's mesmeric effect.

Director Glen Byam Shaw's 1955 production of the play at Stratford, starring Laurence Olivier and Vivien Leigh, is still hailed as a watershed, although photographs of Olivier's extravagant makeup suggest a more stylized portrayal of evil than modern tastes might find acceptable.

In music, Italian composer Giuseppe Verdi first adapted *Macbeth* as an opera in 1847. His longer version, written for the Théâtre Lyrique Paris (1865), is more familiar to operagoers today.

On Screen

Twelve years after his stage production, Orson Welles directed and starred in his film version of *Macbeth*, judged by Welles aficionados to be his least successful screen venture.

Other film adaptations include director Roman Polanski's 1971 *Macbeth*—unfairly judged more for its nude Lady Macbeth sleepwalking scene than Polanski's radical restructuring of the screenplay with the British writer Kenneth Tynan—and the Indian Bollywood production *Maqbool* (2006), directed by Vishal Bharadwaj, in which the role of the Witches is taken by a pair of comic, though extremely manipulative, police inspectors predicting the rise and fall of Maqbool, a local gangland boss. Director Geoffrey Wright's 2006 *Macbeth* is set in contemporary Melbourne, Australia, where Macbeth is a ruthless hitman who is informed by three schoolgirl witches that he will become the ultimate crime boss in the area.

WRITTEN
c. 1606

SETTING AND PERIOD
Alexandria, Rome, and other parts of the Roman Empire, 40–30 BCE

CHARACTERS 37

ACTS 5

SCENES 42

LINES 3,522

Antony and Cleopatra

THE PLOT: *In Egypt, Antony's passion for Cleopatra makes him neglect his political and military duties as one of the Roman triumvirs (with Octavius Caesar and Lepidus). On Antony's return to Rome, Octavius offers marriage to his sister Octavia to strengthen Antony's Roman ties. Octavius eliminates Lepidus, after using him to fight the popular Sextus Pompeius (Pompey), then makes Antony's return to Egypt a pretext for war. When he defeats Antony and Cleopatra at sea, he refuses to negotiate with Antony. Antony successfully strikes back, but suffers a second loss at sea, for which he blames Cleopatra.*

Cleopatra flees and gives out that she has killed herself, whereupon Antony attempts to commit suicide. He bungles the act, however, and, fatally wounded, is hauled up to her monument where he dies in her arms. Once Cleopatra knows Octavius intends to parade her in triumph through Rome, she uses asps to kill herself, anticipating posthumous reunion with Antony. On discovering her body, Octavius acknowledges her regality and decrees that the lovers will be buried together.

In terms of the historical material covered, *Antony and Cleopatra* is a sequel to *Julius Caesar*, but it is a very different kind of tragedy to that earlier work. The play's conflicting political and ideological perspectives are both more personalized and more internalized, resulting in more sympathetic protagonists whose tempestuous relationship demonstrates that the personal and the political are inseparable. *Antony and Cleopatra* is like the other late tragedies in avoiding soliloquy and using debate and satire, but it is more compelling: we always know how Antony is feeling about the conflict between Roman duty and his passion, even if Cleopatra remains fascinating precisely because she is a mystery.

Egyptian Hedonism Versus Roman Duty

Antony and Cleopatra was written in the context of Renaissance sexual and power politics and of that age's general endorsement of Roman values. When Octavius conquered Egypt in 30 BCE, his propaganda ensured that Cleopatra was seen as Rome's enemy, a dissolute foreigner, a woman with inappropriate absolute power. The Romans also colonized Europe and thereby made Roman

BELOW: *A nineteenth-century painting depicts the moment in Act 4, Scene 15 when Antony, mortally wounded, is hauled up to join Cleopatra in her monument.*

Dramatis Personae

Mark Antony, Octavius Caesar, M. Aemilius Lepidus, *triumvirs*
Sextus Pompeius
Domitius Enobarbus, Ventidius, Eros, Scarus, Decretas, Demetrius, Philo, *friends to Antony*
Canidius, *lieutenant-general to Antony*
Maecenas, Agrippa, Dolabella, Proculeius, Thidias, Gallus, *friends to Octavius Caesar*
Taurus, *lieutenant-general to Octavius Caesar*
Menas, Menecrates, Varrius, *friends to Pompey*
Silius, *an officer in Ventidius's army*
Schoolmaster, *acting as an ambassador from Antony to Octavius Caesar*
Alexas, Mardian (a eunuch), Seleucus, Diomedes, *attendants on Cleopatra*
Soothsayer
Lamprius, Rannius, Lucillius, *three Romans appearing as mutes in Act 1, Scene 2*
Clown
Cleopatra, *Queen of Egypt*
Octavia, *sister to Octavius Caesar and wife to Antony*
Charmian, Iras, *attendants on Cleopatra*
Officers, Soldiers, Messengers, and other Attendants

civilization mainstream for Europeans. In Shakespeare's day, Latin was still the universal language of the educated classes, and English people not only tended to identify with the Romans culturally, but to share most of their patriarchal attitudes. These attitudes included the belief that colonization inevitably brought civilization, as well as the conviction that women must be chaste and demure and that sexually assertive women had to be kept in their place.

The dialogue, up until the last long scene, is dominated by Romans, who entrench the play's view of Egypt as a land of hedonism, the opposite of Roman duty. Cleopatra, surrounded by women and eunuchs in an extravagant court supposedly given over to fleshly indulgence, is the very personification of Eastern pleasures. Antony, a Roman who has gone native in Egypt, follows Cleopatra in love games, and, in the play's opening lines, Philo informs Demetrius:

Take but good note, and you shall see in him
The triple pillar of the world transform'd
Into a strumpet's fool ...
(ACT 1, SCENE 1, LINES 11–13)

Octavius responds to Egypt's otherness by demonstrating his power over it without too close an involvement; he is impervious to Cleopatra's appeal. Antony struggles with his Romanness, and in the end must kill himself like a Roman, because the urgency of his attraction to the exotic means it cannot be subdued to his sense of duty and honor. Although both Octavius and Antony are Roman conquerors, they are very different in their responses to Egypt; and Shakespeare uses that difference, and the associated satirical elements in the play, to imply his own attitude to the behavior of the characters.

Inspired By ...

Shakespeare's main source is Sir Thomas North's translation of Greek writer Plutarch's *Lives of the Noble Grecians and Romans*. Enobarbus's barge speech from Act 2, Scene 2 ("The barge she sat in, like a burnish'd throne ...") is North's prose transformed into powerful poetry. Yet, unlike Plutarch, Shakespeare satirizes Roman political machinations just as surely as he represents the hedonism of the Egyptian court.

ABOVE: *Antony is torn between Roman duty and Eastern pleasure. In this scene from a 2005 production at Manchester, England, he listens, enthralled, to Cleopatra, as the queen's bevy of exotic attendants looks on.*

Egypt and England

In presenting Antony and Cleopatra's relationship as a story about love (or sex) and politics, seen from a particular point of view, Shakespeare may also be making allusions to the political situation in contemporary England. Cleopatra's assault on the messenger in Act 2 is possibly based on Elizabeth I's treatment of attendants, and broader parallels between Cleopatra and Elizabeth as powerful, self-dramatizing, and willful queens may also be intended. Like Elizabeth, Cleopatra preserved her power by remaining unmarried. Cleopatra, of course, was no Virgin Queen—her lovers were top Romans, politically powerful men—but, despite her anger at Antony's marrying Octavia, she only articulates thoughts of marriage when she is dying.

Some commentators see an implied parallel between Octavius—who ruled as the Emperor Augustus—and the reigning monarch, James I, who liked to be known as the Second Augustus, and saw himself as bringing about a new peaceful age, just as Augustus's rule had initiated the Pax Romana. Shakespeare's Octavius says, before his final battle with Antony:

The time of universal peace is near.
Prove this a prosp'rous day, the three-nook'd world
Shall bear the olive freely.
(ACT 4, SCENE 6, LINES 4–6)

But the play deals with Octavius's ambitious rise rather than with the statesman who reinvented himself as Augustus, and it is difficult to ignore those elements of the satire directed against the manipulations of Octavius.

Rome Versus Egypt

The themes of the play derive from the conflict between Roman and Egyptian values, which is made literal when Octavius makes war on Antony and Cleopatra, and the accompanying sense of crisis and betrayal, both political and personal. The play emphasizes the unlovely and destructive nature of middle-aged love, but finally endorses the notion that great passion is worth the material loss: the lovers, while political losers,

Cleopatra and the Boy Apprentice

In Shakespeare's day, Cleopatra was the largest and most challenging female role on the English stage. At that time, female parts were played by male apprentice actors. Although the apprentices were often called "boys," we know that at least one of them was still playing female roles at the age of 21, and it is more than likely that the part of Cleopatra was written with a youth in mind, probably the senior apprentice in the company at the time. The apprentice would not only have been competing directly with the star actor himself (Richard Burbage playing Antony), but would have dominated the stage for a whole act after the star's stage death.

ABOVE: *The supposed sensual indulgence of Egypt, and of Cleopatra in particular, has long been a subject of writers and artists. Alexandre Cabanel's* Cleopatra Testing Poisons on Condemned Prisoners *(1887) shows the queen, bare-breasted and lounging on fur and silk, taking a detached interest in poisoning.*

mock
The luck of Caesar, which the gods give men
To excuse their after wrath ...
(ACT 5, SCENE 2, LINES 285–87)

The majority of *Antony and Cleopatra* is concerned with related themes: the conflict in the lovers between duty and passion, the interconnectedness of the personal and the political, and the notion of integrity in action.

Ambiguity and satire complicate the audience's responses throughout the play. Romans close to Antony voice their sense of betrayal at his neglect of duty for sensual indulgence. The disquiet experienced by Enobarbus eventually makes him defect to Octavius's side—only to die of shame in the face of Antony's magnanimity toward him. Cleopatra's way of handling Antony involves changeability and opportunism, and these qualities make her seem capable of betraying him. The lovers also abuse their power in an attempt to resist political reality: Cleopatra beats the messenger bearing news of Antony's marriage in Act 2, Scene 5, and Antony orders the whipping of Octavius's ambassador, Thidias, in Act 3, Scene 13.

The barge she sat in, like a burnish'd throne,/Burnt on the water. The poop was beaten gold,/Purple the sails, and so perfumed that/The winds were love-sick with them ...

—*Enobarbus* (ACT 2, SCENE 2, LINES 191–94)

Nor are Antony's military followers always given their due, as witness Ventidius's comments in Act 3, Scene 1 (lines 12–27), Enobarbus's being put in his place in Act 2, Scene 2 (lines 107–10), and the unnamed Soldier's being sent on his way in Act 3, Scene 7.

Suicide as Redemption

In Antony's own eyes, suicide is an act that will redeem his shortcomings:

> *Not Caesar's valor hath o'erthrown Antony,*
> *But Antony's hath triumph'd on itself.*
> (ACT 4, SCENE 15, LINES 14–15)

Though it is presented ambivalently, Cleopatra's delay in killing herself is arguably caused by her need to try to determine her country's future by negotiation, and demonstrates the way in which, for her, gender and power politics are inextricably linked. When it does come, her death demonstrates her resolution and integrity as ruler of Egypt and as a woman, and her commitment to the dead man she now calls husband. Although both deaths might be seen as the protagonists' attempts to reinvent themselves in a heroic light, they are clearly noble, in a way that very little in or of Rome in the play is noble. Their deaths are an attempt to create an integrity based on individuality, not on loyalty to a political system that resembles a fighting machine.

There is little sign in the play of the statesman that Octavius was to become when he reinvented himself as Augustus. Octavius's empire-building power games are deadly on a grand scale, and we see that internal fighting is an integral part of Roman politics. Octavius is manipulative, treacherous, and deceitful—he disposes of Lepidus, leads his army from the rear, does not trust deserters, attempts to bribe Cleopatra to destroy Antony and to deceive her into thinking that he will not parade her through Rome—and he is mean about feasting his victorious army.

Images of Indulgence and Love

The major groups of images in the play connect the sensuality of Egypt with emasculation and ensnarement (as seen from the Roman imperialist viewpoint). These images operate by connecting the verbal with the visual, and help to maintain Shakespeare's ambiguous, partly satirical, treatment of the lovers.

Antony, once the very embodiment of Roman military values, is under Cleopatra's spell. He has substituted sexual engagements for military ones—a point made by several characters. The play opens with a stage image of Egyptian indulgence and Philo's commentary on Antony's obsession with Cleopatra. Philo sees Cleopatra as being literally fanned by her eunuchs, but metaphorically cooled by Antony's sexual subservience:

> *his captain's heart,*
> *Which in the scuffles of great fights hath burst*
> *The buckles on his breast, reneges all temper,*
> *And is become the bellows and the fan*
> *To cool a gipsy's [Egyptian's] lust.*
> (ACT 1, SCENE 1, LINES 6–10)

Antony's officers think he has been unmanned, ironically made into a military eunuch, by his infatuation. His passion allows Cleopatra to wear the sword in battle as well as in bed, and the result is that the general's sword becomes an instrument of self-destruction. The ultimate price is paid when Antony bungles his own suicide.

Cleopatra's dressing of Antony in women's clothes while she wears his sword (as recounted by Cleopatra to Charmian in Act 2, Scene 5, lines 18–23) is an act of sexual-political, as well as erotic, play. It goes beyond gender-bending to the undermining of Roman dignity and military might, and beyond that again to the subversion of Roman notions of order, conquest, and territorial possession. It is the triumph of Eros (the dis-armer), the god of love, over Mars, the god of war.

As we gather from the cross-dressing incident, Cleopatra's sexual "method" involves unpredictability. Her stage appearance as a "tawny" Egyptian (Act 1, Scene 1, line 6) had important moral implications for the play's original audiences. Her tawny complexion is exotically

> *Age cannot wither her, nor custom stale/ Her infinite variety. Other women cloy/ The appetites they feed, but she makes hungry/Where most she satisfies ...*
>
> 
>
> —*Enobarbus* (ACT 2, SCENE 2, LINES 234–37)

Antony and His Sword

he fishes, drinks, and wastes
The lamps of night in revel; is not more manlike
Than Cleopatra; nor the queen of Ptolomy
More womanly than he ...
—*Caesar* (ACT 1, SCENE 4, LINES 4–7)

Mark Antony
In Egypt sits at dinner, and will make
No wars without-doors ...
—*Pompey* (ACT 2, SCENE 1, LINES 11–13)

and next morn,
Ere the ninth hour, I drunk him to his bed;
Then put my tires and mantles on him, whilst
I wore his sword Philippan.
—*Cleopatra* (ACT 2, SCENE 5, LINES 20–23)

You did know
How much you were my conqueror, and that
My sword, made weak by my affection, would
Obey it on all cause.
—*Antony* (ACT 3, SCENE 11, LINES 65–68)

O, thy vild lady!
She has robb'd me of my sword.
—*Antony* (ACT 4, SCENE 14, LINES 22–23)

but I will be
A bridegroom in my death, and run into't
As to a lover's bed ...
—*Antony* (ACT 4, SCENE 14, LINES 99–101)

ambivalent, neither black nor white. Ultimately, Cleopatra's nobility is confirmed, but in the course of the play many Roman men see her complexion as signifying sensual indulgence. In a cynical moment, Enobarbus calls Cleopatra Antony's "Egyptian dish" (Act 2, Scene 6, line 126)—though it should be noted that Antony's fondness for feasting also marks the magnanimity by which he is contrasted with Octavius. But Antony himself often doubts Cleopatra's loyalty, applying the term "gipsy" to the "false Egyptian" that, he says, "at fast and loose / Beguil'd" him (Act 4, Scene 12, lines 28–29) in the second sea battle. His military dependence on her is visualized in Act 4, Scene 4, where she acts incompetently as his armorer. This scene is a sequel to the offstage cross-dressing: Cleopatra is trying to give him back his generalship.

Cleopatra always takes the lead in love games, and possibly her retreat to her monument, with its dire consequences, is a version of dalliance—though of course she is also running from Antony's violent anger. When he is dying, Cleopatra literally draws the bleeding Antony to her, and, although this might be read as a stage image of the bloody and painful consequences of his ensnarement, Antony is also literally elevated, in keeping with the ultimate dramatic emphasis on the lovers' triumph. When eventually it is Cleopatra's turn to die, she finds another occasion for dressing up—in royal attire that has to do with majestic Eros ("The stroke of death is as a lover's pinch, / Which hurts and is desir'd", Act 5, Scene 2, lines 295–96), rather than the territorial expansionism of a triumphant Mars.

Playing Cleopatra

Although *Antony and Cleopatra* offers the star actress more opportunities than any other play by Shakespeare, the role of Cleopatra confronts traditional Western notions about "appropriate" female behavior: she is sexually dominant and sometimes physically violent, and has absolute political power. This was less of a problem for an apprentice male actor (who would originally have played the role), working within the conventions of the Jacobean theater, than it has been for actresses until quite recent times.

In late seventeenth-century England, two adaptations, one by poet John Dryden, the other by dramatist Charles Sedley, made Cleopatra a more conventionally virtuous figure than Shakespeare's. Shakespeare's Cleopatra was allowed to reassert herself in 1759 at Drury Lane, London, when Mary Ann Yates played the role.

It was not until director Trevor Nunn's 1972 production at Stratford (with Janet Suzman as Cleopatra) that the play became firmly established in the repertoire. The popularization of feminism, and other changing cultural attitudes continue to make the play appealing on stage and in syllabuses. As well as enjoying the play's exploration of the relationship between sexual politics and patriarchal political power, contemporary audiences appreciate the ambiguities inherent in the play's tragic form, with its strong satirical element and its absence of soliloquies.

Since Nunn's, the most successful British production has been director Peter Hall's of 1987 with Anthony Hopkins and Judi Dench. Notable "firsts" on the British stage include the all-black *Antony and Cleopatra*, directed by Yvonne Brewster for the Talawa Theatre Company in 1991, with Jeffery Kissoon and Dona Croll, and the 1999 all-male production in Jacobean dress at the Globe, London, directed by Giles Block, with Paul Shelley as Antony and Mark Rylance as Cleopatra.

Antony and Cleopatra has been staged in the United States since 1838. Katharine Hepburn famously played Cleopatra in 1960. In continental Europe, two directors have staged noteworthy German-language productions: Peter Zadek in Vienna and Peter Stein in Salzburg, both in 1994.

The play has not been much adapted for other media. Samuel Barber's opera, *Antony and Cleopatra* (1966), uses a Shakespeare-based libretto by film director Franco Zeffirelli.

THE HISTORY BEHIND THE PLAY

83 BCE	Birth of Mark Antony
70 or 69 BCE	Birth of Cleopatra
51 BCE	Cleopatra and her brother, Ptolemy XIII, become joint rulers of Egypt
49 BCE	Outbreak of civil war between Julius Caesar and Roman general Pompey
48 BCE	Pompey is assassinated in Egypt; Julius Caesar and Cleopatra become lovers
47 BCE	Cleopatra gives birth to a son, possibly fathered by Julius Caesar
46 BCE	Arrival of Cleopatra in Rome; Julius Caesar is appointed dictator
44 BCE	Assassination of Julius Caesar; Cleopatra returns to Egypt
43 BCE	Formation of the triumvirate—Antony, Octavius Caesar, and Lepidus
42 BCE	Antony and Octavius defeat Julius Caesar's assassins at the Battle of Philippi
41 BCE	Antony and Cleopatra become lovers
40 BCE	Death of Antony's wife, Fulvia; Antony returns to Rome from Egypt, and marries Octavius's sister, Octavia; Cleopatra gives birth to twins fathered by Antony
36 BCE	Antony's expedition against the Parthians fails; Lepidus is removed from the triumvirate; Cleopatra gives birth to Antony's son
35 BCE	Antony returns to Egypt with Cleopatra
33 BCE	Legal end of the triumvirate
32 BCE	Antony divorces Octavia; Octavius declares war on Cleopatra
31 BCE	Octavius defeats Antony and Cleopatra at the Battle of Actium
30 BCE	Octavius and his forces reach Egypt; Antony and Cleopatra commit suicide
27 BCE	Octavius becomes Emperor Augustus Caesar

RIGHT: *Antony (Herbert Beerbohm Tree) dallies with Cleopatra (Constance Collier) while Charmian (Alice Crawford) waits close by, in the spectacularly costumed London production, directed by Tree, of 1906.*

Timon of Athens

THE PLOT: *Timon is one of the richest merchants in Athens, and is immensely generous with his wealth and hospitality. The misanthropic philosopher Apemantus warns him against flatterers. When Timon is unexpectedly ruined financially, his "friends" refuse to help him or reciprocate his past generosity.*

Disillusioned by their ingratitude, Timon rejects society and angrily retreats to the woods. Digging for roots, he finds gold, and broods on its human uselessness and its capacity morally to degrade men—even though, to his disgust, it makes him wealthy again. He meets Alcibiades, formerly a military hero and a general, who resents Athenians for ungratefully banishing him from the city.

Timon gives gold to Alcibiades, to finance a war against Athens in revenge. Timon dies, a misanthrope, on the beach, and Alcibiades reports his death to the now shamed city.

Although formally classed as a tragedy, *Timon of Athens* is in tone a polemical satire raising a series of fundamental questions about society, which places it with the "problem plays" of Shakespeare. The play's stark structure, and its sometimes abrupt plot changes, have led some critics to argue that it is either incomplete, or was coauthored by Shakespeare with another dramatist such as Thomas Middleton—although these views are merely conjectural.

ABOVE: *Timon (Ralph Richardson) is begged for gold by the two prostitutes Phrynia and Timandra in a 1955 production at London's Old Vic. Invoking an image of physical corruption, Timon exhorts them to give their customers venereal diseases.*

Dramatis Personae

Timon of Athens
Lucius, Lucullus, Sempronius, *flattering lords*
Ventidius, *one of Timon's false friends*
Alcibiades, *an Athenian captain*
Apemantus, *a churlish philosopher*
Flavius, *steward to Timon*
Flaminius, *one of Timon's servants*
Servilius, *another*
Lucilius, *another*
Caphis, Philotus, Titus, Hortensius, *several servants to usurers*
Servants *to Varro, Isidore, and Lucius, usurers, and Timon's creditors*
Poet, Painter, Jeweller, Merchant
Old Athenian
Three Strangers, *one named* **Hostilius**
Page
Fool
Phrynia, Timandra, *mistresses to Alcibiades*
Cupid
Certain Maskers, *as Amazons*
Certain Senators and other Lords, Officers, Soldiers, certain Thieves (the Banditti), with divers other Servants and Attendants

WRITTEN
c. 1606–9

SETTING AND PERIOD
Athens and surrounding woods, fourth century BCE

CHARACTERS 33

ACTS 5

SCENES 17

LINES 2,488

Other Characters
Timon
Apemantus
Flavius
Alcibiades
Poet

MAJOR ROLES

Timon is clearly the focus of the play, with some 34 percent of the lines falling to him. The many "other characters," who speak 37 percent of the lines, are largely dishonest flatterers who symbolize Timon's profound disillusionment.

Critical and theatrical neglect may be due to distaste for the play's uncomfortably bitter and bleak tone, which leaves little room for the emphasis on man's innate nobility that is sometimes assumed to redeem Shakespeare's other tragedies. Timon's servants are the only characters who are admirable. However, it can be argued that the play's harsh, socially critical attitudes, alongside our experience of theatrical developments since the time of playwrights Bertolt Brecht and Samuel Beckett, make *Timon of Athens* a play with a contemporary significance that invites reevaluation in light of today's world.

A Mature Shakespeare

The only known sources of the play are a brief account in Thomas North's translation of Greek biographer Plutarch's *Lives of the Noble Grecians and Romans,* and a Greek dialogue by the satirist Lucian, but Shakespeare has added many details and his own gloss to the Classical narrative. Economic casualties littered Shakespeare's time, since with population growth came ever-increasing inflation and extreme economic uncertainty. Many unlucky courtiers were ruined in the way that Timon was, so his experiences and anxieties would have been quite recognizable to the audience.

The play complements Shakespeare's *King Lear* in its themes of flattery and ingratitude, and it may have been written before that play as preparation, or as a spin-off from it. It has a dramatic intensity of its own, and also some knotty and powerful lines of poetry that only the mature Shakespeare could have written:

thou wouldst have plung'd thyself
In general riot, melted down thy youth
In different beds of lust, and never learn'd
The icy precepts of respect, but followed
The sug'red game before thee. But myself,
Who had the world as my confectionary,
The mouths, the tongues, the eyes, and hearts of men
At duty, more than I could frame employment;
That numberless upon me stuck as leaves
Do on the oak, have with one winter's brush
Fell from their boughs, and left me open, bare,
For every storm that blows ...
(ACT 4, SCENE 3, LINES 255–66)

The Corruption of Commerce

Timon is the author of his own downfall since he is tainted by, and enmeshed within, the essentially commercial system that destroys him. His initial generosity is built not because he owns an incorruptible metal like gold, as he does later, but is a result of him "living on credit." He uses his impression of wealth to buffer himself against reality, buying the affection of the men of Athens and deluding himself that commercial generosity creates social and emotional ties.

When his own creditors call in their debts against him, he discovers that wealth is merely an illusion, and that with it friendships can no longer be bought. This realization embitters him and forces him into the opposite position of attacking and condemning a system that corrupts everybody who is involved in it.

RIGHT: *Commissioned by the City of London in 1853 to provide a sculpture for the Lord Mayor's residence, sculptor Frederick Thrupp chose Timon of Athens, "in that part of the drama where Shakespeare describes him retired in the woods," and completed this plaster study the same year.*

The Bard Treads the Boards

Shakespeare was an actor in his company, as well as its leading writer, and it has been surmised (though without evidence) that he played the part of the Poet, who has a surprisingly large number of lines for such a minor character but who, as a character, is just as much an incriminated flatterer as the other Athenians.

Even when Timon discovers gold in the forest and becomes wealthy again, he realizes it is in essence no different from "paper credit" in its capacity to pervert human values and distort moral perceptions:

What is here?
Gold? Yellow, glittering, precious gold?
No, gods, I am no idle votarist;
Roots, you clear heavens! Thus much of this will make
Black white, foul fair, wrong right,
Base noble, old young, coward valiant.
(ACT 4, SCENE 3, LINES 25–30)

In a passage depicting predatoriness among animals, which anticipates the anarchist Pierre-Joseph Proudhon's maxim that "Property is theft," Shakespeare through Timon creates a nightmarish vision of economic exploitation as virtually an incontrovertible law of nature:

I'll example you with thievery:
The sun's a thief, and with his great attraction
Robs the vast sea; the moon's an arrant thief,
And her pale fire she snatches from the sun;
The sea's a thief, whose liquid surge resolves
The moon into salt tears; the earth's a thief,
That feeds and breeds by a composture stol'n
From gen'ral excrement; each thing's a thief.
(ACT 4, SCENE 3, LINES 435–42)

Ingratitude is only a superficial theme, and Timon's true cause of grievance is his sense of betrayal in realizing that an exchange commodity incriminates a whole society. In a series of pageant-like scenes toward the end of the play, Timon in his "feral" state meets representatives of social, commercial, and political interests—prostitutes, bandits, and politicians—allowing Shakespeare to explore how deeply corrupting money is, to the extent of causing wars. Even the Poet and Painter are forced to compromise their integrity, needing to flatter their social betters to ensure patronage.

The only "honest" characters in *Timon of Athens* are socially impotent ones. Timon's humble and devoted steward Flavius is reduced to beggary by his genuine fidelity to his "worthy" master (Act 4, Scene 3, line 511), while Apemantus, the angry satirist, stands outside the system in order to condemn it from a radically critical viewpoint: "Who lives that's not depraved or depraves?" (Act 1, Scene 2, line 140).

The Perversion of Nature

Imagery of disease, and of nature that is rapacious and perverted, runs through the play. The group of prostitutes embodies not only the principle of deceptive dealings driven by economic need, but also the infectious nature of such corruption since, as Timon emphasizes, they infect their customers with venereal diseases. The city and the forest are contrasted—not in a simple opposition of corruption versus innocence, but in a less obvious one of civilized hypocrisy versus elemental clarity.

The sea is another powerful image used sparingly but with significance, as Timon makes the choice to die on the "beached verge of the salt flood" (Act 5, Scene 1, line 216). Water seems the only cleansing element mentioned in the play, but there is a recognition that humans cannot live in the sea and can only die beside it, as though they are too morally polluted ever to be pure.

The Hypocrisy of Wealth

I wonder men dare trust themselves with men.
—*Apemantus* (ACT 1, SCENE 2, LINE 43)

Men shut their doors against a setting sun.
—*Apemantus* (ACT 1, SCENE 2, LINE 145)

Every man has his fault, and honesty is his.
—*Lucullus* (ACT 3, SCENE 1, LINES 27–28)

We have seen better days.
—*Flavius* (ACT 4, SCENE 2, LINE 27)

This yellow slave
Will knit and break religions, bless th' accurs'd,
Make the hoar leprosy ador'd, place thieves,
And give them title, knee, and approbation
With senators on the bench. This is it
That makes the wappen'd widow wed again;
She, whom the spittle-house and ulcerous sores
Would cast the gorge at, this embalms and spices
To th' April day again. Come, damn'd earth,
Thou common whore of mankind, that puts odds
Among the rout of nations, I will make thee
Do thy right nature ...
—*Timon* (ACT 4, SCENE 3, LINES 34–45)

Contrasting banquets, one lavish and the other frugal, highlight Timon's change of attitude. In the first, he dispenses gifts with prodigality, while in the latter he gives nothing.

Animal imagery is used to represent human activities and qualities. Dogs are alluded to some 20 times, and always pejoratively—Timon calls Apemantus "thou issue of a mangy dog" (Act 4, Scene 3, line 366), and suggests that instead of "ingrateful man," the world would be better populated with "tigers, dragons, wolves, and bears" and "new monsters" (Act 4, Scene 3, lines 188–90).

Modern Relevance

Timon of Athens is rarely performed, partly because the text shows signs of being a draft, with some loose ends, and partly because it may seem to lack Shakespeare's more common generosity of spirit. Actors in earlier times preferred his "golden" roles over Timon's "poetry of hatred." However, the play's relentless concentration on the ambiguous power and anxiety-causing uncertainties of the financial system and its contribution to war could be seen as very relevant to the "boom and bust" economic cycles experienced since the Depression of the 1930s, and to the international wars of the twentieth and twenty-first centuries.

Noting this, both Karl Marx and Bertolt Brecht found the play to be an acute critical analysis of capitalism, and in fact Marx was influenced by the play, especially its depiction of the nature of money (*The Power of Money,* 1844). A revival in the theater would be timely, especially since modern drama is often fragmentary and pessimistic, mirroring the mood of its world. In fact, a production in 2008 at the rebuilt Globe in London, directed by Lucy Bailey and billed as a "revival" of the play, was reviewed by the British *Guardian* newspaper as "refreshingly radical," with the staging featuring "a vast net through which actors swoop and dive on the hapless hero like vultures."

ABOVE: *Simon Paisley Day's wild-eyed Timon flings gold at the greedy "Banditti"—Jonathan Bond (left), Sam Parks (right), and Adam Burton (back)—in director Lucy Bailey's 2008 production at the Globe, London.*

Timon hath made his everlasting mansion/
Upon the beached verge of the salt flood,/
Who once a day with his embossed froth/
The turbulent surge shall cover .../
Timon hath done his reign.

—*Timon* (ACT 5, SCENE 1, LINES 215–18, 223)

Coriolanus

THE PLOT: *Cauis Martius, a Roman military hero, leads the Romans to victory against the Volscians, earning himself the name Coriolanus ("conqueror of Corioles"). He is offered a tribuneship by the Senate, dependent on his gaining acceptance by the plebians whom he seeks to represent. Two tribunes, Junius Brutus and Sicinius Velutus, considering Coriolanus's pride and popularity a threat, incite the plebians to turn against Coriolanus and to condemn him to death. Coriolanus, enraged, leaves Rome for Antium to find his military enemy, Aufidius, and lead him and the Volscians in battle against Rome herself. Volumnia, Coriolanus's mother, succeeds in turning him from his purpose and bringing about peace. Coriolanus, returning to Corioles, is murdered by Aufidius, who has become incensed by Coriolanus's failure to attack Rome and his growing power over Aufidius's own armies. Aufidius, realizing he has killed at once his martial counterpart and alter ego, determines to accord Coriolanus a proper burial and memorial acknowledging his military greatness.*

Dramatis Personae

Caius Martius, *afterward* **Caius Martius Coriolanus**
Titus Lartius, Cominius, *generals against the Volscians*
Menenius Agrippa, *friend to Coriolanus*
Sicinius Velutus, Junius Brutus, *tribunes of the people*
Young Martius, *son to Coriolanus*
Roman Herald
Nicanor, *a Roman*
Tullus Aufidius, *general of the Volscians*
Lieutenants to Aufidius and Coriolanus
Conspirators with Aufidius
Adrian, *a Volscian*
Citizen of Antium
Two Volscian Guards
Volumnia, *mother to Coriolanus*
Virgilia, *wife to Coriolanus*
Valeria, *friend to Virgilia*
Gentlewoman, *attending on Virgilia*
Roman and Volscian Senators, Patricians, Aediles, Lictors, Soldiers, Citizens, Messengers, Servants to Aufidius, and other Attendants

Dating from about 1608, *Coriolanus* is the last of Shakespeare's great tragedies. It is, however, generally ranked in critical esteem below *King Lear, Macbeth, Hamlet,* and *Othello,* for it is seen as lacking their psychological insight and depth. Nevertheless, the play provides a fascinating analysis of power and authority, of autocracy and democracy, of political processes and motives, for it demonstrates the complexity and contradictions inherent in those concepts.

Coriolanus himself is, like many tragic heroes in Shakespeare's plays, at least partly responsible for his own downfall. The qualities that bring about his military successes are clear: his autocratic leadership, his sense of honor, and his pride in his military prowess and valor, that "chiefest virtue" (Act 2, Scene 2, line 84). Yet they are also the qualities that precipitate his failure in

WRITTEN
c. 1608
SETTING AND PERIOD
Rome, Corioles, and Antium, early fifth century BCE
CHARACTERS 51
ACTS 5
SCENES 29
LINES 3,752

the political environment of Rome, where they become patrician arrogance, intransigence, and hubris. It is those aspects of Coriolanus, who

has been bred i' th' wars
Since 'a could draw a sword, and is ill school'd
In bolted language . . .
(ACT 3, SCENE 1, LINES 318–20)

that ultimately cannot let him reside in a Rome where "The people are the city" (Act 3, Scene 1, line 199). Thus, inevitably, he is exiled, having no place in the new political life of a city that his military endeavors have helped create.

England and Rome

In addition to Greek biographer Plutarch's "The Life of Caius Martius Coriolanus" in his *Lives of the Noble Grecians and Romans*, Shakespeare's *Coriolanus* draws on Book 7 of *History of Rome* by Roman historian Livy. However, Shakespeare, while adhering to his historical sources in general terms, focuses attention on various contemporary interests and concerns. The Elizabethan and Jacobean fascination with the Greco-Roman heroic warrior ideal is reflected in the play. Also, Shakespeare's depiction of famine-induced civil disorder in Rome during the fifth century BCE would have reverberated strongly with his Jacobean audiences, who were affected by food shortages and the resultant socioeconomic turbulence (such as the Midlands insurrection of 1607) that swept England.

LEFT: *Spattered with gore after the battle at Corioles, Coriolanus (William Houston) is exultant as he celebrates victory, in the Royal Shakespeare Company production at Stratford, 2007.*

Questions of Identity

Personal identity, power, and control are among the play's principal themes. Shakespeare also examines notions of progress and history, of nobility and honor, of masculinity and femininity, of love, friendship, and enmity. All are explored through Coriolanus's character and actions, as well as through the varied responses to him by his friends and enemies, his mother and wife, the Romans and the Volscians.

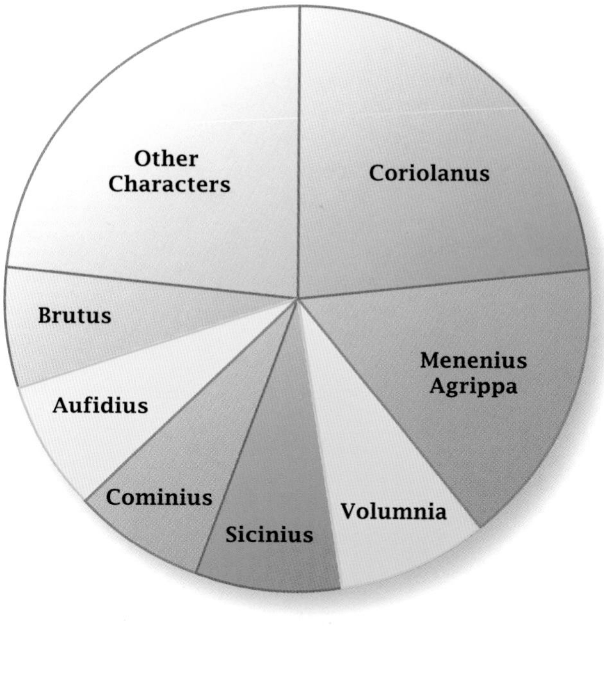

Coriolanus's career as the idealized Roman warrior is the basis of his identity:

Would you have me
False to my nature? Rather say, I play
The man I am.
(ACT 3, SCENE 2, LINES 14–16)

It is an identity crafted for him by his mother, Volumnia; and it is one that, in many ways, exists in the past. Coriolanus, having been bred and nurtured by Volumnia in the tenets of warfare, has no concept that military power and civic control are not the same. Nor does he have a clear or sophisticated concept of historical change in Roman society.

Coriolanus's relationships with Volumnia and Virgilia, his wife, develop Shakespeare's analysis of masculinity and femininity in the Roman world of the play, and likewise demonstrate the ambiguity of nobility and honor in that world. The inflexibility of Volumnia's and Coriolanus's intertwined notions of nobility and honor, regardless of the shifting Roman political environment, comes into sharp focus in Act 3 when Volumnia informs her son that:

The Body in Coriolanus

There was a time when all the body's members
Rebell'd against the belly; thus accus'd it:
That only like a gulf it did remain
I' th' midst a' th' body, idle and unactive,
Still cupboarding the viand, never bearing
Like labor with the rest, where th' other
instruments
Did see and hear, devise, instruct, walk, feel,
And, mutually participate, did minister
Unto the appetite and affection common
Of the whole body . . .
—*Menenius* (ACT 1, SCENE 1, LINES 96–105)

What's the matter, you dissentious rogues,
That rubbing the poor itch of your opinion
Make yourselves scabs?
—*Martius* (ACT 1, SCENE 1, LINES 164–66)

Thy valiantness was mine, thou suck'st it from
me[.]
—*Volumnia* (ACT 3, SCENE 2, LINE 129)

MAJOR ROLES
The lion's share of dialogue is spoken by Coriolanus (some 24 percent) and by his ally and father figure, Menenius (about 16 percent).

ABOVE: *In Scene 2 of Act 3, Volumnia, supported by Titus Lartius, Menenius, and Cominius, counsels Coriolanus (second from the right) to apologize to the plebians who he has offended in the previous scene. He reluctantly agrees, but his attempt at amelioration goes disastrously wrong.*

you can never be too noble,
But when extremities speak. I have heard you say
Honor and policy, like unsever'd friends,
I' th' war do grow together ...
(ACT 3, SCENE 2, LINES 40–43)

Similarly, Shakespeare uses the relationship between Coriolanus and Aufidius to explore themes of masculinity, masculine friendship, homoerotic love, honor, and military enmity.

The Belly Politic

For the most part, Shakespeare uses imagery of two kinds in *Coriolanus*: the body politic and animalism. In Act 1, Scene 1, Menenius's famous use of Aesop's fable in his "belly politic" speech establishes the body politic motif that remains prevalent throughout the play. The notion of the body politic here is that the organic nature of the state tends to require a hierarchical and authoritarian social order:

The kingly-crowned head, the vigilant eye,
The counsellor heart, the arm our soldier,
Our steed the leg, the tongue our trumpeter[.]
(ACT 1, SCENE 1, LINES 115–17)

Throughout *Coriolanus*, Shakespeare uses detailed imagery of the body and its parts to juxtapose the ideal and the reality of the body politic. Concepts of purity and disease, and cleanliness and filth, form part of the assessment of Roman society as a metaphorical body.

It is also through the body metaphor that the theme of warped maternal nurturing is considered and developed, as can be seen from Volumnia's grim belief that:

The breasts of Hecuba,
When she did suckle Hector, look'd not lovelier
Than Hector's forehead when it spit forth blood[.]
(ACT 1, SCENE 3, LINES 40–42)

Shakespeare also uses animal imagery, as he does in *King Lear* and *Othello.* Most notably, he uses it to reflect and explore Coriolanus's attitudes. For example, to Coriolanus the disgruntled Roman citizens are "curs [dogs],"

That like nor peace nor war? The one affrights you,
The other makes you proud. He that trusts to you,
Where he should find you lions, finds you hares;
Where foxes, geese ...
(ACT 1, SCENE 1, LINES 169–72)

Coriolanus elsewhere describes Roman infantrymen and common soldiers as a "herd" (Act 1,

Scene 4, line 31) with "souls of geese" (Act 1, Scene 4, line 34). When Coriolanus is with the Volscians, he in effect considers himself an eagle amid doves:

Cut me to pieces, Volsces, men and lads,
Stain all your edges on me. "Boy," false hound!
If you have writ your annals true, 'tis there
That, like an eagle in a dove-cote, I
[Flutter'd] your Volscians in Corioles.
Alone I did it ...
(ACT 5, SCENE 6, LINES 111–16)

The Roman populace sees Coriolanus somewhat differently, dubbing him "a very dog to the commonality" (Act 1, Scene 1, lines 28–29). Aufidius compares him to a snake: "Not Afric owns a serpent I abhor / More than thy fame and envy" (Act 1, Scene 8, lines 3–4).

Inspired By ...

The plot and major events are based on "The Life of Caius Martius Coriolanus" by Plutarch. But Shakespeare takes considerable license with various aspects of this source to develop the themes and framework of the play. He excludes Plutarch's examination of Coriolanus's previous political experience, focuses attention on food shortages as the reason for the civic unrest in Rome, and transforms Volumnia's role in the downfall of Coriolanus.

Politically Potent

The play's performance history demonstrates the continuing relevance of its political themes and issues. In 1682, at the Theatre Royal, London, playwright Nahum Tate presented his adaptation, *The Ingratitude of a Commonwealth; or, The Fall of Caius Martius Coriolanus,* aimed at lauding the sovereignty of the reigning monarch, Charles II. In 1719, dramatist John Dennis produced an interpretation of *Coriolanus* at Drury Lane, London—*The Invader of His Country; or, The Fatal Resentment*—critical of the 1715 rising of the Jacobites (supporters of the exiled Stuart monarchy). The production closed, to withering disparagement, after only three performances.

In the highly politically charged atmosphere of the 1930s, interest in *Coriolanus* revived. As fascism spread across Europe, the play's concerns with autocracy and democracy held an immediate relevance. So it must have seemed to Anglo-American poet T.S. Eliot, who wrote the overtly fascist poem "Coriolan" in 1931. European productions of the play in this period included both left- and right-wing interpretations. In Nazi Germany, the play was interpreted as supporting the need for the sort of strong leadership that Hitler provided and was consequently banned by the US occupation authorities immediately after World War II because of its potentially seditious nature. Between 1951 and 1953, East German playwright Bertolt Brecht wrote a Marxist adaptation of the play that drew specific attention to the complexity of its politics, both foreign and domestic.

Many leading actors have played Coriolanus, among them, in Georgian England, John Philip Kemble and Edmund Kean, and, in the Victorian era, Henry Irving. In more recent times, Richard Burton, Morgan Freeman, Ian McKellen, Kenneth Branagh, and Ralph Fiennes have distinguished themselves in the role. Laurence Olivier is, however, the most celebrated of the modern Coriolanuses, having first played the role in 1937 at the Old Vic, London, and again in 1959 at the Shakespeare Memorial Theatre, Stratford. His most famous moment was his climactic "death leap," in which he jumped from a 12-foot (3.5-m) high platform toward Aufidius, then hung upside down in the air.

BELOW: *John Philip Kemble was at the peak of his powers when this portrait of him as Coriolanus—a role he made his own—was painted by George Henry Harlow in 1798.*

You common cry of curs, whose breath I hate/As reek a' th' rotten fens, whose loves I prize/As the dead carcasses of unburied men/That do corrupt my air—I banish you!

—*Coriolanus* (ACT 3, SCENE 3, LINES 120–23)

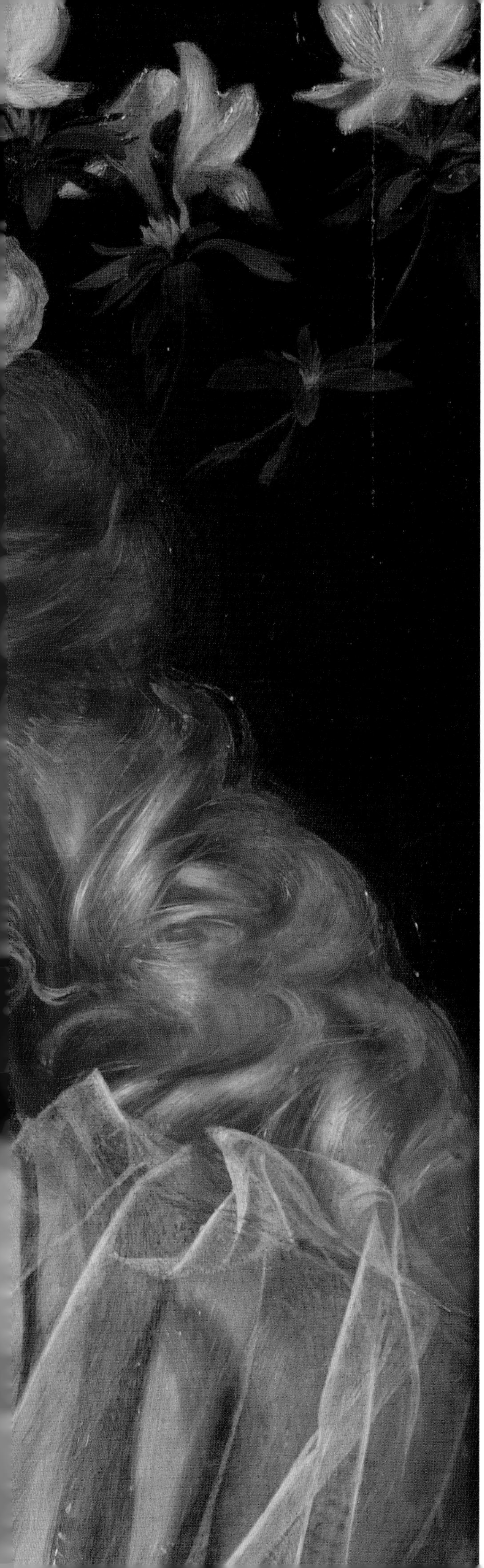

The Romances

The plays Shakespeare wrote toward the end of his career have a character all their own. Full of improbable incidents, and saturated with reference to fictionality, the romances dramatize family reconciliation, especially between parents and children. Predicaments that in earlier plays led to tragedy are here (albeit sometimes uncomfortably) resolved by the healing power of art.

Pericles

THE PLOT: *As a young prince in Tyre, Pericles guesses the answer to a riddle set by the tyrant Antiochus, who has committed incest with his daughter. This knowledge places Pericles's life in danger, and to escape assassination he embarks on years of shipboard wandering. After being shipwrecked at Pentapolis, he weds Thaisa, the daughter of the king.*

In the middle of a violent storm, Thaisa dies in childbirth, although the baby, Marina, survives. Thaisa, buried in a wooden coffin at sea, is washed up on the shore at Ephesus, where she is brought back to life, and becomes a reclusive votaress—a devotee—in the temple of Diana.

Pericles continues his traveling, leaving his daughter at Tharsus with Cleon, the governor of Tharsus, and Dionyza, his wife. When older, Marina is sold into a brothel, but her beauty converts bawds and their clients to virtue, and eventually she is able to negotiate her escape and to live in an "honest house." Years later, a storm at sea drives Pericles to the same shore, and allows him to be reunited with his wife and daughter, both of whom he thought were dead.

Dramatis Personae

Gower, *as Chorus*
Antiochus, *King of Antioch*
Pericles, *Prince of Tyre*
Helicanus, Escanes, *two lords of Tyre*
Simonides, *King of Pentapolis*
Cleon, *Governor of Tharsus*
Lysimachus, *Governor of Mytilene*
Cerimon, *a lord of Ephesus*
Thaliard, *a lord of Antioch*
Philemon, *servant to Cerimon*
Leonine, *a murderer, servant to Dionyza*
Marshal
Pander
Boult, *his servant*
Another Servant
Daughter of Antiochus
Dionyza, *wife to Cleon*
Thaisa, *daughter to Simonides*
Marina, *daughter to Pericles and Thaisa*
Lychorida, *nurse to Marina*
Bawd
Diana, *a goddess appearing to Pericles*
Lords, Ladies, Knights, Gentlemen, Sailors, Pirates, Fishermen, and Messengers

There is general agreement among critics that the first four scenes of *Pericles* were not written by Shakespeare. The probable author is George Wilkins, a minor playwright who was also a publican and petty criminal, notorious for having kicked a pregnant woman in the belly. His verse is stilted and stiff, lacking Shakespeare's free-flowing poetry and dense imagery. However, even if *Pericles* was a collaborative work written partly by a rogue, the play has its own unity, and some very great dramatic poetry in the substantial section contributed by Shakespeare.

BELOW: *"O heavens bless my girl!": the reunion of Pericles and his daughter Marina in Act 5, Scene 1 releases much of the play's emotional tension. Here Pericles (Ray Fearon) and Marina (Kananu Kirimi) embrace in a 2002 production by the Royal Shakespeare Company in London.*

WRITTEN
c. 1606–9

SETTING AND PERIOD
Ancient Greek world and cities (Tyre, Tharsus, Pentapolis, Ephesus, Mytilene), fifth century BCE

CHARACTERS 30

ACTS Originally none; 5 in some modern editions

SCENES 21

LINES 2,459

A Morality Fable

Pericles is accepted as one of Shakespeare's "last plays," which all draw on motifs from romance, the popular mode on the stage at the time, and which mingle tragedy with comedy. As if to highlight the element that led Ben Jonson to dismiss the play as a "mouldy tale ... and stale," the story is introduced by the fourteenth-century medieval poet John Gower, whose epic poem *Confessio amantis* is a primary source for the play. Gower acts as Chorus and presenter, and sets the tone of the romance:

To sing a song that old was sung,
From ashes ancient Gower is come,
Assuming man's infirmities,
To glad your ear and please your eyes.
It hath been sung at festivals,
On ember-eves and holy[-ales];
And lords and ladies in their lives
Have read it for restoratives.
(ACT 1, SCENE 1, LINES 1–8)

The themes, romance material, imagery, and use of language in *Pericles* are consistent especially with *The Winter's Tale* and *The Tempest*, Shakespeare's better known last plays. The poetry of *Pericles* is richly condensed, complex, evocative, and emotionally expressive, but often capped with phrases of moving, eloquent simplicity.

Shakespeare's celebrated gifts for writing with tight dramatic economy and subtle characterization are not evident in this play, since he is striving for a different effect. It is a morality fable, a romance, and an epic drama. Pericles is not individuated but presented as an "everyman," and the play proceeds with an episodic structure.

Wind, rain, and thunder, remember earthly man/ Is but a substance that must yield to you;/ And I (as fits my nature) do obey you./ Alas, the seas hath cast me on the rocks,/ Wash'd me from shore to shore, and left [me] breath/ Nothing to think on but ensuing death.

—*Pericles* (ACT 2, SCENE 1, LINES 2–7)

ABOVE: *The inclusion of the poet John Gower as Chorus in* Pericles *acknowledges Shakespeare's debt to Gower's poem* Confessio amantis *(1393) as a key source for the play.*

Reuniting and Regenerating

Among the themes that recur in Shakespeare's last plays is the relationship between father and daughter, whose reconciliation is one of the most moving human events that gives the protagonist a "second chance." Over a period of many years a family is separated and reunited, allowing time to heal all. Pericles's sheer endurance in adversity is central to the recuperative vision of the play. Greek biographer Plutarch quoted Pericles, the historical Greek statesman, as saying "Time is the wisest counselor of them all," and Shakespeare takes this as his cue for his fictional Pericles:

I see that Time's the king of men,
He's both their parent, and he is their grave,
And gives them what he will, not what they crave.
(ACT 2, SCENE 3, LINES 45–47)

These are sentiments that are consistent with Shakespeare's emphasis on the regenerative quality of time in *The Winter's Tale* and *The Tempest*.

Morality and Desire

Contrasts between natural and unnatural sexual desire provide a less conspicuous but important theme of *Pericles*. The early scenes at the court of

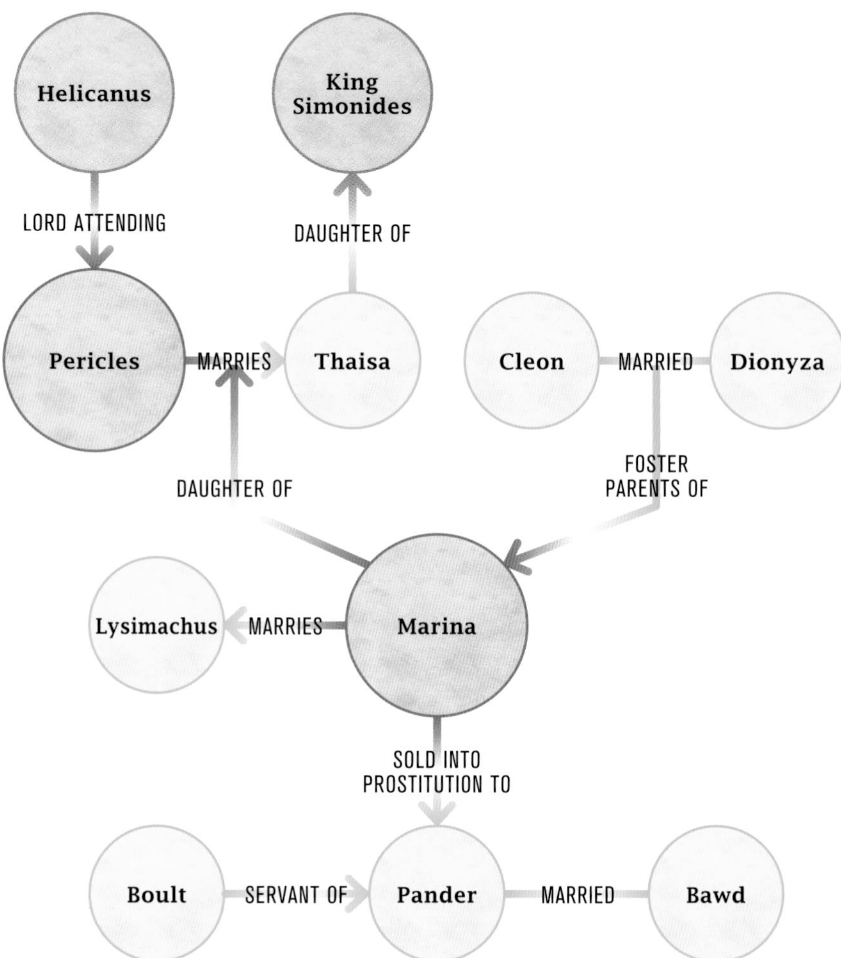

RELATIONSHIPS

Marina, at the center of the relationships in *Pericles,* connects with most of the major characters in the play. Her innocence forms the play's moral core as she survives abandonment, exploitation, and mistreatment to finally reunite with Pericles and Thaisa.

the tyrant Antiochus are haunted by incest, which contrasts later with Pericles's love for Thaisa and the morally redemptive force of Marina's innocence, which reforms those in the brothel. To the guilty all things are guilty, while to the innocent all things are innocent:

> BOULT *What would you have me do? Go to the wars, would you? where a man may serve seven years for the loss of a leg, and have not money enough in the end to buy him a wooden one?*
> MARINA *Do any thing but this thou doest. Empty*
> *Old receptacles, or common shores, of filth,*
> *Serve by indenture to the common hangman:*
> *Any of these ways are yet better than this[.]*
> (ACT 4, SCENE 6, LINES 170–77)

This passage contains rather startling touches of social realism, referring to life in England in the early 1600s—an unexpected exchange in a play of such faraway romance.

In the play, Shakespeare gives human significance even to the most apparently conventional of romance devices. Thaisa recognizes Pericles after so many years of separation not because of some superficial sign or feature, but because she feels the same sexual desire for him as when they married, which is all the proof she requires to confirm his identity.

Images of the Elements

Elemental imagery of water, fire, earth, and the "music of the spheres" (Act 5, Scene 1, line 229) emphasizes the epic scope of the play's action, encompassing lands and sea over many years. Above all, the sea constantly laps through the poetry, as the element upon which Pericles is condemned to travel, suffer, and live. It is not only atmospheric but functional as a continuing emblem of Renaissance ideas about fortune, fate, and providence. The sea is destructive, through storms and shipwrecks, but it also preserves and miraculously returns things that are lost to humans. It is a place of both birth and death, as Pericles discovers when Thaisa appears to die at sea, after giving birth to Marina:

> *A terrible child-bed hast thou had, my dear,*
> *No light, no fire. Th' unfriendly elements*
> *Forgot thee utterly, nor have I time*
> *To give thee hallow'd to thy grave, but straight*
> *Must cast thee, scarcely coffin'd, in [the ooze],*
> *Where, for a monument upon thy bones,*
> *And [e'er-]remaining lamps, the belching whale*
> *And humming water must o'erwhelm thy corpse,*
> *Lying with simple shells ...*
> (ACT 3, SCENE 1, LINES 56–64)

It is implied that fate is not governed by gods or by sheer chance; rather, fate is an amalgam of the human capacity to survive and to tap into a sphere of "natural magic." A goddess, Diana, does appear and speak, but her words suggest that deities exist not to solve humankind's problems, but to help them to understand their world and to solve their own problems in human ways. This is a subtle way of explaining the function and significance of the supernatural in Shakespeare. Likewise, images of

At the Mercy of Fortune

THIRD FISHERMAN Master, I marvel how the fishes live in the sea.
FIRST FISHERMAN Why, as men do a-land; the great ones eat up the little ones.
(ACT 2, SCENE 1, LINES 26–29)

A man whom both the waters and the wind,
In that vast tennis-court, hath made the ball
For them to play upon, entreats you pity him.
—*Pericles* (ACT 2, SCENE 1, LINES 59–61)

The cat, with eyne of burning coal,
Now couches from the mouse's hole[.]
—*Gower* (ACT 3, CHORUS, LINES 5–6)

ABOVE: *In Pericles's lament for Thaisa, whom he believes has died in childbirth at sea (Act 3, Scene 1), Shakespeare evokes images of a pitiless and unforgiving ocean. In this 2003 staging in London, Thaisa's bloodied gown emphasizes the brutal physical toll taken by a life at sea.*

On the Jacobean Stage

Shakespeare was notorious for the scarcity of his stage directions, but *Pericles* contains some of his most cryptically evocative, such as *"Enter* PERICLES *wet," "Enter* PERICLES *a-shipboard," "Enter one with boxes, napkins, and fire,"* and *"*PERICLES *makes lamentation, puts on sackcloth, and in a mighty passion departs."* These directions, together with the use of music, give us invaluable information about Jacobean staging and spectacle.

sleep and dreams represent a source of human self-knowledge and understanding. However, despite the secular explanations for surprising events, the reunions retain an atmosphere of mystery and miracle, heightened by music. Even the revival of Thaisa is given human agency in the form of the physician Cerimon, who realizes that she looks "fresh," and that the warmth of fire—the element antidoting water—will revive her from drowning:

> *A warmth [breathes] out of her. She hath not been*
> *Entranc'd above five hours. See how she gins*
> *To blow into life's flower again ...*
> (ACT 3, SCENE 2, LINES 93–95)

Even in humankind's capacity to survive and act, however, mortality is insignificant in the face of the elements: "The seaman's whistle / Is as a whisper in the ears of death," Pericles laments—it is "Unheard" (Act 3, Scene 1, lines 8–10).

Ignored No More ...

Pericles was apparently very popular when it was first performed in the early seventeenth century, but was then completely neglected until the late twentieth century. Romance was out of fashion on the stage and among critics, until G. Wilson Knight and Northrop Frye wrote discerningly on it in the 1930s and 1940s.

There followed some stage revivals, in particular some spectacular productions in the 1960s and 1970s in the United Kingdom by the Prospect Theatre Company and the Royal Shakespeare Company. In 1973, Prospect's production at the Roundhouse in London featured Derek Jacobi in the title role. The play's theatrical success proven, it is now often performed.

An American theater director, Peter Sellars, saw contemporary significance in *Pericles* in his production in Boston in 1983, creating "a blend of Mel Brooks vulgarity and John Keats romanticism," according to *Newsweek*. The 26-year-old Sellars cast a Boston street performer in the role of Gower, and included extras dressed as homeless people.

Cymbeline

Dramatis Personae

Cymbeline, *King of Britain*
Cloten, *son to the queen by a former husband*
Posthumus Leonatus, *a gentleman, husband to Imogen*
Belarius, *a banished lord disguised under the name of Morgan*
Guiderius, Arviragus, *sons to Cymbeline, disguised under the names of Polydore and Cadwal, supposed sons to Morgan*
Philario, *an Italian, friend to Posthumus*
Jachimo, *an Italian, friend to Philario*
Caius Lucius, *general of the Roman forces*
Pisanio, *servant to Posthumus*
Cornelius, *a physician*
Philarmonus, *a soothsayer*
Roman Captain
Two British Captains
Frenchman, *friend to Philario*
Two Lords of Cymbeline's court
Two Gentlemen of the same
Two Jailers
Apparitions
Queen, *wife to Cymbeline*
Imogen, *daughter to Cymbeline by a former queen*
Helen, *a lady attending on Imogen*
Lords, Ladies, Roman Senators, Tribunes, Dutchman, Spaniard, Musicians, Officers, Captains, Soldiers, Messengers, and other Attendants

WRITTEN
c. 1609–10
SETTING AND PERIOD
Britain under Roman influence, Wales, and Rome around the time of the birth of Jesus
CHARACTERS 36
ACTS 5
SCENES 27
LINES 3,707

THE PLOT: *Imogen, the daughter of King Cymbeline and heir to the British throne, has married Posthumus Leonatus instead of Cloten, the son of her wicked stepmother. Exiled in Rome, Posthumus wagers on Imogen's virtue with Jachimo (often spelled Iachimo), who travels to England to seduce her. Although unsuccessful, Jachimo convinces Posthumus of Imogen's infidelity. Posthumus orders his servant Pisanio to murder her.*

Pisanio reveals the plot and disguises Imogen as Fidele, a page, to travel to Wales to find Posthumus. There she unknowingly encounters her lost brothers, Guiderius and Arviragus, and their abductor Belarius. Cloten, angered at Imogen's rejection, seeks her in Wales, but Guiderius beheads him in combat. Cloten's corpse is placed beside Imogen, who has taken a potion and appears dead. She awakens and thinks the body is her husband's.

Posthumus abandons the Roman army and—with Guiderius, Arviragus, and Belarius—defeats the Romans. In the final scene, the evil queen dies, Imogen is reunited with her father and husband, the princes are acknowledged, and peace between Rome and Britain returns.

Cymbeline is a strange and wonderful play. Written and performed around 1609, it is among the last of Shakespeare's works before his retirement to Stratford. Crammed with incidents and characters, *Cymbeline* includes bold theatrical effects, such as the entry of Jupiter upon an eagle, hurling a thunderbolt (Act 5, Scene 4). It also has two lovely songs. With stolen children identified by a birthmark and an obscure riddle interpreted by a soothsayer, the play operates in the magical realm of romance, and is ultimately concerned with the interrelated themes of reconciliation, reunion, regeneration, and forgiveness. At the end of the play, Posthumus Leonatus tells his enemy, Jachimo:

> *The pow'r that I have on you is to spare you;*
> *The malice towards you, to forgive you. Live,*
> *And deal with others better ...*
> (ACT 5, SCENE 5, LINES 418–20)

LEFT: *Jachimo (Paul Freeman) tries in vain to lure Imogen (Joanne Pearce) into unfaithfulness in the 1997–98 Royal Shakespeare Company production (London, Washington, New York). The* New York Times *reported that "as long as Ms. Pearce is onstage, there's a core of credibility to the extreme circumstances that surround her."*

Sweet Songs

Hark, hark, the lark at heaven's gate sings,
And Phoebus gins arise,
His steeds to water at those springs
On chalic'd flow'rs that lies;
And winking Mary-buds begin to ope their golden eyes;
With every thing that pretty is, my lady sweet, arise:
Arise, arise!
—*Musicians* (ACT 2, SCENE 3, LINES 20–26)

Fear no more the heat o' th' sun,
Nor the furious winter's rages,
Thou thy worldly task hast done,
Home art gone, and ta'en thy wages.
Golden lads and girls all must,
As chimney-sweepers, come to dust.
—*Guiderius* (ACT 4, SCENE 2, LINES 258–63)

Cymbeline also displays the restorative power of nature. Members of the corrupt court exchange their enclosed setting for the Welsh hills and caves, returning healed. The stolen princes grow up away from the court and its distorting influence. As they leave their cave, Belarius exhorts:

[Stoop,] boys, this gate
Instructs you how t' adore the heavens, and bows you
To a morning's holy office. The gates of monarchs
Are arch'd so high that giants may jet through
And keep their impious turbands on ...
(ACT 3, SCENE 3, LINES 2–6)

Tragicomedy and Romance

The genre of *Cymbeline* may have been best communicated by Polonius's humorous description in *Hamlet:* "tragical-comical-historical-pastoral" (*Hamlet,* Act 2, Scene 2, lines 398–99). Although *Cymbeline* was originally printed among the tragedies in the First Folio of 1623, it is Shakespeare's best example of the tragicomic. This new variety of play—an amalgam of comedy and tragedy, drawing on elements of romance, rather than a mixture of the two forms—was popularized by the English playwriting pair Francis Beaumont and John Fletcher in the early seventeenth century.

In tragicomedies, characters undergo the same sorts of suffering that characters in tragedies do, but without the fatal conclusions. Forces at work in the universe keep humankind from making irredeemable mistakes. Pisanio suggests such divine intervention: "Fortune brings in some boats that are not steer'd" (Act 4, Scene 3, line 46). Like a dramatic roller-coaster ride, tragicomedy provides terrifying drops and sharp bends, the sensation of almost hurtling out of control at any moment—then the return of the roller coaster to where it began, with everyone safe and sound.

Most tragicomedies resemble modern grand opera in their use of exotic settings, intricate plots, and high sentiment. In *Cymbeline,* characters speak emotional soliloquies—speeches directed at the audience by characters alone on stage—which resemble operatic arias in their intensity. The most famous examples are in Act 2, Scene 5, during

Jacobean Special Effects

Around 1609–10, the Globe added a spectacular device to produce a lightning bolt on stage, which Shakespeare employed in *Cymbeline:* "*Jupiter descends in thunder and lightning, sitting upon an eagle: he throws a thunderbolt*" (Act 5, Scene 4). In the next three years, actor and playwright Thomas Heywood staged three plays in which Jupiter enters with a lightning bolt.

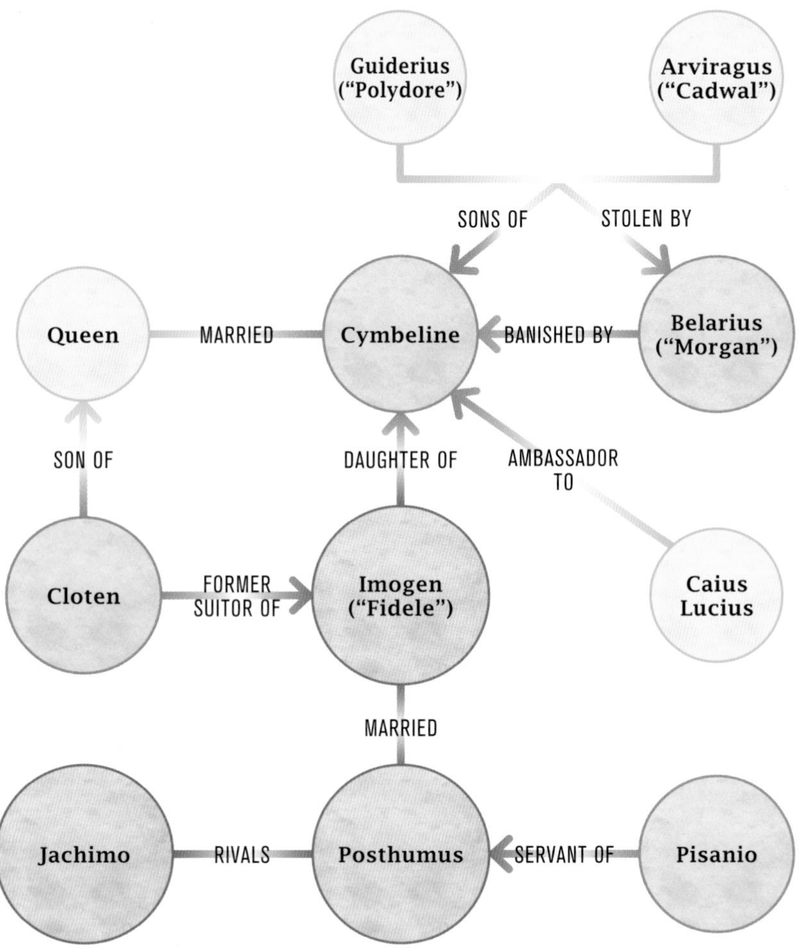

RELATIONSHIPS

Although Imogen is in the center of the play's relationships, she is forced to react to the actions of others, rather than initiate action herself. The strength of her responses to these actions, however, reveals the resilience of her character.

Posthumus's tortured denunciation of women based on his mistaken belief that Imogen has been unfaithful; and in Act 4, Scene 2, lines 295–332, when Imogen awakens from her drug-induced sleep next to the headless body of Cloten. In the former, Posthumus explodes in anger and exposes his own sexual insecurities; in the latter, Imogen gives voice to the anguish she feels at the apparent death of her husband. (Judi Dench considers this speech the most challenging in her Shakespearean experience.) Yet neither situation is what it appears, and the lovers are ultimately reunited.

Recycling Plots

Shakespeare employs plot devices from his earlier plays in *Cymbeline*. Some are minor, such as the potion that makes Imogen appear to be dead and then return to life. The same stratagem is used to allow Juliet to avoid marriage with Paris in *Romeo and Juliet*. In both *Cymbeline* and *Macbeth,* the queens mysteriously die offstage, and the title characters are informed onstage.

Imogen's estrangement from and reconciliation with her father echoes the situation between King Lear and his youngest daughter Cordelia. Like Lear, who does not immediately see the evil in his daughters Goneril and Regan, Cymbeline supports his stepson Cloten's desires to marry Imogen while ignoring the virtues of Posthumus whom he brought up at court but whom, in his anger, he refers to as a "beggar" who will bring only "baseness" to the throne (Act 1, Scene 1, lines 141–42). The genre of tragicomedy, however, assures the audience of a happy reunion between father and daughter.

A more powerful parallel is between Posthumus Leonatus and Othello, the Moor of Venice. Both men are manipulated by villains to believe that their wives have been unfaithful. Both husbands are brought to irrational rage and harbor murderous intents. Hearing of Imogen's supposed adultery, Posthumus says:

> *O that I had her here, to tear her limb-meal!*
> *I will go there and do't, i' th' court, before*
> *Her father ...*
>
> (ACT 2, SCENE 4, LINES 147–49)

Caught in a similar situation, Othello declares, "I'll tear her all to pieces" (*Othello,* Act 3, Scene 3, line 431). And the villains use similar approaches to convince the heroes. Both manufacture sexual incidents to strengthen their tales. After emerging from a trunk in Imogen's bedchamber, Jachimo notices a blemish on Imogen's breast; he later tells Posthumus how he "kiss'd it, and it gave me present hunger / To feed again" (Act 2, Scene 4, lines 137–38). Iago tells Othello that he heard Cassio cry out to Desdemona in his sleep: he

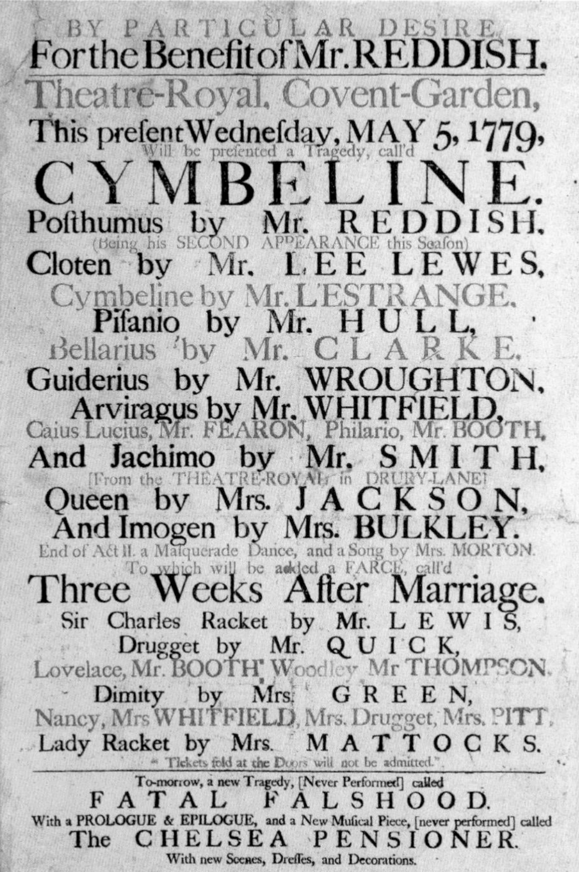

RIGHT: *This poster for a performance of* Cymbeline *in Covent Garden, London, 1779, advertises the play as a "Tragedy." The text of the play, like that of other works by Shakespeare, would have been edited to suit the tastes of its Georgian audience.*

"[sigh'd], and [kiss'd], and then / [Cried], 'Cursed fate that gave thee to the Moor!'" (*Othello,* Act 3, Scene 3, line 426).

The differences between the endings of these two plays reflect the differences between tragedies and tragicomedies. Othello smothers Desdemona, and Iago demonstrates no remorse. Posthumus, on the other hand, commands Pisanio to kill Imogen; the servant preserves her, sending Posthumus a bloody cloth to confirm her death. Posthumus grieves at Imogen's supposed death, but the couple is eventually reunited, and the villain Jachimo repents his evil deeds.

Appearance and Reality

Actual clothing and clothing imagery play an important part in *Cymbeline*. Most of the characters change clothes during the play, but the clothing does not change the essential nature of each individual. To leave court, Imogen dresses in a common riding suit. Pisanio then provides her with the "doublet, hat, hose" (Act 3, Scene 4, line 169) for her disguise as a male, in which she remains for the rest of the play. Cloten dons clothing belonging to Posthumus to humiliate Imogen, planning to wear his rival's clothes while he rapes Imogen and kills Posthumus. Also, the humble garments worn by the two stolen princes, Guiderius and Arviragus, cannot hide the "sparks of nature" (Act 3, Scene 3, line 79) that proclaim their regal ancestry.

Posthumus changes his clothes twice in Act 5, first exchanging his Italian clothing for the dress of a "Britain peasant," (Act 5, Scene 1, line 24) then returning to his Roman garb after helping defeat the Romans. Posthumus articulates the importance of the inner person rather than the clothing: "To shame the guise o' th' world, I will begin / The fashion: less without and more within" (Act 5, Scene 1, lines 32–33).

Cymbeline is, finally, escapist entertainment with unexpected events and a happy ending—not unlike many modern movies. We are told what to think of the characters before we meet them; they are presented rather than developed. The many plotlines cannot stand too much logical scrutiny, but in the rush of events, improbability is not a barrier to enjoyment.

A Performance Rarity

Cymbeline is not often performed, although the role of Imogen has attracted actresses of all periods, from Helen Faucit in the nineteenth century to Helen Mirren in the late twentieth. Early in the twentieth century, two silent films of *Cymbeline* were produced, one in the United States (1913) and one in Germany (1925), but the 1982 BBC TV version, directed by Elijah Moshinsky, is the only significant screen adaptation since. If, however, readers and audiences can suspend their rationality for a while, the play will deliver ample rewards. Like the bumblebee, once thought aerodynamically unsuited to flight, *Cymbeline* can soar.

ABOVE: *Actor Arthur Grenville appeared in a 1906 production of* Cymbeline, *possibly in the role of Cloten. The production ran for a month at the Astor Theater in New York.*

Whom best I love, I cross; to make my gift, / The more delay'd, delighted. Be content, / Your low-laid son our godhead will uplift.

—*Jupiter* (ACT 5, SCENE 4, LINES 101–3)

The Winter's Tale

THE PLOT: *Polixenes, King of Bohemia, has been visiting his childhood friend Leontes, who is the King of Sicilia. Leontes suddenly becomes violently jealous, suspecting an affair between his pregnant wife, Hermione, and Polixenes. Leontes asks one of his lords, Camillo, to poison Polixenes, but instead Camillo warns Polixenes, and the two men flee to Bohemia.*

In a rage, Leontes accuses Hermione of adultery, but she denies it. Leontes imprisons her, nevertheless. When Hermione gives birth, he rejects his new daughter and charges Antigonus to take the baby to some remote location and leave it there. At the queen's trial, Leontes repudiates the pronouncement of her innocence from Apollo's Oracle, but then deeply regrets his actions when he hears of the sudden death of his son, Mamillius. Antigonus's wife, Paulina, announces that Hermione is also dead.

The action moves to Bohemia and then leaps forward 16 years to follow the story of Leontes' daughter, Perdita, who has been raised as the daughter of a shepherd. Polixenes' son, Florizel, and Perdita are in love. Polixenes vehemently opposes the relationship, but the couple escapes to Sicilia and everything is resolved when the true identity of Perdita is revealed. The play ends in joyful reconciliation when Paulina presents the living statue of Hermione, who has been alive and in hiding for the last 16 years.

Dramatis Personae

Leontes, *King of Sicilia*
Mamillius, *young prince of Sicilia*
Camillo, Antigonus, Cleomines, Dion, *four lords of Sicilia*
Polixenes, *King of Bohemia*
Florizel, *prince of Bohemia*
Archidamus, *a lord of Bohemia*
Old Shepherd, *reputed father of Perdita*
Clown, *his son*
Autolycus, *a rogue*
Mariner
Jailer
Hermione, *queen to Leontes*
Perdita, *daughter to Leontes and Hermione*
Paulina, *wife to Antigonus*
Emilia, *a lady attending on Hermione*
Mopsa, Dorcas, *shepherdesses*
Time, *as Chorus*
Other Lords and Gentlemen, Ladies, Officers, and Servants, Shepherds, and Shepherdesses

The Winter's Tale is one of the most daring and outlandish plays in the Shakespearean canon. It breaks all the rules of dramatic unity and plausibility, and it mixes together scenes of intense tragedy, music, comedy, trickery, and romance. The play takes its audience on an emotional roller coaster through a chillingly realistic depiction of pathological jealousy, the death of a much-loved child, incredible coincidences, a love story, and a surprise ending. Its excesses include one of the most bizarre stage directions of all time: *"Exit pursued by a bear"* (Act 3, Scene 3, line 58).

WRITTEN
c. 1610

SETTING AND PERIOD
Sicilia and Bohemia in a mythical pre-Christian past

CHARACTERS 21

ACTS 5

SCENES 15

LINES 3,348

Two-part Structure

The play's strange combination of elements works in the theater because of the play's skillful construction. Its scenes fall into two distinct parts, starting in the first three acts with the depiction of Leontes' jealousy and its tragic consequences. The happy world at the Sicilian court is violently disrupted and Leontes is left without a family, to suffer his grief, guilt, and the reproaches of Paulina. In the closing scene of Act 3, the baby Perdita is discovered by an Old Shepherd on the seacoast of Bohemia, and then his son, the Clown, proceeds to deliver an excited, comic speech about how the ship that carried Perdita was destroyed in a storm while Antigonus was eaten by a bear. There is a strange tension in the play at this moment because we care about Antigonus, yet the Clown makes us laugh. The Old Shepherd sums up the change that is taking place in the mood of the play when he says: "Now bless thyself: thou met'st with things dying, I with things new-born" (Act 3, Scene 3, lines 113–14).

As Act 4 begins, Shakespeare takes the audacious step of introducing the figure of Time, who tells the audience that he is going to turn his hourglass and skip 16 years to show the story of Perdita and Florizel (as "Doricles"). Their romance dominates the second half of the play and is set against the background of a sheep-shearing feast. The rogue-figure Autolycus

LEFT: *Joseph Wright of Derby portrayed Shakespeare's most famous stage direction in* The Storm, Antigonus Pursued by the Bear *(c. 1790).*

Inspired By ...

Shakespeare took much of his story from the prose romance *Pandosto, The Triumph of Time* (1588) by Robert Greene. Greene, who had once called Shakespeare an "upstart crow," also wrote rogue pamphlets describing the tricks used by conmen like Autolycus. Shakespeare changed Greene's story to provide a happy ending for Leontes and Hermione.

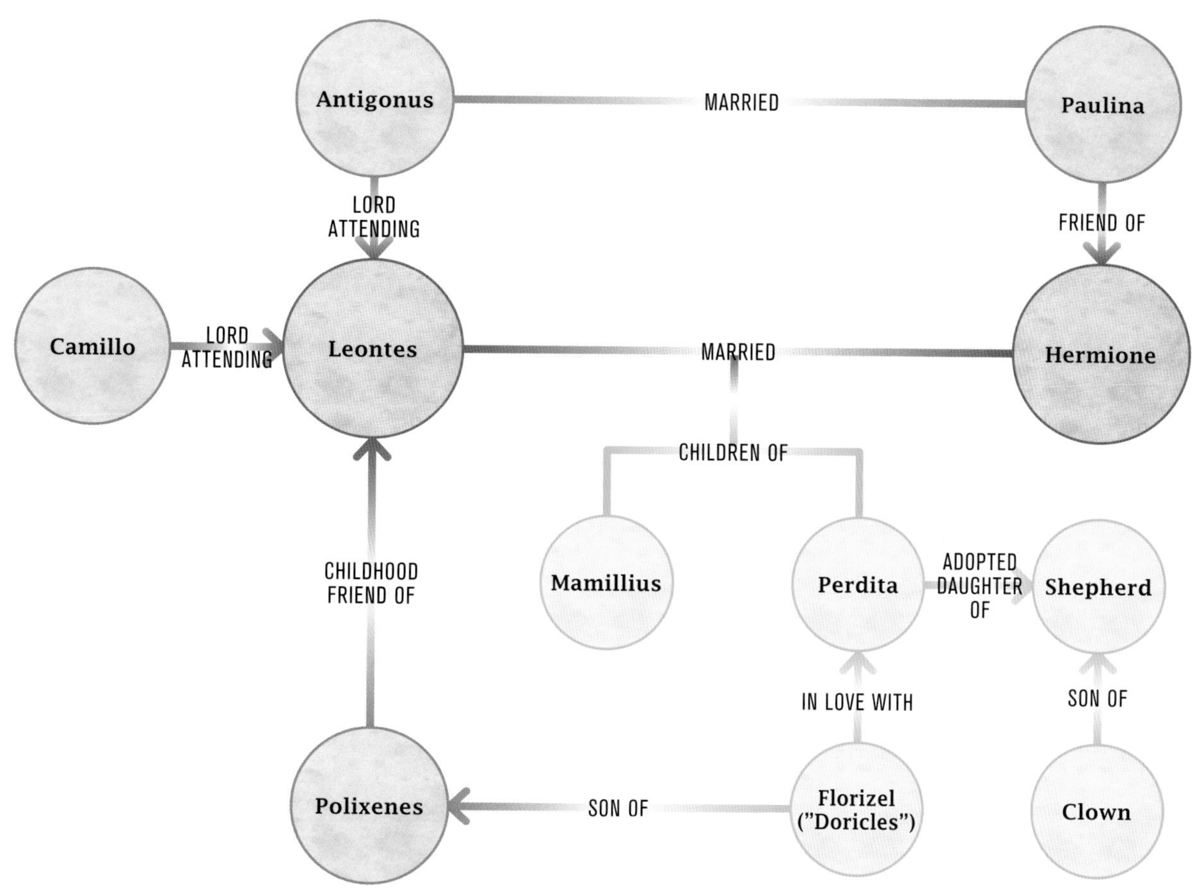

RELATIONSHIPS
At the heart of the play is the family of Leontes and Hermione, broken apart by Leontes' jealousy and only partly reunited at the play's end.

sings songs that make time seem to stand still for a while, and we witness dancing, comic foolery, and courtship. The happy mood is again interrupted, this time by the anger of Polixenes, but Florizel remains a true romantic hero, declaring:

Not for Bohemia, nor the pomp that may
Be thereat gleaned, for all the sun sees, or
The close earth wombs, or the profound seas
hides
In unknown fadoms, will I break my oath
To this my fair belov'd ...
(ACT 4, SCENE 4, LINES 488–92)

It is obvious throughout this second half of the play that things will end happily, yet Shakespeare springs one final surprise on his audience by unexpectedly bringing Hermione back to life to greet her lost child. The ending is at once fantastic wish fulfillment and yet strangely real in its quiet depiction of deep, unspoken emotion.

Despite the different moods evident in the contrasting halves of this play, there are many threads that link them together. When Polixenes explodes in rage against Perdita and Florizel, there is a sense that in the second half of the play history is repeating itself. Camillo again finds himself in a position of divided loyalty as he steps in to help the objects of the king's wrath, and in both halves of the play Perdita undergoes a sea journey that decides her fate. The hourglass that Time refers to is emblematic of this mirroring structure: a winter and a summer movement in the action that remind us of how time operates in cycles, yet also brings profound change.

When a Statue Comes to Life

The improbable but highly emotive statue scene was particularly popular in the nineteenth century and was often staged on its own. It is a difficult scene to perform: lines like Leontes' comment, "But yet, Paulina, / Hermione was not so much wrinkled, nothing / So aged as this seems" (Act 5, Scene 3, lines 27–29), can potentially destroy the mood of solemnity and wonderment. Its staging has been made particularly tricky by the common practice of doubling the roles of Perdita and Hermione. Actresses who have performed both roles include Mary Anderson in 1887, Judi Dench in 1969, and Penny Downie in 1987.

ABOVE: *In 1887, Mary Anderson became the first actress to double the roles of Hermione and Perdita. She is shown here as Perdita.*

A Fairy Tale Grounded in Reality

The play's title signals that this story is a kind of folk or fairy tale and should not be taken too seriously. For Shakespeare's contemporaries, however, its depiction of two kings who behave in a tyrannical way to their families and advisers would have carried significant echoes of their own world. The play was written during the reign of King James I at a time when arrangements for the marriages of James's two eldest children were a key concern. In the matter of royal marriages the king had absolute authority. When his young cousin, Lady Arbella Stuart, secretly married William Seymour in 1610, James promptly sent her to prison and she eventually died in the Tower of London in 1615.

In this context, Polixenes' anger at the decision by his son to marry a mere shepherdess would not seem unusual. Leontes' cruel treatment of Hermione would have carried reminders of the behavior of Henry VIII toward Anne Boleyn. In a world where power and property were always passed on through the male line of inheritance, it was especially disturbing to think that a woman might produce a child who was not the true heir. Leontes' misogynistic fear of female sexuality, his autocratic treatment of his courtiers, and the play's insistence on the importance of finding the true heir to the throne are all aspects of the story that reflect the political and cultural realities of Shakespeare's day.

ABOVE: *Perdita, the lost child of Leontes and Hermione, is at the center of the sunny, life-affirming world of Bohemia in the second half of the play. This portrait of her, by Anthony Frederick Augustus Sandys, dates from c. 1866.*

And many a man there is (even at this present, / Now, while I speak this) holds his wife by th' arm, / That little thinks she has been sluic'd in 's absence, / And his pond fish'd by his next neighbor—by / Sir Smile, his neighbor ...

—*Leontes* (ACT 1, SCENE 2, LINES 192–96)

Beneath the Surface

The Winter's Tale revisits many of the themes and concerns Shakespeare explored in earlier plays. Like *Othello* and *Much Ado about Nothing,* the play depicts the destructive nature of jealousy; like *Romeo and Juliet*, it is a play about young love; and like the other Romances, it focuses on the idea of the lost child and parent–child relationships.

Many moments in the play remind us of fairy tales. At one point the boy, Mamillius, starts to tell his mother a tale. He says:

> *A sad tale's best for winter. I have one*
> *Of sprites and goblins.*
> (ACT 2, SCENE 1, LINES 25–26)

This comment tells us something about the nature of the play: that it is a kind of myth and that like all myths we should look beneath the surface for deeper meanings. *The Winter's Tale* is sometimes seen as carrying a Christian message about the possibility of redemption, especially through its depiction of Hermione's dignified suffering and her resurrection at the play's end.

Dark Comedy

The invitation to look for meanings beneath the surface of *The Winter's Tale* also encourages us to think about its events in terms of the human psyche. The tale is a comedy about the dark side of human experience, about the inner demons that can take control of our actions. Leontes' sudden jealousy is never explained in the play. The confusing language he uses to discuss his suspicions shows that he is tortured by feelings he does not understand, and we feel compelled to seek explanations for him. Has his sense of rivalry with his fellow king, Polixenes, spun out of control? Does he feel repressed desire for his childhood friend, which is projected onto his wife? Is he thrown off balance by his wife's pregnancy and transformation into a maternal figure? In *The Winter's Tale* Shakespeare's mode of writing is often tangled and obscure, inviting us to fill in the gaps. The many references to dreams, fables, and delusions shift focus away from everyday reality and onto what lies beneath in the unconscious mind.

"A Spider Steep'd"

Imagery associated with sleep and dreaming is evident throughout *The Winter's Tale*, and so, too, are images associated with childbirth; words like "womb," "breed," "issue," "delivery," and "pregnant" remind us of where the story started. Many images serve to connect the two parts of the play. Both Leontes in Act 2 and Polixenes in Act 4 resort to accusations of witchcraft against the women who cross them, and echoes of Leontes'

LEFT: *Communal laughter, song, and dance characterize the sheep-shearing feast in Act 4, Scene 4, over which Perdita reigns as "queen." This scene, performed here in 1999 by the Royal Shakespeare Company, forms the pastoral core of the play.*

violent imagination can also be found in the bizarre tortures Autolycus imagines for the shepherds in Act 4:

He has a son, who shall be flay'd alive, then 'nointed over with honey, set on the head of a wasp's nest; then stand till he be three quarters and a dram dead ...
(ACT 4, SCENE 4, LINES 783–86)

Dreams and Delusions

Is whispering nothing?
Is leaning cheek to cheek? is meeting noses?
Kissing with inside lip? stopping the career
Of laughter with a sigh ...
—*Leontes* (ACT 1, SCENE 2, LINES 284–87)

HERMIONE Sir,
You speak a language that I understand not.
My life stands in the level of your dreams,
Which I'll lay down.
LEONTES Your actions are my dreams.
You had a bastard by Polixenes,
And I but dream'd it ...
(ACT 3, SCENE 2, LINES 79–84)

This dream of mine
Being now awake, I'll queen it no inch farther,
But milk my ewes, and weep.
—*Perdita* (ACT 4, SCENE 4, LINES 448–50)

There are also striking differences, however, between the images that dominate each half of the play. In the first half there are many images of disease, infection, poison, and the heat of animal sexuality. When Leontes first starts to feel his jealousy he says:

Too hot, too hot!
To mingle friendship far is mingling bloods.
I have tremor cordis *on me ...*
(ACT 1, SCENE 2, LINES 108–10)

At the thought of his wife and his friend mingling blood through intercourse, Leontes feels a sickening physical pain in his heart. His language is filled with images of sexual disgust, and the knowledge of his wife's supposed adultery operates like poison:

There may be in the cup
A spider steep'd, and one may drink; depart,
And yet partake no venom (for his knowledge
Is not infected), but if one present
Th' abhorr'd ingredient to his eye, make known
How he hath drunk, he cracks his gorge, his sides,
With violent hefts. I have drunk, and seen the spider.
(ACT 2, SCENE 1, LINES 39–45)

Pastoral Images

In the middle of *The Winter's Tale* the image of the violent storm brings the destructive phase of the play to a climax, and after this a new mood is established. In Act 4 Shakespeare draws upon the ancient literary tradition of the "pastoral"—an idealized representation of rural life—and suddenly the play is filled with images of a sweeter version of nature. Autolycus sings about daffodils, the thrush, and the jay, and Perdita delivers a long speech about the meanings of daffodils, violets, pale primroses, oxlips, and lilies. The sheep-shearing scene includes a debate about whether it is right for humankind to try to improve nature by grafting flowers, touching on a topical question about the relative values of art and nature. Autolycus's tricks and cynicism continue to remind us of harsher realities through these scenes, but the dominant images speak lyrically of the transforming power of love:

When you speak, sweet,
I'ld have you do it ever; when you sing,
I'ld have you buy and sell so; so give alms;
Pray so; and for the ord'ring your affairs,
To sing them too. When you do dance, I wish you
A wave o' th' sea, that you might ever do
Nothing but that ...
(ACT 4, SCENE 4, LINES 136–42)

Time, of course, is a fundamental image running through the play, and it is connected to images associated with childhood, memory, and the changing of the seasons. The "wide gap of time" referred to by Leontes in the play's closing lines and encompassed by the action of the play provides space for its characters to age, grow, and learn. Unlike less sprawling plays, *The Winter's Tale* can convey a sense of the way ties of love and friendship can endure and be renewed across the years.

BELOW: *Antony Sher played Leontes in the Royal Shakespeare Company staging of the play in 1999. He showed, according to the* Independent *newspaper, "that the king's manic mistrust is not so much an outbreak of evil as a kind of massive mid-life crisis, at once frightening, farcical and pathetic."*

The Play in Performance

After being cut savagely for stage performance in the eighteenth century, *The Winter's Tale* was rediscovered by performers in the nineteenth century and has been popular on stage ever since. In 1856, English tragedian Charles Kean produced a scenically spectacular production set during the fourth century BCE. Kean was so worried about historical accuracy and the fact that Bohemia did not exist in that period (or have a seacoast) that he changed the locale of Act 4 to Bithynia (an ancient region of Anatolia).

In more recent times, productions of the play have been set in many different times and places. In Britain, director Trevor Nunn's 1969 Royal Shakespeare Company production set the first half of the play within a claustrophobic white box, then contrasted this with a Bohemia that reflected 1960s counterculture, complete with rock music and hippy clothes. At the National Theatre in London in 2001, director Nicholas Hytner took a similar approach by creating a party in Act 4 reminiscent of England's Glastonbury pop music festival. In Germany in 1978, Peter Zadek directed a production in which the stage floor of the Deutsches Schauspielhaus in Hamburg was covered with tons of plastic green slime for Act 4, and Perdita was clad only in branches of forsythia. Several well-known actors have played Leontes over the years, including Ian McKellen, Jeremy Irons, Patrick Stewart, and Antony Sher. *The Winter's Tale* could be adapted into a striking feature film, but that is yet to come.

That she is living,/Were it but told you, should be hooted at/Like an old tale ...

—*Paulina* (ACT 5, SCENE 3, LINES 115–17)

The Tempest

THE PLOT: *Helped by Alonso, King of Naples, Antonio usurps his brother Prospero's dukedom of Milan. Prospero and his daughter, Miranda, are cast out to sea on an open boat. They arrive on an island inhabited only by the spirit Ariel and the savage Caliban. Twelve years later, through his magic, Prospero sees that a boat sailing near the island contains his former enemies. He conjures a storm with Ariel's help. With the ship apparently wrecked, Prospero scatters its men throughout the island. Through his art, Prospero contrives to have Alonso's son, Ferdinand, fall in love with Miranda, and confronts his former foes with their crimes. Caliban conspires with two drunken sailors to murder Prospero, but the plot is foiled. Forgiveness prevails, and with a marriage arranged between Ferdinand and Miranda, Prospero abjures his magic, frees Ariel from his service, and purposes to travel back to Italy, leaving the island to Caliban.*

Dramatis Personae

Alonso, *King of Naples*
Sebastian, *his brother*
Prospero, *the right Duke of Milan*
Antonio, *his brother, the usurping Duke of Milan*
Ferdinand, *son to the King of Naples*
Gonzalo, *an honest old councillor*
Adrian, Francisco, *lords*
Caliban, *a salvage and deformed slave*
Trinculo, *a jester*
Stephano, *a drunken butler*
Master of a ship
Boatswain
Mariners
Miranda, *daughter to Prospero*
Ariel, *an airy spirit*
Iris, Ceres, Juno, Nymphs, Reapers, *spirits*
Other Spirits attending on Prospero

WRITTEN
c. 1610

SETTING AND PERIOD
A fictional island, *c.* seventeenth century

CHARACTERS 18

ACTS 5

SCENES 9 plus Epilogue

LINES 2,283

The Tempest stands first in the 1623 Folio edition of Shakespeare's plays but is his last sole-authored play. While most of Shakespeare's plays have 20 or more scenes, different plotlines, a variety of locations, and action spanning an extended period, *The Tempest* is a condensed play. For the only time since writing *The Comedy of Errors*, nearly two decades earlier, Shakespeare returns to the neoclassical

RIGHT: *In English artist John W. Waterhouse's painting* Miranda—The Tempest *(1916), the artist shows Prospero's daughter watching from the island's shore as a storm—her father's "art"—wrecks the boat carrying Antonio, Alonso, Sebastian, Ferdinand, and Gonzalo.*

idea of the unities: the action of the play happens in one time and place. References to time in the play, such as Prospero's "At this hour / Lies at my mercy all mine enemies" (Act 4, Scene 1, lines 262–63), draw attention to the compression of the action into almost a single afternoon.

Prospero controls most of the action of the play, and his magic has often been seen to mirror Shakespeare's dramatic art. English poet and critic Samuel Taylor Coleridge described Prospero as "the very Shakespeare, as it were, of the tempest." Prospero likens the end of the wedding masque he conjures for Ferdinand and Miranda (Act 4, Scene 1, lines 60–117) to the dismantling of theatrical machinery. The masque has been a "baseless fabric" (line 151), an "insubstantial pageant" (line 155). The vision dissolves like "the great globe itself" (line 153)—a pun on the name of the Globe playhouse in London, where many of Shakespeare's plays were performed.

In the Epilogue to *The Tempest*, Prospero draws attention to himself as a fictional character in a play. Now that the play is ended, his "charms," like those of a playwright, are "all o'erthrown" (line 1).

To be able to travel from the island back to Italy, Prospero requires the permission of the play's audience, in the form of applause: "release me from my bands / With the help of your good hands" (lines 9–10). If *The Tempest* was indeed Shakespeare's last play before he retired to Stratford, Prospero's final speech sounds like the Bard's autobiographical swansong.

The Tempest is often grouped with four of Shakespeare's other late plays, *The Winter's Tale, Cymbeline, Pericles,* and *The Two Noble Kinsmen,* and termed a romance. In an idealistic romance world, a course of events that ought to prove disastrous turns out happily, often through the intervention of some kind of supernatural force. Families, dispersed through treachery, are reunited and, especially in these plays, children are reconciled with erring parents. Shakespeare complicates such simple formulations. For example, in *The Tempest*, is Prospero's concern to have Miranda marry Ferdinand an example of paternal care, or an act of political revenge? How complete is the harmony at the end of the play?

New Realms, New Rulers

European travel and colonialism leave a clear mark on the language of the play. Shakespeare knew members of the Virginia Company, which founded the Jamestown colony in America in 1607.

Caliban's Island

This island's mine by Sycorax my mother,
Which thou tak'st from me ...
(ACT 1, SCENE 2, LINES 331–32)

I prithee let me bring thee where crabs grow;
And I with my long nails will dig thee pig-nuts,
Show thee a jay's nest, and instruct thee how
To snare the nimble marmazet. I'll bring thee
To clust'ring filberts, and sometimes I'll get thee
Young scamels from the rock ...
(ACT 2, SCENE 2, LINES 167–72)

Be not afeard, the isle is full of noises,
Sounds, and sweet airs, that give delight and hurt not.
Sometimes a thousand twangling instruments
Will hum about mine ears; and sometimes voices,
That if I then had wak'd after long sleep,
Will make me sleep again, and then in dreaming,
The clouds methought would open, and show riches
Ready to drop upon me, that when I wak'd,
I cried to dream again.
(ACT 3, SCENE 2, LINES 135–43)

THE ENGLISH EXPLORE THE NEW WORLD

The Tempest was written at a time of intense interest in the exploration and colonization of the New World.

1497	John Cabot reaches the area of Newfoundland, Cape Breton Island, and Labrador
1502	Sebastian Cabot makes the first of a series of voyages to Newfoundland
1560s	Sir John Hawkins makes several slave-trading voyages from Africa to the Caribbean
1576	Sir Martin Frobisher reaches Labrador and Baffin Island
1577–80	Sir Francis Drake circumnavigates the world
1578	Frobisher makes an unsuccessful attempt to found a colony on Baffin Island
1583	Sir Humphrey Gilbert claims Newfoundland for the crown
1585	Sir Walter Raleigh establishes the Roanoke colony in Virginia, which fails by 1590; John Davis explores the eastern coastline of Greenland
1588	Publication of Thomas Harriot's *Brief Report of the New Found Land of Virginia*
1607	The Virginia Company founds the Jamestown colony, Virginia
1610	Henry Hudson explores Hudson Bay and the Hudson River

Gonzalo's vision of a Utopian government of the island (Act 2, Scene 1, lines 148–57), a speech that Shakespeare crafted from the 1603 English translation of French philosopher Montaigne's essay "The Cannibals," is prefaced by the words "Had I plantation of this isle" (line 144), where "plantation" means "colonization." Caliban's name is a near-anagram of "cannibal." Travel narratives such as Thomas Harriot's *Brief Report of the New Found Land of Virginia* (1588) provided early seventeenth-century readers with exotic accounts of strange and wonderful peoples and countries. Trinculo is comically representative of the desire for wonderful strange beings. On first sight of Caliban, he wishes he were in England where

> *[A]ny strange beast ... makes a man. When they will not give a doit to relieve a lame beggar, they will lay out ten to see a dead Indian.*
> (ACT 2, SCENE 2, LINES 31–33)

Royal marriages in pursuit of political reconciliation were much discussed in England throughout Shakespeare's writing career. Mary Tudor was married to Philip II of Spain, and there was public outcry over Elizabeth I's proposed marriage to the Duke of Alençon. In 1613, *The*

ABOVE: *A 1940 production at the Old Vic theater in London featured Jack Hawkins as Caliban, seen at left here alongside Stephano, Ariel, and Trinculo. John Gielgud starred as Prospero.*

Tempest was one of 14 plays staged by Shakespeare's company, the King's Men, as part of the celebrations for the marriage of Elizabeth, daughter of James I, to Prince Frederick, Elector Palatine and later King of Bohemia. It has been suggested that the court masque that Prospero arranges for Ferdinand and Miranda was an addition to the play written especially for this occasion. Whether or not this is the case, dynastic marriage figures prominently in *The Tempest*. Alonso and his men are shipwrecked returning from Carthage, where the King of Naples has just married his daughter Claribel to the King of Tunis. In securing the marriage of Ferdinand and Miranda, Prospero, the deposed Duke of Milan, ensures that his "issue / Should become kings of Naples" (Act 5, Scene 1, lines 205–6).

Inspired By ...

The Tempest's opening storm, and Prospero's reference to the "still-vex'd Bermoothes [Bermudas]" (Act 1, Scene 2, line 229), probably derive from English historian William Strachey's 1610 account of a hurricane that occurred during the previous year's Virginia Company voyage to the Americas, which isolated the governor's ship and drove it toward the Bermudas.

An Ambiguous Magic

For Shakespeare's contemporaries, natural magic was seen as a form of philosophy aligned to the practice of mathematics, astrology, and dream interpretation. Its opposite was demonic magic, especially witchcraft. *The Tempest* shows us both kinds. Before the start of the play, Ariel is imprisoned in a "cloven pine" (Act 1, Scene 2, line 277) through the sorcery of Caliban's mother, "the foul witch Sycorax" (Act 1, Scene 2, line 258), who was banished from Algiers "For mischiefs manifold, and sorceries terrible" (line 264). Caliban calls the god whom his mother served "Setebos" (Act 1, Scene 2, line 373), a name that means "great devil." Ariel is an airy spirit whose interventions in nature are benign. Even while the shipwreck is experienced by its victims as "Hell" with all its "devils" (Act 1, Scene 2, lines 214–15), Ariel contrives it so that

Not a hair perish'd;
On their sustaining garments not a blemish,
But fresher than before ...
(ACT 1, SCENE 2, LINES 217–19)

ABOVE: *Played here by Ralph Richardson in a 1952 Stratford Festival performance, Prospero keeps a tight rein on Ariel (Margaret Leighton) and the other denizens of his island domain.*

Prospero's magic is more ambiguous. While his "art" rescues Ariel from his confinement, we learn that his absorption "in secret studies" (Act 1, Scene 2, line 77) led to his neglect of his political duties and allowed his brother to easily usurp his power. Although Prospero physically injures no one in the play through his magic, Alonso and Ferdinand spend most of the play believing the other is dead, and the Italian nobility stumble around the island in monstrous confusion. When Prospero finally, and magisterially, abjures magic because his project is complete, his words come from a translation of the Roman poet Ovid's *Metamorphoses*, where the speaker is the sorceress Medea:

Ye elves of hills, brooks, standing lakes, and groves,
And ye that on the sands with printless foot
Do chase the ebbing Neptune, and do fly him
When he comes back; you demi-puppets that
By moonshine to the green sour ringlets make . . .
(ACT 5, SCENE 1, LINES 33–37)

Prospero's Authority

Prospero exercises his paternal authority over Ferdinand and Miranda with fierce warnings of the consequences should they give in to sexual desire—for his daughter to become a future queen of Naples, Prospero must keep her chaste. He also exerts the authority of lordship over Ariel and Caliban. Ariel is no more willing a servant than Caliban and spends much of the play appealing for his freedom. He achieves his liberty in the final act only when all his labors have been performed. Prospero calls Caliban his "poisonous slave" and threatens him with cramps and pinches, but tells Miranda they cannot dispense with him because Caliban fetches in their wood and makes their fire.

The problematic nature of authority is also dramatized by the subplot. Caliban, primed with drink, adopts Trinculo and Stephano as his new masters, kneels to them, and promises Trinculo he will be his new subject. Only when Ariel foils their conspiracy to murder Prospero does Caliban realize he was a "thrice-double ass / ... to take this drunkard for a god, / And worship this dull fool!" (Act 5, Scene 1, lines 296–98).

Prospero, who has a study full of books, calls Caliban a savage, "on whose nature / Nurture can never stick" (Act 4, Scene 1, lines 188–89). Caliban's natural instinct is dramatized in his unrepentant desire to have raped Miranda, and yet Shakespeare gives him some of the most beautiful language in the entire play.

Miranda reminds Caliban that he used to be a thing most brutish and gabbled in ignorance of his own meaning, so that she took pity on him and became his tutor. Caliban's retort points at the paradox of such civilizing practices:

You taught me language, and my profit on't
Is, I know how to curse. The red-plague rid you
For learning me your language!
(ACT 1, SCENE 2, LINES 363–65)

Forgiveness and Repentance

At the commencement of Act 5, Prospero finally has all his enemies within his power. Ariel, who has witnessed their terrible afflictions at first hand, even though he is a spirit, and not human, prompts Prospero to recognize that "The rarer action is / In virtue than in vengeance" (Act 5, Scene 1, lines 27–28).

Because he believes his enemies to be penitent, Prospero ultimately resolves to extend his plans no further and to release everyone from his charms. Alonso and Sebastian are truly repentant, but the end of the play sees no transformation in Antonio. There is no rapprochement between Antonio and Prospero, and the apparent harmony and reconciliation at the close of the play fails to resolve the issue of this impenitent usurper and would-be murderer.

Hold the Storm!

Advertisements for late eighteenth-century performances of *The Tempest* hyped the spectacularly theatrical storm effects. By public demand, this resulted in the shipwreck scene that starts the play being delayed until the beginning of Act 2, so that habitual latecomers to the theater did not miss it.

Music and Masque

No other play of Shakespeare's demands more music and spectacle. There are two full-scale masques in *The Tempest*. Staged with spectacular scenery and music, and performed by a mixed cast of royalty, courtiers, and professional actors, masques were especially fashionable in the first decade of the seventeenth century. In the masque for the wedding of Ferdinand and Miranda, spirits take the parts of Juno and Ceres and promise fertility for the newly betrothed couple. The other masque in *The Tempest* is drawn from an episode in *The Aeneid*; it begins when Ariel, in the form of a Harpy, confronts Alonso, Sebastian, and Antonio, "three men of sin," with their crimes (Act 3, Scene 3, lines 53–82). Both masques show Prospero using his art to assert his political power.

Shakespeare also introduces an "antimasque," an entertainment in which, traditionally, grotesque figures danced boisterously in advance of the main masque. Shakespeare, however, positions his antimasque last (Act 4, Scene 1, lines 194–266). It involves Caliban, Stephano, and Trinculo falling into a filthy pool that leaves them smelling of horse urine, and then being chased away by dogs as they attempt to steal clothes from a washing line.

The more graceful masques are accompanied by "soft music" and Juno's and Ceres's song "Honor, riches, marriage-blessing" (Act 4, Scene 1, lines 106–117). In a coarser vein, Stephano enters the play singing a sailor's song (Act 2, Scene 2, lines 42–54), and at the end of the scene a drunken Caliban sings "No more dams I'll make for fish" (lines 180–85). In Act 3, Scene 2, by now thoroughly sozzled, Stephano, Trinculo, and Caliban sing "Flout 'em, and [scout] 'em" to the wrong tune (lines 116–18), while Ariel provides the correct one on a tabor and pipe.

Ariel is associated with music throughout and sings three of Shakespeare's most famous songs. His first song is "Come unto these yellow sands" (Act 1, Scene 2, lines 375–87), followed by "Full fadom five" (lines 397–405). The final song in Act 5 is Ariel's beautifully wistful vision of his long-promised freedom: "Where the bee sucks, there suck I, / In a cowslip's bell I lie" (Scene 1, lines 88–94).

BELOW: *This 2009 production, featuring actors from the Royal Shakespeare Company and South Africa's Baxter Theatre, highlighted, in vivid and original fashion, the importance of music and dance in* The Tempest.

Our revels now are ended. These our actors/ (As I foretold you) were all spirits, and/ Are melted into air,/.../We are such stuff/ As dreams are made on; and our little life/ Is rounded with a sleep ...

—*Prospero* (ACT 4, SCENE 1, LINES 148–50, 156–58)

Sparse Imagery

Surprisingly, *The Tempest* is not rich in figurative diction. The most extended imagery is theatrical, most memorably Prospero's "Our revels now are ended" speech (Act 4, Scene 1, lines 148–58). Prospero also describes Antonio's treachery as wanting "no screen between this part he play'd / And him he play'd it for" (Act 1, Scene 2, lines 107–8). Antonio's plan to murder Alonso with Sebastian is "an act / Whereof what's past is prologue" (Act 2, Scene 1, lines 252–53).

Nature is often personified. Alonso confronts his monstrous crime thus:

> *The winds did sing it to me, and the thunder,*
> *That deep and dreadful organ-pipe, pronounc'd*
> *The name of Prosper; it did base my trespass.*
> (ACT 3, SCENE 3, LINES 97–99)

The sea sighs to the winds with pity, and Ariel describes the island's briars as "tooth'd" (Act 4, Scene 1, line 180). Vivid isolated images include grief as "beauty's canker" (Act 1, Scene 2, line 415); conscience as "candied" (Act 2, Scene 1, line 279), meaning "congealed, glazed, and turned to sugar"; and Prospero's warning to Ferdinand that the "strongest oaths are straw / To th' fire i' th' blood" (Act 4, Scene 1, lines 52–53).

A Malleable Play

The Tempest has proved to be an especially malleable play on stage. Recent productions often make minor revisions, such as cutting Prospero's Epilogue and replacing it with his "Our revels now are ended" speech (Act 4, Scene 1, lines 148–58), or assign to Prospero Miranda's words to Caliban "Abhorred slave, / Which any print of goodness wilt not take" (Act 1, Scene 2, lines 351–52). But these pale into insignificance in light of the play's whole stage history.

When theaters reopened after the Restoration of Charles II, *The Tempest* was one of the first of Shakespeare's plays to be revived, in 1667. Only, what audiences saw was not Shakespeare's *The Tempest*, but John Dryden and William Davenant's *The Inchanted Isle*. In this version, Prospero's most

Movie Spin-offs

Notable film spin-offs of *The Tempest* include *Yellow Sky* (1948), directed by William Wellman, a Western set in a desert, and English director Peter Greenaway's postmodern *Prospero's Books* (1991), a highly stylized and stylish adaptation starring John Gielgud as Prospero, who also narrates the story, and incorporating dance, mime, song, and innovative computer-generated images.

In *Forbidden Planet* (1956), a science-fiction movie directed by Fred Wilcox, the mad scientist Dr. Morbius (Prospero), and his daughter, Altaira, sole survivors of a space mission, live on Planet Alain-4. A crew of astronauts arrives in a spaceship and Commander Adams (an older version of Ferdinand) awakens Altaira's sexuality. While Ariel is transformed into a pliant robot, the film realizes, terrifyingly, the psychological implications of Prospero's description of Caliban as "this thing of darkness I / Acknowledge mine" (Act 5, Scene 1, 275–76). The Caliban of *Forbidden Planet*, an invisible beast who attacks the spaceship and makes it explode into a point of light, is dredged up from Morbius's unconscious. One reviewer called the Freudian id-monster that merges Caliban/ Prospero "a King Kong of space."

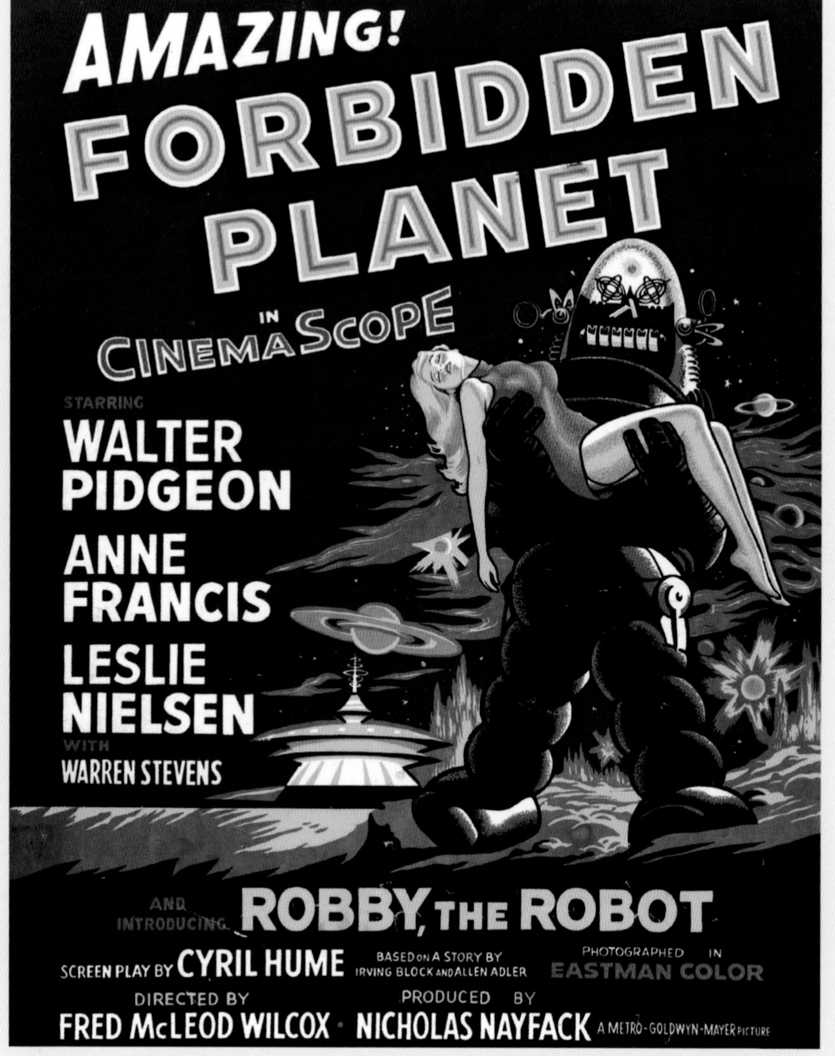

RIGHT: *This promotional poster for Fred Wilcox's 1956 science-fiction film* Forbidden Planet *shows Robby the Robot, based on Ariel in* The Tempest, *rescuing Altaira, a character modeled on Miranda.*

famous speeches were cut and new characters appeared: Miranda's sister Dorinda, who marries Hippolito, the Duke of Mantua, whom Prospero has kept hidden on the island; Caliban's sister, named Sycorax like his mother and memorably termed "Queen Slobber-Chops"; and Milcha, Ariel's spirit consort. *The Inchanted Isle* held the stage until Victorian times, challenged only by an operatic version with words by Thomas Shadwell (1674) and music by Henry Purcell (1690). Even when Shakespeare's text was restored in the nineteenth century, it continued to be a balletic and operatic show, and masques written by Shadwell were still included.

Wholesale revision of Shakespeare's text has not been restricted to the eighteenth and nineteenth centuries. Director Peter Brook's 1968 version at the Roundhouse in London isolated key words from famous speeches, and mixed them disruptively through shards of a mangled plot. At the play's conclusion Prospero spoke a new line, "I forgot the plot," while the other characters began reciting random lines from earlier in the play. The cacophany of chanted fragments ended in silence.

ABOVE: *Featuring in Sam Mendes's 1993 Royal Shakespeare Company production were (left to right) David Bradley (Trinculo), Mark Lockyer (Stephano), David Troughton (Caliban), and Simon Russell Beale (Ariel).*

Playing Ariel and Caliban

The Tempest's stage history has fostered contrasting realizations of Ariel and Caliban. Music has often been used to highlight Ariel's role as a singer and dancer. Even though his is clearly a male part, before 1930 Ariel was often played by a woman, and his/her nonhuman form emphasized: in 1778 Ariel was a dragonfly, and in 1847 an angel. Director Sam Mendes's 1993 Royal Shakespeare Company production cast Simon Russell Beale, an actor of some physical heft, in the part. Equal to Prospero in power, Ariel did not disguise his contempt for him. When Prospero released him from his service, Ariel spat in his face.

Caliban has been played as a drunken sot, a demonic monster, and a Darwinian "missing link." In England in the 1890s, F.R. Benson spent many hours at a zoo, watching apes, to prepare for the role. Caliban has also been played as a kind of fish, snake, lizard, dog, or tortoise. But productions have also stressed his political and humanitarian significance. In director Michael Boyd's 2002 Royal Shakespeare Company production, Geff Francis became the first black actor in the company's history to play Caliban; Ariel was played by a black woman, Kananu Kirimi. Their performances were dignified, while the "civilized" European characters behaved in stark contrast, especially Trinculo, who capered around like a drunken chimpanzee.

> *Full fadom five thy father lies,/ Of his bones are coral made:/ Those are pearls that were his eyes:/ Nothing of him that doth fade,/ But doth suffer a sea-change/ Into something rich and strange.*
>
> 
>
> —*Ariel* (ACT 1, SCENE 2, LINES 397–402)

A Continuing Inspiration

The Tempest has been the inspiration for many new works. English poet W.H. Auden's poem *The Sea and the Mirror* (1942–44) portrays Caliban as the embodiment of suffering humanity. In Caribbean writer Aimé Cesaire's *A Tempest* (1969), Prospero is a decadent imperialist, Ariel a pacifist mulatto slave, and Caliban a black slave; when Caliban's attempted revolution fails, he agrees to stay with Prospero but, if necessary, use violence against him. Australian novelist David Malouf's innovative postcolonial rewriting, *Blood Relations* (1988), explores the spiritual and dream life of an Australian family spending Christmas together. British dramatist Philip Osment's 1989 play *This Island's Mine* uses Caliban's claim to legitimate possession of the island to rally political support against racist and homophobic oppression in Britain.

The Two Noble Kinsmen

WRITTEN
c. 1613–14
SETTING AND PERIOD
Athens, updated to Chaucer's medieval England
CHARACTERS 36
ACTS 5
SCENES 24
LINES 3,261

THE PLOT: *Duke Theseus has returned to Athens victorious after war against Creon, tyrant of Thebes, and now turns his attention to his wedding to Hippolyta. In a ceremonial scene, three Theban queens, widowed by the war, plead with Theseus for the bodies of their husbands, in order to give them burial rites. Theseus eventually agrees.*

The "kinsmen" of the play's title are cousins, Palamon and Arcite, valiant Theban soldiers who are now prisoners of war. Both fall in love with Emilia, Hippolyta's sister, after spying her from their jail window. Hostility over love conflicts with their family loyalties. In a formal combat decreed by Theseus, Arcite prevails and wins Emilia's hand, while Palamon is condemned to die. However, Arcite is accidentally thrown from his horse and dies, so Palamon marries Emilia in the aftermath.

Meanwhile, the Jailer's Daughter goes mad with unrequited love for Palamon, but is finally married to her original wooer, who impersonates Palamon to win her.

Dramatis Personae

Theseus, *Duke of Athens*
Pirithous, *an Athenian general*
Artesius, *an Athenian captain*
Palamon, Arcite, *nephews to Creon, King of Thebes*
Valerius
Six Knights
Herald
Jailer *(also called* **Keeper***)*
Wooer to the Jailer's Daughter
Doctor
Brother, Friends, *to the Jailer*
Gentleman
Gerrold, *a schoolmaster*
Hymen
Hippolyta, *an Amazon, bride to Theseus*
Emilia, *her sister*
Three Queens
Jailer's Daughter
Waiting-Woman to Emilia
Nymphs
Countrymen, Country Girls, Messengers, Taborer, Boy, Executioner, Guard, Servant, Attendants

The Two Noble Kinsmen, a collaborative effort between Shakespeare and John Fletcher, is one of the two last plays Shakespeare worked on. It uses the kind of tragicomic romance material typical of his last, single-authored plays, *The Winter's Tale* and *The Tempest*.

By the time he came to collaborate on *The Two Noble Kinsmen,* Shakespeare was famous enough to work like the great "master" Renaissance painters, such as Leonardo da Vinci and Rubens, adding a scene here and there—just as these revered artists were able to add a face or hands to somebody else's painting. John Fletcher, in his mid-thirties, was a competent playwright, writing conventional rather than startling poetry, and later becoming better known for his part in the writing duo Beaumont and Fletcher. Although two very different hands are at work, *The Two Noble Kinsmen* is nevertheless a dramatically unified piece of writing.

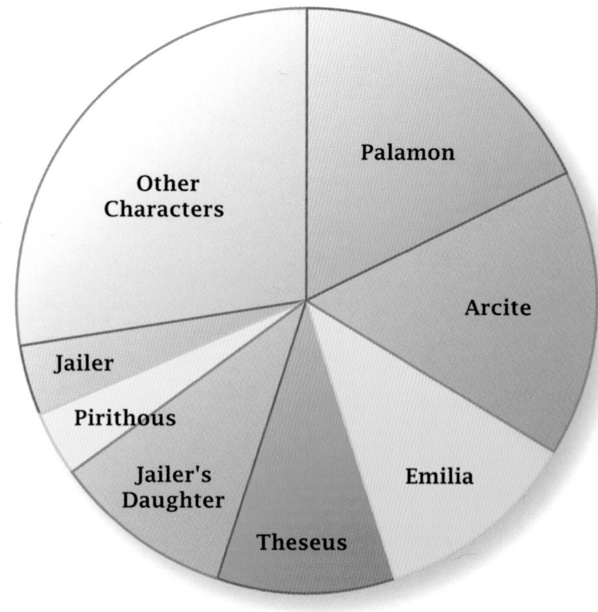

MAJOR ROLES
Between them, the "two noble kinsmen" Palamon and Arcite command 34 percent of the dialogue in the play. Emilia, Theseus, and the lovestruck Jailer's Daughter share 31 percent of the total lines.

A Master Collaborates

The plot is based ultimately on ancient Greco-Roman mythology, but the rustic scenes by Fletcher evoke an idealized English country life, reminding us of the play's direct source: English poet Geoffrey Chaucer's romance narrative *The Knight's Tale,* from *The Canterbury Tales.*

Shakespeare seems to have contributed Act 1; Act 3, Scene 1; most of Act 5 except for Scene 2; and probably the atmospheric third soliloquy of the Jailer's Daughter in Act 3, Scene 2:

The best way is, the next way to a grave;
Each errant step beside is torment. Lo
The moon is down, the crickets chirp, the screech-owl
Calls in the dawn ...

(ACT 3, SCENE 2, LINES 33–36)

These sections have the run-on lines, fertile imagery, and complex but economical syntax familiar in Shakespeare's late plays.

Love and Honor

The plot at times borders on a parody of chivalric conventions of "honor," a medieval code of conduct that was outdated by Shakespeare's time. Each character is compromised by commitment to values of war that are incompatible with kinship and love:

> PALAMON *That we should things desire which do cost us*
> *The loss of our desire! that nought could buy*
> *Dear love but loss of dear love!*
> THESEUS *Never fortune*
> *Did play a subtler game ...*
> (ACT 5, SCENE 4, LINES 110–13)

Palamon prays to Venus, goddess of love, even though he is seeking to kill Arcite; Arcite prays to Mars, god of war, although his deadly campaign against his beloved kinsman is over love; and Emilia prays to Diana, the goddess of chastity, proclaiming that she does not wish to marry any man! There is a strong implication here that male courtship is a threat to women.

Consistent with its tragicomic material, the play begins and ends with preparations for weddings and funerals. Love and war dominate the imagery, with compelling descriptions of the "intertangled roots of love" (Act 1, Scene 3, line 59) set in contrast to passages depicting realistic details of dead bodies on the battlefield—the "pecks of crows in the foul fields of Thebes" and the "stench of our slain lords" (Act 1, Scene 1, lines 42, 47).

On Today's Stage

The Royal Shakespeare Company has shown in its revivals, including director Barry Kyle's samurai-inspired production in 1986, that *The Two Noble Kinsmen* can work effectively on the stage. An enterprising director could bring the play to life by concentrating on its thematic center—the fundamental incompatibility between war and love—and focus on a conflict of ideals that has both tragic and comic outcomes, as relevant today as it ever was.

Women's Dilemmas in Love

The flow'r that I would pluck
And put between my breasts (O then but beginning
To swell about the blossom), she would long
Till she had such another, and commit it
To the like innocent cradle, where phoenix-like
They died in perfume ...
–*Emilia* (ACT 1, SCENE 3, LINES 66–71)

Men are mad things ...
–*Emilia* (ACT 2, SCENE 2, LINE 126)

To marry him is hopeless;
To be his whore is witless ...
—*Jailer's Daughter* (ACT 2, SCENE 4, LINES 4–5)

BELOW: *Depicting a scene from Chaucer's* The Knight's Tale, *this illustration (c. 1387) shows Palamon's duel with Arcite. Although nominally set in ancient Greece,* The Two Noble Kinsmen *reflects the knightly ideals of fourteenth-century England.*

Palamon desireth to slay his foe Arcite

The Poetry

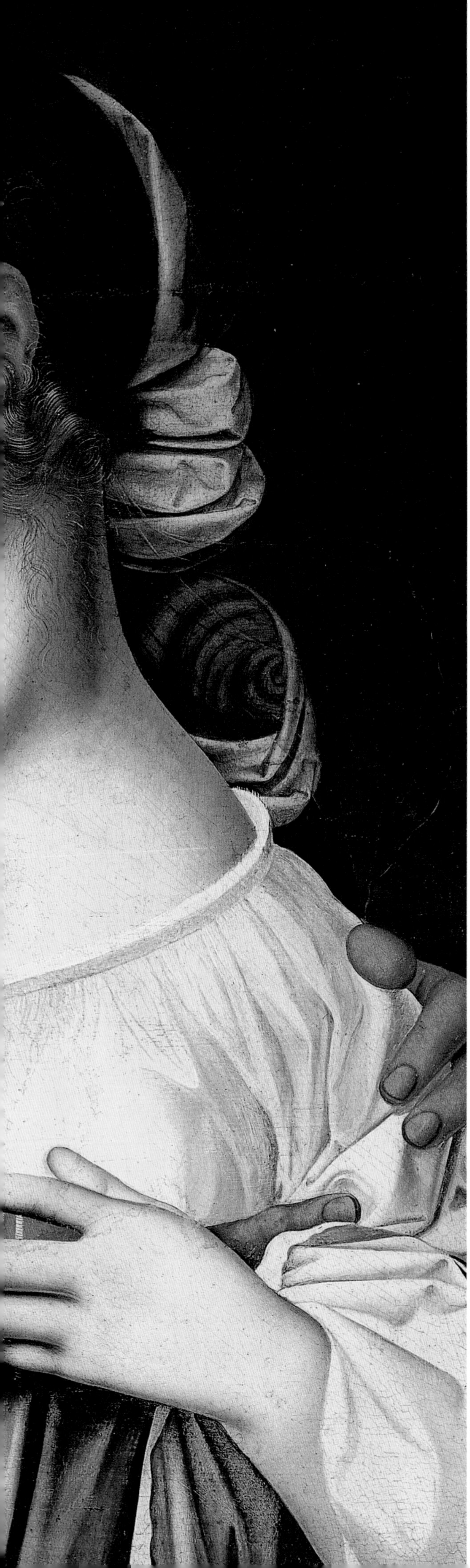

The Poems

During his lifetime, Shakespeare was as famous for his poetry as for his dramatic works. His most notable triumphs were the witty and erotic Venus and Adonis *and the more somber* The Rape of Lucrece. *His reputation as a lyric poet was reinforced by his occasional poems, including* The Phoenix and Turtle, A Lover's Complaint, *and* The Passionate Pilgrim.

Venus and Adonis

THE PLOT: *Venus, the goddess of love, is infatuated with a beautiful young mortal, Adonis. She uses various arguments to seduce him but Adonis resists, declaring that he is too young for love and would rather go hunting. When he attempts to leave, his horse runs off in pursuit of a female, leaving Adonis at Venus's mercy. The next day, he goes boar-hunting, despite Venus's warnings, and is killed. Where his blood has fallen, an anemone springs up, which Venus plucks and wears in her bosom. She promises that henceforth love will always end in sorrow.*

WRITTEN *c.* 1592–93
LINES 1,194
STANZAS 199
FORM Sixains

LEFT: *From 1593, Henry Wriothesley, 3rd Earl of Southampton, was Shakespeare's patron. He is depicted here in an 1824 portrait by Edmund Lodge. The Earl's enthusiasm for whiling away his time in playhouses was well noted among his contemporaries.*

Shakespeare's *Venus and Adonis* is a beguiling mix of the tragic and the comic. In telling the story of Adonis's death, it focuses on the insatiability of desire and the inexorability of time, but it combines these tragic themes with comic slapstick, bawdy humor, and, above all, the comic predicament of Venus as a goddess who cannot satisfy her desire.

The poem was the first work published under Shakespeare's own name (he called it "the first heir of my invention" for this reason), and one of only two texts to which he attached a dedication. It was written during a period in which theaters were closed due to plague, and the dramatist may have been motivated by financial necessity to seek noble patronage. Both *Venus and Adonis* and *The Rape of Lucrece* are dedicated to Henry Wriothesley, the 3rd Earl of Southampton, a young aristocrat renowned for his pleasure in theater, who some scholars believe may also have been the addressee of at least the first 17 of the sonnets. However, Shakespeare seems also to have had a wider readership in mind.

Exploring the Erotic

During the 1580s and 1590s, a kind of poem, now called the "epyllion," or minor epic (plural "epyllia"), became extremely popular with university students, gallants, and courtiers. The epyllion was written in a self-consciously witty style and based on an erotic and mythological narrative, usually taken from the Roman poet Ovid's book *Metamorphoses* (the Venus and Adonis story appears in Book 10). Although there was a long tradition of moralizing Ovid's tales (Arthur Golding, whose 1567 translation of Ovid's work was certainly known by Shakespeare, described Book 10 as "reproving most prodigious lusts"), what was particularly characteristic of the epyllion writers was their emphasis on the erotic pleasures of the narrative and of language itself.

Venus and Adonis went through 16 editions before 1640, and its extraordinary success seems to have been largely attributable to its powers of seduction. In Thomas Middleton's comic play, *A Mad World, My Masters* (*c.* 1608), the jealous Harebrain describes his attempts to make his young wife stay faithful: "I have conveyed away all her wanton pamphlets, as *Hero and Leander, Venus and Adonis,* oh, two luscious marrow-bone pies [aphrodisiacs] for a young married wife."

Love and Transformation

Perhaps the main theme of *Venus and Adonis* is love's power to transform deities and mortals

Who's Who

The two major characters in *Venus and Adonis* are Venus, goddess of love, and Adonis, a beautiful adolescent male. Their tale is related by a narrator who, though often a prominent character in other epyllia (for example, in Christopher Marlowe's *Hero and Leander*), is here relatively unobtrusive. All the other characters within the poem are animals: Adonis's horse who takes up with a female ("jennet") in the forest; the hare, Wat, imagined as the subject of a hunt; and the boar that kills Adonis. One character who appears in other versions of the legend but is missing here is Cupid. Shakespeare focuses his attention on the goddess as a representation of love, and omits to explain how her infatuation began.

alike. Venus appears comically—and desperately—mortal. She weeps over Adonis, pants and sweats with exertion, and, for all her supernatural power, cannot force him to have sex with her (lines 41–42). She is further degraded by the bestialism associated with lust, to the point that she identifies with the boar: "Had I been tooth'd like him, I must confess, / With kissing him [Adonis] I should have kill'd him first" (lines 1117–18).

Meanwhile, Adonis is also discovered at a transitional moment. He refers to his extreme youth and to the fact that he does not yet know himself (lines 524–25), but rather than be transformed by love, he wishes to achieve adult masculinity through hunting (a ritualized form of war) and male companionship. This ambition finds some sympathy with the narrator: Venus is depicted as a suffocating maternal figure who will impede Adonis's transition to adulthood. The irony is, of course, that it is Adonis's very efforts to avoid love which result in the poem's most literal transformation: the metamorphosis of his blood into the "new-sprung" anemone flower (line 1171).

A related theme is that of gender reversal. Venus's authority naturally identifies her as male in Elizabethan culture (although it is justified by her divinity), just as the power of Queen Elizabeth was explained by her sovereignty—and some parallels have been seen between the two figures. At the same time, the poem also emphasizes the way in which desire can destabilize gender. For example, the fact that the goddess takes not only an active but a physically aggressive role in the courtship—she is able to pluck the "tender" Adonis from his horse (lines 30–31)—identifies her with the male.

While Venus takes on this more masculine role, Adonis is increasingly feminized by his virginity, his passivity, and even his physical appearance:

RIGHT: Venus and Adonis, *by Italian sculptor Antonio Canova (1757–1822), depicts Adonis preparing to leave for the hunt. The poses of the figures clearly suggest Venus's adoration and Adonis's casual carelessness.*

"Fie, No More of Love!"

Shakespeare's major alteration to Ovid's narrative in *Metamorphoses* is to have Adonis refuse Venus's advances. This approach may have been suggested by Titian's painting *Venus and Adonis* (1554), which was exhibited in London from that date. The image suggested by the poem's line "With this he breaketh from the sweet embrace" (line 811) is particularly reminiscent of Titian's work.

> *"Thrice fairer than myself," thus she began,*
> *"The field's chief flower, sweet above compare,*
> *Stain to all nymphs, more lovely than a man,*
> *More white and red than doves or roses are[.]*
> (LINES 7–10)

Even the mode of Adonis's death feminizes him: he is penetrated by the tusk of the boar, bleeds, and is transformed into a flower (the term "flowers" was often used to denote women's menstrual bleeding).

The Cycle of Time

We might also observe the poem's fascination with the effects of time. In his commentary on *Metamorphoses,* published in 1632, George Sandys observed that one of the morals of the Adonis story was "the frail condition and short continuance of beauty." The main argument by which Venus hopes to seduce Adonis is that his attractions will fade, and he should "Make use of time" (line 129) and seize the erotic opportunity presented to him. But if the poem demonstrates the destructiveness of time through Adonis's death, it also holds out a kind of consolation. The structure of the poem is itself cyclical. On day one, Venus tries to seduce Adonis and fails. On day two, she fails to prevent him from pursuing the boar and Adonis is killed. But at the end of the second day, Adonis is transformed into the anemone flower, which confers a kind of immortality upon him:

> *A purple flow'r sprung up,*
> *check'red with white,*
> *Resembling well his pale cheeks and the*
> *blood*
> *Which in round drops upon their whiteness*
> *stood.*
> (LINES 1168–70)

Individual flowers die, but the species lives on—as does the poem itself.

Beauty's Colors

One of the most obvious image patterns in *Venus and Adonis* is the repetition of red and white. These were the colors identified with ideal beauty in the period (specifically, a white complexion with red cheeks and lips), but they are mainly used here to describe Adonis. The figure of Adonis is clearly an object of homoerotic desire, perhaps reflecting Shakespeare's own erotic interests (many of the sonnets are directed to a "lovely boy"), but also the kinds of desire conventionally produced by the epyllion. The red and white of Adonis implies his distinction from Venus—"She red and hot as coals of glowing fire, / He red for shame, but frosty in

BELOW: *Shakespeare may have been inspired by Titian's* Venus and Adonis *(1554) in deciding to have Adonis reject the attentions of the goddess in the poem, and in depicting the emotional and physical desperation of Venus's doomed love.*

ABOVE: *In* Venus and Adonis: A Masque for Puppets *for the Royal Shakespeare Company, 2004 (revived in 2007), director Gregory Doran and director of puppetry Steve Tiplady created an innovative blend of music, narration, and puppet show that proved a sell-out hit in London.*

desire" (lines 35–36)—but also his passionate (and potentially erotic) fluctuations of feeling.

As suggested above, animal imagery is central to the poem. Not only do we have the interlude in which Adonis's horse shows his master how it should be done by wooing a female horse (lines 259–324), but the characters themselves become animals, suggesting that the pursuit of love is also a kind of hunt. Thus, Venus describes Adonis as a deer that she will allow to graze "where thou wilt" in her parkland (lines 229–34), while Venus's kissing is likened to a ravenous eagle, which:

Tires with her beak on feathers, flesh, and bone,
Shaking her wings, devouring all in haste,
Till either gorge be stuff'd, or prey be gone[.]
(LINES 56–58)

Finally, some of Shakespeare's most admired nature writing can be found in *Venus and Adonis.* There is an affecting description of the hare's pursuit by hounds across the fields—"Each envious brier his weary legs do scratch" (line 705)—while Venus's withdrawal at the sight of Adonis's death is likened to that of "the snail, whose tender horns being hit, / Shrinks backward in his shelly cave with pain" (lines 1033–34). Some commentators have suggested that the poem reveals Shakespeare's nostalgia for the countryside in Stratford he had left behind to pursue his London career.

She's Love, she loves, and yet she is not lov'd.

(LINE 610)

Renewed Interest

After languishing in obscurity and critical opprobrium on and off since the eighteenth century, there was a revival of interest in *Venus and Adonis* in the late twentieth century, due partly to its relevance for feminist and queer theory. More generally, the poem has been given a new lease of life on the stage. In 2004 and 2007, the poem's dramatic potential and its artificiality were exploited in a production directed by Gregory Doran in London using giant puppets. A musical version, directed by Marion Potts, was performed in Melbourne, Australia, in 2008, reimagining the poem as an Elizabethan masque with music.

The Rape of Lucrece

WRITTEN
c. 1593–94
LINES 1,855
STANZAS 265
FORM Rhyme royal

THE PLOT: *At the siege of Ardea, a group of Roman noblemen has been competing over the virtue of their wives. Collatine makes such a persuasive case for the chastity of his wife, Lucrece, that he enflames the king's son, Tarquin, with lust for her. Tarquin visits Lucrece when Collatine is away from home and is welcomed as a guest. In the night, he attempts to rape her. She begs him to preserve both their honors, but Tarquin threatens to murder her and a servant, and make it look as though they were in bed together, so Lucrece submits.*

The next morning, she sends a message to Collatine, who arrives with other Roman nobles, including her father. She tells them her misfortune, makes them swear an oath of revenge, then stabs herself and dies. The men determine to carry her body through the streets and to publicize Tarquin's crime; consequently, the Tarquin clan is banished from Rome.

In the dedication to *Venus and Adonis,* Shakespeare anticipated the production of a "graver labour." This was *The Rape of Lucrece,* a poem related to its predecessor through its erotic and Classical theme and its rhetorical ambitions, but now emphasizing the tragic consequences of the fulfillment of desire and the failure of language.

Shakespeare's source for the poem was ancient Roman history, as retold in the Roman historian Livy's *Historia* and the poet Ovid's *Fasti* (*Chronicles*), both of which were studied in Elizabethan grammar schools. However, Lucrece's tragedy also had a more recent artistic history: it was a poetic theme for the fourteenth-century poets Geoffrey Chaucer and John Gower, and a favorite with Renaissance painters (including Lucas Cranach and Titian), who depict a violent Tarquin stealing into Lucrece's bedchamber, or Lucrece holding a dagger to her breast.

By writing the poem, Shakespeare engaged in a debate over the justification for Lucrece's suicide that had gone on for centuries. Its celebrated political consequences (the shift from monarchy to republicanism) were emphasized by Livy and Ovid, and Lucrece was praised for her loyalty to Rome. However, Christian commentators inevitably condemned it, with Catholic theologian St. Augustine arguing that Lucrece had acted out of pride, being moved "not by her love of chastity but her irresolute shame."

Shakespeare incorporates these ambiguities into the poem by having Lucrece anachronistically consider the pagan and Christian arguments about suicide, and ask whether she is spiritually guilty if her transgression was enforced (Augustine insisted not). Nevertheless, the poem's treatment of rape may also strike contemporary readers as surprisingly modern. Not only does it insist that this is an act motivated as much by power as by lust, but Lucrece's feeling of guilt that she did not do enough to prevent it and her sense of psychological as well as physical violation are easily recognizable.

The Power of Shame

One of the poem's most pervasive themes is the destructive effect of shame. Lucrece warns Tarquin that if he performs this crime he will not only have betrayed himself but he will be forever alienated from his identity as "Tarquin" (lines 155–57). The latter's own painful understanding of this fact, even as he proceeds in his rape, has suggested to some critics that he represents a rough draft for Macbeth:

I have debated, even in my soul,
What wrong, what shame, what sorrow I shall
breed,
But nothing can affection's course control,
Or stop the headlong fury of his speed.
(LINES 498–501)

For Lucrece, self-loss is even more acute, since she is divided from all the public roles that have created her identity. She can no longer be Collatine's wife because she has defiled the marriage bed; she can no longer be the ideal mother, since she may now be pregnant with an illegitimate child; she is no longer even a proud Roman, since she has been forced to betray the principal Roman values of chastity, loyalty, and honor for which she once stood. Her suicide is clearly an attempt to reintegrate her shattered sense of self before an audience of her husband

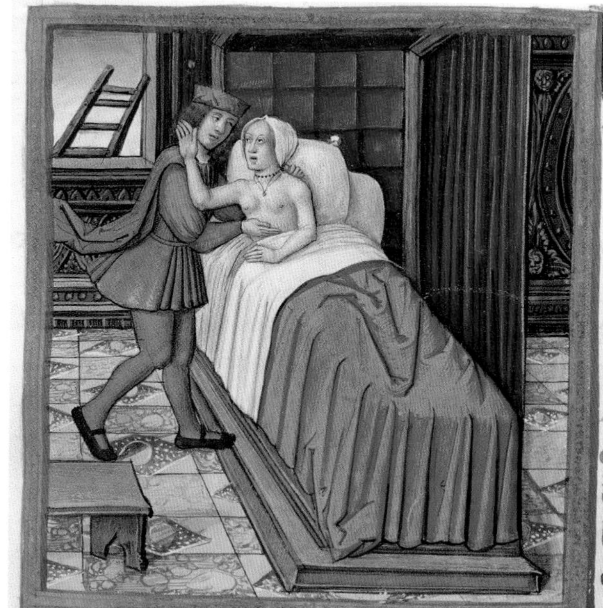

ABOVE: *"The treasure of his happy state" (line 16): this illustration from a French manuscript, c. 1505, presents a rarely portrayed aspect of Lucrece—her willing acceptance of her husband, Collatine, into her bed.*

and father, paradoxically reaffirming her commitment to marriage and to Rome through an act of self-destruction.

What partly explains this decision is the poem's relentless politicization of rape. Not only does Tarquin's act recall the crime that was perpetrated against Rome when his father murdered the rightful king and usurped his seat, the poem also sees the destruction of Troy as a consequence of Helen's rape (line 1369)—though "rape" here may refer to her abduction by Paris rather than her physical violation. As Lucrece points out, it seems wrong that the "private pleasure" of an individual should bring such widespread destruction to an entire city (lines 1478–84).

But perhaps more pressing is our sense of the private being subjugated to the public. Lucrece's personal loss is entirely subsumed by its Roman (and masculine) meaning. Her tragedy inspires first a tussle between her husband and her father over who had superior rights of ownership in Lucrece (lines 1791–1806), before Brutus decides to exploit it as an opportunity to oust the Tarquins (lines 1814–34). Even Lucrece sees the act as one that has been committed more against her husband than herself, to be revenged by men.

Who's Who

The poem's main protagonists are Lucrece, a Roman wife, famed for her beauty and chastity; Tarquin, the son of the Roman king, Lucius Tarquinius Superbus; and Collatine, Lucrece's husband. Other characters are the Roman lords whom Collatine brings with him to the house, including Brutus, a Roman who has long been dissatisfied with the Tarquins' reign, and Lucrece's father, Lucretius. Also significant are those figures who appear not in the flesh but as the subjects of a painting on the fall of Troy, in particular the deceitful Sinon, a prototype for Tarquin, and Hecuba, a model for Lucrece's grief.

Interpreting the World

Another powerful theme in the poem is that of reading and interpretation. One of the reasons that Lucrece is apparently vulnerable to Tarquin is not simply her husband's boasting (though that does come in for a share of blame), but her inability to read in Tarquin's appearance or behavior any signs of his wicked intent (lines 99–105). This

OPPOSITE: *The story of Lucrece (also spelled Lucretia) and Tarquin has inspired countless artists and writers since ancient Roman times. Lucas Cranach's* The Suicide of Lucretia *(1538) is just one of the famous depictions of Lucrece's suicide.*

ABOVE: Lucretia *(1834), by Spanish sculptor Damian Campeny y Estrany, suggests the graceful nobility of the dying Lucrece. Shakespeare's heroine precedes her suicide with an anguished denouncement of Tarquin's act.*

What win I if I gain the thing I seek?/ A dream, a breath, a froth of fleeting joy./ Who buys a minute's mirth to wail a week?/ Or sells eternity to get a toy?

(LINES 211–14)

is attributed to Lucrece's own goodness—she cannot imagine anyone harboring such a design, having "touched no unknown baits, nor fear'd no hooks" (line 103)—but also reveals how circumscribed her life has been, so that in attempting to keep her safe, Collatine has actually put her at risk.

After the rape, Lucrece learns to read much better. In a famous passage, she contemplates a painting of the siege of Troy (lines 1366–1582). The figure of the grief-stricken Hecuba provides some comfort, but it is the image of Sinon that seems to offer Lucrece a second chance. At first, she cannot reconcile Sinon's famous treachery with the picture of innocence that she sees before her in the painting but, drawing upon her experience with Tarquin, she concludes the opposite: "It cannot be, I find, / But such a face should bear a wicked mind" (lines 1539–40). With this new understanding of the possibilities of misinterpretation, Lucrece proceeds to stage her own suicide, controlling the meaning of her tragedy through narrative and gesture.

Burning Lust, Cold Death

The contrast between Tarquin's lust and Lucrece's chastity is evocatively depicted through the imagery of hot and cold. The poem begins with the "lightless fire" (line 4) that consumes Tarquin. This image is then literalized in the burning torch that guides him through the house. Yet even when the flame blows out, Tarquin's heat does not die until he has sated his lust. Meanwhile, Lucrece is described not merely in terms of cold, hard substances such as ivory and stone, but as a corpse. When she is first seen asleep, her head between the pillows appears "entombed" (line 390) and her whole body resembles "a virtuous monument" (line 391), suggesting that she has already become her own funereal sculpture. This strain of imagery anticipates the conclusion of the poem, but it also suggests a deeper (potentially misogynistic) identification between chastity and death: not only that chastity is essentially static, but that death is the only way to ensure it remains intact.

"In This Blemish'd Fort ..."

Another recurrent image is the siege, which recalls Ardea (where the narrative begins) but is also applied to the consequences of rape. The souls of both Tarquin and Lucrece are described as ruined buildings:

Her house is sack'd, her quiet interrupted,
Her mansion batter'd by the enemy,
Her sacred temple spotted, spoil'd, corrupted,
Grossly engirt with daring infamy[.]
(LINES 1170–73)

The progress of Tarquin through Lucrece's house toward the bedchamber is also likened to an invasion. "Affection" leads him (line 271), as he pushes through the various doors that try to resist, then places his hand like a battering ram on the "ivory wall" of Lucrece's breast (line 464). Lucrece's self-wounding, which releases two streams of blood, transforms her body into a "late-sack'd island" (line 1740), suggesting that Lucrece has now taken on Tarquin's role, and become the besieger of herself.

Finally, Tarquin and Lucrece are transformed into something less than human by their violent encounter. The bestial images into which Tarquin is translated are inevitably predatory, such as the ravenous "wolf" (line 677) and "lurking serpent" (line 362), but they also include the "night-owl" (line 360) and the "foul night-waking cat" (line 554), all creatures of the Night that Lucrece personifies as being partly to blame for her rape (lines 764–805):

> *O comfort-killing Night, image of hell,*
> *Dim register and notary of shame,*
> *Black stage for tragedies and murthers fell,*
> *Vast sin-concealing chaos, nurse of blame!*
> *Blind muffled bawd, dark harbor for defame[.]*
> (LINES 764–68)

Meanwhile, Lucrece's innocence and physical inferiority are emphasized through her description as a "weak mouse" (line 555), "poor lamb" (line 677), and "frighted deer" (line 1149).

Arguing Over the "Argument"

The Rape of Lucrece is prefaced by a plot summary or "Argument," but not all of the actions it describes make it into the poem. This suggests either that Shakespeare did not write the Argument, or that he wanted to provide an official narrative that would then offset his own less political, more psychologically realized poem.

The Poem and its Audiences

Despite being initially popular (it was reprinted six times before 1616) and inspiring dramatic imitations by Thomas Middleton and Thomas Heywood, *Lucrece* remains one of Shakespeare's most neglected works. One of its notable modern defenders was the poet Ted Hughes, who argued in his book *Shakespeare and the Goddess of Complete Being* (1992) that it was central to the dramatist's tragic vision. Since then, the poem has also found a slightly wider audience in performance. In 2008, for example, Gerard Logan gave a remarkable solo recitation at the Rose Theatre in London.

BELOW: *Benjamin Britten's opera* The Rape of Lucretia *is based on Andre Obey's 1931 play* Le Viol de Lucrece, *which was in turn inspired by Shakespeare's poem. Here, Lucretia attempts to ward off Tarquin's advances in a 2004 performance of the opera in London.*

The Passionate Pilgrim

WRITTEN *c.* pre-1598

FORMAT A collection of 20 poems

FORM Various, including sonnets and ballads

The Passionate Pilgrim is an assorted collection of 20 poems published by William Jaggard in 1599 and attributed to "W. Shakespeare." However, only five have been positively identified as actually written by Shakespeare himself. These are the two opening poems, which were later reprinted as Sonnets 138 and 144, and three poems taken from *Love's Labor's Lost*. Among the contemporaries of Shakespeare thought to have contributed the rest are Christopher Marlowe, Sir Walter Raleigh, and Richard Barnfield.

An Enthusiastic Audience

How Shakespeare first responded to this anthology is not recorded, but in 1612 when *The Passionate Pilgrim* was republished, the dramatist Thomas Heywood reported that Shakespeare was "much offended" with Jaggard for having "presumed to make so bold with his name." Various theories have been put forward as to its origins. It may be that Jaggard found a manuscript miscellany in which he recognized some Shakespearean poems and genuinely believed others to be by him also, or he may only have been able to find copies of five Shakespeare poems and decided to pass off others as his, even though some had already been printed under other names.

Jaggard's sense that there was an audience for a Shakespeare anthology was probably based not only on the popularity of his narrative poems but also on the praise of Shakespeare by clergyman and literary critic Francis Meres in his book *Palladis Tamia: Wits Treasury* (1598). In addition to his liberal praise of Shakespeare's work generally—asserting, for example, that "the sweet, witty soul of Ovid lives in mellifluous & honey-tongued Shakespeare"—Meres also observed that certain of Shakespeare's "sugred sonnets" were circulating "among his private friends," perhaps whetting a reader's appetite for the purchase of such poems.

The title that Jaggard gave his collection also strengthens its identification with Shakespeare. Meres had described the poet as "passionate in bewailing the perplexities of love," and readers might also have detected an allusion to *Romeo and Juliet* (published the year before) in which Juliet

POEM	AUTHOR	THEME/GENRE
1	Shakespeare (Sonnet 138)	Female duplicity
2	Shakespeare (Sonnet 144)	On his two loves—male and female
3	Shakespeare	Longaville's sonnet to Maria in *Love's Labor's Lost* (Act 4, Scene 3, lines 58–71)
4	Uncertain. Possibly Bartholomew Griffin	Venus's courtship of Adonis
5	Shakespeare	Berowne's sonnet to Rosaline in *Love's Labor's Lost* (Act 4, Scene 2, lines 105–18)
6	Unknown	Venus and Adonis
7	Unknown	On a deceitful mistress
8	Richard Barnfield	On music and poetry
9	Unknown	Venus and Adonis
10	Unknown	Elegy for a friend
11	Possibly Bartholomew Griffin	Venus and Adonis
12	Possibly Thomas Deloney	Contrast between youth and age
13	Unknown	On beauty
14	Unknown	Lovers' farewell
15	Unknown	On a woman's dilemma between two lovers
16	Shakespeare	Dumaine's poem to Katherine in *Love's Labor's Lost* (Act 4, Scene 3, lines 99–118)
17	Possibly Thomas Weelkes	Pastoral, mourning the end of love
18	Possibly Joseph Hall	On women's wiles
19	Christopher Marlowe and Sir Walter Raleigh	Pastoral love lyric
20	Richard Barnfield	Pastoral love lyric

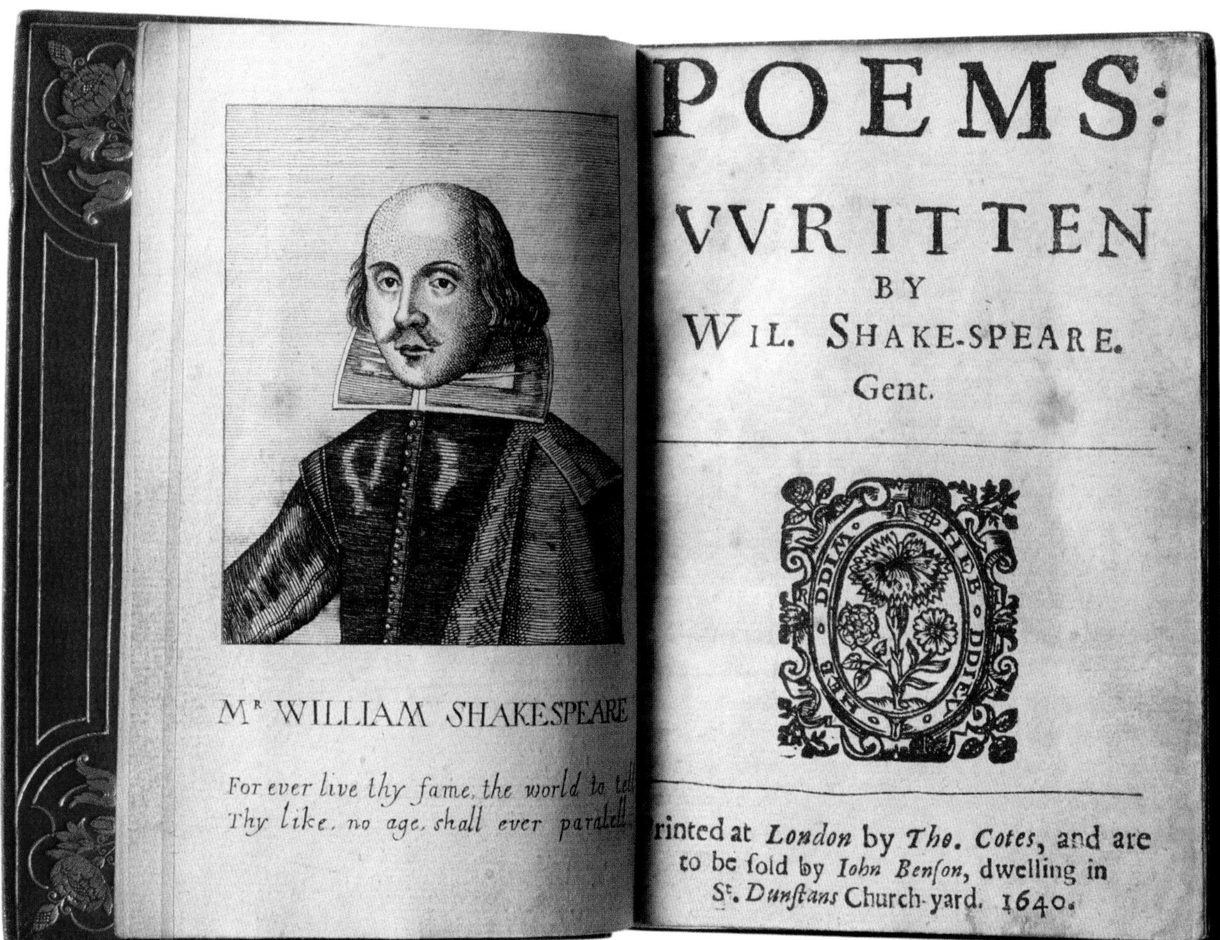

Mr WILLIAM SHAKESPEARE

For ever live thy fame, the world to tell
Thy like, no age, shall ever paralell.

POEMS:
VVRITTEN
BY
WIL. SHAKE-SPEARE.
Gent.

Printed at London by Tho. Cotes, and are to be sold by Iohn Benson, dwelling in St. Dunstans Church-yard. 1640.

LEFT: *John Benson's 1640 edition of Shakespeare's poems included several of the poems from* The Passionate Pilgrim, *as well as most of the sonnets, in addition to works by Ben Jonson, Christopher Marlowe, Sir Walter Raleigh, and others.*

addresses Romeo as "Good pilgrim" (*Romeo and Juliet,* Act 1, Scene 5, line 97).

Fashioning a Reputation

What is perhaps most interesting about the publication of *The Passionate Pilgrim* is the way in which it shaped Shakespeare's public image as a poet before the publication of the sonnets. Readers of *The Passionate Pilgrim* would have started with two of his most cynical sonnets: the first on the duplicity of the mistress and her "false-speaking tongue" (line 7), the second describing the fair youth and the dark lady as betraying the speaker. The theme of treachery and oath-breaking was then continued in Poem 7—"Fair is my love, but no so fair as fickle" (line 1)—and Poem 18 (written by authors unknown).

Shakespeare's fame as the creator of *Venus and Adonis* perhaps suggested the inclusion of the four Venus and Adonis poems (once thought to be by him but now often identified with Bartholomew Griffin), poems which would have strengthened Shakespeare's reputation as heir to the erotic Roman poet, Ovid, and reiterated his fondness for mythological tales. Above all, what unites the collection is its use of the first-person voice (appearing in 15 out of the 20 poems), perhaps intended to be read as that of Shakespeare himself.

On a day (alack the day!)/Love, whose month was ever May,/Spied a blossom passing fair,/Playing in the wanton air./Through the velvet leaves the wind/All unseen gan passage find,/That the lover, sick to death,/Wish'd himself the heavens' breath.

—*Poem 16* (LINES 1–8)

Who Was William Jaggard?

Jaggard (d. 1623) was a London printer and publisher, and an unscrupulous admirer of Shakespeare's work. Not only did he publish the unauthorized *Passionate Pilgrim,* but in 1619 he printed nine quartos of Shakespeare's plays for Thomas Pavier, whose intention to make them into a collection incurred the wrath of the King's Men. Nevertheless, when the company decided to produce their own collected works of Shakespeare, they turned to Jaggard, who published the First Folio in 1623.

The Phoenix and Turtle

WRITTEN c. 1601

LINES 67

STANZAS 18

FORM Quatrains and tercets

RIGHT: *The dove—or "turtle," meaning turtledove—may symbolize the Virgin Mary, or the Christian Church, in the poem. This depiction is from a nineteenth-century mosaic in the Basilica of the Rosary, part of the Sanctuary of Lourdes in France.*

THE PLOT: *The poem begins with a call to mourning for the phoenix and the turtledove, who represent an ideal of chaste, married, and indivisible love. The "bird of loudest lay" (perhaps another phoenix) requests the eagle, swan, and crow to attend, but deliberately excludes the owl and other birds of prey. An anthem follows, perhaps sung by the birds, in which the phoenix and turtledove's love is celebrated as a union that defied Reason by transforming two into one. In the final third, Reason responds with a "threnos," or mourning song, emphasizing what the world has lost through their extinction.*

The untitled lyric now known as *The Phoenix and Turtle* was first published in a collection of poems by Robert Chester called *Love's Martyr ... Allegorically Shadowing the Truth of Love in the Constant Fate of the Phoenix and Turtle* (1601). Shakespeare's contribution appears in the section entitled "Diverse Poeticall Essaies," whose contents are described as "newly written ... by the best and chiefest of our moderne writers," which includes George Chapman, Ben Jonson, and John Marston.

The poem has long invited a range of allegorical readings, partly on the basis that its protagonists are birds, and partly due to the elliptical description of the love between them, which may be read as Neoplatonic, religious, or political. Although there is some doubt as to whether Shakespeare wrote the whole poem, the "threnos" that bears his name is notably the most pessimistic section of the work, standing out from the other contributions in the volume for its insistence that "Truth and Beauty buried be" (line 64).

The Inseparable Lovers

The indivisibility of the lovers is depicted in the form of the poem itself, which merges a kind of epithalamium, or marriage song, with an elegy. In life, the phoenix and turtle were united by marriage, as suggested by the echo of the wedding service from the Book of Common Prayer: "Hearts remote, yet not asunder" (line 29). In death, they were consumed by one mutual fire (line 24), and are now united in the funeral urn:

Beauty, Truth, and Rarity,
Grace in all simplicity,
Here enclos'd, in cinders lie.
(LINES 53–55)

This imagery of love's union has been one of the focal points for allegorical readings of the poem. Critics have observed the Neoplatonic theory inherent in the notion of the turtledove "Flaming in the Phoenix' sight" (line 35), until they dissolve into one another.

The poem has also been read by some critics in Christian terms, as deploying the language of the Holy Trinity:

love in twain
Had the essence but in one,
Two distincts, division none:
Number there in love was slain.
(LINES 25–28)

Birds and Poets

The various contributors to *Love's Martyr* may be identified by the birds described in the opening to *The Phoenix and Turtle.* Shakespeare may have been "the bird of loudest lay" (line 1) given that he was the most famous. The "priest in surplice white" (line 13) might be John Marston, who would take holy orders in 1609, and the crow (line 17) George Chapman, who had published poems under the title *The Shadow of Night* (1594).

Moreover, the phoenix was a potential symbol of Christ, while the turtledove was identified with the Church, the Virgin Mary, or the soul. Thus, the union of the two might express the Church's betrothal to Christ.

Political Readings

The poem may also have had a more obvious political intent. *Love's Martyr* in its entirety was dedicated to Sir John Salusbury, a Welsh nobleman, who was a cousin of Queen Elizabeth. He was knighted by the queen for the part he played in suppressing the Essex rebellion in the same year as *Love's Martyr* was published, and he may even have commissioned the volume. In the course of 1601, Salusbury was trying to get elected as a Member of Parliament for Denbighshire, so the collection may have been intended to express the faithful love and service offered by the loyal turtledove (Salusbury) to "his queen" (line 31), Queen Elizabeth I.

While Shakespeare's poem clearly contributes to this panegyric—it may refer to Salusbury's parliamentary ambitions in the allusion to "this session" (line 9)—it is potentially subversive in its refusal to accept one of the phoenix's unique abilities: its power to rejuvenate. By 1601, when the poem was written, Elizabeth was too old to produce an heir and would refuse to name her successor until her deathbed. Poems of the 1590s to early 1600s written in her praise (among which we should include *Love's Martyr*) tended to obfuscate this political problem by poetic means, describing Elizabeth as a phoenix who would generate her own offspring, or rise again from the flames of her own destruction. Nevertheless, Shakespeare ends his poem with the prospect only of death, the pair "Leaving no posterity" (line 59). In this respect, he occupies the role of the owl, which was associated with the approach of death, in predicting the end of the Tudor dynasty.

The phoenix, which not only combined all virtues in one but was an emblem for chaste and eternal love, was a popular motif for Queen Elizabeth. In 1599, Thomas Holland observed in a sermon on the anniversary of her accession: "How rare a Phenix *[sic]* the Queen of England hath beene, & how bright a starre in these daies." Moreover, Shakespeare himself had referred to Elizabeth as such in his play *Henry VIII,* where she is described as a "maiden phoenix" (*Henry VIII,* Act 5, Scene 4, line 40).

Here the anthem
doth commence:/
Love and Constancy is dead.

(LINES 21–22)

Recent Views

More recently, some scholars have suggested that *The Phoenix and Turtle* may be a lament for a Catholic martyr, with its central pair modeled on a historical figure such as Robert Southwell, Henry Walpole, or Anne Lyne, who was executed in 1601. Other critics argue, however, that this is unlikely in a volume dedicated to John Salusbury, given Salusbury's need to disassociate himself from Catholicism to secure Elizabeth's continuing patronage, particularly since his brother, Thomas, had been executed in 1586 for his involvement in the plot to replace Elizabeth with Mary Stuart.

BELOW: *The so-called "Phoenix Portrait" of Queen Elizabeth I (c. 1575), attributed to court painter Nicholas Hilliard, includes a phoenix pendant in the center of the queen's breast, just above her hand.*

A Lover's Complaint

WRITTEN *c.* 1602–5
LINES 329
STANZAS 47
FORM Rhyme royal

THE PLOT: *The narrator overhears the lament of a young woman who weeps and casts love-gifts and letters into the river. An old man, grazing his cattle, sits down by the maid and asks her to explain her woes. She describes how she was seduced by a beautiful but promiscuous young man who insisted that all his previous relationships were based on lust, and that she was the first to have won his affections. Despite his subsequent betrayal, the maid confesses that were she to have the choice again, she might still be seduced by him.*

A Lover's Complaint is the shortest of all Shakespeare's narrative poems, published for the first time in the 1609 edition of his sonnets. Much recent criticism of *A Lover's Complaint* has focused on its possible connections with Shakespeare's sonnets, not least the similarity between their protagonists. The maid knows that the young man is promiscuous, but she is seduced by him anyway, just as Shakespeare's male speaker in the sonnets attests to the truth about his beloved's lack of chastity and yet cannot resist.

Rhetoric and Morality

Perhaps the poem's most obvious theme is its suspicion of rhetoric's affective power. On the one hand, elaborate speech is a source of pleasure. The unknown narrator lies down in order to appreciate the lament more fully, imitating the reader's own preparations to read/hear. On the other hand, it is the male lover's eloquence that proves the maid's undoing: "He had the dialect and different skill, / Catching all passions in his craft of will" (lines 125–26). The fact that the male seducer also uses gestures, such as weeping,

Thus merely with the garment of a Grace/The naked and concealed fiend he cover'd,/ That th' unexperient gave the tempter place,/Which like a cherubin above them hover'd./ Who, young and simple, would not be so lover'd?

(LINES 316–20)

RIGHT: *"In top of rage the lines she rents" (line 55): appearing wistful rather than vengeful in this watercolor from Charles Robinson's* Songs and Sonnets of Shakespeare *(c. 1915), the abandoned maid tears up her lover's letters and casts them into the river.*

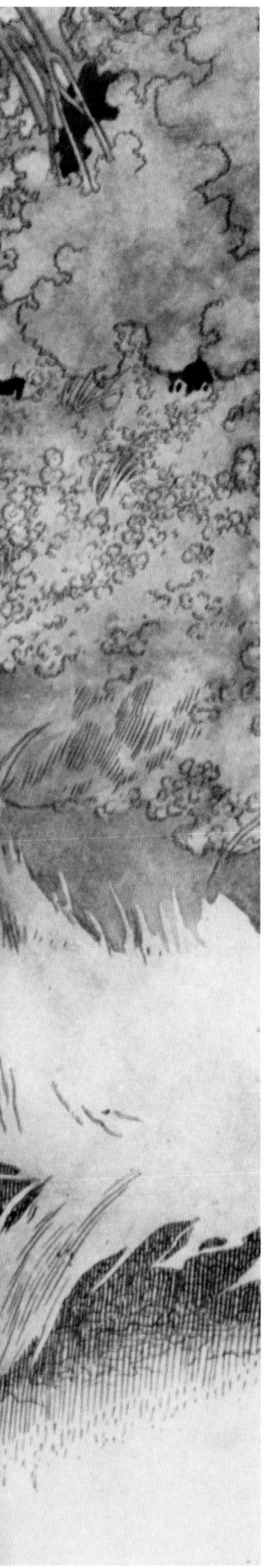

to convince the maid suggests that Shakespeare was commenting not only upon the poet's artifice (a theme that recurs in both *Venus and Adonis* and *The Rape of Lucrece*) but also upon the treacherous arts of the actor.

The poem also creates an intriguing moral ambiguity around the figure of the maid. In line 5, she is described as "fickle," most likely meaning "changeable," "disturbed," or "agitated," but also implying "morally unstable" in an allusion to her sexual fall. Moreover, at the end of the poem, she admits that the youth's eloquence and "false fire" (line 324) might entrance her again:

O, that sad breath his spungy lungs bestowed,
O, all that borrowed motion seeming owed,
Would yet again betray the fore-betray'd,
And new pervert a reconciled maid!
(LINES 326–29)

Does "reconciled" mean that she has atoned for her sin and been welcomed back by the church? Or does it mean "calmed" or "acquiescent" through the process of relating her story? It might be argued that in reliving the persuasions of her beloved, her passion has actually been re-aroused. In comparison with other complaints, Shakespeare's is unusually open-ended. The old man had asked the maid to speak in the hopes that he might assuage her suffering (lines 68–70), but we never hear him offer her advice; nor does the narrator reappear at the end to relate what the maid did next.

Changeable Imagery

The way in which tears and blood change their meaning in the poem suggests the difficulty of judging true from false emotion. The poem's location is watery, with the maid discovered by a river "Upon whose weeping margent she was set" (line 39). This was a conventional setting for the abandoned and/or betrayed female, recalling *Hamlet*'s Ophelia, and the "willow" song that Desdemona sings in *Othello* (Act 4, Scene 3). The river acted as a receptacle for the woman's tears, but also suggested that Nature sympathized with the protagonist's plight. In the course of Shakespeare's poem, however, water imagery (specifically tears) is co-opted by the male lover. It is partly the fact that he weeps that persuades the maid to abandon her chastity, causing her to expostulate to the old man:

O father, what a hell of witchcraft lies
In the small orb of one particular tear!
But with the inundation of the eyes
What rocky heart to water will not wear?
(LINES 288–91)

The Complaint Genre

A Lover's Complaint belongs to a genre of lyric poetry called the "complaint"—specifically, the "female complaint"—in which the protagonist describes her betrayal by a charming but unscrupulous seducer. Such poems were popularized by the collection *The Mirror for Magistrates* (1559, 1563), and by the ballad tradition. However, in the 1590s, the complaint also began to be associated with the sonnet sequence, providing a dual perspective on love. Where the sonnets featured a male speaker, blaming his chaste beloved for spurning his advances, the complaint gave the perspective of an unchaste woman who lamented the fact that she had succumbed to the male's rhetoric.

Similarly, the language of "blood" is initially deployed as a sign of heartfelt emotion. The maid possesses letters written in that substance, declaring "O false blood, thou register of lies" (line 52) before she tears them up, while the male lover describes the "rubies red as blood" (line 198) that he has been given as tokens of affection. However, blood becomes synonymous with lust when the male lover admits that his former seductions were only "errors of the blood, none of the mind; /Love made them not" (lines 184–85). The image of "proofs new-bleeding" in line 153 further reminds us of the shattered virginities that the fickle seducer leaves in his wake.

Critical Attention

Appreciation of *A Lover's Complaint* has been largely overshadowed by uncertainty about its authorship and by the relative inaccessibility of the text. It is only from the 1960s onward that the poem has received any sustained critical attention. Since then, it has been discussed alongside the rest of Shakespeare's poetry and in relation to his plays, particularly *Hamlet* and *All's Well That Ends Well* which share some thematic similarities in their depiction of women seduced and spurned by men.

Doubtful Authorship

Shakespeare's authorship of *A Lover's Complaint* continues to be disputed, partly on the basis of stylistic tests and partly due to the unreliability of Thomas Thorpe, its original publisher. In 2007, Brian Vickers argued that the poem was actually written by John Davies of Hereford.

The Sonnets

Shakespeare remains the chief practitioner of the English or Shakespearean sonnet. No ordinary love poems, Shakespeare's sonnets analyze love's many facets, and evoke emotions ranging from joy, hope, and desire to despair, shame, and frustration. Four centuries old, these rich and passionate poems continue to speak to and for lovers across the world.

Introduction

Shake-speares Sonnets. Never before Imprinted appeared as a quarto volume published by Thomas Thorpe of London, in 1609. It constituted a group of 154 sonnets and a long poem entitled *A Lover's Complaint*.

It is unclear whether the publication of *The Sonnets* was authorized by the poet. It is possible, although most scholars believe that it is unlikely, that the text of the 1609 volume was arranged and printed without Shakespeare's involvement.

The Sonnet Vogue

The sequence appeared conspicuously late: the sonnet vogue was at its height in the 1590s. Nevertheless, in several crucial ways, *Shake-speares Sonnets* were innovative and new rather than derivative and outmoded.

Most obviously, this sonnet sequence is barely a sequence at all. It contains a distinct group of sonnets (1–17) that seek to persuade an unnamed fair young man to marry and procreate, a larger group of love poems addressed apparently to the same young man (18–126), several poems focused on the poet's competition for the young man's love/patronage with an unidentified rival poet (78–80 and 82–86), and a further group of sonnets that are concerned with the poet's tawdry affair with an anonymous dark mistress (127–54).

ABOVE: *There has been some speculation that Nicholas Hilliard's* Young Man Leaning Against a Tree Among Roses *(c. 1588) is a portrait of Robert Devereux, Earl of Essex, and possibly the "fair young man" of the sonnets.*

Generic Conventions

Typically, sonnet sequences of Shakespeare's time were addressed to an idealized—but unavailable—female beloved, and focused on an unending and frustrated desire. Shakespeare's sonnets were radically different: they addressed both a male and a female beloved, revealed the imperfections of both beloveds, suggested the inconstancy of love, and explored both heterosexual and homoerotic desire.

In marked contrast to the chief model for sonnet sequences—Petrarch's *Canzoniere,* which was written in the mid-fourteenth century and describes the endurance of the poet's love for Laura, even years after her death—Shakespeare explores love's changing courses, and its capacity to debase rather than ennoble man. The fair and beautiful beloved is problematically transformed into a promiscuous, vain, and powerful man. Meanwhile, the poet's mistress is dark rather than fair-haired and she appears—most famously in Sonnet 130—as a parody of Petrarch's Laura. The dark lady's eyes are:

nothing like the sun;
Coral is far more red than her lips' red;
If snow be white, why then her breasts
are dun;
If hairs be wires, black wires grow on
her head.

(LINES 1–4)

SHAKE-SPEARES

SONNETS.

Neuer before Imprinted.

AT LONDON
By G. Eld for T. T. and are
to be solde by Iohn Wright, dwelling
at Christ Church gate.
1609.

LEFT: *This is the title page of* Shake-speares Sonnets, *published in 1609 by Thomas Thorpe—"T.T"—and "solde by John Wright," a London bookseller. Thorpe was an unorthodox publisher, never owning a printery or bookshop, instead commissioning printers and licensing booksellers to sell his books. He also published Christopher Marlowe, Ben Jonson, and George Chapman.*

Although she is subjected to the conventional blazon, or description, of her features, this dark mistress does not merely lack Laura's fair coloring (red lips, pale skin, and blonde hair), rather she precisely inverts those characteristics. Likewise, although she causes the poet sexual frustration, this is not because she denies him sex, but rather because—in sleeping with him—she infects him with lust (and possibly with a venereal disease, as Sonnet 129 infamously suggests).

Date and Structure

Although first published as a sequence in 1609, it is not clear when the sonnets were written, and their structural and thematic relationship to one another also remains uncertain. External evidence suggests that they were not composed as a whole sequence after the vogue of the 1590s, but rather in clusters over a decade or more.

We know that some of the sonnets were circulating by 1598, when, in his commonplace book *Palladis Tamia: Wits Treasury,* Francis Meres alluded to manuscript copies of Shakespeare's "sugred Sonnets" being read among a group of "private friends." (The Meres book also lists Shakespeare's plays up until 1598.)

Early versions of Sonnets 138 and 144 were published in a volume of poetry, *The Passionate Pilgrim,* in 1599, and it is probable that a number of others were composed around the same time, when the plague forced the closure of the theaters in London and Shakespeare may have turned to writing patronage poetry for wealthy aristocrats, such as Henry Wriothesley, Earl of Southampton.

Shakespeare's sonnets, unusually among sonnet sequences, vary considerably in style and tone. Some—including the widely anthologized Sonnet 18 ("Shall I compare thee to a summer's day?")—recall the style and idealistic themes of the Elizabethan cycles, even though the "beloved" is problematically male. Others—the acerbically misogynistic Sonnet 135 ("Whoever hath her wish, thou hast thy *Will*"), for example—are deeply cynical in tone; they focus intensely on betrayals and disappointments suffered by the poet, evoking feelings of profound disillusion. Full of the language of disease and economics, signaling a concern with the prostitution of both love and of poetry, such sonnets are far removed from the Petrarchan conventions. Indeed, their preoccupations are often those of contemporary satire. In Sonnet 137 ("Thou blind fool, Love, what dost thou to mine eyes"), then, the poet images the mistress's body as a "bay where all men ride" (line 6), suggesting a promiscuous woman, and he deploys plague metaphors in order to articulate the corruption of desire in the modern city.

ABOVE: *The frontispiece of a fifteenth-century edition of* Canzoniere, *love sonnets to Laura by the Italian Francesco Petrarch (1304–74), includes a portrait of the poet.*

Shakespeare's Complaint

When *The Sonnets* were first published they were followed in the same collection by *A Lover's Complaint.* This 329-line narrative poem belongs to a genre of lyric poetry known as the "female complaint," in which a woman laments the tragic events of her life. Shakespeare was following the two-part structure common among English sonneteers, and which originates with Samuel Daniel's publication in 1592 of *Delia ... with the Complaint of Rosamund.*

Scholars disagree about the strength of the formal connections between *The Sonnets* and *A Lover's Complaint.* Indeed, modern editors often omit the *Complaint,* doubting it is Shakespeare's work. Nevertheless, *The Sonnets* and *A Lover's Complaint* share significant stylistic features as well as strong thematic connections. Moreover, they both break with convention by neglecting to name the beloved and the complainant. Their complementary plays on gender implicitly align male and female experiences of love, and both feature speakers—opposite in their genders—who are faithful lovers of a narcissistic and promiscuous man who sexually betrays them.

Themes, Allusions, and Imagery

The cryptic title page of *Shake-speares Sonnets* announces a mystery that has compelled readers over the centuries. The dedication appears as an inscription; it is addressed to the "ONLIE. BEGETTER. OF. THESE. INSUING. SONNETS. MR. W. H." The sonnets are evidently intended to deliver "THAT. ETERNITIE. PROMISED. BY. OUR. EVER-LIVING. POET." to the dedicatee of the poems. But who is "Mr. W. H."?

Recent editors of the sonnets have tended to favor William Herbert, Earl of Pembroke, as the most likely "Mr. W. H."—he is known to be Shakespeare's patron and was the dedicatee of the First Folio edition of Shakespeare's works, which was published in 1623. Another likely contender is Henry Wriothesley, Earl of Southampton, to whom Shakespeare had dedicated his narrative poems *Venus and Adonis* and *The Rape of Lucrece* in the 1590s. It has also been suggested that "W. H." is simply a printing error, or a pun on the poet's name, denoting "William Himself."

Mystery identities aside, we might think of the dedication to *Shake-speares Sonnets* as its own paradox: it claims to deliver on a promise to immortalize the man who inspired them, but it fails to reveal his identity. Indeed, the only man who really receives the "eternitie" promised in the dedication is the "ever-living poet" himself—the sonnets are finally *Shake-speares*.

The Personae of the Sonnets

When—in a sonnet published in 1827—William Wordsworth warned the critic to "Scorn not the Sonnet," he specifically admonished the failure to comprehend the worth of a poetic form that was used by Petrarch to "ease [... love's] wound," and by Shakespeare to "unlock ... his heart." For Wordsworth, as for most contemporary readers, *The Sonnets* express deeply personal sentiments

LEFT: *This portrait of Henry Wriothesley, Earl of Southampton, was made during his imprisonment in the Tower of London for supporting the Earl of Essex's 1601 rebellion. Wriothesley, one of Shakespeare's patrons, is sometimes proposed as the dedicatee of* The Sonnets.

RIGHT: *This dedication in the first printing of* Shake-speares Sonnets *has mystified scholars for centuries. Who is "Mr. W. H."?*

TO.THE.ONLIE.BEGETTER.OF.
THESE.INSVING.SONNETS.
M^r.W.H. ALL.HAPPINESSE.
AND.THAT.ETERNITIE.
PROMISED.
BY.
OVR.EVER-LIVING.POET.
WISHETH.
THE.WELL-WISHING.
ADVENTVRER.IN.
SETTING.
FORTH.

T. T.

born of real psychological suffering. But should we read them as autobiographical in nature, as keys to Shakespeare's life? Rightly or wrongly, readers have tended to find the temptation to do so impossible to resist. As well as the attempts to discover the identity of "Mr. W. H.," speculation about the identities of *The Sonnets'* other personae continues, driven perhaps by the sense that these 154 sonnets hold the key to all the mysteries of the life of Shakespeare.

Apart from the poet himself, the three chief personae of *Shake-speares Sonnets* are the fair young man, who dominates the early sonnets; the dark lady or mistress, who features in those sonnets beginning with Sonnet 127; and the rival poet, who is introduced in Sonnet 78.

As the fair young man is urged by the poet to marry and reproduce himself in Sonnets 1 to 17, he is often identified as an aristocrat and, possibly, "Mr. W. H." himself. Addressed in Sonnet 20 as the "master mistress" of the poet's passion (line 2), and praised as his "all the world" in Sonnet 112 (line 5), the young man is an object of homoerotic desire; even after declaring him a subject that is "too dear" for his "possessing" in Sonnet 87 (line 1), it is very clear that the poet cannot let him go.

Nevertheless, the poet is also involved with the dark lady, who is described in terms of sexual obsession in Sonnet 129. In Sonnet 134, the poet expresses fears this apparently voracious mistress has stolen the young man from him. Deploying one of many economic metaphors of the sequence, in this sonnet the poet complains that though the young man "pays the whole" (line 14) by sleeping with the poet's mistress—ostensibly in order to "free" (line 14) the poet from the mistress's will, to which he is "mortgag'd" (line 2)—the mistress does not relinquish either of the men, but rather keeps and enjoys both of them. "[T]hou hast both him and me" (line 13), the poet complains rather desperately, before launching into an explicit reflection about her "large and spacious" genitals/sexual appetite in the next poem (Sonnet 135, line 5).

BELOW: *William Herbert, 3rd Earl of Pembroke, may have been the "Mr. W. H." to whom* The Sonnets *is dedicated. Herbert had an affair with Mary Fitton, who some believe to be the dark lady.*

As with the fair young man, there have been attempts to identify the dark lady with a real person—Elizabeth I's maid of honor, Mary Fitton, and the poet Aemilia Lanyer have been popular suggestions—but she is finally an abstraction of carnal desire, described as a "hell" to which the poet is drawn by his sensual appetites (Sonnet 129, line 14).

As for the rival poet, scholars have made cases for Christopher Marlowe, George Chapman, and Samuel Daniel, among others, but the man who, we assume, uses the "new-found methods" mentioned in Sonnet 76 (line 4) of praise to compete for the young man's love (Sonnets 78 to 86) is ultimately indistinct. Indeed, he might not even be singular, but rather be representative of all the poet's rivals for the young man's affections and/or for patronage of an influential supporter.

The Poetic "I"

Even if the personae of *Shake-speares Sonnets* ultimately function as abstractions, readers invariably find it a challenge to separate the poems' poetic "I" from Shakespeare himself. In that regard, they are encouraged by the poet's frequent punning on "Will"—as in Sonnet 135, in which he exploits the word's multiple meanings to advance a crude joke about the mistress's sexual appetite—as well as the apparent connection between *The Sonnets'* "onlie begetter" and the fair young man that they address. Naturally, that has led to some claims that *The Sonnets* suggest Shakespeare was either bisexual or homosexual, and to readings of the poems as psychological explorations of the actual life experiences of Shakespeare.

Narcissus Figures

Throughout *The Sonnets,* and especially in the "procreation" sequence (Sonnets 1 to 17), Shakespeare makes use of the myth of Narcissus as it is rendered by the Roman epic poet Ovid in *Metamorphoses*. Like Narcissus, the fair young man is imagined as having fallen in love with his own image—in Sonnet 4, he is a "beauteous niggard" (line 5) because he has "traffic" only with himself (line 9), thus causing the destructive waste of his "unus'd beauty" (line 13). The young man is not the only Narcissus figure in *The Sonnets.* The poet himself confesses the "[s]in of self-love" (line 1) in Sonnet 62, and explores the idea that—in loving the young man—he, too, is guilty of a form of narcissism, because he sees himself in, or projects himself onto, his portrait of the young man, which he adores.

LEFT: *In Ovid's Narcissus myth, the young man falls in love with his own image in a pool, as in this fresco from Pompeii. Realizing his love can never be acted upon, he dies, fulfilling a prophecy that he was doomed if he "come to know himself".*

The Nature of Love and Desire

Even those who deny that Shakespeare's *Sonnets* should be read in these autobiographical terms tend to agree that the persona of the poet is a means for Shakespeare to articulate his true feelings about the nature of love. In Sonnet 147, for example, the poet's apparent psychic division and suffering in a love, which he describes as a fever that leaves him pitiably "[p]ast cure … / And frantic mad with evermore unrest," is raw and powerful (lines 9–10).

The true relation of the sonnets to the life of Shakespeare cannot be known, of course, but their exploration of the compulsions and contradictions of erotic love is nevertheless compelling. To take an important example, in Sonnet 20 the young man is figured as a hermaphrodite, and advances a joke that his physical perfection is marred for the poet by nature's one selfish "addition"—a phallus:

And for a woman wert thou first created,
Till Nature as she wrought thee fell a-doting,
And by addition me of thee defeated,
By adding one thing to my purpose nothing.
(LINES 9–12)

The sonnet's ingenuity may provoke a reader's smile, but it has a real point to make about the arbitrary nature of desire. The poet's mourning that his love has been "prick'd … out for women's pleasure" (line 13), and his attempt to comfort himself with the idea that only he truly possesses the youth's "love," draw the reader into the poet's exploration of desire's potential for destruction.

The Poet's Two Loves

In Sonnet 144 the poet famously images his "Two loves" (line 1) as angels: "The better angel is a man right fair, / The worser spirit a woman color'd ill" (lines 3–4). Imagining the two loves in the vein of the contradictory Virtue and Vice figures from a medieval morality play, he depicts them in battle for control of his psyche:

To win me soon to hell, my female evil
Tempteth my better angel from my [side],
And would corrupt my saint to be a devil,
Wooing his purity with her foul pride.
(LINES 5–8)

Nevertheless, the polarized perspective of the poet cannot be sustained because the good angel is not sufficiently virtuous or true to resist the temptations of the bad angel. The poet suspects, in fact, that his two loves have been engaged in an affair that will only be revealed at such time as the young man manifests the symptoms of syphilis—in other words, when his "bad angel fire[s]" his "good one out" (line 14).

The sonnet is unique in that it compares the young man and the dark lady directly, and because it illuminates the nature of the love triangle that defines the poet's experience of desire. His doubt now about his own capacity to distinguish fair, good, true, from black, bad, false is tangible and interconnects with a broader anxiety about authenticity that runs throughout.

In Sonnet 17 the poet imagines that "[t]he age to come would say, 'This poet lies['"] (line 7); and in Sonnet 84 he expresses to the young man regret that language is finally inadequate in articulating the truth—"that you alone are you" (line 2). By Sonnet 144, the lines between fair, good, true, and black, bad, false have been blurred to such an extent that the poet fears they have collapsed altogether: he articulates his disillusionment and disorientation through a disturbing image of the young man coupling with the dark mistress: "... being both from me, both to each friend, / I guess one angel in another's hell" (lines 11–12).

Problems of Authenticity

His concern with authenticity regularly leads the poet to torturous self-analysis. When it does, he focuses typically on two destructive aspects of his desire: namely, that it cannot be satisfied, and that it distorts his judgment and deprives him of clear sight. In turn, those twin concerns unsettle his faith in true love (or the truth of his love/lover), and also in the integrity of his verse. In the final sonnets of the sequence, the poet complains that "cunning Love" has made him incapable of reason (Sonnet 148, line 13). Blinded by love, he reflects that his own eye has caused him ("I") to perjure himself (Sonnet 152, line 6).

The poet's perjury appears to be related to his praising the dark mistress; however, the validity of his praise of the young man is also in doubt. Sonnets 40 to 42, for example, suggest that the young man has betrayed the poet's love by stealing his mistress, while Sonnets 78 to 86 express fears that the poet has lost the affections/patronage of

ABOVE: *US stage actress Katharine Cornell is pictured here as Mary Fitton—thought to be the "dark lady"—in English dramatist Clemence Dane's* Will Shakespeare. *The play enjoyed a long run in London in the 1920s.*

BELOW: *The subject of* Allegory of Vice and Virtue *by Anthuenis Claeissens (1536–1613) would have been very familiar to Shakespeare's readers in the 1600s: from the Middle Ages, the Vices and Virtues personified often played major roles in morality plays.*

the young man to a rival poet. Particularly because his addressee is socially superior, younger, and evidently more physically attractive than the poet, who has described himself as "chopp'd with tann'd antiquity" (Sonnet 62, line 10), he is frequently worried that his praise is transmuted to flattery. Thus, in Sonnet 72, he declares that he is "sham'd by that which I bring forth" (line 13), and goes on, in Sonnet 84, to castigate the young man for his vanity, which makes the true praise of the poet appear as flattery.

Nevertheless, when he finds that his verse is in competition with that of a rival poet, and feels that the young man has slighted his love/verse in favor of fresher praise, the poet claims that the great strength of his writing rests in its sincerity, constancy, and truth. Specifically, in Sonnet 82, those qualities readily distinguish it from the "gross painting" of his rival (line 13). Rhetorically excusing the young man for seeking some "fresher stamp" (line 8), on the grounds that the poet's skill in praise cannot match its subject's virtues, the poet nevertheless implies that he alone is capable of rendering the young man faithfully:

Thou, truly fair, wert truly sympathiz'd
In true plain words by thy true-telling friend;
And their gross painting might be better us'd
Where cheeks need blood, in thee it is
abus'd.

(LINES 11–14)

Poetic Reticence

Deploying the topos, or theme, of inexpressibility, the poet claims that his reticence in praise articulates his true love—his "dumb thoughts, speaking in effect" (Sonnet 85, line 14). After a period of absence, in which his verse is apparently impoverished, the poet returns to penning praise of the fair youth in Sonnet 105. In these lines he denies that his love is idolatrous, and once again he asserts the truth of his verse:

Kind is my love to-day, to-morrow kind,
Still constant in a wondrous excellence,
Therefore my verse, to constancy confin'd,
One thing expressing, leaves out difference.
"Fair," "kind," and "true" is all my argument,
"Fair," "kind," and "true" varying to other
words,
And in this change is my invention spent,
Three themes in one, which wondrous scope
affords.

(LINES 5–12)

BELOW: *Shakespeare's contemporary, the dramatist, poet, and translator George Chapman, is a strong candidate to be the "rival poet" of* The Sonnets.

Despite the poet's claim that the truth of his love is beyond expression, the poet repeats his sentiments through several sonnets; and, though he is at pains to assert that the fairness, kindness, and truth of the youth, and praise of the youth, is all he can write about, 22 sonnets later he shifts his attention to a mistress.

Time and Endurance in Shakespeare's Sonnets

That inconsistency connects with an important theme in *The Sonnets*: time and the (in)capacity of love to endure. Early in *The Sonnets*, the poet has promised to preserve the young man/his love against the ravages of time in his "eternal lines" (Sonnet 18, line 12), and he famously defines true love in opposition to fickle change in Sonnet 116, as he asserts that "love is not love / Which alters when it alteration finds" (lines 2–3). Again, in Sonnet 123, he is confident of his love's victory, when he addresses time as an adversary and insists that he will never be able to "boast" of the poet's changeability in love (line 1). Nevertheless, the transformative power of Time's "continual haste" (line 12) is finally inevitable, and the poet does admit that he can only "be true despite [Time and his] scythe" (line 14).

The sonnets generally avoid particularities, but in Sonnet 104 there is an unusual reference to the young man's ageing, the poet specifically assuring the youth that "[t]hree winters cold" (line 3) have done nothing to detract from his beauty and that—to the poet at least—he "never can be old" (line 1). Even this, however, is qualified with a reference to the inevitability of change. The poet wonders at the youth's apparent sameness since he first saw him "fresh" (line 8) three years earlier, and concludes that his own eye "may be deceiv'd" (line 12) for, though "no pace [is] perceiv'd" (line 10) in the young man's decline, his "sweet hue" (line 11) nevertheless has "motion" (line 12).

A similar paradox is evident in Sonnet 107 in the allusion to Queen Elizabeth I as the "mortal moon" (line 5). Usually understood to refer to Elizabeth's death in 1603 and the beginning of a "balmy time" of peace under the first Stuart king, James I (which turned out to be somewhat of an illusion), this sonnet images Queen Elizabeth as the changeable but eternally cyclical moon, who is constant even in death. The endurance of the virgin queen beyond her "eclipse" (line 5) affirms the power of art to preserve mortal greatness against time, but it also imagines a world that is enduring continual change.

BELOW: *The funeral procession of Queen Elizabeth I in 1603 marked the end of the great Elizabethan period of renaissance. It is thought that Shakespeare alluded to the queen's death in Sonnet 107.*

Significance and Influence

ABOVE: *The 1998 film* Shakespeare in Love *starred Joseph Fiennes as Shakespeare and Gwyneth Paltrow as his love. It includes a scene in which the young Shakespeare starts a sonnet with "Shall I compare thee to a summer's day?"*

Shakespeare's sonnets were not widely read in their own age. In fact, when an opportunistic John Benson republished most of the sonnets in 1640 in a volume that also included a selection of other poems by Shakespeare and some of his contemporaries, the publisher was famously able to get away with asserting that they had never been published before. In the late eighteenth century, the Shakespeare scholar Edmond Malone returned readers to the original quarto text of 1609, but in the intervening years Benson's now discredited text had been the standard.

When we consider how significantly Benson's volume varied from the quarto in its arrangement—for example, the prominent Sonnet 18 was among several of the sonnets that were omitted entirely, others appeared out of the original order, and Benson replaced several male pronouns with female ones to make the sequence correspond with the expectations of the genre—we can get a sense of how unsatisfactory that situation was. Unsurprisingly, the publication of the far more careful and scholarly edition of the poems by Malone in 1780 signaled a turning point in *The Sonnets'* history and popularity.

In Obscurity

The Sonnets was almost entirely forgotten among Shakespeare's works in the eighteenth century—partly because of the want of an authoritative text, partly because the sonnet form was unfashionable until its revival by the Romantic poets in the late eighteenth and the early nineteenth centuries, and partly because the sonnets Shakespeare wrote did not conform to the conventions of love poetry.

After the death of John Milton in 1674, the next widely acclaimed practitioner of the sonnet was not writing for over a century. But, early in his career, even William Wordsworth expressed concerns that the sonnet form was "tedious" and suggested that it was an outdated mode of poetic expression—quaint rather than innovative, and obscure rather than direct and engaging. In 1827, however, he published his famous "Scorn not the Sonnet," in which he imagined the sonnets as keys with which Shakespeare "unlocked his heart." Along with Malone's editing of the quarto text, that defense of the sonnet by Wordsworth, with specific reference to Shakespeare's innovative use of the form, marked a watershed moment in the history of *The Sonnets*.

Love in the Nineteenth Century

John Keats continued the trend Wordsworth had begun; although he never achieved widespread acclaim for his writing during his own lifetime, and despite his own criticism of the sonnets' "dull rhymes," Keats wrote several sonnets that are now considered to be among his finest poems. His beautiful reflection on temporality and love in "When I have fears that I may cease to be" (1816) is Shakespearean, not only in form but also in its thematic focus and its emotional intensity. Shortly before he died in 1821, Keats wrote "Bright Star," a reflection on constancy and love's immortality, which picks up Shakespeare's cosmic metaphors of "those gold candles fix'd in heaven's air" (Sonnet 21, line 12). Poignantly, Keats wrote his sonnet on a page in a copy of *The Sonnets* that had been gifted to him by a close friend, which suggests that Shakespeare's poetry—and *The Sonnets* in particular—was already associated, in Keats's mind at least, with what W.H. Auden would term "naked autobiographical confession."

It is that characteristic intensity of feeling that arguably led to *The Sonnets'* widespread popularity in the nineteenth century and, especially, in the twentieth century. The influence of Shakespeare is apparent in the sonnets of countless poets, such as Henry Wadsworth Longfellow, Oscar Wilde, Elizabeth Barrett Browning, and Christina Rossetti. The latter's evocative "Remember Me" specifically echoes Sonnet 71's complex memorializing urge to the young man not to mourn the death of the poet, but rather to let him "be forgot" in his "sweet thoughts" (line 7). As Rossetti's poem testifies, and as Matthew Arnold claimed in his sonnet on "Shakespeare" published in 1849, Shakespeare's poetry was understood to articulate universal suffering: all "pains the immortal spirit must endure" thus found their voice in his work, and thus Shakespeare's sonnets found great and varied contemporary relevance.

Sex, the Law, and Poetry

As many commentators note, George Steevens's refusal to include the sonnets in his 1793 edition of Shakespeare's works probably marks the first real moral objection to the homoeroticism of the sequence. Overlooked in part in the Victorian period because of their ambiguous representations of love, the sonnets were considered unwholesome, and poets such as Robert Browning were thus considered to be far more accomplished—and, of course, respectable. As a result, Shakespeare was only acclaimed as a dramatist.

In 1889, however, Oscar Wilde published *The Portrait of Mr. W. H.,* a story confronting the debate about the homoeroticism of Shakespeare's poetry

LEFT: *John Keats, portrayed on his deathbed in 1821 by Joseph Severn, employed the sonnet form in the early nineteenth century.*

BELOW: *One of the first Americans to write widely in the sonnet form, Henry Wadsworth Longfellow wrote a memorial sonnet on the death of his second wife, "The Cross of Snow."*

directly. Taking the identity questions surrounding the sonnets as the inspiration for his fiction, Wilde has his story revolve around an assertion that "Mr. W. H." was William Hughes, a young actor with whom Shakespeare is represented as having had a physical relationship. Despite *The Sonnets'* obvious homoerotic tone and concerns, the story by Wilde marked the first direct assertion that their author was engaged in homosexual relations, and that *The Sonnets* was begotten, so to speak, by a homosexual lover. When Wilde was put on trial for his own transgressive sexuality six years later, in 1895, however, he effectively denied that reading by referring to Shakespeare's sonnets as examples of the Greek tradition of platonic love between men, and by using that argument as a means of defending his own relationships with men.

Following the legalization of homosexuality in 1967 in Britain (though much later in the United States and elsewhere), the reception of *The Sonnets* shifted significantly, and contemporary culture now tends to embrace the homoeroticism of the poems, often struggling more to reconcile itself with the explicit misogyny of the sequence.

The Sonnets and Modern Love

In contemporary culture, Sonnets 18 and 116, in particular, have been appropriated as models for modern love, and both are among those most regularly reprinted and adapted. Sonnet 18 has arguably been rendered a cliché of love by throw-away appearances (often just the first few lines are recited) in such films as *Dead Poets Society* (1989, directed by Peter Weir), *Clueless* (1995, directed by Amy Heckerling), and *Shakespeare in Love* (1998, directed by John Madden).

Yet, when adapted sensitively, as in the 2006 film *Venus* (directed by Roger Michell), in which Peter O'Toole, as Maurice, reads the complete Sonnet 18 to the too-young object of his desire, the poem remains a captivating expression of love and beauty as vehicles for battling the inevitable ravages of time. Addressed to "Venus," the sonnet is reimagined as an articulation of Maurice's compelling desire for youth and love (for Venus, goddess of love), even in the face of old age and death. Perhaps, too, it attains a new relevance in a vanity-driven society in which beauty is an insistent mantra. Confronted with the odd pairing of an aged and failing Maurice and a young, unpredictable Venus, the audience is forced to reassess the relationship between beauty and love, and led to question the power of love to conquer time, which finds such confident expression in the eternizing conceit of Sonnet 18:

But thy eternal summer shall not fade,
Nor lose possession of that fair thou ow'st,
Nor shall Death brag thou wand'rest in
his shade,

Sci-fi's Shakespeare

Among many appropriations of Shakespeare's *Sonnets* in popular culture, sci-fi television series warrant special mention.

Star Trek is littered with Shakespearean references, and some of the sonnets have even been translated into the fictional language of "Klingon." In *The Next Generation* series, Captain Jean-Luc Picard regularly refers to his personal copy of Shakespeare's works and, in episodes entitled "Perfect Mate" and "Ménage à Troi," quotes from *The Sonnets* in order to analyze the transformative nature of desire.

An episode of *Doctor Who* entitled "The Shakespeare Code" reflects humorously on the absurdity of academic debate about *The Sonnets'* mysteries and what they may or may not indicate about the sexuality of Shakespeare. The episode implies Shakespeare's/the poet's homosexuality—he flirts with Doctor Who—and plays with *The Sonnets'* history of floating gender pronouns. It also emphasizes the importance of the idea that it might be possible to "decode" them. "Shakespeare" thus produces Sonnet 18—the most famous sonnet of the young man sequence—to farewell Martha, the Doctor's assistant and the "dark lady" of the episode.

LEFT: *In* Star Trek: The Next Generation, *the Shakespearean actor Patrick Stewart, playing Captain Jean-Luc Picard (center front), keeps his copy of* The Complete Works *close.*

LEFT: *In the 2006 film* Venus, *directed by Roger Michell, Peter O'Toole's character reads the whole of Sonnet 18 to his much younger lover, played by Jodie Whittaker.*

When in eternal lines to time thou grow'st.
So long as men can breathe or eyes can see,
So long lives this, and this gives life to thee.
(LINES 9–14)

The Sonnets in the Marketplace

Commonly referenced in popular television, in film, and in print, Shakespeare's *Sonnets* have been published in 52 languages around the world, and they have run through more than 1,500 editions since Thorpe's text of 1609. New editions of Shakespeare's sequence appear every year, and selections of sonnets or single sonnets feature in poetry anthologies too numerous to estimate. The sequence continues to be mined by the print industry for quotable lines on love, and variously reproduced in and on everything, from greeting cards to coffee-table books. Intertextual references to *The Sonnets* appear in many modern novels, including Virginia Woolf's *To the Lighthouse* (1927), Anthony Burgess's *Nothing Like the Sun* (1964), and Lennard J. Davis's *The Sonnets: A Novel* (*c.* 2001).

Audio readings of *The Sonnets* on tape and compact disk have been produced by Penguin (1995) and Airplay Audio (2000), to mention just two. Countless Internet sites include texts of individual sonnets or videos of sonnet readings: Alan Rickman can be found reading Sonnet 130 on YouTube, for example. Composers, including Igor Stravinsky and Benjamin Britten, have set sonnets to music; individual sonnets have become popular music recordings—including Brian Ferry's recording of Sonnet 18—and they have been the inspiration for popular songs, such as The Beatles' "In My Life," which was inspired by Sonnet 30. The Royal Shakespeare Company ran a major project, "Nothing Like the Sun," commissioning composers working in an eclectic range of styles to set *The Sonnets* to music in 2007.

LEFT: *Virginia Woolf references* The Sonnets *in her novel* To the Lighthouse. *In* A Room of One's Own, *Woolf famously suggests that when women have the freedom and space in which to write, "the dead poet who was Shakespeare's sister ... will be born."*

SHAKESPEAR
1623.

Reference

Timeline

YEAR	SHAKESPEARE'S LIFE	HISTORICAL AND LITERARY EVENTS
1558		Mary Tudor dies and is succeeded by Elizabeth I
1560		Publication of the Geneva Bible
1564	William Shakespeare is born in Stratford-upon-Avon. His date of birth is unknown, but assigned by tradition to April 23	
1567		Mary, Queen of Scots is compelled to abdicate, and James VI, her son, assumes the Scottish throne. Publication of Arthur Golding's translation of Ovid's *Metamorphoses*
1577–80		Sir Francis Drake sails round the world
1580		Publication of Michel de Montaigne's *Essais*
1582	Shakespeare marries Anne Hathaway, who is eight years his senior	
1583	Birth of Susanna, first child of William and Anne, five months after her parents' marriage	
1585	The twins, Judith and Hamnet, are born to William and Anne	
1585–92	Shakespeare leaves Stratford, joins a company of actors, and at some point takes up a theatrical career in London	
1586		First performance of Thomas Kyd's *The Spanish Tragedy* Death of Sir Philip Sidney
1588		Destruction of the Spanish Armada Publication of Thomas Hariot's *A Brief and True Report of [...] Virginia* First performance of Christopher Marlowe's *Doctor Faustus*
1589–90	Shakespeare probably begins to write his plays, possibly with *The Two Gentlemen of Verona* but perhaps with *Henry VI*. His plays' dates of composition are in most cases uncertain. Over roughly the next two decades he will write—or coauthor—a couple of plays every year	
1590		Publication of Sidney's *Arcadia* Publication of Edmund Spenser's *The Faerie Queene*, Books 1–3
1591		Publication of Sidney's *Astrophil and Stella*

YEAR	SHAKESPEARE'S LIFE	HISTORICAL AND LITERARY EVENTS
1592	Robert Greene's *A Groats-worth of Wit* famously derides Shakespeare as being an "upstart crow" in the world of the London theater Plague causes closure of the playhouses, and Shakespeare probably begins to write his nondramatic verse at this time	John Donne's earliest poems circulate in manuscript
1593	Shakespeare probably begins to write the *Sonnets*	Marlowe's *Hero and Leander* is entered in the Stationers' Register (but published in 1598) Death of Marlowe
1594	Shakespeare acts with the Lord Chamberlain's Men, along with celebrity performers William Kemp and Richard Burbage. At some point, Shakespeare becomes part-owner of that theatrical troupe *The Rape of Lucrece* is printed	
1596	Death of Hamnet	Publication of Spenser's *The Faerie Queene,* Books 4–6
1597	Shakespeare buys New Place in his native Stratford, the second-largest house in the town	
1599	The Lord Chamberlain's Men lease land on which they build the Globe theater. The playhouse opens in this year	Death of Spenser
1601	The Lord Chamberlain's Men are paid to perform *Richard II* the day before the Earl of Essex stages his failed rebellion. They are deemed not to be involved in the plot and are not punished	
1603	King James grants a patent to the Lord Chamberlain's Men. They take the title the "King's Men" to honor their new patron	Death of Elizabeth I and succession of James VI of Scotland as James I of England
1605		Failure of the Gunpowder Plot, an attempt by Catholic conspirators to blow up Parliament and assassinate King James
1608	The King's Men lease the Blackfriars theater, which had permanent roofing and artificial lighting. However, in this year and through the next, London theaters close because of an outbreak of plague	
1609	Publication of *Shake-speares Sonnets*. It is not known whether publication of the *Sonnets* is authorized by Shakespeare	
1611		Publication of the Authorized Version ("King James" Version) of the Bible
1613	The Globe theater is destroyed by fire	Publication of Elizabeth Cary's *The Tragedy of Mariam*
1616	Death of Shakespeare, in April. He is buried in Holy Trinity Church, Stratford-upon-Avon, on the 25th of that month	Publication of Ben Jonson's *Works*
1623	Publication of the First Folio	

Further Reading

Shakespeare's Life, Contexts, and Works

Shakespeare's Life and Times

Ackroyd, Peter. *Shakespeare: The Biography*. London: Chatto & Windus, 2005.

Bryson, Bill. *Shakespeare: The World as Stage*. New York: HarperCollins, 2007.

Dobson, Michael, and Stanley Wells. *The Oxford Companion to Shakespeare*. Oxford: Oxford University Press, 2001.

Dutton, Richard. *William Shakespeare: A Literary Life*. London: Macmillan, 1989.

Honan, Park. *Shakespeare: A Life*. Oxford: Oxford University Press, 2000.

Wells, Stanley. *Shakespeare: The Poet and His Plays*. London: Methuen, 1997.

Wood, Michael. *Shakespeare*. London: BBC Worldwide, 2003.

Shakespeare's Works

Greg, W.W. *The Shakespeare First Folio: Its Bibliographical and Textual History*. Oxford: Clarendon Press, 1955.

Hinman, Charlton. *The Printing and Proof-Reading of the First Folio of Shakespeare*. Oxford: Clarendon Press, 1963.

Maguire, Laurie E. *Shakespearean Subject Texts: The "Bad" Quartos and Their Contexts*. Cambridge: Cambridge University Press, 1996.

Muir, Kenneth. *Shakespeare as Collaborator*. London: Methuen, 1960.

Pollard, Alfred W., et al. *Shakespeare's Hand in the Play of Sir Thomas More*. Cambridge: Cambridge University Press, 1923.

Theobald, Lewis. *Double Falsehood, or The Distressed Lovers*. London: J. Watts, 1728.

Tucker-Brooke, C.F. *The Shakespeare Apocrypha*. Oxford: Clarendon Press, 1908.

Wells, Stanley, and Gary Taylor, et al. *William Shakespeare: A Textual Companion*. Oxford: Clarendon Press, 1987.

Shakespeare's Language

Hope, Jonathan. *Shakespeare's Grammar*. London: The Arden Shakespeare, 2003.

Kermode, Frank. *Shakespeare's Language*. Harmondsworth: Penguin, 2000.

King, Ros. "'Action and Accent Did They Teach Him There': Shakespeare and the Construction of Soundscape." In *Shakespeare and the Mediterranean: Selected Proceedings of the International Shakespeare Association World Congress, Valencia 2001,* edited by Tom Clayton, Susan Brock, and Vicente Forés, 189–93. Newark: University of Delaware Press, 2004.

Lennard, John. *But I Digress: The Exploitation of Parenthesis in English Printed Verse*. Oxford: Clarendon Press, 1991.

Nuttall, A.D. *Shakespeare the Thinker*. New Haven: Yale University Press, 2007.

Parkes, M.B. *Pause and Effect: An Introduction to the History of Punctuation in the West*. Aldershot: Scolar Press, 1992.

Smith, Bruce R. *The Acoustic World of Early Modern England: Attending to the O-factor*. Chicago: University of Chicago Press, 1999.

Wright, George T. *Shakespeare's Metrical Art*. Berkeley and Los Angeles: University of California Press, 1988.

Shakespeare's Legacy

Bate, Jonathan, and Russell Jackson, eds. *Shakespeare: An Illustrated Stage History*. Oxford: Oxford University Press, 1996.

Burnett, Mark Thornton, and Romana Wray. *Screening Shakespeare in the Twenty-First Century*. Edinburgh: Edinburgh University Press, 2006.

Linton, Joan Pong. *Romance of the New World: Gender and the Literary Formations of English Colonialism*. Cambridge: Cambridge University Press, 1998.

Loomba, Ania. *Gender, Race, Reniassance Drama*. Manchester: Manchester University Press, 1989.

Rothwell, Kenneth S. *A History of Shakespeare on Screen*. Cambridge: Cambridge University Press, 2004.

Shaughnessy, Robert. *The Cambridge Companion to Shakespeare and Popular Culture*. Cambridge: Cambridge University Press, 2007.

Smith, Emma. *The Cambridge Introduction to Shakespeare*. Cambridge: Cambridge University Press, 2007.

Travedi, Harish. *Colonial Transactions*. Manchester: Manchester University Press, 1995.

Wells, Stanley, ed. *The Cambridge Companion to Shakespeare Studies*. Cambridge: Cambridge University Press, 1986.

The Plays

Henry VI, Parts 1–3

Blanpied, John W. *Time and the Artist in Shakespeare's English Histories*. Newark: University of Delaware Press; London and Toronto: Associated University Presses, 1983.

Cartelli, Thomas. "Jack Cade in the Garden: Class Consciousness and Class Conflict in *2 Henry VI*." In *Enclosure Acts: Sexuality, Property, and Culture in Early Modern England,* edited by Richard Burt and John Michael Archer, 48–67. Ithaca and London: Cornell University Press, 1994.

Cottegnies, Line. "Lies Like Truth: Oracles and the Question of Interpretation in Shakespeare's *Henry VI, Part 2*." In *Les Voix de Dieu: Littérature et prophétie en Angleterre et en France à l'âge baroque,* edited by Line Cottegnies, C. and T. Gheeraert, and A.-M. Miller-Blaise, 24–36. Paris: Presses de la Sorbonne Nouvelle, 2008.

Dessen, Alan C. "Stagecraft and Imagery in Shakespeare's *Henry VI*." *Yearbook of English Studies* 23 (1993): 65–79.

Fitter, Chris. "'Your Captain is Brave and Vows Reformation': Jack Cade, the Hacket Rising, and Shakespeare's Vision of Popular Rebellion in *2 Henry VI*." *Shakespeare Studies* 32 (2004): 173–219.

Greenblatt, Stephen. "Murdering Peasants: Status, Genre, and the Representaion of Rebellion." In *Representing the English Renaissance,* edited by Stephen Greenblatt, 1–29. Berkeley: University of California Press, 1988.

Hattaway, Michael. "Rebellion, Class Consciousness, and Shakespeare's *2 Henry VI.*" *Cahiers élisabéthains* 33 (1988): 13–22.

Kastan, David Scott. *Shakespeare and the Shapes of Time.* Hanover: University Press of New England, 1982.

Patterson, Annabel. *Shakespeare and the Popular Voice.* Oxford: Basil Blackwell, 1989.

Pendleton, Thomas A, ed. *"Henry VI": Critical Essays.* New York and London: Routledge, 2001.

Rackin, Phyllis. *Stages of History: Shakespeare's English Chronicles.* Ithaca: Cornell University Press, 1990.

Tillyard, E.M.W. *Shakespeare's History Plays.* London: Chatto & Windus, 1944; New York: Collier Books, 1962.

Richard III

Colley, John Scott. *Richard's Himself Again: A Stage History of "Richard III."* New York: Greenwood Press, 1992.

Saccio, Peter. *Shakespeare's English Kings: History, Chronicle, and Drama.* Oxford: Oxford University Press, 2000.

Sher, Antony. *Year of the King: An Actor's Diary and Sketchbook.* London: Chatto & Windus, 1985.

Richard II

Drouet, Pascale, ed. *Shakespeare au XXème siècle: Mises en scène, mises en perspective de King Richard II.* Rennes: Presses Universitaires de Rennes, 2007.

Forker, Charles R., ed. *King Richard II.* London: The Arden Shakespeare (3rd series), 2002.

Gilman, Ernest B. "*Richard II* and the Perspectives of History." In *Renaissance Drama, New Series VII: Drama and the Other Arts,* edited by J.H. Kaplan, 85–115. Evanston: Northwestern University Press, 1976.

Shrewing, Margaret. *King Richard II.* Shakespeare in Performance series. Manchester: Manchester University Press, 1998.

King John

Anderson, Thomas. "'Legitimation, Name, and All Is Gone': Bastardy and Bureaucracy in Shakespeare's *King John.*" *Journal for Early Modern Cultural Studies* 4, no. 2 (Fall/Winter 2004): 35–61.

Braunmiller, A.R. "*King John* and Historiography." *English Literary History* 55 (1988): 309–32.

Gieskes, Edward. "'He Is But a Bastard to the Time': Status and Service in *The Troublesome Raigne of John* and Shakespeare's *King John.*" *English Literary History* 65 (1998): 779–98.

Levin, Carole. "'I Trust I May Not Trust Thee': Women's Visions of the World in Shakespeare's *King John.*" In *Ambiguous Realities: Women in the Middle Ages and Renaissance,* edited by Carole Levin and Jeanie Watson, 219–34. Detroit: Wayne State University Press, 1987.

Pugliatti, Paola. "The Scribbled Form of Authority in *King John.*" In *Shakespeare the Historian,* 77–101. New York: Macmillan Press, 1996.

Henry IV, Part 1

Berger Jr., Harry. *Making Trifles of Terrors: Redistributing Complicities in Shakespeare.* Edited by Peter Erickson. Stanford: Stanford University Press, 1997.

Greenburg, Bradley. "Romancing the Chronicles: *1 Henry IV* and the Rewriting of Medieval History." *Quidditas* 27 (2006): 34–50.

Greenfield, Matthew. "*1 Henry IV*: Metatheatrical Britain." In *British Identities and English Renaissance Literature*, edited by David J. Baker and Willy Maly, 71–80. Cambridge: Cambridge University Press, 2002.

Highley, Christopher. "Wales, Ireland, and *1 Henry IV.*" *Renaissance Drama*, n.s., 21 (1990): 91–114.

Kastan, David Scott. "'The King Hath Many Marching in His Coats': or, What Did You Do During the War, Daddy?" In *Shakespeare Left and Right*, edited by Ivo Kamps, 241–58. New York: Routledge, 1991.

Womersley, David. "Why Is Falstaff Fat?" *The Review of English Studies* 47 (1996): 1–22.

Henry IV, Part 2

Berger Jr., Harry. "The Prince's Dog: Falstaff and the Perils of Speech-Prefixity." *Shakespeare Quarterly* 49 (1998): 40–73.

Crewe, Jonathan. "Reforming Prince Hal: The Sovereign Inheritor in *2 Henry IV.*" *Renaissance Drama*, n.s., 21 (1990): 225–42.

Levine, Nina. "Extending Credit in the *Henry IV* Plays." *Shakespeare Quarterly* 51 (2000): 403–31.

Scoufos, Alice-Lyle. *Shakespeare's Typological Satire: A Study of the Falstaff–Oldcastle Problem.* Athens: Ohio University Press, 1979.

Wiles, David. *Shakespeare's Clown: Actor and Text in the Elizabethan Playhouse.* Cambridge: Cambridge University Press, 1987.

Henry V

Altman, Joel. "'Vile Participation': The Amplification of Violence in the Theatre of *Henry V.*" *Shakespeare Quarterly* 42 (1991): 1–32.

Berger, Harry Jr. "Harrying the Stage: *Henry V* in the Tetralogical Echo Chamber." In *Shakespeare International Yearbook: Where Are We Now in Shakespeare Studies?,* edited by Graham Bradshaw, et al, 131–55. Aldershot: Ashgate Press, 2003.

Greenburg, Bradley. "'O for a Muse of Fire': *Henry V* and Plotted Self-Exculpation." *Shakespeare Studies* 36 (2008): 182–206.

Quint, David. "'Alexander the Pig': Shakespeare on History and Poetry." *Boundary 2,* 10 (1982): 49–63.

Rabkin, Norman. "Rabbits, Ducks, and *Henry V.*" *Shakespeare Quarterly* 28 (1977): 279–96.

Henry VIII

Frye, Susan. "Queens and the Structure of History in *Henry VIII.*" In *A Companion to Shakespeare's Works, Vol. 4: Poems, Problem Comedies, Late Plays*, edited by Richard Dutton and Jean E. Howard, 427–44. Malden: Blackwell, 2003.

Hodgdon, Barbara. *The End Crowns All: Closure and Contradiction in Shakespeare's History.* Princeton: Princeton University Press, 1991.

Kermode, Frank. "What is Shakespeare's *Henry VIII* About?" In *Shakespeare, The Histories: A Collection of Critical Essays*, edited by Eugene M. Waith, 168–79. Englewood Cliffs: Prentice-Hall, 1965.

Noling, Kim H. "Grubbing Up the Stock: Dramatizing Queens in *Henry VIII*." *Shakespeare Quarterly* 39 (1988): 291–308.

Wegemer, Gerard. "*Henry VIII* on Trial: Confronting Malice and Conscience in Shakespeare's *All Is True*." *Renascence* 52 (2000): 111–30.

The Two Gentlemen of Verona

Berry, Ralph. *Shakespeare's Comedies: Explorations in Form*. Princeton: Princeton University Press, 1972.

Kirsch, A.C. *Shakespeare and the Experience of Love*. Cambridge: Cambridge University Press, 1981.

Mangan, Michael. *A Preface to Shakespeare's Comedies*. London: Longman, 1996.

Schlueter, Kurt, ed. *The Two Gentlemen of Verona*. Cambridge: Cambridge University Press, 1990.

The Comedy of Errors

Cartwright, Kent, ed. *The Comedy of Errors*. London: The Arden Shakespeare (3rd series), forthcoming.

Henning, Standish, ed. *The Comedy of Errors*. New Variorum edn. New York: MLA, forthcoming.

Miola, Robert S., ed. *"The Comedy of Errors": Critical Essays*. New York: Garland, 1997.

Tillyard, E.M.W. *Shakespeare's Early Comedies*. London: Chatto & Windus, 1965.

The Taming of the Shrew

Fineman, Joel E. "The Turn of the Shrew." In *Shakespeare and the Question of Theory*, edited by Patricia Parker and Geoffrey Hartman, 138–160. New York and London: Methuen, 1985.

Gay, Penny. *The Cambridge Introduction to Shakespeare's Comedies*. Cambridge: Cambridge University Press, 2008.

Haring-Smith, Tori. *From Farce to Metadrama: A Stage History of "The Taming of the Shrew."* Westport: Greenwood Press, 1985.

Holdernes, Graham. *The Taming of the Shrew*. Shakespeare in Performance series. Manchester: Manchester University Press, 1989.

Love's Labor's Lost

Carroll, William C. *The Great Feast of Language in "Love's Labour's Lost."* Princeton: Princeton University Press, 1976.

Elam, Keir. *Shakespeare's Universe of Discourse: Language-games in the Comedies*. Cambridge: Cambridge University Press, 1984.

Ellis, Herbert A. *Shakespeare's Lusty Punning in "Love's Labour's Lost."* The Hague: Mouton, 1973.

A Midsummer Night's Dream

Halio, Jay L. *A Midsummer Night's Dream*. Shakespeare in Performance series. Manchester: Manchester University Press, 1994.

Montrose, Louis. *The Purpose of Playing: Shakespeare and the Cultural Politics of the Elizabethan Theatre*. Chicago: University of Chicago Press, 1996.

Williams, Gary Jay. *Our Moonlight Revels: "A Midsummer Night's Dream" in the Theatre*. Iowa: University of Iowa Press, 1997.

Young, David P. *Something of Great Constancy: The Art of "A Midsummer Night's Dream."* New Haven: Yale University Press, 1966.

The Merchant of Venice

Bloom, Harold, ed. *William Shakespeare's "Merchant of Venice."* New York: Chelsea House, 1986.

Bulman, James. *The Merchant of Venice*. Shakespeare in Performance series. Manchester: Manchester University Press, 1991.

Edelman, Charles, ed. *The Merchant of Venice*. Shakespeare in Production series. Cambridge: Cambridge University Press, 2002.

Gross, John. *Shylock: Four Hundred Years in the Life of a Legend*. London: Chatto & Windus, 1992.

McCarthy, Mary. *Venice Observed*. New York: Reynal, 1956.

Shapiro, James. *Shakespeare and the Jews*. New York: Columbia University Press, 1996.

The Merry Wives of Windsor

Carroll, William C. "Falstaff and Ford: Forming and Reforming." In *The Metamorphoses of Shakespearean Comedy*, 183–201. Princeton: Princeton University Press, 1985.

Melchiori, Giorgio. "Reconstructing the Garter Entertainment at Westminster on St. George's Day 23 April 1597." In *Shakespeare's Garter Plays: Edward III to Merry Wives of Windsor*, 92–112. Newark: University of Delaware Press, 1994.

Ross, Charles. "Shakespeare's Merry Wives and the Law of Fraudulent Conveyance." *Renaissance Drama*, n.s., 25 (1994): 145–69.

Tiffany, Grace. "Falstaff's False Staff: 'Jonsonian' Asexuality in *The Merry Wives of Windsor*." *Comparative Drama* 26 (1992): 254–70.

Wall, Wendy. "Why Does Puck Sweep?: Fairylore, Merry Wives, and Social Struggle." *Shakespeare Quarterly* 52 (2001): 67–106.

As You Like It

Chakravorty, Swapan. "Translating Arden: Shakespeare's Rhetorical Place in *As You Like It*." In *Shakespeare and the Mediterranean*, edited by Tom Clayton, Susan Brock, and Vicente Forés, 156–67. Newark: University of Delaware Press, 2004.

Colie, Rosalie L. *Shakespeare's Living Art*. Princeton: Princeton University Press, 1974.

Dusinberre, Juliet. "Pancakes and a Date for *As You Like It*." *Shakespeare Quarterly* 54 (2003): 371–405.

Howard, Jean E. *The Stage and Social Struggle in Early Modern England*. New York: Routledge, 1994.

Marshall, Cynthia. "The Doubled Jaques and Constructions of Negation in *As You Like It*." *Shakespeare Quarterly* 49 (1988): 375–92.

Montrose, Louis. "'The Place of the Brother' in *As You Like It*: Social Process and Comic Form." *Shakespeare Quarterly* 32 (1981): 28–54.

Neely, Carol Thomas. *Distracted Subjects: Madness and Gender in Shakespeare and Early Modern Culture*. Ithaca: Cornell University Press, 2004.

Traub, Valerie. *Desire and Authority: Circulations of Sexuality in Shakespearean Drama*. New York: Routledge, 1992.

Wilson, Richard. *Will Power: Essays on Shakespearean Authority*. Hemel Hempstead: Harvester Wheatsheaf, 1993.

Much Ado about Nothing

Brown, John Russell, ed. *"Much Ado about Nothing" and "As You Like It": A Casebook*. London: Macmillan, 1979.

Cox, John F., ed. *Much Ado about Nothing*. Shakespeare in Production series. Cambridge: Cambridge University Press, 1997.

Leiter, Samuel L., ed. *Shakespeare Around the Globe: A Guide to Notable Postwar Revivals*. New York: Greenwood Press, 1986.

Madelaine, Richard. "Oranges and Lemans: *Much Ado about Nothing*, IV.i.31." *Shakespeare Quarterly* 33 (1982): 491–92.

Madelaine, Richard, and John Golder, eds. *"O Brave New World": Two Centuries of Shakespeare on the Australian Stage*. Sydney: Currency Press, 2001.

Wynne-Davies, Marion, ed. *"Much Ado about Nothing" and "The Taming of the Shrew."* New Casebooks series. Basingstoke: Palgrave, 2001.

Twelfth Night

Barber, C.L. *Shakespeare's Festive Comedies*. Princeton: Princeton University Press, 1959.

Coddon, Karin S. "'Slander in an Allow'd Fool': *Twelfth Night*'s Crisis of the Aristocracy." *Studies in English Literature, 1500–1900*, 33, no. 2 (Spring 1993): 309–25.

Elam, Keir. "The Fertile Eunuch: *Twelfth Night*, Early Modern Intercourse, and the Fruits of Castration." *Shakespeare Quarterly* 47, no. 1 (Spring 1996): 1–36.

Freund, Elizabeth. "*Twelfth Night* and the Tyranny of Interpretation." *English Literary History* 53, no. 3 (Autumn 1986): 471–89.

Schalkwyk, David. "Love and Service in *Twelfth Night* and the Sonnets." *Shakespeare Quarterly* 56, no. 1 (Spring 2005): 76–100.

All's Well That Ends Well

Styan, J.L. *All's Well That Ends Well*. Shakespeare in Performance series. Manchester: Manchester University Press, 1984.

Waller, Gary, ed. *"All's Well That Ends Well": New Critical Essays*. New York: Routledge, 2007.

Zitner, Sheldon. *All's Well That Ends Well*. New York: Harvester Wheatsheaf, 1989.

Measure for Measure

Baines, Barbara. "Assaying the Power of Chastity in *Measure for Measure*." *Studies in English Literature* 30 (1991): 283–301.

Bennett, Josephine Waters. *"Measure for Measure" as Royal Entertainment*. New York: Columbia University Press, 1966.

Dollimore, Jonathan. "Transgression and Surveillance in *Measure for Measure*." In *Political Shakespeare: Essays in Cultural Materialism*, edited by Jonathan Dollimore and Alan Sinfield, 72–87. 2nd edn. Manchester: Manchester University Press, 1994.

Hawkins, Harriet. *Measure for Measure*. Boston: Twayne Publishers, 1987.

Kamps, Ivo, and Karen Raber. *"Measure for Measure": Texts and Contexts*. Boston: Bedford/St. Martin's, 2004.

Knight, G. Wilson. *The Wheel of Fire: Interpretations of Shakespearian Tragedy*. 2nd edn. London: Methuen, 1949.

Korda, Natasha. *Shakespeare's Domestic Economies: Gender and Property in Early Modern England*. Philadelphia: University of Pennsylvania Press, 2002.

McLuskie, Kathleen. "The Patriarchal Bard: Feminist Criticism and Shakespeare: *King Lear* and *Measure for Measure*." In *Shakespeare, Feminism and Gender*, edited by Kate Chedgzoy, 24–48. Basingstoke: Palgrave, 2001.

Maus, Katharine Eisaman. *Inwardness and Theater in the English Renaissance*. Chicago: University of Chicago Press, 1995.

Shell, Marc. *The End of Kinship: "Measure for Measure," Incest and the Ideal of Universal Siblinghood*. Chicago: Stanford University Press, 1988.

Shuger, Deborah Kuller. *Political Theologies in Shakespeare's England: The Sacred and the State in "Measure for Measure."* New York: Palgrave, 2001.

Taylor, Gary. "Shakespeare's Mediterranean *Measure for Measure*." In *Shakespeare and the Mediterranean: Selected Proceedings of the International Shakespeare Association World Congress, Valencia 2001*, edited by Tom Clayton, Susan Brock, and Vicente Forés, 243–69. Newark: University of Delaware Press, 2004.

Wheeler, Richard P. *Shakespeare's Development and the Problem Comedies: Turn and Counter-Turn*. Berkeley: University of California Press, 1981.

Titus Andronicus

Bate, Jonathan, ed. Introduction to *Titus Andronicus*. London: The Arden Shakespeare (3rd series), 1995: 1–121.

Kendall, Gillian Murray. "'Lend me thy Hand': Metaphor and Mayhem in *Titus Andronicus*." *Shakespeare Quarterly* 40, no. 3 (Autumn 1989): 299–316.

Palmer, D.J. "'The Unspeakable in Pursuit of the Uneatable': Language and Action in *Titus Andronicus*." *Critical Quarterly* 14 (1972): 320–29.

Rowe, Katherine. "Dismembering and Forgetting in *Titus Andronicus*." *Shakespeare Quarterly* 45, no. 3 (Autumn 1994): 279–303.

Waith, Eugene. "The Metamorphosis of Violence in *Titus Andronicus*." *Shakespeare Survey* 10 (1957): 39–59.

Willis, Deborah. "'The Gnawing Vulture': Revenge, Trauma, Theory, and *Titus Andronicus*." *Shakespeare Quarterly* 53, no. 1 (Spring 2002): 21–52.

Romeo and Juliet

Brooke, Nicholas. *Shakespeare's Early Tragedies*. London: Methuen, 1968.

Davis, Lloyd. "'Death-marked Love': Desire and Presence in *Romeo and Juliet*." *Shakespeare Survey* 49 (1996): 57–67.

Earl, A.J. "*Romeo and Juliet* and the Elizabethan Sonnets." *English* 27 (1978): 99–119.

Kahn, Coppélia. "Coming of Age in Verona." In *The Woman's Part: Feminist Criticism of Shakespeare*, edited by Carolyn Ruth Swift Lenz, Gayle Greene, and Carol Thomas Neely, 171–93. Urbana: University of Illinois Press, 1980.

Leech, Clifford. "The Moral Tragedy of *Romeo and Juliet*." In *English Renaissance Drama*, edited by Standish Henning, Robert Kimbrough, and Richard Knowles, 59–75. Carbondale: Southern Illinois University Press, 1976.

Levenson, Jill. "The Definition of Love: Shakespeare's Phrasing in *Romeo and Juliet*." *Shakespeare Studies* 15 (1982): 21–36.

Loehlin, James N. "'These Violent Delights Have Violent Ends': Baz Luhrmann's Millennial Shakespeare." In *Shakespeare, Film, Fin de Siècle*, edited by Mark Thornton Burnett and Ramona Wray, 121–36. London: Macmillan, 2000.

Slater, Ann Pasternak. "Petrarchanism Come True in *Romeo and Juliet*." In *Images of Shakespeare: Proceedings of the Third Congress of the International Shakespeare Association 1986,* edited by Werner Habicht, D.J. Palmer, and Roger Pringle, 129–50. London: Associated University Presses, 1988.

Snyder, Susan. *The Comic Matrix of Shakespeare's Tragedies.* Princeton: Princeton University Press, 1979.

———. "Ideology and the Feud in *Romeo and Juliet*." *Shakespeare Survey* 49 (1996): 87–96.

Julius Caesar

Carnegie, David. *Julius Caesar.* Shakespeare Handbooks series. Basingstoke: Palgrave, 2009.

Miles, Geoffrey. *Shakespeare and the Constant Romans.* Oxford: Clarendon, 1996.

Miola, Robert S. *Shakespeare's Rome.* Cambridge: Cambridge University Press, 2008.

Sohmer, Steve. *Shakespeare's Mystery Play: The Opening of the Globe Theatre, 1599.* Manchester: Manchester University Press, 1999.

Hamlet

Burnett, Mark Thornton. "The 'Heart of My Mystery': *Hamlet* and Secrets." In *New Essays on Hamlet*, edited by Mark Thornton Burnett and John Manning. New York: AMS Press, 1994.

Curran, John E. *"Hamlet," Protestantism and the Mourning of Contingency.* Aldershot: Ashgate Press, 2006.

De Grazia, Margreta. *"Hamlet" without Hamlet.* Cambridge: Cambridge University Press, 2007.

Greenblatt, Stephen. *Hamlet in Purgatory.* Princeton: Princeton University Press, 2001.

Howard, Tony. *Women as Hamlet: Performance and Interpretation in Theatre, Film and Fiction.* Cambridge: Cambridge University Press, 2007.

Lyons, Bridget Gellert. "The Iconography of Ophelia." In *English Literary History* 44 (1977): 60–74.

McGee, Arthur. *The Elizabethan Hamlet.* New Haven: Yale University Press, 1987.

Mercer, Peter. *"Hamlet" and the Acting of Revenge.* Iowa: University of Iowa Press, 1987.

Mullaney, Stephen. "Mourning and Misogyny: *Hamlet, The Revenger's Tragedy*, and the Final Progress of Elizabeth I, 1600–1607." *Shakespeare Quarterly* 45, no. 2 (Summer 1994): 139–62.

Neill, Michael. *Issues of Death: Mortality and Identity in English Renaissance Tragedy.* Oxford: Oxford University Press, 1997.

Pirie, David. "*Hamlet* without the Prince." *Critical Quarterly* 14 (Winter 1972): 293–314.

Showalter, Elaine. "Representing Ophelia: Women, Madness, and the Responsibilities of Feminist Criticism." In *Shakespeare and the Question of Theory*, edited by Patricia Parker and Geoffrey Hartmann, 77–94. New York and London: Methuen, 1985.

Stanton, Kay. "Hamlet's Whores." In *New Essays on "Hamlet,"* edited by Mark Thornton Burnett and John Manning, 167–84. New York: AMS Press, 1994.

Troilus and Cressida

Crewe, Jonathan, ed. *The History of Troilus and Cressida.* New York: Penguin, 2000.

Elton, G.R. *"Troilus and Cressida" and the Inns of Courts Revels.* Aldershot: Ashgate Press, 2000.

McCandless, David. *Gender and Performance in Shakespeare's Problem Comedies.* Bloomington: Indiana Press, 1997.

Othello

Adamson, Jane. *"Othello" as Tragedy: Some Problems of Judgement and Feeling.* Cambridge: Cambridge University Press, 1980.

Appelbaum, Robert, "War and Peace in 'The Lepanto' of James VI and I." *Modern Philology* 97, no. 3 (February 2000): 333–63.

Bradshaw, Graham. *Misrepresentations: Shakespeare and the Materialists.* Ithaca: Cornell University Press, 1993.

Hampton-Reeves, Stuart. *Othello.* Shakespeare Handbooks series. Basingstoke: Palgrave, 2008.

Heilman, Robert B. *Magic in the Web: Action and Language in "Othello."* Louisville: University of Kentucky Press, 1956.

Honigmann, E.A.J. *The Texts of "Othello" and Shakespearean Revision.* London: Routledge, 1996.

Jones, Eldred. *Othello's Countrymen: The African in English Renaissance Drama.* Oxford: Oxford University Press, 1965.

King, Ros. "'The Disciplines of War': Elizabethan War Manuals and Shakespeare's Tragicomic Vision." In *Shakespeare and War*, edited by Ros King and Paul Franssen. Basingstoke: Palgrave, 2008.

Kingsley, Ben. *"Othello."* In *Players of Shakespeare 2*, edited by Russell Jackson and Robert Smallwood, 167–78. Cambridge: Cambridge University Press, 1988.

Rosenberg, Marvin. *The Masks of Othello: The Search for the Identity of Othello, Iago, and Desdemona by Three Centuries of Actors and Critics.* Newark: University of Delaware Press, 1992.

Snyder, Susan. *The Comic Matrix of Shakespeare's Tragedies.* Princeton: Princeton University Press, 1979.

Vaughan, Virginia Mason. *Othello: A Contextual History.* Cambridge: Cambridge University Press, 1994.

Wain, John, ed. *"Othello": A Casebook.* Rev. edn. London: Macmillan, 1994.

King Lear

Bate, Jonathan, and Eric Rasmussen, eds. *"King Lear": The RSC Shakespeare.* New York: Palgrave, 2009.

Booth, Stephen. *"King Lear", "Macbeth", Indefinition, and Tragedy.* New Haven: Yale University Press, 1983.

Holland, Peter, ed. *"King Lear" and its Afterlife: Shakespeare Survey 55.* Cambridge: Cambridge University Press, 2002.

Kahan, Jeffrey, ed. *"King Lear": New Critical Essays.* New York: Routledge, 2008.

Leggatt, Alexander. *"King Lear."* 2nd edn. Shakespeare in Performance series. Manchester: Manchester University Press, 2004.

Nuttall, A.D. *Why Does Tragedy Give Pleasure?* Oxford: Clarendon Press, 1996.

Ryan, Kiernan, ed. *King Lear.* New Casebooks series. New York: Palgrave, 1992.

Taylor, Gary, and Michael Warren, eds. *The Division of the Kingdoms: Shakespeare's Two Versions of "King Lear."* Oxford: Clarendon Press, 1983.

Macbeth

Adelman, Janet. "'Born of Woman': Fantasies of Maternal Power in *Macbeth.*" In *Cannibals, Witches, and Divorce: Estranging the Renaissance*, edited by Marjorie Garber, 90–121. Baltimore: Johns Hopkins University Press, 1987.

Calderwood, James L. *If it Were Done: "Macbeth" and Tragic Action.* Amherst: University of Massachusetts Press, 1986.

Dollimore, Jonathan. *Radical Tragedy: Religion, Ideology, and Power in the Drama of Shakespeare and his Contemporaries.* Chicago: University of Chicago Press, 1984.

Kastan, David Scott. *Shakespeare after Theory.* New York: Routledge, 1999.

Mullaney, Steven. *The Place of the Stage: License, Play, and Power in Renaissance England.* Chicago: University of Chicago Press, 1988.

Orgel, Stephen. *The Authentic Shakespeare, and Other Problems of the Early Modern Stage.* New York: Routledge, 2002.

Quarmby, Kevin. "A Twenty-fifth Anniversary Study of Rehearsal and Performance Practice in the 1980 Royal Court *Hamlet* and the Old Vic *Macbeth*: An Actor's View." *Shakespeare* 1 (2005): 174–87.

Wells, Robin Headlam. *Shakespeare on Masculinity.* Cambridge: Cambridge University Press, 2000.

Williams, George Walton. "'*Macbeth*': King James's Play." *South Atlantic Review* 47 (1982): 12–21.

Antony and Cleopatra

Brown, John Russell, ed. *Shakespeare's "Antony and Cleopatra": A Casebook.* Rev. edn. Basingstoke: Palgrave Macmillan, 1991.

Deats, Sara Munson, ed. *"Antony and Cleopatra": New Critical Essays.* London: Routledge, 2006.

Drakakis, John, ed. *Antony and Cleopatra.* New Casebooks series. New York: St. Martin's Press, 1994.

Madelaine, Richard, ed. *Antony and Cleopatra.* Shakespeare in Production series. Cambridge: Cambridge University Press, 1998.

Timon of Athens

Knight, G. Wilson. "'The Pilgrimage of Hate': An Essay on *Timon of Athens.*" In *The Wheel of Fire: Interpretations of Shakespearian Tragedy*, 207–39. 4th edn. London: Methuen, 1949.

Nuttall, A.D. *Timon of Athens.* Hemel Hempstead: Wheatsheaf Harvester, 1989.

White, R.S. "Marx and Shakespeare." *Shakespeare Survey* 45 (1993): 89–100.

Coriolanus

Barton, Anne. "Livy, Machiavelli, and Shakespeare's *Coriolanus.*" In *Shakespeare Survey Volume 38: Shakespeare and History*, edited by Stanley Wells. Cambridge: Cambridge University Press, 1986.

Bloom, Harold, ed. *William Shakespeare's "Coriolanus."* New York: Chelsea House, 1988.

Heuer, Hermann. "From Plutarch to Shakespeare: A Study of *Coriolanus.*" In *Shakespeare Survey Volume 10: The Roman Plays*, edited by Allardyce Nicoll. Cambridge: Cambridge University Press, 1957.

Kahn, Coppélia. *Roman Shakespeare: Warriors, Wounds, And Women.* London, New York: Routledge, 1997.

Stevenson, Kay. "'Hear Me Speak': Listening to *Coriolanus.*" In *Shakespeare: Readers, Audiences, Players*, edited by R.S. White, Charles Edelman, and Christopher Wortham, 233–47. Perth: University of Western Australia Press, 1998.

Wheeler, David, ed. *"Coriolanus": Critical Essays.* New York: Garland, 1995.

Pericles

Felperin, Howard. *Shakespearean Romance.* Princeton: Princeton University Press, 1972.

Jackson, MacDonald P. *Defining Shakespeare: "Pericles" as a Test Case.* Oxford: Oxford University Press, 2003.

Knight, G. Wilson. "The Writing of *Pericles.*" In *The Crown of Life: Essays in Interpretation of Shakespeare's Final Plays,* 32–76. Oxford: Oxford University Press, 1947.

White, R.S. *"Let Wonder Seem Familiar": Endings in Shakespeare's Romance Vision.* London: Athlone Press, 1985.

Cymbeline

Gillies, John. "The Problem of Style in *Cymbeline.*" *Southern Review* 15 (1982): 269–90.

Knight, G. Wilson. "*Cymbeline.*" In *The Crown of Life: Essays in Interpretation of Shakespeare's Final Plays,* 129–202. Oxford: Oxford University Press, 1947.

Leggatt, Alexander. "The Island of Miracles: An Approach to *Cymbeline.*" *Shakespeare Studies* 10 (1977): 191–209.

Simonds, Peggy Muñoz. *Myth, Emblem, and Music in Shakespeare's "Cymbeline": An Iconographic Reconstruction.* Newark: University of Delaware Press, 1992.

The Winter's Tale

Bartholomeusz, Dennis. *"The Winter's Tale" in Performance in England and America 1611–1976.* Cambridge: Cambridge University Press, 1982.

King, Ros. *The Winter's Tale*. Shakespeare Handbooks series. Basingstoke: Palgrave, 2008.

Nutt, Joe. *An Introduction to Shakespeare's Late Plays*. Basingstoke: Palgrave, 2002.

Orgel, Stephen, ed. *The Winter's Tale*. Oxford: Oxford University Press, 1996.

Ryan, Kiernan, ed. *Shakespeare: The Last Plays*. London: Longman, 1999.

Snyder, Susan, and Deborah T. Curren-Aquino, eds. *The Winter's Tale*. Cambridge: Cambridge University Press, 2007.

Warren, Roger. *Staging Shakespeare's Late Plays*. Oxford: Clarendon Press, 1990.

The Tempest

Clark, Sandra, ed. *The Tempest*. London: Penguin, 1986.

Knight, G. Wilson. *The Crown of Life: Essays in Interpretation of Shakespeare's Final Plays*. Oxford: Oxford University Press, 1947.

Orgel, Stephen, ed. *The Tempest*. Oxford: Oxford University Press, 1998.

Palmer, D.J., ed. *"The Tempest": A Casebook*. Rev. edn. Basingstoke: Palgrave, 1991.

The Two Noble Kinsmen

Bawcutt, N.W., ed. Introduction to *The Two Noble Kinsmen*, 1–50. Harmondsworth: Penguin, 1977.

Thompson, Ann. "*The Two Noble Kinsmen.*" In *Shakespeare's Chaucer: A Study in Literary Origins*, 166–215. Liverpool: Liverpool University Press, 1978.

The Poetry

Venus and Adonis

Bate, Jonathan, *Shakespeare and Ovid*. Oxford: Clarendon Press, 1993.

Belsey, Catherine. "Love as Trompe-l'oeil: Taxonomies of Desire in *Venus and Adonis*." *Shakespeare Quarterly* 46 (1995): 257–76.

Cheney, Patrick, ed. *The Cambridge Companion to Shakespeare's Poetry*. Cambridge: Cambridge University Press, 2007.

Dubrow, Heather. *Captive Victors: Shakespeare's Narrative Poems and Sonnets*. Ithaca and London: Cornell University Press, 1987.

Hyland, Peter. *An Introduction to Shakespeare's Poems*. Basingstoke: Palgrave, 2003.

Keach, William. *Elizabethan Erotic Narratives: Irony and Pathos in the Ovidian Poetry of Shakespeare, Marlowe and their Contemporaries*. New Brunswick: Rutgers University Press, 1977.

Smith, Peter J. "A 'Consummation Devoutly to Be Wished': The Erotics of Narration in *Venus and Adonis*." *Shakespeare Survey* 53 (2000): 25–38.

The Rape of Lucrece

Donaldson, Ian. *The Rapes of Lucretia: A Myth and its Transformations*. Oxford: Clarendon Press, 1982.

Fernie, Ewan. *Shame in Shakespeare*. London and New York: Routledge, 2002.

Kahn, Coppélia, "The Rape in Shakespeare's *Lucrece*." *Shakespeare Studies* 9 (1976): 45–72.

Miola, Robert S. *Shakespeare's Rome*. Cambridge: Cambridge University Press, 1983.

Vickers, Nancy. "'The Blazon of Sweet Beauty's Best': Shakespeare's *Lucrece*." In *Shakespeare and the Question of Theory*, edited by Patricia Parker and Geoffrey Hartman, 95–115. New York and London: Methuen, 1985.

The Passionate Pilgrim

Burrows, Colin, ed. *The Complete Sonnets and Poems*. Oxford: Oxford University Press, 2002.

Cheney, Patrick. *Shakespeare, National Poet-Playwright*. Cambridge: Cambridge University Press, 2004.

The Phoenix and Turtle

Ellrodt, Robert. "An Anatomy of *The Phoenix and the Turtle*." *Shakespeare Survey* 15 (1962): 99–110.

Finnis, John, and Patrick Martin. "Another Turn for the *Turtle*." *The Times*, April 18, 2003.

Matchett, William. *"The Phoenix and the Turtle": Shakespeare's Poem and Chester's "Loues Martyr."* The Hague: Mouton, 1965.

Stetner, Clifford. "Shakespeare's Shrieking Harbinger: *The Phoenix and the Turtle* and the End of the Tudor Myth." http://phoenixandturtle.net/papers.html.

A Lover's Complaint

Craik, Katherine. "Shakespeare's *A Lover's Complaint* and Early Modern Criminal Confession." *Shakespeare Quarterly* 53 (2002): 437–59.

Jackson, MacDonald P. *Shakespeare's "A Lover's Complaint": Its Date and Authenticity*. Auckland, 1965.

Kerrigan, John, ed. *Motives of Woe: Shakespeare and Female Complaint. A Critical Anthology*. Oxford: Clarendon Press, 1991.

Sharon-Zisser, Shirley, ed. *Critical Essays on Shakespeare's "A Lover's Complaint": Suffering Ecstasy*. Aldershot: Ashgate Press, 2006.

Vickers, Brian. *Shakespeare, "A Lover's Complaint" and John Davies of Hereford*. Cambridge: Cambridge University Press, 2007.

The Sonnets

Cousins, A.D. *Shakespeare's Sonnets and Narrative Poems*. London: Longman, 2000.

Dubrow, Heather. *Captive Victors: Shakespeare's Narrative Poems and Sonnets*. Ithaca and London: Cornell University Press, 1987.

Duncan-Jones, Katherine, ed. *Shakespeare's Sonnets*. London: The Arden Shakespeare (3rd series), 1997.

Edmondson, Paul, and Stanley Wells. *Shakespeare's Sonnets*. Oxford: Oxford University Press, 2004.

Fineman, Joel. *Shakespeare's Perjured Eye: The Invention of Poetic Subjectivity in the Sonnets*. Berkeley: University of California Press, 1986.

Hyland, Peter. *An Introduction to Shakespeare's Poems*. Basingstoke: Palgrave, 2003.

Schiffer, James, ed. *Shakespeare's Sonnets: Critical Essays*. New York and London: Garland, 1999.

Glossary

ASIDE A remark or observation made by a character in a play, which the audience hears but which the other characters onstage do not.

BLANK VERSE Verse composed of iambic pentameter lines (that is, lines with five metrical stresses, such as, "The curfew tolls the knell of parting day") that do not rhyme. Most of Shakespeare's verse is in iambic pentameter.

CANON, THE That group of literary texts which, at any given time, a culture deems to have most influenced its development and to be essential to its literary history.

CHORUS A character who delivers the prologue and epilogue to a play, commenting on its other characters and events.

COMMEDIA DELL'ARTE An Italian comic mode, from about the 1500s to the 1700s, in which actors improvise on the basis of stock situations and characters.

COMPLAINT A poetic form in which a speaker—for example, a famous historical personage or figure from mythology—laments the tragic events of his or her life.

DE CASIBUS Traditional stories of eminent personages and their falls from power and prosperity. Such stories offer warnings about the fragility and transience of success, the futility of pride, and the unpredictability of existence.

DOUBLING When an actor takes on more than one role in a play.

DRAMATIS PERSONAE The characters in a play.

EPITHALAMIUM A marriage poem celebrating the bride and groom.

EPYLLION A minor or, in effect, miniature epic poem, focusing on the erotic rather than on the heroic and drawing heavily on mythology.

FEMALE COMPLAINT A complaint (see *Complaint*, above) in which the speaker is a woman. In England during the 1590s, the female complaint became a fashionable literary form and writers who contributed to it include Shakespeare, with his *The Rape of Lucrece*.

FIRST FOLIO The book entitled *Mr. William Shakespeares Comedies, Histories, & Tragedies*, printed in 1623, in which Shakespeare's colleagues, John Heminges and Henry Condell, brought together most of his plays for the first time. A second, corrected edition (the Second Folio) was published in 1632, and this was followed by the Third Folio (1663), the Fourth Folio (1685), and the Fifth Folio (*c.* 1700).

FOLIO A sheet of paper folded once: thus, a book made up of sheets of paper that have been folded once. This format was generally used to produce prestigious, expensive editions.

FOOL The jester (as in, court jester) whose job was to amuse his noble employers—and who might dare, under the cover of jest, to tell them uncomfortable truths about themselves and their actions.

HISTORY A play about notable historical events, such as those in the reign of a particular king, and usually focusing on royalty and aristocracy.

KING'S MEN The name that Shakespeare's acting company, the Lord Chamberlain's Men, took in honor of King James I when, in 1603, he became their new patron.

LATE PLAYS As the phrase suggests, the plays written in Shakespeare's later years—broadly speaking, between 1608 and 1613. Usually the term refers particularly to the romances and thus to *Pericles, The Winter's Tale, The Tempest, Cymbeline,* and *The Two Noble Kinsmen*.

LORD CHAMBERLAIN'S MEN The company of actors that Shakespeare joined around 1594, and of which he subsequently became part-owner.

NEOPLATONIC A school of philosophy that diversely elaborated on and developed the doctrines of Greek philosopher Plato. It emphasized, among other things, the ephemeral nature of the physical world and the ultimate reality of the spiritual world.

PANEGYRIC A speech or written text in praise of someone or something.

PATRON A person, who might have social eminence or wealth, or both, from whom a writer or, say, an actor might gain or seek support. The support might or might not be simply financial and usually the "client" would dedicate his or her work to the person in question.

PLAY-WITHIN-THE-PLAY A play—or part of a play—contained within the play that one is reading or watching. Within the action of *Hamlet,* for example, part of a play *(The Mousetrap)* is performed before the Danish court.

PROBLEM PLAYS A term that usually refers to *All's Well That Ends Well*, *Troilus and Cressida,* and *Measure for Measure*. The term suggests that the plays are primarily concerned with exploring moral and social problems lacking or seeming to lack solutions. Some commentators prefer to identify the so-called "problem plays" as tragicomedies.

QUARTO The size of a piece of paper when it is folded twice and so has four leaves. Thus, a book made up of paper of that size. Many of Shakespeare's plays were published in this format. The quarto format was cheaper and smaller than the more prestigious folio format (see *Folio*, above).

RENAISSANCE A European cultural phenomenon, from about 1300 to 1450, connected especially with a revived knowledge of and interest in ancient Greece and Rome. England did not experience that phenomenon until the 1490s. The English Renaissance can be said to last from approximately then until around 1660.

REVENGE TRAGEDY An Elizabethan and Jacobean form of tragedy derived chiefly from the plays of Roman philosopher Seneca. The main character in such plays is known as "the revenger," a person who must avenge a crime committed against himself and (or) his family because he cannot find justice in his society. The revenger himself is therefore someone operating outside the law.

RHETORIC The ancient art of speaking or writing effectively with the help of techniques aimed at creating belief and sympathy in the hearer or reader.

RHYME ROYAL A stanza of seven lines, in iambic pentameter and rhyming *ababbcc*.

ROMANCE A play emphasizing the marvelous and the coincidental as it brings harmony out of discord, comedy out of tragedy. Often a romance will emphasize a quest, redemption, and the restoration of a broken family.

SIXAIN A stanza of six lines, in iambic pentameter and most often rhyming *ababcc.*

SOLILOQUY A monologue delivered by a character in a play, in which he or she literally "speaks alone"—that is, talks at length to himself or herself, thinking aloud, and not to the play's other characters.

SONNET A lyric form, usually having 14 lines of iambic pentameter verse. The so-called Shakespearean sonnet rhymes *abab cdcd efef gg.*

STATIONERS' REGISTER The record book of the Stationers' Company of London, in which a bookseller, for a fee, could register the right to publish and have copyright in a literary or other work.

STICHOMYTHIA Dialogue spoken in alternating lines, typically by characters who are sharply in dispute.

TETRALOGY A series of four plays. Shakespeare wrote two tetralogies: the first consists of the three *Henry VI* plays and *Richard III,* the second of *Richard II,* the two *Henry IV* plays, and *Henry V.*

THRENOS A lament.

Index

Plain page numbers refer to the main body text, italic page numbers to illustrations or illustration captions, and bold numbers to text within feature boxes. The initials W.S. refer to William Shakespeare.

Acknowledgments

The Publisher would like to thank Sophia Oravecz for her help during the conceptualization process prior to production, as well as Rochelle Deighton for her help in the early stages of the book's production. Special thanks go to Kylie Mulquin for creating the graphics (relationship diagrams, family trees, and pie charts).

The quotations and extracts from Shakespeare's works used in *The Shakespeare Encyclopedia* are taken from EVANS, *The Riverside Shakespeare,* 1E. © 1974 Houghton Mifflin Company. Reproduced by permission. www.cengage.com/permissions

Captions for preliminary pages and openers

Page 1 A theater program illustrated by Chas A. Buchel from a 1901 production of *Twelfth Night* at Her Majesty's Theatre, London

Page 2 A portrait of Shakespeare, *c.* nineteenth century, unknown artist

Pages 4–5 Actors take a curtain call at the Shakespeare Memorial Theatre, Stratford, 1963

Page 7 A Royal Shakespeare Company actor returns to the stage via the auditorium during a performance of *Richard II*, Stratford, 2008

Pages 8–9 Views of the reconstructed Globe theater, London.

Pages 10–11 Preparing for a performance of *Richard II* by the Royal Shakespeare Company, Stratford, 2008

Pages 12–13 *Shakespeare and His Friends at the Mermaid Tavern* (1851) by John Faed

Pages 42–43 *Cordelia Comforting Her Father, King Lear, in Prison* (1886) by George William Joy

Pages 44–45 Henry V (Laurence Olivier) addresses his army in a scene from the 1944 film of *Henry V*, directed by Olivier

Pages 84–85 Puck (Stanley Tucci, left) and Oberon (Rupert Everett) in a scene from the 1999 film of *A Midsummer Night's Dream*, directed by Michael Hoffman

Pages 150–51 Othello (Eamonn Walker) and Desdemona (Zoe Tapper) in a 2007 production of *Othello* at Shakespeare's Globe, London

Pages 228–29 *Miranda* (1869) by Anthony Frederick Augustus Sandys

Pages 254–55 *The Awakening of Adonis* (1899) by John William Waterhouse

Pages 256–57 *Tarquin and Lucretia* by Jan Massys (1509–75)

Pages 272–73 *A Young Woman Reading a Love Letter* by Pietro Antonio Rotari (1707–62)

Pages 286–87 A copy of the First Folio (1623)

Page 298 A nineteenth-century engraving of the Swan (left) and Globe (right) theaters

Picture Credits

b = bottom, c = center, l = left,
r = right, t = top
AA = Picture Desk – The Art Archive
AKG = AKG Images
CB = Corbis
GI = Getty Images
IMP= Imagestate Media Partners
KC = Picture Desk – The Kobal Collection
PL = Photolibrary.com
PS = Donald Cooper/photostage.co.uk
SH = Shutterstock

1 GI, **2** GI, **4–5** GI, **7** GI, **8**tl GI, **8**tr GI, **9**tr SH, **10–11** GI, **12–13** GI, **14**b AA, **15**l PL, r PL, **16**t AA, **17**b GI, t GI, **18**t PL, **19**b CB, t CB, **20**b PL, **21**b GI, tl GI, tr PL, **22**bl AA, br PL, **23**t CB, **24**t AA, **25**b PS, t CB, **26**b KC, t CB, **27**t GI, **28**t PS, **29**bl PL, br PS, **30**b GI, **31**bl CB, tr IMP, **32**t GI, **33**b KC, t CB, **34**b CB, **35**b "Te Tangata Whai Rawa o Weniti" *The Maori Merchant of Venice*, photograph by Kirsty Griffin, t AA, **36**b GI, t CB, **37**t PS, **38**t KC, **39**b CB, t CB, **40**b CB, t KC, **41**b KC, **42–43** GI, **44–45** GI, **46**t AA, **47**b PS, **50**t PS, **52**c KC, **53**b PL, **55**b CB, **56**t CB, **57**b KC, **59**l GI, **60**b PS, **61**t AA, **62**l CB, **65**b CB, **66**t PL, **67**b KC, **68**t CB, **70**b CB, **71**t GI, **72**r PL, **74**b CB, **75**t AA, **76–77** KC, **78**l PL, **79**b PS, **80**t AA, **82**t GI, **83**b PS, **84–85** KC, **87**t AKG, **88**t PL, **89**b PS, **91**t PS, **92**b GI, **94**b CB, **95**t PL, **96**t CB, **97**r PL, **98**b CB, **101**b KC, **102–3** GI, **105**t KC, **106**b CB, **107**t GI, **108**b CB, **109**t KC, **110**b CB, **113**b KC, **114**b PL, **115**t GI, **116**t CB, **118**t PL, **119**b CB, **120**t CB, **122**b CB, **124**l KC, **125**t KC, **126–27**b CB, **128**l AA, **129**r AA, **130**t CB, **131**b PL, **132** KC, **134**b CB, **136**l AA, **137**r CB, **138**b PL, **139**t KC, **140**t GI, **141**b CB, **143**t PS, **144**b GI, **145**t AA, **146**r IMP, **148**b CB, **150–51** GI, **153**b PS, **154**t CB, **155**b KC, **156–57** KC, **158**t PL, **159**b PS, **160**b KC, **162**t PL, **163**b KC, **164**b PL, **165**b CB, **167**t KC, **168**t CB, **169**b KC, **171** CB, **173**t AA, **174**b GI, **175**t KC, **176–77**b KC, **176**t AA, **178**t KC, **179**b CB, **180**t CB, **181**b PL, **183**l CB, **184–85**t PL, **186**b GI, **187**r PL, **188**l CB, **189**r KC, **190**l PL, **191**t GI, **193**t CB, **194**b AA, **197** GI, **198**t AA, **199**b KC, **200**b KC, **201**t CB, **202**b PS, **203**t PL, **204–5**t AA, **206**t CB, **208**t CB, **209**r IMP, **210**t KC, **211**b CB, **212**b KC, **213**t KC, **214**l AA, **215**t PL, **216–217** AA, **219**r IMP, **220**t GI, **221**b IMP, **223**t PS, **224**r CB, **226**t PS, **227**b AA, **228–29** GI, **230**b PL, **231**t PL, **233**t CB, **234**t CB, **236**b AA, **237**t GI, **238**t GI, **240**b CB, **241**t GI, **242**t PS, **243**b CB, **244–45** AKG, **247**t CB, **248**t CB, **249**b CB, **250**b KC, **251**t PS, **253**b PL, **254–55** GI, **256–57** GI, **258**t IMP, **259** AA, **260**b IMP, **261**t PS, **262**b PL, **263**t PL, **264**t CB, **265**b CB, **267**t CB, **268**t PL, **269**b IMP, **270** By permission of the Folger Shakespeare Library, **272–73** GI, **274**b PL, t PL, **275**t AA, **276**b CB, **277**b PL, t By permission of the Bodleian Library, Oxford, **278**t AA, **279**b PL, t CB, **280**bl GI, **281**b PL, **282**t KC, **283**b GI, t AA, **284**b KC, **285**b GI, t KC, **286–87** GI, **298** GI.